Listening to
Their Voices

Studies in Rhetoric/Communication

Thomas W. Benson, Series Editor

Listening to Their Voices

*The Rhetorical
Activities of Historical Women*

Edited by Molly Meijer Wertheimer

University of South Carolina Press

To Carroll C. Arnold, teacher and friend

Published in Columbia, South Carolina, by the
University of South Carolina Press

Manufactured in the United States of America

01 00 99 98 97   5 4 3 2 1

Library of Congress Cataloging-in-Publication Data

Listening to their voices : essays on the rhetorical activities of historical
    women / edited by Molly Meijer Wertheimer.
        p. cm. — (Studies in rhetoric/communication)
    Includes bibliographical references and index.
    ISBN 1–57003–171–1 —ISBN 1–57003–172–X (pbk.)
        1. Rhetoric—History. 2. Women—Language. I. Wertheimer, Molly
Meijer. II. Series.
P301.L57 1997
808'.0082—dc21   97–4866

When one reads historical works covering long spans of time there are no more traces of our [women's] names to be found than there are traces to be found of a vessel crossing the ocean.

Anna Maria von Schurmann

Contents

Contents

Editor's Preface

In *Listening to Their Voices* Molly Meijer Wertheimer presents the voices of a fascinating group of feminist scholars who have recovered for contemporary readers the rhetorical activities of historical women. In this wide-ranging series of essays the authors undertake the recovery of marginalized voices, provide gendered re-readings of taken-for-granted theory and practice in rhetoric, and re-create theory from feminist perspectives. The resulting book contributes to rediscovering women in the history of rhetorical practice and re-writing women into the history of rhetorical theory.

Whether by explicit prohibition, by circumstance, by definition, or by naturalizing assumptions, women have been in various ways excluded from the history of rhetoric. And yet, as the authors in this book demonstrate, women have found ways to overcome such exclusions. The theoretical and ethical problems created by the gendered history of rhetoric seem to require simultaneous pursuit of what may seem conflicting paths. It is important to recover the history of the ways in which women's voices have been stifled. It is, in contrast, equally important to recover the history of those exceptional women who were able to be heard in the male public sphere. In contrast yet again, it is important to revise our definitions of rhetoric itself by asking what feminist rhetorical perspectives might do to re-write rhetorical theory—both as a way of making visible the assumptions of canonical rhetorical theory and as a way of generating productive theories for our own uses. In turn, re-reading the history of women's communicative activities from the perspective of feminist rhetorical theories allows us to recover misunderstood or unheard voices, some of which have been hiding in the open in such activities as letter writing and conversation.

Listening to Their Voices is a welcome addition to the University of South Carolina Press series Studies in Rhetoric/Communication.

Thomas W. Benson

Preface and Acknowledgments

This book was instigated by a weird combination of serendipity and calculation. During the summer of 1990 I attended a National Endowment for the Humanities Summer Seminar for College Teachers in London. The theme of the seminar was "Eighteenth-Century British Sources of Early American Rhetoric"; the director was Lloyd F. Bitzer. My research project was to trace the transformation from deductive to inductive logic in rhetorical theory, a transformation that occurred amid much debate and intermediate forms. While reading Isaac Watts's *Logic* one day in the British Museum, I chanced to sit next to the historian Hilda L. Smith, who introduced me to her bibliography, *Reason's Disciples: Seventeenth-Century English Feminists*. That work became increasingly significant during the fall, when I stepped into the classroom to teach an introductory rhetorical theory course. During that semester I became more and more irritated by the absence of women in the history of rhetoric and especially by the lack of critical studies of women's voices that could correct the defect. I decided to edit a collection of essays on the rhetorical activities of historical women and circulated a call for contributors.

I would like to thank Winifred B. Horner, James J. Murphy, and Carroll C. Arnold for blind reviewing the dozens of abstracts I received. I followed their recommendations, especially Arnold's idea to make sure that the selected essays not only introduced historical women to the field but also contributed something new to rhetorical theory. All of the essays included make this sort of double contribution.

My interest in rhetoric and appreciation of its historically undulating domain come from graduate studies in the departments of speech communication and philosophy at the Pennsylvania State University. I am grateful to the following persons for helping me to understand core issues in rhetorical history, theory, and criticism: Thomas W. Benson, Herman Cohen, Richard B. Gregg, Gerard A. Hauser, Gerald M. Phillips, and Eugene E. White. I would also like to thank Henry Johnstone Jr., whose graduate courses on "philosophical methodology" (the intersections of philosophy and rhetoric) challenged me to find intellectual satisfaction in such perverse activities as testing the validity of all 256 possible syllogisms with Venn diagrams. My thanks go especially to Carroll C. Arnold, dissertation director, whose sensitive criticisms became increasingly rigorous in proportion to my growing confidence as a thinker and writer.

I would like to acknowledge Harold W. Aurand, who has directed the academic program at the Hazleton campus for the last ten years. Under his leadership I have been able to teach a variety of speech communication and women's studies courses, to hold appointments in both departments, and to enrich my understanding of the overlapping areas. Thanks also go to my students, many of whom were returning adult women; some were often just as mystified and angry as I was at the absence of studies of women from their courses in the humanities, arts, and sciences. In addition, I thank my colleagues for their useful comments on my introduction: Harold W. Aurand and Eugene Miller, history department; R. Alan Price, English department; and George Tseo, geography department and novelist.

Warren Slesinger, then senior editor at the University of South Carolina Press, helped me draft the book's "Prospectus," and Peggy Hill, managing editor, has been very helpful in the assemblage and production of the manuscript. Jerry Murphy, as senior adviser on this project, has given me valuable suggestions about the organization of essays as well as the headings of sections. Tom Benson, Studies in Rhetoric/Communication series editor, has been encouraging from the day I first discussed this project with him in fall 1991.

My husband and son deserve public recognition too. Without Frits's technical knowledge of various software programs this book would have taken much longer to see publication. And without Aaron's unspoiled joyfulness to sustain me, moments of sheer drudgery would have been much harder to take.

Listening to
Their Voices

Introduction
Roses in the Snow

Molly Meijer Wertheimer

You are the only maiden living who handles a book instead of wool,
a reed pen instead of make-up, a metal stylus instead of a needle,
and who smears not her skin with white lead, but rather paper with
ink. This indeed is as extraordinary, as rare, as new, as if violets took
root amid ice, roses in snow or lilies in frost.
    Angelo Poliziano, "Encomium to Cassandra Fedele"

I

In the fifteenth century Cassandra Fedele was an exception who
proved the rule (King and Rabil 1992). She was a well-educated and
eloquent woman. She delivered orations at the University of Padua,
before the people of Venice, and to the Venetian ruler. She was invited to
join the court of Queen Isabella of Aragon and Sicily, and in 1488 the
Venetian Senate denied her permission to emigrate since she was considered too much of a prodigy to lose. Admired for her wisdom and
eloquence during her youth, Fedele was, in her world, a rare flower.[1] Yet
she shared a common fate with women speakers and writers who came
both before and after her: none has appeared in the history of rhetoric.

Traditionally, women have not been considered part of this history.
Authors of most, if not all, current and older histories situate rhetoric in
the public arena and define the term as "persuasive argumentation practiced by citizens." For most of Western history women have been denied
citizenship rights and have not been able to participate in public life
(Riesenberg 1992). By definition, they have been shifted to a realm outside of rhetoric. Though marginalized, many have left traces of other
sorts of rhetorical activities in speeches and writings—for example, on
sturdy shards of pottery, in the secondary accounts of philosophers and
historians, in silent collaborations, in writings published under pseud-

onyms, and more. The purpose of this book is to recollect some of their voices, thereby enriching our definitions of rhetoric and our knowledge of rhetorical theory.

This collection is part of a larger effort by scholars in several disciplines to include the accomplishments of women in the history of rhetoric. Feminist historians and rhetoricians examine accounts of women's lives and the situations in which women have lived for evidence of significant rhetorical activity, broadly considered. Until recently information about historical women was limited, primarily because women, having no public voices of their own, were known mainly through a veil of misogynist assumptions. Firsthand data about their lives and their works were not considered important enough to preserve (Duby and Perrot 1992). In *The Creation of Feminist Consciousness*, for example, Gerda Lerner reports that "up to 1700 there are fewer than 300 learned women in Western Europe known to historians" (1993, 29). But as historians—mostly female—have developed the will to know about women and have expanded what they are willing to examine as evidence, more and more rhetorically significant women are coming to the fore. In writing their two-volume *History of Their Own: Women in Europe from Prehistory to the Present,* Anderson and Zinsser claim to have used "hundreds of works written since 1970 on women in Europe" and to have located "subject matter for thousands of doctoral dissertations" (1988, 1: vix, xviii).

Motivating this enterprise are the beliefs that "rhetoric" as a human activity has been too narrowly conceived for most of its history and that feminism can provide important kinds of enrichment. Borrowing notions from Walter Ong, Robert Connors claims that the traditional conception of rhetoric was "shaped by [the] discursive and psychological agendas" of men. Male consciousness, he says, typically perceives and responds as though in a contest and settles interactions by the formation of hierarchies (1992, 65–67). Here it is interesting to consider the ancient Greeks Corax and Tisias, usually cited as the inventors of rhetorical argument (Kennedy 1994, 34). Corax, the teacher, and Tisias, the student, argue in court over the payment of a fee. Tisias argues: "I shouldn't have to pay Corax for his alleged services. If I win the case, then I don't have to pay him. But if I lose the case, then I didn't learn enough from him, so I shouldn't have to pay him." Alternatively, Corax argues that Tisias should pay the fee: "If I win the case, then he should have to pay me. But if I lose the case, then he has learned from me sufficiently, so he should have to pay me." In either case, according to both, each wins. Their story has come down as a leading metaphor for rhetoric—a conception of rhetoric as agonistic debate that turns on probabilities and ends with a winner and a loser.

Many scholars have challenged such foundational stories of Western rhetoric. Many agree that the agonistic view of rhetoric is too limited—large portions of historical populations and significant kinds of suasory activities have been left out of account. They disagree, however, over how to reconceive rhetorical theory and history anew. One area of debate has developed precisely over this question of how to include the voices, interests, and, to use an old-fashioned word, the sensibilities of women in this history. Positions have seemed to polarize between those who seek to recover and to insert exceptional women, such as Cassandra Fedele, alongside their male counterparts in traditional accounts, and those who favor the identification of oppressive forces that have kept women silent.[2] The first group seems willing, at least provisionally, to accept the agonistic view of rhetoric, while the second seems more eager to root out cultural biases that have held that notion fast.

The differences between these two positions seem less problematic, however, when research, from either perspective, is pursued deeply enough. For example, using the notion of "constraints" from Lloyd Bitzer's "The Rhetorical Situation" (1968), a traditional critic of public address might begin with an individual speaker, Cassandra Fedele, then through research discover constraining forces (oppressions) upon all women in the Italian Renaissance and the exceptional circumstances—of class and family—that allowed one woman or a small group of women to speak in public. Another scholar might begin with a study of oppressive religious beliefs and civil legislation silencing women in the Renaissance, and end by describing the special circumstances that allowed some Italian women, such as Cassandra Fedele, some degree of release from their hold. Both sorts of studies would map overlapping terrains.

Proponents of each position agree, however, that the basic conception of rhetoric as agonistic debate needs revision. For example, in "Border Crossings: Intersections of Rhetoric and Feminism" (1995) Lisa Ede, Cheryl Glenn, and Andrea Lunsford usefully suggest some of the ways, on a canon-by-canon basis, feminism could change traditional notions of rhetoric. They suggest, for example, how the canon of invention might change if the agonistic underpinnings of the notion were recast according to feminist thinking about subjectivity, knowledge, and human relationships. Other scholars have taken different approaches or developed ideas differently;[3] for example, Sonja K. Foss and Karen A. Foss promote a view of "presentational speaking" as an "invitation to transformation" wherein "the speaker's invitation is an offering, an opening, an availability—not an insistence" and the auditor's "transformation occurs . . . through the process of self-change . . ." (1994, 4). By stressing listeners' voluntary change, they highlight the self-rhetoric of personal growth.

As editor of this volume, I have chosen to forego top-down pronouncements privileging any single method of revision. My belief is that the controversy among feminists in rhetoric is mostly an artifact, being instigated by a genre of scholarship that makes polemic an obligatory part of scholarly work. Journal editors and conference program planners often arrange clashes between scholars to garner the attention of readers and listeners.[4] In the popular media journalists also use conflict as an editorial device for the same purpose. A good example is the combative framework constructed by journalists who published stories about the ice skaters Nancy Kerrigan and Tonya Harding with such headlines as "The Cold Wars" (Ryan 1994) and "With Blades Drawn" (Duffy 1994).

The position taken here is the promotion of pluralism, a position consistent with much feminist thinking today. Most contemporary feminists admit their differences and agree to disagree. For example, Joanna Crosby says, "Feminism . . . is not one point of view, it is not one set of right practices, nor should feminist theory or philosophy limit itself to what one group may find appropriate" (1994). This very sentiment was expressed well in a recent article in *Ms*, "Let's Get Real about Feminism." The article celebrated discussion and debate: "That there is diversity and room for debate in feminism is one of the joys of our movement. But too often, we've muted our discussions for fear of being misconstrued by our critics. Well, it's time to turn up the volume" (Vaid et al. 1993, 4: 2). A similar perspective was adopted by Alison M. Jaggar and Paula S. Rothenberg in *Feminist Frameworks* (1993); the authors contend that differences of opinion and outlook among feminists reveal genuine differences among women and the situations in which they—we—live and have lived. Thus, pluralism pervades the contemporary scene among feminists, including those who are active in the political arena.

In July 1992 four hundred women from forty-three countries met in Dublin to discuss the subject of leadership for women. The participants advocated a model of plurality, even in describing the women for whom they were all committed to work (Pavlou 1993). Ruth Bamela Engo-Tjego, from Cameroon, Africa, explained that each society has its own way of marginalizing women. So, those who seek to recover women rhetoricians must be responsive to the differing cultural and historical situations in which women live and have lived.

The essays in this volume illustrate the fruitfulness of encouraging scholars to start with a woman from the past, a piece of writing or a speech, a compelling idea, an anomaly, or an oppression and to go wherever their research leads. The conclusions reached by the authors of chapters in this volume are consistent with the conclusions of many art historians who are writing women into the history of art. Nancy Heller (1991), for instance, has found that, on the one hand, some of the works of women painters are indistinguishable from the works of their male contemporaries: both painted portraits of royalty in exactly the same styles. On the other hand, some of the works are different in kind or degree: for example, women were barred from academies, were not allowed to paint from nude models, and did not have the same access to the materials of art. Consequently, art historians find more still lifes of household objects, more self-portraits, and more miniatures among female painters than their male colleagues (11–13). Similar results emerge from the studies collected in this volume; some of the rhetorical works produced by women are indistinguishable from those produced by men, while other works are different in kind or degree, such as the rhetoric of mother's manuals and an unusually heavy emphasis placed on private conversation.

II

I have grouped the essays in this volume in thematic categories, believing that doing so would help the reader to understand some of the themes that emerge in this research. To a certain extent the themes used are arbitrary in that another editor might have sorted the essays differently. On the other hand, significant threads do run through the essays, and grouping them as I have done helps to make these threads explicit.

Part 1: Making Delicate Images

Essays in this section show the intellectual dexterity often required to recover information about the rhetorical activities of historical women, even when the women and works recovered are fairly recent. This section reminds us of the patriarchal conditions that rendered the achievements of women all but invisible. Cheryl Glenn's "Locating Aspasia on the Rhetorical Map" introduces Aspasia as an intellectual and speechwriter whose greatest work, "The Funeral Oration," was credited to a man—her lover Pericles. Glenn contends that we know about Aspasia the same way we know about Socrates: from comments made about her in secondary accounts. From these less than perfect statements made in passing, tissuelike in their thinness, emerges the faint image of a woman who participated actively in a powerful circle of thinkers and leaders. Regrettably, little of her life and work has been preserved. Glenn's study reminds us that rhetoric has been conceived from a patriarchal, misogynist perspective; consequently, many women have never been able to enter its history.

Virginia Allen's essay, "*On Liberty* and Logic: The Collaboration of Harriet Taylor and John Stuart Mill," reinforces Glenn's indictment of the long-standing cultural bias against women—one that denies women roles in creating anything intellectual. Allen recounts the "curlicued logic" she uncovered as she probed sources to discover Harriet Taylor's contributions to *On Liberty*, the classic statement on liberalism that she wrote collaboratively with John Stuart Mill, her lover and companion. Allen traces the difficulty of getting a clear picture of Taylor to nineteenth-century assumptions about women's physiology and psychology that were championed by Mill's biographer, Alexander Bain.

Can we assume that scholars who seek information about contemporary women rhetoricians face little of the difficulty Virginia Allen encountered? Barbara Warnick's essay, "Lucie Olbrechts-Tyteca's Contribution to *The New Rhetoric*," provides a case study of the difficulty Warnick had when she tried to find information about Olbrechts—only recently deceased. Warnick's tactic was to examine Olbrechts's single authored work to see what she could have contributed to *The New Rhetoric*. Through an analysis of *Le Comique du discours* and "Les Couples philosophiques," Warnick identifies Olbrechts's major intellectual interests and cognitive style. Operating as critics, if we apply their notion of "philosophical pairs" metaphorically to Chaïm Perelman and

Olbrechts as a writing team, we can say that in trying to "dissociate" each author's contribution from the other's a hierarchy was assumed. Perelman became the more valuable contributor, given a double cultural bias: to value logic and the construction of frameworks over empirical, taxonomic work, and to value the male over the female.

Part 2: A Sampler of Rhetorical Practices

The four essays in Part 2 examine some of the rhetorical practices of historical women. One of the most significant points to emerge from these essays, in fact from all of the essays, is that the research makes a contribution *both* to the literature on women's rhetoric and to rhetorical theory, a point illustrated well by the first essay, "The Rhetoric of Women in Pharaonic Egypt."

Little has been written about Egyptian rhetoric. The most significant work to date is probably Michael Fox's "Ancient Egyptian Rhetoric" (1983). Barbara Lesko challenges his characterization of "ideal Egyptian speech," saying that it is based on a study of the wisdom literature, which are texts used to teach young boys to be "efficient, loyal civil servants in a totalitarian state." Confining herself to the texts of women, Lesko examines other sources: the words of ordinary women, princesses and queens, and women in love. Her conclusion is that ordinary women speak boldly and directly, perhaps because, owing to their gender, they did not receive a scribal education. The royal words of princesses and queens, however, are every bit as boastful as the words of their male counterparts—presumably because they used forms of speech learned from their royal educations.

Robert W. Cape Jr. presents an analysis of both the private and public speaking of ancient Roman women. In "Roman Women in the History of Rhetoric and Oratory" he argues that ancient Rome might be a more fruitful place to look for female rhetoric and rhetoricians than ancient Greece. Cape contends that some of these women, at least in the respectable classes, led public lives and had public voices. He presents the characteristics of *sermo* or conversation, then shows how sample texts of both men and women conform to those rules. Cape also discusses several Roman women who gave speeches in public and the unusual conditions under which they were allowed to speak.

In "Women, Commerce, and Rhetoric in Medieval England" Malcolm Richardson examines the business correspondence of women in England during the later Middle Ages, about 1401–1500. Most extant business documents come from estate-managing women of the middle to upper classes who wrote to their often absent husbands. The "voices" in these letters, according to Richardson, are indistinguishable from the "voices" in letters written by men. His finding is consistent with research conducted today on contemporary women's business correspondence: the more role-bound and formulaic the communication, the more female and male voices sound alike. Richardson cites a surprising number of gutsy, brisk, commanding letters written by women to men, and he wonders whether the formal requirements of the *dictamen* gave them their power.

African American women engaged in considerable rhetorical activity in the nineteenth century as described in Shirley Wilson Logan's "Black Women on the Speaker's Platform (1832–1899)." Many used their oratorical skills to address a "panoply of issues challenging peoples of African descent throughout America," including slavery, woman's rights, and racial dignity. According to Logan, "they spoke their minds from platform and pulpit," leaving little textual record of all they said and did. These speakers were the embodiments of their messages: the fact that they spoke so eloquently authenticated their arguments such that "the messenger was the message." Both known and unknown, all contributed to the noble purpose expressed well by Lucy Stone Blackwell, "Make the world better."

Many of the women Logan presents were empowered to speak by virtue of their religious faith. Divine sanction has early been a factor giving women the authority and courage to speak; as Lesko shows, even Hatshepsut claimed divine birth and the favor of the Gods as she created her monumental messages in stone. Though inspired by different Gods and conceptions of God, many women have relied on the divine to authorize their speaking and writing—the theme of Part 3.

Part 3: Authorized by Faith

In "Dhuoda's *Handbook for William* and the Mother's Manual Tradition" Clella I. Jaffe describes the religious warrant that gave Dhuoda, a ninth-century Carolingian noblewoman, the courage to author a manual to instruct her son William (and his baby brother), who had been taken away from her, "a virtual hostage to guarantee his father's loyalty" to the Crown. She felt empowered not only by her religious convictions but also by her sense of motherhood—her duty to instruct her children though they were far away from her. Jaffe places Dhuoda's text in a larger tradition, suggesting that mother's manuals may have been invented by several different women, without knowledge of each other, over a period of several hundred years. She also suggests that mother's manuals may be an early form of today's etiquette handbooks.

In "The Visionary Rhetoric of Hildegard of Bingen" Julia Dietrich provides an analysis of the rhetorical activities of Hildegard, an eleventh-century mystic and abbess. How was Hildegard able "to authorize herself as a theologian," and what were the "rhetorical means" she used to "create . . . a space for her particular vision"? In the *Scivias*, according to Dietrich, Hildegard makes God the ultimate source of wisdom and herself the mere vehicle through which he speaks. Hildegard uses tropes, especially allegory, reversal, and modesty, and writes as an outsider, recasting the institutional church as female and suggesting that women become "spiritual men" through virginity and sanctity. Dietrich places Hildegard's influential work in an apocalyptic tradition—"less obvious to historians of rhetoric than the tradition running from Aristotle to the scholastics into modern practice."

Laurel Carrington's "Women, Rhetoric, and Letter Writing: Marguerite d'Alençon's Correspondence with Bishop Briçonnet of Meaux" traces the spiritual friendship that developed through the exchange of letters between a woman who would become queen of France and a bishop who required her patronage during a time of church reform. Carrington examines the ways in which these two correspondents used the *dictamen* to negotiate an exchange of support, the bishop providing Marguerite with spiritual support and Marguerite providing the bishop with royal protection. As Carrington says, their exchange is a valuable case study of how a man and a woman attempt to work out "issues of power, gender, and spirituality in an epistolary exchange, at a time when the rules of language and writing were changing."

Vicki Tolar Collins's essay, "Women's Voices and Women's Silence in the Tradition of Early Methodism," traces John Wesley's liberal policies toward women preachers and writers. With his support, many Methodist women engaged in a variety of rhetorical activities, for example, leading classes in spiritual discussion or interpreting biblical passages to audiences, some traveling the circuit with male preachers or even preaching alone. Wesley encouraged both preachers and laity—men and women—to keep spiritual journals. He published some of them in part or whole. After his death, however, nearly all of these activities stopped. Using the spiritual journal of Hestor Ann Rogers as an example, Collins shows how her work was edited by later Methodist leaders and used as a tool to silence Methodist women.

Part 4: Women's Intellectual Desires

These essays examine some of the rhetorical strategies women have used to appropriate intellectual and educational territories held exclusively by men. Christine Mason Sutherland's analysis of Margaret Cavendish, for example, shows dramatically that there have been women who have wanted to speak and write not only as mothers or religious servants but also in their own voices as intelligent, learned women. In "Aspiring to the Rhetorical Tradition: A Study of Margaret Cavendish" Sutherland traces Cavendish's life and relevant works, showing how Cavendish did everything she could to increase her intellectual skills. Ultimately, Cavendish wanted to be "a man of letters." She pursued her goal actively, benefiting from her husband's support as mentor and patron as well as through his circle of learned friends. He also encouraged her to publish under her own name, paid for the publication of her works, and wrote laudatory prefaces to them. Though she failed to achieve eminence among literary and scientific communities, Cavendish, as Sutherland says, "performed an essential service for the women who followed her. The idea that women might wish to publish their work was not unknown after her time. She got the issue, as it were, on the table."

Nancy Weitz Miller and Ekaterina V. Haskins also examine the rhetorical strategies some women have used to argue for women's capacity to achieve in matters of intellect and virtue. In "Ethos, Authority, and Virtue for Seventeenth-century Women Writers: The Case of Bathsua Makin's *An Essay to Revive the Antient Education of Gentlewomen* (1673)" Miller discusses Makin's authorial decisions to write her essay anonymously and to adopt the persona of a well-educated gentleman interested in the education of his daughter. Miller claims that Makin makes modest demands and justifies them with arguments that appeal to the self-interest of men; for example, an educated woman makes a good helpmate for her husband and a valuable educator for her sons.

In "A Woman's Inventive Response to the Seventeenth-century *Querelle des Femmes*" Haskins describes the rhetorical strategies and arguments Judith Drake uses in her *An Essay in Defence of the Female Sex*. Writing anonymously in a female persona, Drake uses a combination of character portraits and contemporary philosophy to press her claims about the abilities of women. Highlighting empiricism, her portraits seem drawn from observation of actual persons rather than from the classical, literary tradition, largely unavailable to women. She uses the Cartesian notion that a scholastic education is not necessary to the discovery of knowledge or truth, and the Lockean idea that learning comes from experience—from access to education. Her essay provides a "creative amalgamation" of rhetorical styles and philosophical reasoning from the late Renaissance and the Enlightenment.

Part 5: Appropriating the Rhetorical Tradition

Essays in Part 5 present a variety of revisions that women have already made to the rhetorical traditions they inherited. In "'As Becomes a Rational Woman to Speak': Madeleine de Scudéry's Rhetoric of Conversation" Jane Donawerth presents a revised view of Renaissance rhetoric for use by aristocratic women in the salon society of seventeenth-century France. Scudéry revises Renaissance rhetoric conservatively: the characters in her dialogues are fictional, and she places them in mythological settings. Nonetheless, the characters are female and they discuss rhetoric and other subjects philosophically. She shows how sophistic values in rhetoric—appropriateness, agreeableness, and so on—are better suited to her female contemporaries than are the scholastic practices of public argument and debate. She bases her theory of speaking on conversation, her idea of letter writing on extended conversation. In the end, she blurs the line between public and private, as Donawerth suggests, probably because in a monarchy public speech is limited and private speech can be used to influence material and social events.

In "The Uses and Problems of a 'Manly' Rhetoric: Mary Wollstonecraft's Adaptation of Hugh Blair's *Lectures* in Her Two *Vindications*," Julia Allen provides a feminist reading of Blair's *Lectures on Rhetoric and Belles Lettres*. She examines assumptions about class, morality, and gender that are embedded in Blair's eighteenth-century conception of rhetoric. Allen claims that Wollstonecraft shared many religious, social, and political beliefs with Blair and so felt comfortable using his *Rhetoric;* yet her ideas about gender and human rights differed significantly from his. Allen traces the modifications Wollstonecraft made to Blair's theory, especially in terms of his gender typing when discussing the orator's or writer's use of emotion and figures of speech. In the end, Wollstonecraft severed the connection between biological sex and gender assumptions about language—about masculine and feminine (effeminate) prose styles. She saw her own prose as written with manly simplicity and virtue.

In "Textbooks for New Audiences: Women's Revisions of Rhetorical Theory at the Turn of the Century" Jane Donawerth examines the ways in which rhetoric and composition handbooks were modified to accommodate new students—females and African Americans who began to attend American colleges after the Civil War. Donawerth analyzes the texts and communication theories of Gertrude Buck and two of her lesser-known colleagues, Hallie Quinn Brown and Mary Augusta Jordan. Donawerth's thesis is that these three authors did not write the same kinds of textbooks as did their male counterparts; instead, "they offer alternatives, accommodating women's experience, most frequently by using conversation, rather than public discourse, as a model." In addition, they cite the experiences of women in their theory and use alternating male and female pronouns. Hallie Quinn Brown also modifies her theory in terms not only of gender but of race.

Epilogue

Diane Helene Miller offers an analysis of the attempts made by contemporary feminists in communication and rhetoric to revise the field. In "The Future of Feminist Rhetorical Criticism" Miller details the achievements of feminist literary critics and the use feminist rhetorical critics have made of their works. Some rhetorical critics have borrowed "the women's history approach"—inserting neglected yet deserving women into traditional histories. Using criticism from other scholars as well as her own insights, Miller summarizes some of the shortcomings of this approach. She outlines an alternative, one that presupposes a "deconstructionist" view of language. Admitting that there is "no one prescription for feminist revision," she promotes "revisionary rereading as an umbrella term encompassing a variety of approaches, some already delineated and many more yet to be articulated or attempted."

All of the chapter authors offer their studies as contributions to the growing literature on women and the history of rhetoric. We hope that many of our readers will find the works stimulating enough to want to undertake their own studies, for much remains to be done.

Notes

1. Cassandra Fedele was married off sometime around 1497 to a physician. Although she was considered a prodigy when she was young, she was not encouraged to continue her studies. She produced almost nothing after her marriage; what survives are two letters written after her husband's death, one to Pope Leo X in 1521, the other to Pope Paul III in 1547. In both letters she explains her financial distress and asks for aid. After prodding by Pope Paul, the Venetian Senate granted her a position as prioress of an orphanage, a position she held for eleven years—until her death at ninety-three in 1558 (King and Rabil 1992, 22). Fedele is a good example of an "extraordinary woman"—wealthy and educated—who nonetheless was "disadvantaged and oppressed" when compared to her male counterparts (Campbell 1994, xvi).

2. The two approaches are: the rescue of neglected women and their works, and the rereading of traditional lore through the lens of gender to uncover sexist assumptions that have silenced women. Diane Miller has summarized this controversy in "The Future of Feminist Rhetorical Criticism," included as the epilogue in this volume.

3. Sonja Foss and Karen Foss challenge the assumption that speech uttered in public is more significant than speech uttered in private (1991, 13–16) and that individuals "are solely responsible for the texts they create" (11–12). Many texts are the products of collaboration that often goes unacknowledged (Ede and Lunsford 1990). Some say that distinctively feminine forms of knowledge and communication have not been considered in rhetorical theory. Feminist philosophers, for example, challenge the identification of the ideals of masculinity with the ideals of human reason—the privileging, for example, of linear chains of reasoning over more narrative forms (Nye 1990; Code 1991; Harding 1991; Lloyd 1993).

4. Barbara Biesecker launched a fairly strident attack against Karlyn Kohrs Campbell's "women's history approach" in her essay "Coming to Terms with Recent Attempts to Write Women into the History of Rhetoric" (1992). I have read Biesecker's essay several times and believe that she did use Campbell's work rhetorically—as a foil against which to develop her own views; she could have written her essay without the polemical confrontation, but the clash gave the piece a kind of gutsy energy. Unfortunately, what may have been originally a capitulation to "scholastic" form became transformed into genuine conflict—somewhat personal in nature—by the journalistic practice of allowing an author who was attacked the opportunity to defend herself in print. Campbell thus wrote: "Biesecker Cannot Speak for Her Either" (1993, 153–59). But the exchange was further exacerbated when the editor of *Philosophy and Rhetoric* showed Biesecker a prepublication copy of Campbell's "rebuttal" and gave her another opportunity to comment in the next number, for which she produced

"Negotiating with Our Tradition: Reflecting Again (without Apologies) on the Feminization of Rhetoric" (1993, 237–42). Biesecker ends that article with the hope that Campbell and other readers will be able to find "enabling points of contact" between the two projects instead of concluding "that an intractable distance remains between them" (238). An enabling point of contact may be found in Lloyd Bitzer's notion of "constraints" (1968).

References

Anderson, Bonnie S., and Judith P. Zinsser. 1988. *A History of Their Own: Women in Europe from Prehistory to the Present.* 2 vols. New York: Harper and Row.

Biesecker, Barbara. 1992. "Coming to Terms with Recent Attempts to Write Women into the History of Rhetoric." *Philosophy and Rhetoric* 25.2: 140–61.

———. 1993. "Negotiating with Our Tradition: Reflecting Again (without Apologies) on the Feminization of Rhetoric." *Philosophy and Rhetoric* 26.3: 237–42.

Bitzer, Lloyd F. 1968. "The Rhetorical Situation." *Philosophy and Rhetoric* 1.1: 1–14.

Campbell, Karlyn Kohrs. 1993. "Biesecker Cannot Speak for Her Either." *Philosophy and Rhetoric* 26.2: 153–59.

———. 1994. *Women Public Speakers in the United States 1925–1993: A Bio-Critical Sourcebook.* Westport, Conn.: Greenwood Press.

Code, Lorraine. 1991. *What Can She Know? Feminist Theory and the Construction of Knowledge.* Ithaca: Cornell University Press.

Connors, Robert. 1992. "The Exclusion of Women from Classical Rhetoric." In *A Rhetoric of Doing: Essays on Written Discourse in Honor of James L. Kinneavy,* edited by Stephen P. Witte et al., 65–78. Carbondale: Southern Illinois University Press.

Crosby, Joanna. 1994. "Comment." On SWIP-L (Society for Women in Philosophy Information and Discussion List), 13 November.

Duby, George, and Michelle Perrot. 1992. "Writing the History of Women." In *A History of Women.* Vol. 1: *From Ancient Goddesses to Christian Saints,* ix–xxi. Cambridge: The Belknap Press of Harvard University Press.

Duffy, M. 1994. "With Blades Drawn." *Time* 143 (21 February): 52–56.

Ede, Lisa, Cheryl Glenn, and Andrea Lunsford. 1995. "Border Crossings: Intersections of Rhetoric and Feminism." *Rhetorica* 13.4: 401–41.

Ede, Lisa, and Andrea Lunsford. 1990. *Singular Texts/Plural Authors: Perspectives on Collaborative Writing.* Carbondale: Southern Illinois University Press.

Foss, Karen A., and Sonja K. Foss. 1991. *Women Speak: The Eloquence of Women's Lives.* Prospect Heights, Ill.: Waveland Press.

Foss, Sonja K., and Karen A. Foss. 1994. *Inviting Transformation: Presentational Speaking for a Changing World.* Prospect Heights, Ill.: Waveland Press.

Harding, Sandra. 1991. *Whose Science? Whose Knowledge?* Ithaca: Cornell University Press.

Heller, Nancy. 1991. *Women Artists: An Illustrated History,* rev. ed. New York: Abbeville Press.

Jaggar, Alison M., and Paula S. Rothenberg. 1993. *Feminist Frameworks: Alternative Theoretical Accounts of the Relations between Women and Men,* 3rd ed. New York: McGraw-Hill.

Kennedy, George A. 1994. *A New History of Classical Rhetoric.* Princeton: Princeton University Press.

King, Margaret L., and Albert Rabil Jr. 1992. *Her Immaculate Hand: Selected Works by and about the Women Humanists of Quattrocentro Italy.* Binghamton, N.Y.: Medieval & Renaissance Texts & Studies.

Lerner, Gerda. 1993. *The Creation of Feminist Consciousness: From the Middle Ages to Eighteen-seventy.* New York: Oxford University Press.

Lloyd, Genevieve. 1993. *The Man of Reason.* 2nd ed. Minneapolis: University of Minnesota Press.

Nye, Andrea. 1990. *Words of Power: A Feminist Reading of the History of Logic.* New York: Routledge.

Pavlou, Kay, dir. 1993. *Not a Bedroom War: New Visions of Leadership for Women.* Produced by Anne Deveson and Anna Grieve. Princeton: Films for the Humanities.

Riesenberg, Peter. 1992. *Citizenship in the Western Tradition: Plato to Rousseau.* Chapel Hill: University of North Carolina Press.

Ryan, Joan. 1994. "The Cold Wars." *San Francisco Chronicle Magazine,* 27 March, 1.

Vaid, Urvashi, Naomi Wolf, Gloria Steinem, and bell hooks. 1993. "Let's Get Real about Feminism: The Backlash, the Myths, the Movement." *Ms.* 4 (September/October): 34–43.

Part 1

Making Delicate Images

And it may hap that many a clerk
Will claim as his what is my work.
But such pronouncements I want not!
It's folly to become forgot.

Marie de France

Locating Aspasia on the Rhetorical Map

Cheryl Glenn

Land he thought already mapped was now found to have been done so in a mist. . . . But the discovery of the mist was the clearest sign of his progress.
Juliet Mitchell, *Psychoanalysis and Feminism*

In philosophy, literature, language, writing, social science, theology, history, education, reading, and psychology feminist scholars have been recovering and establishing women's colonies on the broad cultural map. More recently feminist historians of rhetoric have joined the effort, focusing *their* lens on the rhetorical map.[1] While some scholars (Bizzell 1992; Glenn 1992, 1994, 1995; Jarratt 1992) anticipate and account for various disruptions that realign and regender the rhetorical terrain,[2] others (Biesecker 1992; Collins 1996) "forge a new storying of our tradition that circumvents the veiled cultural supremacy operative in mainstream histories of Rhetoric" (Biesecker 1992, 147). These challenges restore women to rhetorical history and rhetorical history to women, and the restoration itself revitalizes theory by shaking the conceptual foundations of rhetorical study.[3] Of course, more than theory is at stake here, for feminist historiography is performative—it *does* something. While it challenges the dominant stories of the West, feminist historiography also challenges the contemporary academic and cultural scenes as well.

As part of the feminist challenge to the history of rhetoric, I want to reconstruct Aspasia of Miletus, a woman whose life and manuscripts have been colonized by men. In the fifth century B.C.E. Miletus was a Far Eastern Greek subject-ally, a cultivated city (in what is now Turkey) renowned for its literacy and philosophies of moral thought and nature.[4] A non-Athenian, citizen-class Greek, Aspasia arrived in Athens brilliantly educated by means that have never been fully explained.[5] Whether she was educated within a literate Milesian family or within a school for hetaerae,[6] she was exceptionally fortunate, for "there is no evidence at all that in the classical period girls attended schools, and it is entirely consistent with what we know about the seclusion of women in Athens that Athenian girls did not do so (some other cities may have been less benighted in this respect)" (Harris 1989, 96). Married at an early age, Athenian women neither attended schools nor participated in the polis. Yet the system of the polis, which implied both civic consciousness and "the extraordinary preeminence of speech over all other instruments of power" (Vernant [1962] 1982, 49), tripped the mechanism that powered the active diffusion and acquisition of literacy among Greek males (proper citizens). We must assume that at least a few Athenian or Athenian-colony women of the citizen class, even those defined by good families and cultural constraints, became literate—and became conscious of civic rights and responsibilities (Cole 1981, 222–23; Harris 1989, 103, 107).[7] Aspasia of Miletus was one of those women.

As a free woman brought up in the transitional society of Asia Minor, Aspasia was freed from the rigidity of traditional marriage and from the identity that arose from that fixed role. Upon emigrating from Miletus, Aspasia emerged in Athens linked with the great statesman Pericles (fl. 442 B.C.E.), the aristocratic democrat who placed Athenian democratic power "in the hands not of a minority but of the whole people," with everyone equal before the law (Thucydides 2.37.1). Thus, this non-Athenian, this stranger-woman, was subject to Athenian law but did not have citizen rights. Nor was she accountable to the severe strictures of aristocratic Athenian women, whose activities, movements, educations, marriages, and rights as citizens and property holders were extremely circumscribed by male relatives. Aspasia could ignore—even rupture—the traditional enclosure of the female body. She could subvert Pericles' advice for ideal womanhood: "Your greatest glory is not to be inferior to what God has made you" (Thucydides 5.46.2). She could—and she did.

We know about Aspasia exactly the same way we know about Socrates: from secondary sources, for the work of neither exists in primary sources. Although the historical tradition has readily accepted secondary accounts of Socrates' influence, teaching, and beliefs, the same cannot be said about any female counterpart, especially a woman described so briefly in so few accounts. But the fact that Aspasia is even mentioned by her male contemporaries is remarkable, for rare is the mention of any intellectual woman. Surviving fragments and references in the work of male authors provide tantalizing indications that the intellectual efforts of Aspasia were, at least occasionally, committed to writing. When other women were systematically relegated to the domestic sphere, Aspasia seems to have been the only woman in classical Greece to have distinguished herself in the public domain. Her reputation as both a rhetorician and philosopher was memorialized by Plato (437–328 B.C.E.), Xenophon (fl. 450 B.C.E.), Cicero (100–43 B.C.E.), Athenaeus (fl. 200 C.E.), and Plutarch (46 C.E.–circa 120)—as was, of course, her enduring romantic attachment to Pericles. For those authors Aspasia clearly represented the intelligentsia of Periclean Athens. Therefore, I want to consider seriously this woman who merited such documentation, particularly in terms of her intellectual contributions to rhetoric.

The best-known source of information about Aspasia is Plutarch's *Lives of the Noble Grecians and Romans* (100 C.E.), an account written several hundred years after her existence. Nevertheless, all earlier mentions of Aspasia confirm this

inquiry about the woman, what art or charming faculty she had that enabled her to captivate, as she did, the greatest statesmen, and to give the philosophers occasions to speak so much about her, and that, too, not to her disparagement. That she was a Milesian by birth, the daughter of Axiochus, is a thing acknowledged. And they say it was in emulation of Thargelia, a courtesan of the old Ionian times, that she made her addresses to men of great power. Thargelia was a great beauty, extremely charming, and at the same time sagacious; she had numerous suitors among the Greeks. . . . Aspasia, some say, was courted and caressed by Pericles upon account of her knowledge and skill in politics. Socrates himself would sometimes go to visit her, and some of his acquaintances with him; and those who frequented her company would carry their wives with them to listen to her. Her occupation was anything but creditable, her house being a home for young courtesans. . . . In Plato's *Menexenus*, though we do not take the introduction as quite serious, still thus much seems to be historical, that she had the repute of being resorted to by many of the Athenians for instruction in the art of speaking. Pericles's inclination for her seems, however, to have rather proceeded from the passion of love. He had a wife that was near of kin to him, who had been married first to Hipponicus, by whom she had Callias, surnamed the Rich; and also she brought Pericles, while she lived with him, two sons,

Xanthippus and Paralus. Afterwards, when they did not well agree, nor like to live together, he parted with her, with her own consent, to another man, and himself took Aspasia, and loved her with wonderful affection; every day, both as he went out and as he came in from the market-place, he saluted and kissed her. (1932, 200–201)

By every historical account, Aspasia ventured out into the common land, distinguishing herself by her rhetorical accomplishments, her sexual attachment to Pericles, and her public participation in political affairs. Her alleged connection with the courtesan life is important only insofar as it explains her intellectual prowess and social attainments—and the surprise of an Athenian citizenry unaccustomed to (or perhaps jealous or suspicious of) a public woman.[8] As Marie Delcourt wrote in her study of Pericles: "No one would have thought the less of Pericles for making love to young boys, . . . but they *were* shocked by his treating [Aspasia] like a human being—by the fact that he *lived* with her instead of relegating her to the *gynaikeion* [women's quarters], and included his friends' wives when he issued invitations to dinner. It was all too amazing to be proper; and Aspasia was so brilliant she could not possibly be respectable" (1939, 77).

Aspasia opened an academy for young women of good families (or a school for hetaerae, according to some sources[9]) that soon became a popular salon for the most influential men of the day: Socrates, Plato, Anaxagoras, Sophocles, Phidias, and Pericles. Aspasia's appearance was unprecedented at a time when the construction of gender ensured that women would be praised only for such attributes as their inherent modesty, for their inborn reluctance to join males (even kinsmen) for society or dining, and for their absolute incapacity to participate as educated beings within the polis; at a time when a woman's only political contribution was serving as a nameless channel for the transmission of citizenship from her father to her son[10] (Keuls 1985, 90); and at a time when Pericles pronounced that "the greatest glory of a woman is to be least talked about by men, whether they are praising . . . or criticizing" (Thucydides 5.46.2).[11] It is difficult to overemphasize how extraordinary the foreign-born Aspasia—a public woman, philosopher, political influence, and rhetorician—would have been in fifth-century B.C.E. Athenian society, given the male-dominated character of Athenian political and rhetorical culture.

Fifth-century B.C.E. Athens, Periclean and Aspasian

In the burgeoning democracy of Periclean Athens men were consciously forming human character in accordance with the new cultural ideals of military strength and justice (*dikē*), tempered by traditional concepts of *aretē* (excellence of virtue, usually associated with the well-born and wealthy citizen class[12]). Only aristocratic male citizens, equal in their *homonoia* (being of one mind), argued for civic and political aretē, the essential principle of government by the elite—a democratic oligarchy. Yet the Platonic Socrates called for aretē according to social role, be it male or female, free or slave (*Republic* 353b), and later Aristotle would write that both the rulers and the ruled, males and females alike, "must possess virtue" and that "all must partake of [moral virtues], . . . in such measure as is proper to each in relation to his own function" (*Politics* 1260a5, 1260a7). Thus, a complex tension existed between elitist aretē and a more democratic homonoia.

In *The Origins of Greek Thought* Jean-Pierre Vernant tells us that "Greek political life aimed to become the subject of public debate, in the broad daylight of the agora, between citizens who were defined as equals and for whom the state was the common undertaking" ([1962] 1982, 11). Such public oratory fed the spirit of panhellenism, a doctrine sorely needed to unify the Greek city-states, just as it satiated the male appetite for public display. Vernant describes the polis as a system implying "the extraordinary preeminence of speech over all other instruments of power, [speech becoming] the political tool par excellence, the key to all authority in the state, the means of commanding and dominating others" (49). In what would be an inestimable contribution to a democratic oratory informed by aristocratic characteristics, former logographer (speech writer) Isocrates practiced rhetoric as a literary form, one imbued with civic, patriotic, and moral purpose. Confident in the power of words, he practiced and taught a morally influenced and rhetorically based system of general culture that propounded individual responsibility as well as political and social action. No longer were men deferring to their sovereign or the gods, who could reinforce *nomos* (beliefs, customs, laws—enforced by universal opinion) with *physis* (nature, reality). "With this denial of the absolute status of law and moral things, the stage [was] set for a controversy between the two . . . [and for drawing] different practical conclusions from it" (Gutherie 1969, 3: 60). Individuals would be responsible for their own actions and collectively responsible for the actions of the democratic state, the polis. Significantly, these individuals did not include women.

The Athenian polis was founded upon the exclusion of women, just as, in other respects, it was founded upon the exclusion of foreigners and slaves (Vidal-Naquet 1986, 145). Although females born of Athenian-citizen parents belonged to the citizen-class and were subjects within the polis, they were not "citizens-to-be" in any sense. Nor could foreign-born women or men hope for citizenship, regardless of their political influence, civic contributions, or intellectual ties with those in power. Therefore, noncitizens such as Protagoras, Gorgias, Prodicus, Thrasymachus, Anaxagoras, and Aspasia functioned within the polis, yet remained outside its restraints.

If we think of gender as a cultural role, a social rank, "a social category imposed on a sexed body" (Scott 1988, 32), or as "a primary way of signifying relations of power" (Laqueur 1990, 12), then we can more easily trace Aspasia's movement across gendered boundaries of appropriate roles for women and men in fifth-century B.C.E. Athens. She seems to have profited by her excursion into the male domain of politics and intellect, even at the expense of her respectability, reputation, and authority. Named among the rather short "list of Athenian citizen[-class] women" known to us from literature (Schaps 1977, 323), the assertively intelligent Aspasia has been interpreted as self-indulgent, licentious, immoral. Historical records have successfully effaced the voice of the ideal Greek woman, rendering silent her enclosed body. Those same historical records have defaced any subversion of that ideal woman, rendering her unconfined body invalid.

Thus, even though Aspasia's contributions to rhetoric are firmly situated and fully realized within the rhetorical tradition, those contributions have been directed through a powerful gendered lens both to refract toward and reflect Socrates and Pericles. Paradoxically, then, Aspasia's accomplishments and influence have been enumerated by men and most often attributed to men—or installed in the apocryphal, the safest place for wise (and therefore fictitious) women. As for Aspasia's popular salon, it is often accredited to Pericles instead of to his female companion.

Aspasia's Contested Role in Periclean Eloquence

The circle in which Aspasia moved belonged to Pericles, perhaps the most socially responsible, powerful, and influential of Athenians. Indeed, he was surrounded by the greatest thinkers of his age: Sophists, philosophers, architects, scientists, and rhetoricians. In his *Mass and Elite in Democratic Athens* Josiah Ober refers to Pericles' intellectual circle as the "'educated elite' of late fifth-century Athens," "a brain trust"; Ober describes the Sophists as "experts in political manipulation who were flocking to Athens from other Greek *poleis*"; and places the "educated courtesan Aspasia . . . among Pericles' closest associates," calling her "the power behind the throne" (1989, 89–90).[13]

For forty years the Athenians applauded Pericles' eloquence, often invoking his wise and excellent companions, including the rhetorician Aspasia and the philosopher Anaxagoras. In the *Phaedrus* the Platonic Socrates calls Pericles "the most perfect orator in existence" and attributes Pericles' eloquence to the successful combination of his natural talents with the high-mindedness he learned from Anaxagoras, who "filled him with high thoughts and taught him the nature of mind . . . and from these speculations [Pericles] drew and applied to the art of speaking what is of use to it" (269e4ff.). Cicero later concurred that Pericles' teacher was indeed Anaxagoras, "a man distinguished for his knowledge of the highest sciences; and consequently Pericles was eminent in learning, wisdom and eloquence, and for forty years was supreme at Athens both in politics and at the same time in the conduct of war" (*De Oratore* 3.34.138–39).

Yet, several centuries later, Philostratus (fl. 250 C.E.) wrote in his *Epistle* 73 that "Aspasia of Miletus is said to have sharpened the tongue of Pericles in imitation of Gorgias," with "the digressions and transitions of Gorgias' speeches [becoming] the fashion" (qtd. in Sprague 1972, 41–42). Philostratus echoes Plato, the earliest writer to mention Aspasia. In the *Menexenus* the Platonic Socrates reveals Aspasia to be the author of Pericles' funeral oration (*Epitaphios*), an assertion I explore below. Aspasia becomes implicated even more in Pericles' education if we consider the "familiar knowledge at Athens that Aspasia had sat at the feet of Anaxagoras in natural philosophy" (Courtney 1912, 491). Several hundred years later, when Quintilian (100 C.E.) examined Pericles' written works, he concluded that some other pen had composed them: "I have been unable to discover anything in the least worthy of [Pericles'] great reputation for eloquence, and am consequently the less surprised that there should be some who hold that he never committed anything to writing, and that the writings circulating under his name are the works of others" (*Institutio Oratoria* 3.1.12). The rhetorician most closely associated with Pericles would no doubt have served as his logographer, as logography was commonly the province of rhetoricians. Hence, Aspasia most probably supplied Pericles with those speeches that both established him as a persuasive speaker and informed him as the most respected citizen-orator of the age.[14]

Although Plutarch credits Aspasia with contributing greatly to intellectual life, specifically to philosophy, politics, and rhetoric, many scholars have since discredited her. In the aforementioned "Life of Pericles" Plutarch draws on a now-incomplete work of Aeschines (450 B.C.E.) to describe Aspasia, but neither his nor Aspasia's case has been strengthened by the fragments of Aeschines that survived. Those fragments present a controversial statement on gender equality: "the goodness of a woman is the same as that of a man," an assertion Aeschines illustrates with the political abilities of Aspasia (qtd. in Taylor 1960, 278).[15] Both Xenophon and Cicero (and later the medieval abbess Heloise, perhaps best known for her attachment to Abelard[16]), however, tap that same complete text, giving credence to the text—as well as to the existence of a historical, rhetorical Aspasia.[17]

According to several ancient authors, all of whom knitted together secondary sources to shape a reliable view of Socrates, Socrates deeply respected Aspasia's thinking and admired her rhetorical prowess, disregarding, it seems, her status as a woman and a hetaera. In Xenophon's *Memorabilia,* for instance, Socrates explains to Critobulus the "art of catching friends" and of using an intermediary: "I can quote Aspasia. . . . She once told me that good matchmakers are successful only when the good reports they carry to and fro are true; false reports she would not recommend for the victims of deceptions hate one another and the matchmaker too. I am convinced that this is sound, so I think it is not open to me to say anything in your praise that I cannot say truthfully" (2.36).

In Xenophon's *Oeconomicus* Socrates ascribes to Aspasia the marital advice he gives to Critobulus: "There's nothing like investigation. I will introduce Aspasia to you, and she will explain the whole matter [of good wives] to you with more knowledge than I possess" (3.15). Plutarch writes that "Socrates sometimes came to see her [Aspasia] with his disciples, and his intimate friends brought their wives to her to hear her discourse . . . as a teacher of rhetoric" (200); Athenaeus calls Aspasia "clever . . . to be sure, . . . Socrates' teacher in rhetoric" (5.29) and goes on to account for the extent of Aspasia's influence over Socrates:

In the verses which are extant under her name and which are quoted by Herodicus, . . . [she says]: "Socrates, I have not failed to notice that thy heart is smitten with desire for [Alcibiades]. . . . But hearken, if thou wouldst prosper in thy suit. Disregard not my message, and it will be much better for thee. For so soon as I heard, my body was suffused with the glow of joy, and tears not unwelcome fell from my eyelids. Restrain thyself, filling thy soul with the conquering Muse; and with her aid thou shalt win him; pour her into the ears of his desire. For she is the true beginning of love in both; through her thou shalt master him, by offering to his ear gifts for the unveiling of his soul."

So, then, the noble Socrates goes a-hunting, employing the woman of Miletus as his preceptor in love, instead of being hunted himself, as Plato has said, being caught in Alcibiades' net. (5.219)

Furthermore, in the *Menexenus*, the Platonic Socrates agrees that were the Council Chamber to elect him to make the recitation over the dead (the *Epitaphios*) he "should be able to make the speech . . . for she [Aspasia] who is my instructor is by no means weak in the art of rhetoric; on the contrary, she has turned out many fine orators, and amongst them one who surpassed all other Greeks, Pericles" (235–36). It was Pericles—not Aspasia—who delivered that speech.

Plato's *Menexenus* contains Plato's version of Socrates' version of Aspasia's version of Pericles' funeral oration, further recognition of Aspasia's reputation as a rhetorician and philosopher as well as influential colleague in the sophistic movement, a movement devoted to the analysis and creation of rhetoric—and of truth. Moreover, the funeral oration itself held political, philosophical, and rhetorical significance: by its delivery alone, the oration played out "rhetoric's important role in shaping community" (Mackin 1991, 251). In *The Invention of Athens: The Funeral Oration in the Classical City* Nicole Loraux clarifies the funeral oration as an "*institution*—an institution of speech in which the symbolic constantly encroached upon the functional, since in each oration the codified praise of the dead spilled over into generalized praise of Athens" (1986, 2). Besides conflating praise of the Athenians with praise of Athens, this institutionalized and specialized epideictic was useful for developing "consubstantiality [*homonoia*]" and creating a "similar rhetorical experience" for everyone present, be they citizens, foreigners, or women related to the dead.[18] The shared experience of this rhetorical ritual linked everyone present even as it connected them "with other audiences in the past" (Mackin 1991, 251). As "one of the authorized mouthpieces of classical Athens," the funeral oration translated into "Greek patriotism"—"Athenian eloquence . . . adapted to the needs of a given historical situation" (Loraux 1986, 5). As such, the issues of translation and adaptation easily connect the *Epitaphios* with sophistic philosophy.

In *Rereading the Sophists* Susan C. Jarratt reminds us that "for the Sophists, human perception and discourse were the only measure of truths, all of which are contingent"; therefore, they focused on "the ability to create accounts of communal possibilities through persuasive speech" (1991, 64, 98). Loraux tell us that in every epitaphios, "a certain idea that the city wishes to have of itself emerges, beyond the needs of the present" (1986, 14). Thus, the beliefs and practices of Sophists overlapped beautifully one basic requirement of an epitaphios: "the personality of the orator has to yield to the impersonality of the genre . . . as an institution and as a literary form" (11). Aspasia's sophistic training, political capacity, and powerful influence on Pericles' persuasive oratory easily translate into Socrates' pronouncement to Menexenus that she composed the famous funeral oration delivered by Pericles: "I was listening only yesterday to Aspasia going through a funeral speech for [the Athenians]. . . . She rehearsed to me the speech in the form it should take, extemporizing in part, while other parts of it she had previously prepared, . . . at the time when she was composing the funeral oration which Pericles delivered" (Plato's *Menexenus*, 236b).

That Aspasia may well have composed Pericles' speech makes sense: after all, being honored by the opportunity to deliver the *Epitaphios*, he would have prepared well, seeking and following the advice of his colleagues, including Aspasia, on points of style and substance. That she wrote it becomes more convincing when we consider Loraux's assurance that "the political orator must have the ascendance over the logographer" (1986, 11) and that the Sophist would preserve the "essential features of the civic representations" (107). For reasons of Aspasia's proximity to Pericles and her intellectual training, Quintilian was right, then, to doubt the originality of Pericles' work.

Before demonstrating her expertise at composing moving, patriotic epideictic oratory, Aspasia reminds Socrates of the efficacy of rhetoric. In the *Menexenus* the Platonic Aspasia explains that "it is by means of speech finely spoken that deeds nobly done gain for their doers from the hearers the meed of memory and renown" (236e)—an accurate description of contingent truth. Jarratt explains the sophistic rhetorical technique and its social-constructionist underpinning with her definition of *nomos* as a "self-conscious arrangement of discourse to create politically and socially significant knowledge . . .; thus it is always a social construct with ethical dimensions" (1991, 60).

Hence, the author of the *Epitaphios* makes clear the power of oratory to influence the public's belief that its history was other than it was. Loraux explains that "a Sophist and a rhetor [would have] used the official oration in order to write a fictitious logos; within the corpus, then, the 'false' follows hard upon the 'true'" (1986, 9). Accordingly, the most aggressive exploits of Attic imperialism are represented as "[bringing] freedom [to] all the dwellers of this continent" (Plato's *Menexenus*, 240e), as "fighting in defense of the liberties of the Boeotians" (242b), as "fighting for the freedom of Leontini" (243a), as "setting free . . . friends" (243c), and as "saving their walls from ruin" (244c). This version of Pericles' funeral oration, an exaggerated encomium abounding with historical misstatements and anachronisms, makes explicit Plato's feeling about the use of rhetoric—just as Thucydides' version makes explicit the necessary subjection of individual citizenship to the polis: "A man who takes no interest in politics is a man who . . . has no business here at all" (2.40).

Thinly disguised in the *Menexenus* is Plato's cynicism. In his opinion, the development of oratory had negative consequences for Athens, the most glaring defect of current oratory being its indifference to truth. A rhetorician such as Aspasia was, indeed, more interested in believability than in truth, more interested in constructing than delivering truth, more interested in nomos (beliefs, customs, laws) than physis (nature, reality), interests leading to Thucydides' claims that such "prose chroniclers . . . are less interested in telling the truth than in catching the attention of their public" (1.21). In the opening dialogue of the *Menexenus* the Platonic Socrates disparages the orators in much the same way he does in the *Symposium*, saying that "in speeches long beforehand . . . , they [orators] praise in such splendid fashion, that . . . they bewitch our souls. . . . Every time I listen fascinated [by their praise of me] I am exalted and imagine myself to have become all at once taller and nobler and more handsome . . . owing to the persuasive eloquence of the speaker" (235b). Thus, Plato recoils from the touch of rhetoric.

Aspasia's Influence

Aspasia was at the center of the most famous intellectual circle, her influence radiating out to such well-known thinkers as Socrates and to such exemplary orators as Pericles. Most important, her influence extended to Plato, coloring his concept of rhetoric as well. By her example Aspasia taught Plato that belief and truth are not necessarily the same, a sentiment Plato makes evident in his *Gorgias* when Gorgias admits that rhetoric produces "[mere] belief without knowledge" (454). She also revealed to him that rhetoric, which is the daughter of truth-disclosing philosophy, does not always carry on the family tradition; rhetoric can be used to obscure the truth, to control and deceive believers into belief. In the *Gorgias* his Socrates says, "Rhetoric seems not to be an artistic pursuit at all, but that of a shrewd, courageous spirit which is naturally clever at dealing with men; and I call the chief part of it flattery" (463). In the *Phaedrus* Plato writes that "in the courts, they say, nobody cares for truth about these matters [things which are just or good], but for that which is convincing; and that is probability" (272e).

Like Aspasia, Plato approved of a rhetoric of persuasion; he too sees the political potential of public rhetoric. But his rhetoric is foremost a search for the truth; only truth—not fictive effect over accuracy—should constitute persuasive rhetoric. His perfect orator of the *Phaedrus* "must know the truth about all the particular things of which he speaks or writes . . . [and] must understand the nature of the soul" (277c), for the ideal rhetorician speaks "in a manner pleasing to the gods" (273e). What Plato could learn, then, from Aspasia is the potentially harmful uses of rhetoric as a branch of philosophy as well as the as yet uncalibrated potential of rhetoric to create belief.

In addition to influencing Socrates and Plato, Aspasia also had an effect on Xenophon and his wife, teaching them the art of inductive argument. In *De Inventione* Cicero uses her lesson in induction as the centerpiece for his argumentation chapter. Like others before him, Cicero too acknowledges Aspasia's influence on Socrates as well as the existence of the Aeschines text:

In a dialogue by Aeschines Socraticus[,] Socrates reveals that Aspasia reasoned thus with Xenophon's wife and with Xenophon himself: "Please tell me, madam, if your neighbour had a better gold ornament than you have, would you prefer that one or your own?" "That one," she replied. "Now, if she had dresses and other feminine finery more expensive than you have, would you prefer yours or hers?" "Hers, of course," she replied. "Well now, if she had a better husband than you have, would you prefer your husband or hers?" At this the woman blushed. But Aspasia then began to speak to Xenophon. "I wish you would tell me, Xenophon," she said, "if your neighbour had a better horse than yours, would you prefer your horse or his?" "His," was his answer. "And if he had a better farm than you have, which farm would you prefer to have?" "The better farm, naturally," he said. "Now, if he had a better wife than you have, would you prefer yours or his?" And at this Xenophon, too, himself was silent. Then Aspasia: "Since both of you have failed to tell me the only thing I wished to hear, I myself will tell you what you both are thinking. That is you, madam, wish to have the best husband, and you, Xenophon, desire above all things to have the finest wife. Therefore, unless you can contrive that there be no better man or finer woman on earth you will certainly always be in dire want of what you consider best, namely, that you be the husband of the very best of wives, and that she be wedded to the very best of men." To this instance, because assent has been given to undisputed statements, the result is that the point which would appear doubtful if asked by itself is through analogy conceded as certain, and this is due to the method employed in putting the question. Socrates used this conversation method a good deal, because he wished to present no arguments himself, but preferred to get a result from the material which the interlocutor had given him—a result which the interlocutor was bound to approve as following necessarily from what he had already granted. (1.31.51–53)

Few women participated in the intellectual life of ancient Greece. Aspasia is a striking exception.

Although Aspasia was a powerful force in Periclean Athens and seems to have affected the thinking of Plato and Socrates, few Greek thinkers accepted women as mental equals. Aristotle makes no provision for the intellectual woman, except for his nod to Sappho: "Everyone honours the wise. . . . The Mytilenaeans Sappho, though she was a woman" (*Rhetoric* 1389b.12). Otherwise, Aristotle denied any philosophical or rhetorical contributions of women. He quotes Sophocles when he writes, "'Silence gives grace to woman'—though that is not the case likewise with a man" (*Politics* 1.5.9). Reasoning from Aristotle's basic premise, Aspasia could not have become a teacher, much less a rhetorician. By the principle of entelechy (the vital force urging one toward fulfilling one's actual essence), she would have naturally followed her predetermined life course, her progress distinctly marked off and limited to a degree of perfection less than that for a man. The power politics of gender, the social category imposed on each sexed body, establishes the social creation of ideas about appropriate roles for women and men. Denied the telos of perfect maleness, Athenian women were denied a passport into the male intellectual battleground of politics, philosophy, rhetoric. But Aspasia had approached the border—and trespassed into masculine territory.

For the most part, Aristotle's accounts of woman, buttressed by the defective scientific understanding of reproduction and biological processes, belie woman's participation in the making of culture, leaving her daughters without access to any knowledge of a female tradition or intellectual underpinning. For Aristotle men and women differed only in outward form—but the inequality is permanent. Unlike Plato, he could not see beyond the contemporary and seemingly permanent inferior status of Greek women. In the *Politics* Aristotle writes that "between the sexes, the male is by nature superior and the female inferior, the male ruler and the female subject" (1.2.12); in the *Poetics* he pronounces goodness as possible "even in a woman . . . though [she] is perhaps an inferior . . . ; but it is not appropriate in a female Character to be manly, or clever" (15.1454a20–24); and in the *Rhetoric* he writes that "one quality or action is nobler than another if it is that of a naturally finer being: thus a man's will be nobler than a woman's" (1.9.15).

Those "naturally finer" beings—men—were awarded a public voice, which enabled them to participate as speakers, thinkers, and writers in the polis, in the "good" of public life. A public voice was the right and privilege of those who were declared to possess reason and goodness to its fullest extent—men only. In the polis, the public sphere of action, the realm of highest justice, the world of men, women, and slaves should be invisible and aphonic. "Naturally," then, women and slaves—inferior beings in every way—were condemned to silence as their appointed sphere and condition. Most women spoke no memorable alternative—that is, except for Aspasia. But even Aspasia's voice is muted, for she speaks only through men.

Aspasia's Challenge to the History of Rhetoric

Aspasia colonized the patriarchal territory, but her colony was quickly appropriated by males. Although she herself escaped enclosure, although she publicly articulated her intelligence and her heterosexual love, she did not escape those who defined her. Her influence has been enclosed within the gendered rhetorical terrain—and neutralized. "And the trouble is that the map of an enclosed space describes only the territory inside the enclosure," writes Myra Jehlen. "Without knowing the surrounding geography, how are we to evaluate this woman's estate" (1991, 80)? Few of us have ever heard of Aspasia of Miletus, teacher of rhetoric. But if we locate her colony within "its larger context" and "examine the borders along which [she] defined herself" (81)—the writings of the men she influenced, Plato, Socrates, and Pericles—we can better map out how Aspasia was perceived by those men and, perhaps, how she perceived her estate within the surrounding geography.

But even now Aspasia's intellectual estate seems to be "off-limits." In the nineteenth-century print titled *Alcibiades and Aspasia* French artist J. L. Gerome (best known for transfusing his journeys to the East with an exotic and erotic charm) presents, in beautiful detail, "Our Mother of Rhetoric" reclining seductively on Alcibiades, her hand cupping his breast, while Alcibiades looks away from her and reaches out to clasp Socrates' hand. Thus, Aspasia—lifelong companion of Pericles and influential colleague of famous men—comes down to us as an odalisque. Alcibiades—arrogant, dissolute, untrustworthy, love-object of Socrates— comes to us wreathed in laurel and the object of Aspasia's attention. This inaccurate and unfair example of Aspasia as harem girl to a masterful Alcibiades brings to the fore the whole notion of women's place in rhetoric. Where on that landscape we call rhetorical history should we look for women? How many women remain hidden in the shadows of monumental rhetoricians? How many others remain misidentified as holes and bulges on out-of-the-way territories? How much of rhetorical history is itself, as Carole Blair describes, "rhetorical iterations, saturated with the impure representations, intrinsic interestedness, and general obstreperousness of any discourse" (1992, 417).

If we acknowledge that rhetorical history is not neutral territory, Aspasia's challenge to the history of rhetoric has ramifications for past studies as well as implications for future examinations. The most powerful ramification is an awareness of women's place on the rhetorical terrain—hence, this collection of essays. Surveying the fault line of gender from many angles in this and the other essays in this book reveals that women have, indeed, participated in and contributed to the rhetorical tradition, and that fault line reverberates down the corridors of past scholarship to the foundations of the Greek intellectual tradition. Our first obligation, then, as rhetorical scholars is to look backwards at all the unquestioned scholarship that has come before as we begin to remap our notions of rhetorical history. After all, any history or product of the past is not only active in the present but also shapes the future in knowable ways.

In *Language as Symbolic Action* Kenneth Burke tells us that any narrative, any history, any mapping is a subjective presentation: "Even if any terminology is a *reflection* of reality, by its very nature as a terminology it must be a *selection* of reality; and to this extent it must function also as a *deflection* of reality" ([1966] 1968, 45). All historical accounts, then, even those seeming objective, are stories, tellings, choosings. "So," as Burke would say, "where are we now?"

We are now realizing that the proliferation of new rhetorical maps as well as new interpretations of those maps are allowing us to see that no historiographic rhetorical map ever reflects a neutral reality. In choosing what to show and how to represent it, these maps *do* something: they subtly shape our perceptions of a rhetoric englobed. By simply choosing which men and women to show and how to represent them, we also shape the perceptions of our profession and encourage recognition of more women on our intellectual landscape. We also, of course, shape the perceptions of our students, both female and male, enabling and encouraging them to participate in communities of discourse in which they are uninterested or from which they have felt excluded.

Fortunately, rhetorical scholars—females and males alike—around the country are involved in various feminist historiographic and cartographic projects.[19] We can turn to new maps, often partially completed maps, that reflect and coordinate our current institutional, intellectual, political, and personal values, all of which have become markedly more diverse and elastic in terms of gender, race, and class. We all seem to agree that our new maps are "doing" differently what maps do: they are taking us more places, introducing us to more people, complicating our understanding in more ways than did the previous map. These cartographic achievements are serving to challenge the history of rhetoric to recognize the full range of its texts, its practices, and its theories. Aspasia's contribution to rhetoric is just one of many stories that disrupt and then enrich what has long been held as patriarchal territory. Until recently we did not seem to realize that the rhetorical map had flattened out the truth, leaving scarcely a ridge that could suggest all the women and the otherwise disenfranchised who are buried beneath the surface.

If historical narratives are primarily motivated actions to *do* something, and if that something has to do with power, then perhaps we should find ways to connect our current rhetorical inquiries, histories, and mappings with our contemporary academic and social concerns. After all, the only way we can displace the old map of rhetoric, that monolithic chart of public, political, virile performance, is to replace it with maps that *do* something else, whether that is to search for lost voices, to compare favorably "other" works with canonized works, or to reconceptualize the definition of rhetorical practice in such a way as to challenge the lineal dominance of masculine discourse and to include "others." Each time we encourage such remappings and reconceptualize basic assumptions, whether in our theories or our practices, we are redrawing the boundaries of rhetoric to include new practitioners and new practices. Indeed, the significance of Aspasia's challenge to the history of rhetoric lies in the establishment of her own colony in what has long been thought to be the patriarchal territory of exclusionary rhetoric. The future of rhetoric, the rhetorical frontier, awaits our further explorations, settlements, and mappings.

Notes

1. Previous and ongoing feminist scholarship has helped to create a space for reconceiving and thereby transforming the rhetorical tradition (Ballif 1992; Biesecker 1992; Bizzell and Herzberg 1990; Blair and Kahl 1990; Collins 1993; Glenn 1992, 1994, 1995; Jarratt and Ong 1995; Lunsford 1995; Peaden 1989; Swearingen 1991).

2. Edward P. J. Corbett anticipated women's rhetorical contributions, writing "Rhetoric is one of the most patriarchal of all the academic disciplines. But because of the active feminist movement, we may be on the verge of recovering the names of women who could lay claim to being rhetors" (1990, 577). A regendered history of rhetoric, such as my 1997 *Rhetoric Retold: Regendering the Tradition from Antiquity through the Renaissance*, neither reproduces nor reduces the power politics of that concept referred to as "gender." After all, "gender" is merely a concept borrowed from grammar that connotes "a socially agreed upon system of distinctions rather than an objective description of inherent traits" (Scott 1988, 29). A regendered history, then, examines gender as a relationship among distributions of power,

a relationship that plays itself out within cultural constraints and demands.

3. Joan Kelly tells us that "women's history has a dual goal: to restore women to history and to restore our history to women. . . . In seeking to add women to the fund of historical knowledge, women's history has revitalized theory, for it has shaken the conceptual foundations of historical study" (1984, 1). Carole Blair (1992) contests the histories of rhetoric both when she interrogates the politics of preservation as well as when, with Mary L. Kahl (1990), she argues for revising the history of rhetorical theory. Barbara Herrnstein Smith's "Contingencies of Value" (1988) eloquently demonstrates how such inclusions do and must problematize genres.

4. Miletus had relatively large numbers of literate citizens, among them the philosophers Anaximander, Anaximenes, and Thales (Harris 1989, 63; Kirk and Raven 1962, 73ff.; Vernant [1962] 1982, 127; Vernant [1965] 1983, 343ff.). In *Myth and Society in Ancient Greece* Jean-Pierre Vernant writes that alongside moral thought, "a philosophy of nature starts to develop . . . in the Greek cities of Asia Minor. The theories of these first 'physicists' of Ionia have been hailed as the beginning of rational thought as it is understood in the West" ([1974] 1980, 96).

5. Most scholars (for instance, Bloedow 1975; Flaceliere [1960] 1962; Halperin 1990; Just 1989; Keuls 1985; Licht 1932; Ober 1989) have labeled Aspasia a courtesan, schooled in intellectual and social arts. But both Eva Cantarella ([1981] 1987) and William Courtney (1912) argue that the Athenian suspicion and misunderstanding of such a powerful, political, non-Athenian, unmarriageable woman living with their controversial leader, Pericles, led automatically to the sexualized and undeserved label of hetaera; Nicole Loraux (1986) refers to Aspasia as a foreigner and as a nonpolitician; Mary Ellen Waithe calls her "a rhetorician and a member of the Periclean Philosophic circle" (1987, 75); and Susan Guettel Cole writes only of Aspasia's intellectual influence and measure of literacy (1981, 225).

6. Eva Cantarella clearly describes the hetaera as "more than a casual companion," "more educated than a woman destined for marriage, and intended 'professionally' to accompany men where wives and concubines could not go [namely social activities and discussions]" ([1981] 1987, 30). "This relationship was meant to be somehow gratifying for the man, even on the intellectual level, and was thus completely different from men's relationships with either wives or prostitutes" (31). Robert Flaceliere agrees that "in practice, if not in law, they [hetaerae] enjoyed considerable freedom" ([1960] 1962, 130). He goes on to quote Athenaeus's *Deipnosophists* (XIII) that the hetaerae "applied themselves to study and the knowledge of the sciences" (131).

7. Keuls suggests that a female educational underground might have been the source of male anxiety, for the philosopher Democritus wrote, "Let a woman not develop her reason, for that would be a terrible thing" (Fragment 110, qtd. in Keuls 1985, 104). A character in a lost play by Menander pronounced that "he who teaches letters to his wife is ill-advised: He's giving additional poison to a horrible snake" (Fragment 702 K, ibid.).

8. Roger Just reminds us that "Aspasia's notoriety and the popular resentment her supposed influence aroused should . . . be remembered—a resentment transmuted into mockery by comedy" (1989, 21). In the *Acharnians* Aristophanes writes that the Megarians "abducted *two* whores from Aspasia's stable in Athens" (1969, 523); Plutarch writes that Cratinus "in downright terms, calls her a harlot": "To find him a Juno the goddess of lust / Bore that harlot past shame, / Aspasia by name" (1932, 201). Flaceliere assures us that "the Athenian comic poets never tired of repeating that Aspasia led a life of debauchery, though apparently she was as well behaved as she was well informed, and even a scholar" ([1960] 1962, 131). Cantarella writes, "It is not surprising that many Athenians hated Aspasia. She was not like other women; she was an intellectual" ([1981] 1987, 54–55).

9. See Pomeroy (1975, 89) and Just (1989, 144). But Hans Licht (a pseudonym for Paul Brandt) explains that "the preference for Aspasia shown by Pericles afforded a welcome excuse for his opponents to attack him; people would not hear of a woman having anything to say in political life, especially one who was not an Athenian but was brought from abroad, and even from Ionia . . . , which was notorious for the immorality of its women. . . . Hence she was severely criticized by the comic poets. . . . According to a statement in Athenaeus . . . she was said to have maintained a regular brothel. . . . When she was accused of *asebeia* (impiety) and procuring, Pericles defended her and secured her acquittal" (1932, 352–53).

10. Pierre Vidal-Naquet writes that "the sole civic function of women was to give birth to citizens. The conditions imposed upon them by Pericles' law of 451 was to be the mother of a citizen and a citizen's daughter" (1986, 145).

11. Women of low reputation could be spoken of publicly and freely; for some Aspasia fit such a category. For others Aspasia's intellectual and political gifts earned her a measure of public distinction. David Schaps asserts that there were three categories of women whose "names could be mentioned freely: disreputable women, opposing women, and dead women" (1977, 329).

12. *Arete* is referred to as various manifestations of human excellence: as virtue (the prerequisite of a good human life; cf. Democritus's "On *Arete* or Manly Virtue"); as a combination of self-control, courage, and justice; as moral nobility; or as valor; see Gutherie (1969, 3: 253ff.).

13. The tautology of Jean Bethke Elshtain's argument rightly encompasses Aspasia: "I am not impressed with the claims made for powerful women who influenced men through their private activities—in Athenian society this claim is frequently made for the *hetaera*. . . . Were such 'women-behind-the-men' to have attempted to enter the public arena to speak with their own voices, they would have been roundly jeered, satirized, and condemned" (1987, 14–15, n. 11).

14. Centuries later, in his *Letter of Consolation to Apollonius,* the pseudo-Plutarch would call Pericles "the Olympian" because of his extraordinary powers of speech and understanding (qtd. in Sprague 1972, 23).

15. Taylor quotes from the fragments of the *Aspasia* collated in H. Dittmar's *Aeschines von Sphettos.*

16. In her epistolary arguments with Abelard, Heloise relies on ancient authorities. In one particular case, her crown *auctoritas* is Aspasia. Quoting from the now-missing text of Aeschines, Heloise argues for the excellence of a good wife and a good husband (Moncrieff 1942, 58). In her reading of Heloise's letters, Andrea Nye challenges the philosophical community to be "informed by Heloise's and Aspasia's wisdom, their subtle, sensitive, mobile, flexible women's tongues." She also wants us to admit that "a woman can be the teacher of a man" (1992, 17).

17. In addition, Aspasia is memorialized in a fresco over the portal of the University of Athens, in the company of Phidias, Pericles (on whom she leans), Sophocles, Antisthenes, Anaxagoras, Alcibiades, and Socrates.

18. Thucydides writes, "Everyone who wishes to, both citizens and foreigners, can join in the procession, and the women who are related to the dead are there to make their laments at the tomb" (1954, 2.34).

19. For example, recent issues of both *College Composition and Communication* (October 1992) and *Rhetoric Society Quarterly* (Winter 1992) center on feminist readings of rhetoric and composition, theories and practices. Also see notes 1, 2, and 3.

References

Aristophanes. 1969. *The Acharnians.* In *Four Comedies,* edited by William Arrowsmith. Trans. Douglass Parker, 99–112. Ann Arbor: University of Michigan Press.

Aristotle. 1977. *Politics.* Trans. H. Rackham. Cambridge: Loeb-Harvard University Press.

———. 1984. *The Rhetoric and Poetics of Aristotle.* Trans. W. Rhys Roberts and Ingram Bywater. New York: Modern Library.

Athenaeus. 1967. *The Deipnosophists.* Trans. Charles Burton Gulick. Cambridge: Harvard University Press.

Ballif, Michelle. 1992. "Re/Dressing Histories; Or, On Re/Covering Figures Who Have Been Laid Bare by Our Gaze." *Rhetoric Society Quarterly* 22 (Winter): 91–98.

Biesecker, Barbara. 1992. "Coming to Terms with Recent Attempts to Write Women into the History of Rhetoric." *Philosophy and Rhetoric* 25.2: 140–61.

Bizzell, Patricia. 1992. "Opportunities for Feminist Research in the History of Rhetoric." *Rhetoric Review* 11 (Fall): 50–58.

Bizzell, Patricia, and Bruce Herzberg. 1990. *The Rhetorical Tradition: Readings from Classical Times to the Present.* Boston: Bedford-St. Martin's Press.

Blair, Carole. 1992. "Contested Histories of Rhetoric: The Politics of Preservation, Progress, and Change." *Quarterly Journal of Speech* 78 (November): 403–28.

Blair, Carole, and Mary L. Kahl. 1990. "Introduction: Revising the History of Rhetorical Theory." *Western Journal of Speech Communication* 54 (Spring): 148–59.

Bloedow, Edmund F. 1975. "Aspasia and the 'Mystery' of the Menexenos." *Wiener Studien (Zeitschrift fur Klassiche Philologie und Patristic)* Neu Folge 9: 32–48.

Burke, Kenneth. [1966] 1968. *Language as Symbolic Action.* Berkeley: University of California Press.

Cantarella, Eva. [1981] 1987. *Pandora's Daughters.* Baltimore: Johns Hopkins University Press.

Cicero. 1972. *De Oratore (Book III), De Fato, Paradoxa Stoicorum, Partitiones Oratoriae.* Trans. H. Rackam. Cambridge: Harvard University Press. 2–188.

———. 1976. *De Inventione, De Optimo Genere, Oratorum, Topica.* Trans. H. M. Hubbell. Cambridge: Harvard University Press. 1–348.

Cole, Susan Guettel. 1981. "Could Greek Women Read and Write?" In *Reflections of Women in Antiquity,* edited by Helene P. Foley, 219–45. New York: Gordon.

Collins, Vicki Tolar. 1993. "Perfecting a Woman's Life: Methodist Rhetoric and Politics in *The Account of Hester Ann Rogers.*" Ph.D. diss., Auburn University.

———. 1996. "Walking in Light, Walking in Darkness: The Story of Women's Changing Rhetorical Space in Early Methodism." *Rhetoric Review.*

Corbett, Edward P. J. 1990. *Classical Rhetoric for the Modern Student.* New York: Oxford University Press.

Courtney, William. 1912. "Sappho and Aspasia." *Fortnightly Review* 97: 488–95.

Delcourt, Marie. 1939. *Pericles.* N.p.: Gallimard Press.

Elshtain, Jean Bethke. 1987. *Public Man, Private Woman.* Princeton: Princeton University Press.

Flaceliere, Robert. [1960] 1962. *Love in Ancient Greece.* Trans. James Cleugh. London: Frederick Muller.

Glenn, Cheryl. 1992. "Author, Audience, and Autobiography: Rhetorical Technique in *The Book of Margery Kempe.*" *College English* 53 (September): 540–53.

———. 1994. "sex, lies, and manuscript: Refiguring Aspasia in the History of Rhetoric." *College Composition and Communication* 45 (May): 180–99.

———. 1995. "Remapping Rhetorical Territory." *Rhetoric Review* 13 (Spring): 287–303.

———. 1997. *Rhetoric Retold: Regendering the Tradition from Antiquity through the Renaissance.* Carbondale: Southern Illinois University Press.

Gutherie, W. K. C. 1969. *A History of Greek Philosophy.* 6 vols. Cambridge: Cambridge University Press.

Halperin, David M. 1990. *One Hundred Years of Homosexuality.* New York: Routledge.

Harris, William V. 1989. *Ancient Literacy.* Cambridge: Harvard University Press.

Jarratt, Susan C. 1991. *Rereading the Sophists: Classical Rhetoric Refigured.* Carbondale: Southern Illinois University Press.

———. 1992. "Performing Feminisms, Histories, Rhetorics." *Rhetoric Society Quarterly* 22 (Winter): 1–6.

Jarratt, Susan C., and Rory Ong. 1995. "Aspasia: Rhetoric, Gender, and Colonial Ideology." In *Reclaiming Rhetorica: Women in the Rhetorical Tradition*, edited by Andrea A. Lunsford, 9–24. Pittsburgh: University of Pittsburgh Press.

Jehlen, Myra. 1991. "Archimedes and the Paradox of Feminist Criticism." In *Feminisms*, edited by Robyn R. Warhol and Diane Price Herndl, 75–96. New Brunswick: Rutgers University Press.

Just, Roger. 1989. *Women in Athenian Law and Life*. London: Routledge.

Kelly, Joan. 1984. *Women, History, and Theory: The Essays of Joan Kelly*. Chicago: University of Chicago Press.

Keuls, Eva C. 1985. *The Reign of the Phallus*. New York: Harper.

Kirk, G. S., and J. E. Raven. 1962. *The Presocratic Philosophers*. Cambridge: Cambridge University Press.

Laqueur, Thomas. 1990. *Making Sex*. Cambridge: Harvard University Press.

Licht, Hans [Paul Brandt]. 1932. *Sexual Life in Ancient Greece*. London: Abbey Library.

Loraux, Nicole. 1986. *The Invention of Athens: The Funeral Oration in the Classical City*. Trans. Alan Sheridan. Cambridge: Harvard University Press.

Lunsford, Andrea A., ed. 1995. *Reclaiming Rhetorica: Women in the Rhetorical Tradition*. Pittsburgh: University of Pittsburgh Press.

Mackin, James A. Jr. 1991. "Schismogenesis and Community: Pericles' Funeral Oration." *Quarterly Journal of Speech* 77.3: 251–62.

Mitchell, Juliet. 1975. *Psychoanalysis and Feminism*. New York: Vintage-Random.

Moncrieff, C. K. 1942. *The Letters of Abelard and Heloise*. New York: Knopf.

Nye, Andrea. 1992. "A Woman's Thought or a Man's Discipline? The Letters of Abelard and Heloise." *Hypatia* 7 (Summer): 1–22.

Ober, Josiah. 1989. *Mass and Elite in Democratic Athens*. Princeton: Princeton University Press.

Peaden, Catherine. 1989. "Feminist Theories, Historiographies, and Histories of Rhetoric: The Role of Feminism in Historical Studies." In *Rhetoric and Ideology: Compositions and Criticisms of Power*, edited by Charles Kneupper, 116–26. Arlington, Tex.: Rhetoric Society of America.

Plato. 1952. *Gorgias*. Trans. W. C. Helmbold. Indianapolis: Bobbs-Merrill.

———. 1977. *Euthyphro, Apology, Crito, Phaedo, Phaedrus*. Trans. H. N. Fowler. Cambridge: Harvard University Press. 405–579.

———. [1929] 1981. *Timaeus, Critias, Cleitophon, Menexenus, Epistles*. Trans. R. G. Bury. London: Heinemann-Loeb.

———. 1982. *Republic*. 2 vols. Trans. Paul Shorey. Cambridge: Harvard University Press.

Plutarch. 1932. *The Lives of the Noble Grecians and Romans*. Trans. John Dryden, rev. Arthur Hugh Clough. New York: Modern Library.

Pomeroy, Sarah. 1975. *Goddesses, Whores, Wives, and Slaves*. New York: Schocken.

Quintilian. [1920] 1969. *Institutio Oratoria.* 4 vols. Trans. H. E. Butler. London: Heinemann.

Schaps, David M. 1977. "The Woman Least Mentioned: Etiquette and Women's Names." *Classical Quarterly* 27: 323–31.

Scott, Joan Wallach. 1988. *Gender and the Politics of History.* New York: Columbia University Press.

Smith, Barbara Herrnstein. 1988. "Contingencies of Value." In *Contingencies of Value,* edited by Barbara Herrnstein Smith, 30–53. Cambridge: Harvard University Press.

Sprague, Rosamond Kent, ed. 1972. *The Older Sophists.* Columbia: University of South Carolina Press.

Swearingen, C. Jan. 1991. *Rhetoric and Irony.* New York: Oxford University Press.

Taylor, A. E. 1960. *Plato, the Man and His Work.* 7th ed. London: Methuen.

Thucydides. 1954. *History of the Peloponnesian War.* Trans. Rex Warner. London: Penguin.

Vernant, Jean-Pierre. [1974] 1980. *Myth and Society in Ancient Greece.* New York: Zone.

———. [1962] 1982. *The Origins of Greek Thought.* Ithaca: Cornell University Press.

———. [1965] 1983. *Myth and Thought among the Greeks.* London: Routledge.

Vidal-Naquet, Pierre. 1986. *The Black Hunter.* Trans. Andrew Szegedy-Maszak. Baltimore: Johns Hopkins University Press.

Waithe, Mary Ellen, ed. 1987. *A History of Women Philosophers.* Vol. 1: *600 bc–500 ad.* Dordrecht: Martinus Nijhoff.

Xenophon. 1988. *Memorabilia and Oeconomicus.* Trans. E. C. Marchant. Cambridge: Harvard University Press.

On Liberty and Logic
The Collaboration of Harriet Taylor and John Stuart Mill

Virginia Allen

Who can tell how many of the most original thoughts put forth by
male writers, belong to woman by suggestion, to themselves only
by verifying and working out? If I may judge by my own case, a
very large portion indeed.
John Stuart Mill
The Subjection of Woman

Collaborative writing, like the "self," is not a stable or coherent
construct.
Lisa Ede and Andrea Lunsford,
Singular Texts / Plural Authors

The Problem Stated

Despite the strict social constructionists' denial of the possibility of
individual authorship, those of us with an unregenerate biographical
bent in our natures find questions about authorship and relative degrees of co-authorship not only intriguing but amenable to investigation.
It is against this conflicted theoretical backdrop that I propose to reexamine the most famous case of dubious co-authorship in the history of
Western civilization, the composition of *On Liberty,* written by John Stuart
Mill and—if we can take his word for it—his wife Harriet Taylor Mill.
Whether Mill's judgment about his wife's contribution to his work can,
in fact, be trusted has been a much debated biographical question for an
extended period of time (Anschutz 1955; Bain 1882; Diffenbaugh 1923;
Hayek 1951; Himmelfarb 1965, 1974; Mazlish 1988; Mineka 1963; Packe
1954; Pappé 1956, 1960; Robson 1966, 1968; Rose 1983; Rossi 1970; Soper
1983; Stillinger 1969, 1983; Stove 1993; Trilling 1952, to cite some of the
more prominent). From a historical perspective, the extraordinary thing
about the case is that so much of the archival evidence for a reasonable

judgment about her influence and what has happened to her reputation is still retrievable.

Although they may strike the hyper-sophisticated postmodern reader as naive, three distinct but intertwined questions have beset discussions of the case for more than a century: Is *On Liberty* a "great" work? Was Harriet a collaborator on the text? Was Harriet a genius? The conclusion of most commentators has been that *On Liberty* is undeniably a great achievement and that, therefore, Harriet, who was no genius, could not have been a serious co-author. The conclusion of the conservative opposition has been that *On Liberty* is not a great work and the cause for its deficiency is the overpowering influence of Harriet, who was no genius, upon John during the years of its composition. The common ground has been the unarguable certainty that Harriet was no genius.

That the liberal and conservative explanations—based on the same data—contradict one another as to the nature and extent of her influence has not been recognized as even a minor obstacle in the controversy. Since it has appeared patently impossible to so many readers that Harriet could have been an equal collaborator as John maintained both in his *Autobiography* (1873) and prominently in the dedication to *On Liberty* (1859), the problem has been to explain away his persistent unwarranted claim. Once the problem is pointed out, the curlicued logic around the evidence that persists in denying Harriet's small claim to fame is not difficult to analyze, and the odd twist in the evidence against her is not difficult to trace through the archival record and the commentary upon such evidence.

One might prefer that Mill had merely appended his wife's name to the title page of *On Liberty* as co-author, but he did not. However, his wish that she be openly regarded as his collaborator was no whimsical or passing claim. Fearing the imminent approach of his own death from consumption, on 29 August 1853 he wrote to her:

> We must finish the best we have got to say, & not only that, but publish it while we are alive. I do not see what living depository there is likely to be of our thoughts, or who in this weak generation that is growing up[1] will even be capable of thoroughly mastering & assimilating your ideas, much less of re-originating them—so we must write them & print them, & then they can wait until there are again thinkers. But I shall never be satisfied unless you allow ou[r][2] best book the book which is to come, to have our two names on the title page. It

ought to be so with everything I publish, for the better half of it all is yours, but the book which will contain our best thoughts, if it has only one name to it, that should be yours. I should like everyone to know that I am the Dumont & you the originating mind, the Bentham, bless her! (Hayek 1951, 185)

But in this, as in most decisions, he deferred to Harriet's judgment, and it was her judgment that a subject of such grave importance—"the nature and limits of the power which can be legitimately exercised by society over the individual" (Mill [1859] 1976, 1)—ought not be diminished in its impact by having her name interfere with its reception (Hayek 1951, 124). When this short treatise, recognized as the classic statement of liberalism, was published the year following Harriet Mill's death, it bore this effusive dedication:

To the beloved and deplored memory of her who was the inspirer, and in part the author, of all that is best in my writings—the friend and wife whose exalted sense of truth and right was my strongest incitement, and whose approbation was my chief reward—I dedicate this volume. Like all that I have written for many years, it belongs as much to her as to me; but the work as it stands has had, in a very insufficient degree, the inestimable advantage of her revisions; some of the most important portions having been reserved for a more careful re-examination, which they are now never destined to receive. Were I but capable of interpreting to the world one half the great thoughts and noble feelings which are buried in her grave, I should be the medium of a greater benefit to it, than is ever likely to arise from anything that I can write, unprompted and unassisted by her all but unrivaled wisdom. (Mill 1859, versa 1)

About this sort of praise John M. Robson makes a fair assessment: "[J. S. Mill's] hyperbolic statements about [Harriet Taylor Mill's] powers have *offended* [my emphasis] successive generations, and not least the present one which, if it has no living memory of her, has more literary evidence" (1966, 168).

What Counts as Evidence?

Three kinds of evidence, in fact, have been brought to bear on the case. First, literary or textual evidence, long declared to be nonexistent, has recently come under scrutiny. The second and most popular kind of evidence has been the testimony of observers, most of which is hearsay, especially after about 1840 when the unmarried couple withdrew from social life, purportedly as a result of being made aware of the malicious gossip that followed in their wake. Finally and most persuasive has been the evidence of numerous impassioned appeals to what "everybody knows" about how husbands and wives collaborate.

Adherence to the principle of parsimony undoubtedly has operated here: Mill clearly had all the intellectual ability and literary skill necessary to write the text without his wife, so why complicate the hypothesis that he wrote holding the pen and shaping the arguments with, perhaps, her kibitzing and niggling editorial suggestions? Still, when a commentator's judgment leaks forth either contempt or defensiveness for a woman more than a century in the grave, we need not ascribe incontestable scientific objectivity to our own judgment to guess fairly that something odd and very personal is going on. Where reports of witnesses conflict with one another, that is just the point at which we ought to set up our biographical excavating equipment.

Looking back at the record of commentary on the case, it is not always apparent when one type of evidence has blended into the next as presupposition or interpretation, and in the way of too much research based largely in secondary source material, what was stated as opinion in one place has been passed on as fact in the next.

The Written Record: Where's the Proof?

What evidence remains of the independent personality and literary production of Harriet was collected in 1951 by F. A. Hayek in *John Stuart Mill and Harriet Taylor: Their Correspondence and Subsequent Marriage,*[3] and its publication incited a spate of commentary on the relationship in the 1950s that bears the peculiar misogynistic mark of that period in history. Along with the letters Hayek includes an early, unpublished essay by Harriet Taylor that, he says with due caution, "*curiously* [my emphasis] anticipates some of the arguments of *On Liberty*" (26). Far more typical is commentary by Bruce Mazlish, who warns us that "we must not overvalue Harriet's contribution" (1988, 383). Mazlish points out that Mill in his *Autobiography* says he had "first planned and written it as a short essay in 1854" (382), and Mill does write from Rome (15 January 1855): "I wish I had brought with me here the paper on Liberty that I wrote for our volume of Essays—perhaps my dearest will kindly read it through

& tell me whether it will do as the foundation of *one part* [my emphasis] of the volume in question" (Hayek 1951, 216).

Prominent among the conservatives who attribute what deficiencies may appear in Mill's literary production to the influence of his wife is Gertrude Himmelfarb. She calls Harriet Taylor "a mediocre mind" and opines that Mill was lucky to be freed from her dogmatic and ideological influence by her early death, but her most serious charge is that *On Liberty* is a flawed effort to find "simple principles" to justify the rights of individuals against the demands of society. She attributes the insight that the liberty of women was central to the argument of the treatise to the man history remembers primarily as "Mill's friend," Alexander Bain: "'The Subjection of Women' was deplored by most of Mill's friends, by Alexander Bain as much as the others. But Bain saw what the rest did not. Mill's 'strongest case' in *On Liberty*, he wrote, was the 'relationship of the sexes' which was 'little more than hinted at' [Bain 1882, 108]. Bain did not elaborate upon this comment. But it may provide us with matter for thought" (Himmelfarb 1974, 183).

Himmelfarb believes that there are "Two Mills" (1965). In her opinion, the most articulate refutations of the extreme liberalism expressed in *On Liberty* are found in the writings of J. S. Mill himself before his relationship with Harriet began and after her death. Whoever may have held the pen while the couple wrote together, the thesis of *On Liberty*—and a sorry thesis she thinks it to be—she attributes wholly to Harriet Taylor Mill. The "one very simple principle" of *On Liberty* is "that the sole end for which mankind are warranted, individually or collectively, in interfering with the liberty of action of any of their number is self-protection" (1974, qtd. 3). She notes first that, having rejected the greatest happiness principle of Benthamite utilitarianism, "Mill had intimate experience with attempts to base an entire philosophy upon a single principle, and he had dramatically rejected those attempts—rejected not only the particular principle at issue but the *simplistic view of human nature and social affairs* [my emphasis] implied in the assertion of such a principle" (1974, 4).

To support her contention that John was demonstrably more conservative (and intelligently so) than Harriet, Himmelfarb cites Alice Rossi's observation (1970) that *The Enfranchisement of Women* (which Rossi convincingly attributes primarily to Harriet) approves of the employment of women, while *The Subjection of Women* (which Rossi attributes primarily to John) "disapproved of such employment except in special circumstances" (1974, 185–86).

Stripped down to bare proposition, the principal claim against Harriet's serious collaboration with John is that praise so extreme could not possibly be true; this claim is reinforced by the seemingly reasonable call for objective evidence. With a tone of unexceptionable objectivity, Bain frames the prevailing opinion: "If Mill had been content with putting forward these explanations as to his wife's concurrence in his labours, the world would have accepted them as given, and would have accorded her a reputation corresponding. Unfortunately for both, he outraged all reasonable credibility in describing her matchless genius, without being able to supply any corroborating testimony" (1882, 171).

The recurrent plea for evidence of Harriet's independent genius carries with it the unexamined presumption that genius is the result of the solitary artist working alone. Falsifying Robert Connors's claim that the agonistic impulse is a male-against-male phenomenon (1992), Diana Trilling makes the presumption explicit:

> If Mrs. Taylor[4] was as talented as Mill says, why, we must ask, did she leave no independent record of it? What writer is content to be vicarious forever? (After all, even Jane Carlyle wrote more and better letters than circumstances required.) Or again, if Mrs. Taylor was so luminous a character, why was her light visible only to Mill? We can dismiss Carlyle's poor opinion of her, for who would take Carlyle's opinion of anybody; and we can accuse Mrs. Carlyle of cattiness. Still shouldn't there have been someone from the Mill-Taylor circle, however small that became, to bear witness in Mrs. Taylor's defense? (1952, 115–16)

Without going too far afield, we might note in passing that the witnesses on Harriet's behalf were among the Unitarian radicals led by William J. Fox. That a woman might choose to submerge her work in the work of her husband rather than not work at all is not argued against: it is only presumed that genius does not work that way. Rossi ponders that while a great deal of effort has been expended on discrediting Harriet's genius, no one has wondered what she might have done had John not provided her a powerful means for getting her ideas before a hostile public (1970, 33).

The Testimony of Firsthand Witnesses

Two putative firsthand witnesses to the Taylor/Mill affair command special attention: Thomas Carlyle and Alexander Bain. While Carlyle's assessment is recognized as extreme, self-justifying, and inconsistent, repeatedly Bain has been taken as the unbiased voice of reason. Every student of literature knows that in 1835 John Mill inadvertently put Carlyle's manuscript of the first volume of *The French Revolution* in a pile of paper to be used in the fireplace, and the housemaid destroyed all but a few scraps. No one, to my knowledge, has realized that much of Bain's knowledge of Harriet, whom he never met face-to-face, came to him only through Carlyle and Carlyle's intimates.

The focus of my own interest in the case was not originally on "the myth of Harriet Taylor" (a nominalization that prejudges the evidence) but on Bain. When I first started to try to find out more about Bain, I kept coming across him not in the text of the lives of the various Mills but in the subtext, in the footnotes.

Bain has a great deal to say about the Mill family. He wrote a biography of Mill's father and a quasi-biography of the younger Mill, titled, honestly enough, *John Stuart Mill: A Criticism with Personal Recollections.* Among Bain's many complaints about the son was that it was his filial duty to write a biography of his great father, but as he failed in that duty, it finally fell to Bain to carry out the responsibility. Both biographies were published in 1882, a decade following J. S. Mill's death and the coincident publication of his *Autobiography* in 1873 but—perhaps significantly—a year after the death of Carlyle.

Since Bain is used as a primary source of information about all the various Mill relationships and since he is in everything I have ever read always treated as a disinterested observer, we ought to look more closely at what facts there are to support his often-cited assessments of the Mill family. The fact that his characterizations of James Mill as the prototype of the self-made man and Harriet Mill as the domineering wife with the unexceptional intellect have taken on the status of truth is not his fault; nor should he be blamed for the prolonged controversy that his hearsay testimony has supported. I make a point of this because in her defense of Bain, Andrea Lunsford protests the fact that he has become "a popular whipping boy" among composition theorists (1982, 290). As she insists with some justice, Bain was not personally responsible for caging discourse theory inside the four forms of discourse (1982, 297), nor should he be blamed for being more appreciated as a biographer than as a psychologist or rhetorician. Had Bain never taken up his pen, the controversy would still have developed; Carlyle would have seen to that. In the nineteenth century what Bain did was to rationalize and give a scientific voice to the prevalent misogyny.

Testimony as Evidence: Telling the Tale

The story of Mill's ill-considered infatuation with Mrs. Taylor has been told and retold, and the reputation of the lady has, if anything, deteriorated through the retellings. Every narrative, of course, involves the selection and arrangement of detail. What is left out may be as significant as what is put in or relegated to a footnote.

It is customary to begin the story with the circumstances of their first meeting. When Mill, recovering from his 1828 mental breakdown, met Harriet Taylor in 1830, she was twenty-three years old, unhappily married to a somewhat older, wealthy, but dull businessman, and the mother of two sons; a daughter was born shortly after. It is generally agreed that Fox introduced them in an effort to assuage Mrs. Taylor's intellectual restlessness. John Mill, by all accounts, was utterly smitten. In a famous letter Carlyle describes the situation to Charles Eliot Norton upon hearing of Mill's death in 1873:

A verra noble soul was John Mill, quite sure, beautiful to think of. I never could find out what more than ordinary there was in the woman he cared so much for; but there was absolute sincerity in his devotion to her. She was the daughter of a flourishing London Unitarian tradesman, and her husband was the son of another, and the two families made the match. Taylor was a verra respectable man, but his wife found him dull; she had dark, black, hard eyes, and an inquisitive nature, and was ponderin' on many questions that worried her, and could get no answers to them, and that Unitarian clergyman you've heard of, William Fox by name, told her at last that there was a young philosopher of very remarkable quality, whom he thought just the man to deal with her case. And so Mill with great difficulty was brought to see her, and that man, who up to that time, had never looked a female creature, not even a cow, in the face, found himself opposite those great dark eyes, that were flashing unutterable things, while he was discoursing the utterable concernin' all sorts o' high topics. (Hayek 1951, 287; Norton 1974, 496–97)

Carlyle tells a great story, so saturated with verisimilitude that one could hardly doubt he was there on the spot to view the bewitching. However, he himself did not actually meet Mill until 1831, and there is no evidence that he was aware of Harriet Taylor at the time. (It may be only coincidence that Bain mistakenly dates the couple's meeting in 1831.) Again, Hayek makes the point: "Much of the information we have about Mill and Harriet Taylor during the early years after their friendship had become intimate comes at second hand. For a few years in the middle of the 1830s they apparently made little attempt to conceal their intimacy until they became aware of the inevitable gossip which they had caused and withdrew almost completely from all social contacts" (1951, 79).

The Carlyles were out of London from 1832 until 1834—during the Taylors' trial separation and the "arrangement" between the Taylors and Mill that followed—but the affair was the first piece of gossip they picked up on when they returned. If we take Carlyle's own words in a letter to his brother as evidence, the extravagance of his 1873 account was constructed well after the fact: "*Thomas Carlyle to Dr. John Carlyle, May 1834:* Mrs. Austin had a tragical story of [John Mill's] having fallen desperately in love with some young philosophic beauty (yet with all the innocence of two sucking doves), and being lost to all his friends and to himself, and what not; but *I traced nothing of this in poor Mill* [my emphasis]; and even incline to think that what truth there is or was in the adventure may have done him good. Buller also spoke of it but in the comic vein" (Hayek 1951, 80).

My first inclination is to rely entirely on Hayek's reconstruction of the dates, and Buller's soirée and the subsequent falling out after the reported amusement in 1834 do not necessarily contradict Hayek's guess that the fateful soirée, which led to the end of Mill's closeness with John Roebuck, may have taken place on 15 June 1835. If so, that would put the soirée and the subsequent falling out after the accidental burning of the manuscript while it was in Mill's possession (6 March 1835). Hayek says: "It [the soirée] cannot have been before 1835, since it was only the beginning of that year that the Bullers came to live in London" (291). (Serious archival scholarship is not a job for the fainthearted.)

In any case, on the occasion of a soirée given by Mrs. Buller, Roebuck was astonished into taking action: "Mill entered the room with Mrs. Taylor hanging on his arm. The manner of the lady, the evident devotion of the gentleman, soon attracted universal attention, and a suppressed titter went round the room. My affection for Mill was so warm and sincere that I was hurt by anything which brought ridicule upon him. I saw, or thought I saw, how mischievous might be this affair, and as we had become in all things like brothers, I determined, most unwisely, to speak to him on the subject" (Hayek 1951, 79–80). Roebuck's account is that he went to Mill at the India House where Mill listened to his complaint in utter silence. The warmth of their friendship was over, and Roebuck considered himself the aggrieved party. This is represented as the first of many such terminations on account of Mrs. Taylor.

The years 1834 and 1835 must have been extraordinarily stimulating to this celebrated London circle. The Unitarian minister Fox was romantically, but probably not sexually, involved with his ward Eliza Flower—the father of Eliza and her sister having died in 1829 after appointing Fox executor and trustee. Mrs. Fox apparently made her complaint public in 1834, and a fight for the congregation followed. Fox won but in the process lost 46 of his 120–member flock. He separated from his wife and lived with Eliza and two of his children ("at their request"), according to Bruce Mazlish (1988, 295), until Eliza's death in 1846.

Bain says that when he first went to London in 1842, "the friendship [between John and Harriet] had lasted eleven years," and the affair was "the familiar talk of all the circle" (1882, 163). Mrs. Grote (but not Grote himself), Mrs. Austin, and Harriet Martineau were all "under the ban" (164), but the open break with the Carlyles had not yet come. Bain intimates that Martineau,[5] "who had special opportunities of knowing the history of the connexion, and also spoke her mind freely concerning it" (164), was another firsthand witness from whom his secondhand view was derived, but Hayek's assertion that "Bain's discretion has refrained from passing her story on to us" (36) presupposes first that Bain was discreet and second that there may have been some tidbit of information in Martineau's story that he withheld. Neither presumption is necessary, nor—I think—justified. Everything Bain tells us about Harriet Taylor Mill has the status of hearsay, and the freedom of Martineau's gossip ensured that she was one of the women put "under the ban" by Mill. Bain's *Criticism* of John Mill was not motivated by discretion, and the purpose of his invoking the women as sources for the story he tells— while, coincidentally minimizing Carlyle and Grote's importance as sources—is to give authority to events he himself was in no way privy to while at the same time characterizing gossip as a feminine enterprise. Hayek says that Carlyle never seemed to understand that his long-standing habit of gossip was what finally came between him and Mill (88–89).

R. P. Anschutz, in a telling description, says that after finishing *Sartor Resartus* (1834), Carlyle seems "to have found himself only to lose his publishers" (1955, 66). Carlyle was having difficulty placing the review articles he depended upon for a living when Mill attached himself as a kind of disciple, which Carlyle found quite congenial. Norton writes that he was the first to inform Carlyle of Mill's death in 1873: "He had not even heard of his illness, and he was deeply moved. . . . 'it's so long since I've seen him, and he was the friendliest of men to me when I was in need of friends'" (Norton 1974, 495). As Anschutz puts it: "The death of his father enabled Mill to open *The London and Westminster Review* to all writers 'who were in sympathy with progress' as he understood it. And from this time Carlyle became a frequent contributor" (1955, 73).

Even before Carlyle's manuscript was burned, the Carlyles' assessment of Harriet was somewhat unstable. In a correspondence of 22 July 1834 Carlyle describes her to his brother as "a living romance heroine, of the clearest insight, of the royalest volition, very interesting, of questionable destiny" (Hayek 1951, 80). In August, Carlyle wrote to his mother that "Jane has made a most promising acquaintance, of a Mrs. Taylor; a young beautiful reader of mine and 'dearest friend' of Mill's, who for the present seems 'all that is noble' and what not. We shall see how that wears." Later in August, Carlyle said to his brother: "Mrs. Taylor herself did not yield unmixed satisfaction, or receive it. She affects, with a kind of sultana noble-mindedness, a certain girlish petulance, and felt that it did not wholly prosper." In September, walking to call on Mrs. Taylor, the Carlyles came unexpectedly upon her and her husband: "pale she, and passionate and sad-looking: really felt a kind of interest in her" (Hayek 1951, 81). By October, again to his brother, Carlyle waxed philosophical about people "very indignant at marriage and the like" who find themselves "obliged to divorce their own wives, or be divorced: for though the world is already blooming (or is one day to do it) in everlasting 'happiness of the greatest number,' these people's own houses (I always find) are little Hells of improvidence, discord, unreason. Mill is far above all that, and I think will not sink in it; however, I do wish him fairly far from it. . ." (82). And in correspondence of 12 January 1835 Jane Carlyle reports: "There is a Mrs. Taylor who I could really love, if it were safe and she were willing; but she is a dangerous looking woman and engrossed with a dangerous passion, and no useful relation can spring up between us" (Hayek 1951, 82). To this comment, Carlyle amends that "she was worse than dangerous—she was patronizing" (Diffenbaugh 1923, 202).

At some point about this time, in the days before carbon paper and Xerox machines, Mill borrowed the only copy of the ill-fated manuscript. It does seem beyond belief that in a bookish household anyone would burn paper without first getting explicit permission, but the story is that on 6 March 1835 the housemaid used it to start a fire. Carlyle's version, as recorded by Norton, is that Mill took the manuscript "to that woman Mrs. Taylor in whom he had discovered so much that no one else could find. And so she had it at her house on the riverside at Kingston, and I never shall forget the dismay on John Mill's face one day when he came to tell me the housemaid lighted the fire with it, and it was gone. . . . Oh, as for her I never heard that it very much diminished her content in life" (1974, 496).

The story is that in his anguish Mill and Mrs. Taylor rushed to the Carlyle house in a carriage. Hayek suspects it to be a later addition to the story for dramatic effect, but upon seeing the carriage and the evident haste, Jane is reported to have cried out, "Gracious Providence, he has gone off with Mrs. Taylor." Mill dashed up the stairs alone, begging Jane to run down to the carriage and speak to Harriet. What the Carlyles felt at first was great relief that they were not witnessing an elopement, but as the enormity of the real news sank in, Hayek suggests that "they seem to have conceived of the idea that Mrs. Taylor was responsible for the destruction of the manuscript"; Hayek continues, "their various hints to that effect were later exaggerated by others into the scarcely veiled allegation that Mrs. Taylor had deliberately destroyed it" (83).

James Mill died in July 1836. Carlyle wrote to Jane: "There was little sorrow visible in their house, or rather none, nor any human feeling at all; but the strangest *unheimlich* kind of composure and acquiescence, as if all human spontaneity had taken refuge in invisible corners. Mill himself talked much, and not stupidly—far from that—but without emotion of any discernible kind." Carlyle describes his thirty-year-old friend as "withered" and his eyes as "twinkling and jerking with wild lights and twitches." Finally, "It seemed to me the strangest thing what this man could want with me, or I with such a man so *unheimlich* to me." Jane's sagacious reply is directly to the point: "Poor Mill! He really seems to have 'loved and lived'; his very intellect seems to be failing him in its strongest point:—his implicit admiration and subjection to you" (Hayek 1951, 84–85).

By 1837 Carlyle was back to his gossipy self, writing to John Sterling of Mill: "His Platonica and he are constant as ever: innocent I do believe as sucking doves, and yet suffering the clack of tongues, worst penalty of guilt" (Mazlish 1988, 301). That Carlyle himself did much to keep the tongues clacking, he never seemed fully to admit. "Sometime in the middle 'forties,'" Hayek says, "Mill and Mrs. Taylor had suddenly become aware of the talk that was going on about them and not only broke radically with all those whom they suspected of gossip but altogether withdrew from society. To have offended in this connection was the one thing that Mill never forgave" (Hayek 1951, 89).

Enter Alexander Bain. The man whom every history book records as "Mill's friend Alexander Bain" traces his first letter to Mill to 1839, when he was nineteen and a student at Marischal College, Aberdeen. First Bain "assiduously perused the back numbers of the *London* and *London and Westminster Reviews,* as well each new number as it appeared" until he pretty much had Mill by heart "and was thus able to exchange ideas with him on his own subjects" (1882, 62–63). He came to London from Aberdeen for five months beginning in 1842: "The day after arriving, I walked down to the India House with Robertson, and realized my dream of meeting Mill in person" (1882, 64).

In his own *Autobiography* Bain meets Mill on page 124, versa, and Carlyle on page 125, recto: "It was not long ere Robertson in his zeal was able to introduce me to Carlyle, after a little hesitation as to whether I should be welcome. However, he obtained the requisite permission; and Carlyle was quite friendly and gracious" (1904, 125). Bain was just the sort of fellow Carlyle liked best, a disciple. Bain says that he believes it was in 1841 that he read *Heroes* "and derived from it a portion of the stimulation that it gave to the then young generation. From that time forth, I was a reader of his works as they appeared, and may be said to have acquired a thorough mastery of them all" (1904, 126).

It is no great stretch to conjecture that Bain also mastered Carlyle's opinion of Harriet Taylor. In his *Autobiography* Mill adds insult to the injury of the burned manuscript when he describes Harriet as "more of a poet than Carlyle" and more of a thinker than himself—her only equal being his father—thus dividing up intellectual culture into the abstract and scientific, which he takes unto himself, and the imaginative and poetic, which he renders unto Carlyle, save for their mutual superior, Harriet. Bain accepts the categories except for the detail that he knocks

Harriet off her pedestal. He grants that she has a poetic mind, like Carlyle, but he denies the possibility that she is capable of scientific thinking at all. He sees himself, like Mill, as one of the abstract, scientific sort of men; Harriet, like Carlyle, he takes on the authority of both Carlyle and Mill himself (when he is not outraging credibility with hyperbole) to have "the groundwork of an imaginative intellect" undeveloped, by necessity, because of the reproductive burden. As a footnote to Mill's quoted remark that the "abstract and purely scientific" part of his production generally belonged to himself alone, Bain says that "Carlyle, when led to refer to Mrs. Taylor, used to describe her in his own way. That phrase that he most usually employed was, I think, 'veevid'; which the reader may compare with the terms that he used in his supercilious mood when he penned the 'reminiscences'" (1882, 169).

It seems reasonable to suppose that it was Bain who led Carlyle to discuss one of his favorite subjects, and the phrase "usually employed" suggests that the subject came up regularly. By comparison, Bain is quite specific about his conversations with Mill on the subject of his wife. He says that all of Mill's friends "abstained from all allusions to Mrs. Taylor" (1882, 164), but when the *Political Economy* came out with a few "Gift copies" carrying a dedication—remembered by Bain as "To Mrs. John Taylor, who, of all persons known to the author, is the most highly qualified, either to originate or to appreciate speculation of social advancement, this work is, with the highest respect and esteem, dedicated"—Bain decided that "to continue ignoring her existence was a mistaken delicacy." He ventured to speak of her and was treated to "a eulogy of her extraordinary powers" sufficient in intensity that he says: "I confess, I did not feel disposed to renew the reference very often: I alluded to her again only two or three times, and not till after their marriage" (1882, 165–66)—and this, keep in mind, over a period of seventeen years until her death and another fourteen until the death of John.

Testimony as Interpretation: Reading the Record

The one contemporary complaint made about Bain's quasi-biography of J. S. Mill was that he told so little of what he was perhaps uniquely positioned to observe. An unsigned review in *The Nation*, 11 May 1882, expresses this disappointment:

Mr. Bain's "John Stuart Mill" will, we regret to say, not prove anything like the life which Mill's followers wish for. The "Criticism, with

Personal Recollections," is a book of some merit, for it gives in *a precise and accurate form* [my emphasis] information which is of interest and value. But the author of the work is a Scotchman, a logician, and a grammarian. His treatise, therefore, is dull, pragmatical, and ill-written. It abounds in criticism which might well have been shorter; it contains a small number of personal anecdotes of Mill, which, considering the writer's opportunities, might have been more numerous. (403)

The reviewer's slighting jab at Bain here serves, ironically, to validate both Bain's limited observations and his extended criticisms. Who could suppose that one so dull and pragmatic might have his ego deeply entangled in the subject he recorded? That, however, is precisely my thesis. Jack Stillinger's introduction to the popular Riverside Edition of Mill's *Autobiography* is typical in its assessment of the role of Harriet Taylor Mill and in its acceptance of Bain's authority. Stillinger remarks with a tone of judicious objectivity: "Few readers have suspended disbelief over Mill's encomiums [to his new wife], which are, it has to be admitted, a blemish on the work—not because we squirm at the notion that Mill owed so much to another, but simply because the claims do not carry conviction: we should object to such extravagances in fiction, and similarly must object to them in autobiography" (1969, xvii).

If appending her name to the title page along with his own would have been more persuasive, such a gesture might well have doomed the book to a hundred years of obscurity. What is of particular interest here is Stillinger's warrant for his belief: "It is reasonably clear in fact that Harriet was no originator of ideas, however much she may have aided Mill by *ordinary wifely* [my emphasis] discussion and debate. (Bain's view, probably the *most reasonable among contemporaries* [my emphasis], is that she helped set Mill's faculties in motion by intelligently controverting his ideas.) What must be grasped is the symbolic role she plays. Mill himself raises her to the symbolic level when he calls her influence "the presiding principle of my mental progress" (xvii–xviii). Where Bain is extremely careful, those who accept his account as veridical are much less so. In a 1956 article that does not cite Bain in a single footnote, H. O. Pappé borrows not only Bain's critical opinion about John's relationship to his family after he felt Harriet was being slighted by them, but his very words.

Here is Pappé: "John Stuart Mill must have caused much pain to his mother, his sisters, and his brother George when he broke off relations with them at the time of his marriage in 1851. He had been the joy and the light of the house while he was living with the family" (1956, 19).

Here is Bain's assessment with all the precise verbal parallels intact: "It is a painful fact that his marriage was the occasion of his utter estrangement from his mother and sisters. He had been the joy and light of the house when he lived with the family" (1882, 172).

Unlike Pappé, Bain himself goes on to qualify his judgment: "I speak, of course, from one-sided knowledge, which is never held conclusive; but all parties concerned have been under powerful motives to put the best possible construction upon his conduct" (172). Pappé makes no secret of the fact that he does not care for Harriet as a personality, but he maintains a good measure of respect for her husband. He says without a word of support, for example, "she was obviously more wilful than John and not plagued with his overdeveloped conscience in matters intellectual and moral" (1956, 23).

When Pappé does cite Bain four years later in his monograph, *The John Stuart Mill and the Harriet Taylor Myth,* he credits him with an intimacy he simply did not have: "According to Alexander Bain, who knew the Mills *intimately* [my emphasis], Mill outraged all reasonable credibility in describing Harriet's matchless genius; Mill's statements are explained as the natural outcome of extraordinary hallucination and overwhelming passion" (Bain 1882, 171; Pappé 1960, 5). Bain's putatively close observations of the Mill family and his record of the opinions of others often count as hard evidence for the claims of critics about Harriet, but Hayek is the only commentator I have found who notices in passing that Bain never met (nor, I would add, ever claims to have met) John's wife face-to-face (1951, 182).

Despite the representations of those who rely on Bain's authority to discredit her, the only thing Bain himself really takes exception to in Mill's account of her influence is his "hyperbolic language of unbounded laudation, which has been the cause of so much wonderment" (1882, 168). Bain allows Harriet's influence, as claimed by John, in the composition of *On Liberty.* It was, Bain says, "the chief production of his married life: and in it, she bore a considerable part" (170). He also grants *The Subjection of Women,* published a decade after her death, "to have been the result of their joint discussions for many years; Miss Helen Taylor [Harriet's daughter] assisting in the composition" (171). What Bain does not allow is that either of the works touched by Harriet's influence is among John Mill's great works, nor a fortiori that Harriet was the intellectual genius John took her to be. The only special knowledge he claims is his knowledge of John Mill, as becomes clear when the passage continues:

> It is not a true account of Mill to say that he was pleased by the simple giving back of his own thoughts. Of course, this would have been preferable to contradicting him at every point, or to gross misconception of his meaning. Judging from my own experience of him, I should say that what he liked was to have his own faculties set in motion, so as to evolve new thoughts and new aspects of old thoughts. This might be done better by intelligently controverting his views than by merely reproducing them in different language. And I have no doubt that his wife did operate upon him in this very form. But the ways of inducing him to exert his powers in talk, which was a standing pleasure of his life, cannot be summed up under either agreement or opposition. It supposed *independent resources* on the part of his fellow talker, and *a good mutual understanding* [my emphases] as to the proper conditions of the problem at issue. (1882, 173)

The only explanation Bain can come up with for Mill's failure of good sense in so overestimating his wife is "the influence of over-weening passion" (171) or "the witchery of the other sex" (172). Bain tells us, "Mill was not such an egotist to be captivated by the echo of his own opinions," and he provides as examples Mill's relationships with John Sterling and W. T. Thornton. Both men, Bain intimates, "overflowed with suggestive talk, which Mill took up and improved upon in his own way" (173).

The breakdown in Mill's perceptiveness is resolved in part by the limited range of his ideas that, in Bain's judgment, Harriet was likely to have been able intelligently to controvert. When Bain allows John's claim about the details of his wife's influence on *On Liberty*, he believes that he is not conceding much to her. Mill's *System of Logic*—which Bain tells us in his own *Autobiography* and elsewhere in the *Criticism*—he himself worked over carefully, inserting examples and correcting mistakes, "owed nothing to [Harriet Taylor], except the minutiae of composition" (1882, 168), and to demonstrate that what Bain regarded as most manly and important in all Mill's work came only from Mill, he quotes Mill himself: " 'What was abstract and purely scientific was generally mine; the properly human element came from her; in all that concerned the application of philosophy to the exigencies of human society and progress, I was her pupil, alike in boldness of speculation and cautiousness of practical judgment' " (1882, 169).

Rossi notes that "positive assessments of Harriet Taylor" have been few, and that when they do occur, they are "far outweighed by harshly negative assessments." She illustrates this history of negativity with Harold Laski's often-quoted response to Justice Holmes's query about the troublesome woman:

> I believe that he [Mill] was literally the only person who was in the least impressed by her. Mrs. Grote said briefly that she was a stupid woman. Bain said she had a knack of repeating prettily what J. S. M. said and that he told her it was wonderful; Morley told me that Louis Blanc told him he once sat for an hour with her and that she repeated to him what afterwards turned out to be an article Mill had just finished for the Edinburgh. . . . If she was what he thought, someone else should have given us indications. (Rossi 1970, 33–34; Stillinger 1961, 24–25)

The commonplace notion that three independent judgments constitute a reliable consensus collapses under any kind of reasonable analysis of this often-cited passage. First, Mrs. Grote's judgment arguably referred to Harriet's dangerous (ergo stupid) flouting of the sanctity of marriage conventions and not her intellectual ability, at least so far as anyone to my knowledge has demonstrated. Morley's judgment gotten secondhand from Blanc assumes without argument that the good wife was merely parroting an article written by her husband rather than, as Mill would have us believe, that the couple were close collaborators and that what appeared under his name was their joint production. However, the opinion attributed to Bain is most troublesome of all as proof of her intellectual deficiency. First, it is the "observation" attributed to Bain, who never once observed Harriet Taylor Mill—her habit of repeating whatever Mill said—that lends credence to what Laski said Morley told him Blanc had said.

To my knowledge, only Himmelfarb has recognized Laski's error. "In fact," Himmelfarb tells us, "Bain described this as the opinion of some of Mill's other friends, which he himself did not share" (1974, 224n.).

In fact, to go even further than Himmelfarb, in his *Criticism* of his supposed friend, Bain convincingly debunks the theory Laski attributes to him: "The more common way of representing Mrs. Mill's ascendancy, is to say that she imbibed all his views, and gave them back in her own form, by which he was flattered and pleased. This is merest conjecture: the authors of the surmise never saw Mill and his wife together; and, in all probability, misconceived the whole situation" (1882, 173). If Bain, in fact, ever expressed such a belief to Laski, our judgment of him must be even harsher than I think is necessary, and Laski's apparently reasonable call for evidence is, in my opinion, nothing more than a rhetorical flourish to demonstrate his own superior good sense; as proof against Harriet Mill's intellect, the story just does not hold up.

It is plain enough that the love of Mill's life inspired a good deal of animosity, but the specific charges against her are always laden with contradiction. Perpetuating a common opinion that Harriet invented offenses against herself, Himmelfarb includes Mrs. Grote in a list of such innocents: "the bitter experiences of those early years, the long period during which she endured the aspersions, or *fancied aspersions* [my emphasis], of Mrs. Grote, Mrs. Carlyle, Miss Martineau, and others, gave her a stake in unconventionality, a lasting commitment to it" (1974, 266). Now either Mrs. Grote called her stupid or Harriet Taylor Mill imagined aspersions, but both charges cannot be held against the poor woman at the same time.

It seems evident that a good measure of Bain's opinion about Harriet came from Mrs. Grote herself. "When I first knew [John]," Bain tells us, "he was completely alienated from Mrs. Grote, while keeping up his intercourse with Grote himself; and as she was not the person to have an opinion without freely expressing it, I inferred the estrangement had some reference to Mrs. Taylor" (1882, 163–64). Bain dutifully records what we can reasonably infer was George Grote's often-repeated comment upon the affair: "Grote used to say—'only John Mill's reputation could survive such displays'" (167). (What Mrs. Grote had to say when Mr. Grote later took up openly with a lovely young sculptress is not part of Bain's narrative.)

Throughout his analysis Bain compares his own relationship to Mill with Harriet's relationship to John, but using the rhetorical strategy he always employs in assessing his own worth, Bain leaves it to posterity to piece together the evidence he provides and figure out for ourselves that it is his own intellect that has been undervalued. In another context

Bain says: "If you wanted, at any time, to commend yourself to [Mill's] favourable regards, you had but to start a doctrinal discussion—to bring a new logos to his view" (1882, 143). But he implicitly denies that same power to Harriet when he continues the paragraph above: "As I have just remarked, it was comparatively few of his ideas that she *could* [my emphasis] render back in an intelligent form" (173). When we compare this judgment with Blanc's indignity at feeling duped by Harriet's reciting an article John and/or she had prepared for the Edinburgh, we unpack the commonplace assumption that female intellect was a consequence of memory without understanding, an assumption promoted by the psychologist Bain. His certainty is warranted not by observation but by inference.

Bain was so put off by John's public encomiums to Harriet that while he was reading proof for the *Autobiography,* he intervened with a letter to Helen Taylor, Mill's stepdaughter and literary executor, urging her to delete "those sentences where he declares her to be a greater poet than Carlyle . . . and a greater thinker than himself—and again, a greater leader than his father (or at all events an equal)" (Mineka 1963, 302). But despite his best efforts, the words have come to be among those most often quoted—albeit with derision—from the record of the life of Harriet Taylor Mill.

Thomas Carlyle thrived on the admiration of disciples, and among them he counted Harriet Taylor, John Mill, and Alexander Bain. I conjecture that John Mill's dragging Carlyle's name into his often-quoted characterization of his wife was the complete undoing of Harriet's reputation in history.

The Testimony of Science: Interpreting the Evidence

If it was the purportedly platonic extramarital affair going on for twenty years that distressed the women, it was Mill's claims regarding her brilliance that offended the men, and the warrant for their objection was purely scientific. It was Bain who articulated the warrant.

In addition to being a Scotchman, a logician, and a grammarian, for two or three brief decades Bain was the British voice of authority at the birth of nineteenth-century psychology as a scientific discipline until it was displaced by the New Psychology driven by the evolutionary hypothesis. He turned the weight of that authority against the intellectual aspirations of women, but to be scrupulously fair to Bain, he did not believe that women's political rights should be dependent upon their abilities. Mill was in no way dissuaded from his belief in the intellectual equality of men and women by Bain's concession to their political rights (Bain 1882, 131).

As a scientist objectively—to his way of thinking—studying the human animal, Bain believed that Mill's greatest theoretical error was "his doctrine of the natural equality of men." It was, Bain tells us, a mistake Mill inherited from his father, and he "could neither learn nor unlearn in regard to it . . . ; my contention is that he did not allow what *every competent physiologist* [my emphasis] would now affirm to be the facts . . . his feelings operated in giving his mind a bias" (1882, 147). And Bernard Semmel tells us a century later, "Mill's *close friend* [my emphasis] and biographer, Alexander Bain, noted his unwillingness to accept even the possibility of such innate differences, though Bain, also a steadfast associationalist psychologist, *patiently* [my emphasis] pointed out to Mill the difficulties of a starkly environmentalist position" (29). As a psychologist, Bain was a generation beyond the faculty psychologists, who saw the mental faculties (memory, reason, imagination, to name a few) as independently functioning powers of the mind: Bain knew that the mind and the body were interrelated, but the unfortunate conclusion he drew was that overdevelopment in one area of functioning must necessarily cause a deficit in another area.

It was patently clear to Bain that Mill was guilty of "overstraining" when he applied the "evils of subjection in general" to "the disabilities of women" (1882, 130). "In the intensity of his special pleading on this question," Bain says, "he hardly avoids contradicting himself; when he postulates a degree of equality that does not chime in with the experience of *the least biased observers* [my emphasis]." But the individual woman, Harriet, becomes lost, essentially irrelevant in the overpowering scientific abstraction. Bain continues: "[Mill] grants that women are physically inferior, but he seems to think this does not affect their mental powers. He never takes account of the fact, that the large diversion of force for the procreative function must give some general inferiority in all things where that does not come in, unless women are made on the whole much stronger than men" (131).

When Bain says that Mill's feelings have given his mind a bias, he is arguing tu quoque to Mill's acceptance in *The Subjection of Women* that the burden of proof lies with whoever argues against established opinion. Mill says:

So long as an opinion is strongly rooted in the feelings it gains rather than loses in stability by having a preponding weight of argument against it. For if it were accepted as a result of argument, the refutation of the argument might shake the solidity of the conviction; but when it rests solely on feeling, the worse it fares in argumentative content, the more persuaded its adherents are that their feeling must have some deeper ground, which the arguments do not reach; and while the feeling remains, it is always throwing up fresh entrenchments of argument to repair any breach in the old. (Rossi 1970, 126)

Mill's answer to the appeal to the authority of science is the most direct response he ever made to Bain's 1861 book *On the Study of Character,* which Mill had hoped would add scientific authority to his belief in the mental equality of women. Mill proclaims: "I have before repudiated the notion of its being yet certainly known that there is any natural difference at all in the average strength or direction of the mental capacities of the two sexes, much less what that difference is." His dismissal of Bain's book is an unavoidable conclusion,[6] and it gives scant comfort to the rest of Bain's psychological doctrine. Mill continues:

Nor is it possible that this should be known, so long as the psychological laws of the formation of character have been so little studied, even in a general way, and in the particular case never scientifically applied at all; so long as the most obvious external causes of difference of character are habitually disregarded—left unnoticed by the observer, and looked down upon with a kind of *supercilious contempt* [my emphasis][7] by the prevalent schools both of natural history and of mental philosophy: who, whether they look for the source of what mainly distinguishes human beings from one another, in the world of matter or in that of spirit, agree in running down those who prefer to explain these differences by the different relations of human beings to society and life. (Rossi 1970, 200–201; Soper 1983, 122–23)

Mill argues that until social conditions change so that women have both the opportunity and the encouragement to develop their faculties, it is impossible to know what they may be capable of. In this belief he parallels Archbishop Richard Whately's argument for the equality of primitive peoples made in his lecture "On the Origin of Civilization," in which Whately compares the so-called natural state of "savages" of primitive civilizations to a tree growing in poor soil along a snow line: if transplanted to fertile soil in a congenial climate a little lower down the mountain, a tree that once grew to a height of two or three feet may achieve a height of fifty or sixty yards. "In like manner," Whately assures us: "the natural state of Man must, according to all fair analogy, be reckoned, not that in which his intellectual and moral growth are as it were stunted and permanently repressed, but one in which his original endowments are—I do not say brought to perfection, but—enabled to exercise themselves, and to expand like the foliage and flowers of a plant . . ." (1854, 7–8).

In like manner, Mill proclaims that the bias against women's intellectual capacities is in the observer who forms hasty generalizations based "upon the first instances which present themselves" (Rossi 1970, 201). Although history has accepted Bain's judgment about Harriet Mill's intellectual deficiency, it has erased his judgment about her contribution to *On Liberty*. To that point he says: "The book has unsurpassed excellencies, and, as I think, some defects. How far these are to be partitioned between the two co-operating minds, there is probably no means of discovering" (1882, 170–71).

After pondering whether Mill's early breakdown from "severe intellectual strain" had made him more susceptible to an emotional abreaction, such as his intemperate passion for Mrs. Taylor, Bain continues: "The fact must be faced that, on his own showing, she was an intellectual companion, only in a very small portion of his range of studies. He had no sympathy or help from her during perhaps the most intense and exciting work that he ever went through—the composition of the Logic" (172). Mill's modest companion in that work was Bain himself. "To my mind," Bain says elsewhere, "the best piece of work that he ever did, was the Third Book of the Logic—Induction" (146).

Regrettably for Bain, that implacable agent time has tested Mill's influence and his genius and rendered a different judgment: among his greatest achievements (as Mill himself thought) is the classical statement of liberalism, *On Liberty*, and, as the contorted reasoning process goes, therefore, Harriet Mill could not have been his co-author. On close examination, it can be shown that a persistent warrant for the claim that Harriet Mill was no real co-author is Bain's studied demonstration that the lady, whom he knew only through hearsay, was no genius.

Prevailing Opinion: Without Whom . . .

The significance of the treatise *On Liberty* need not be argued: cases regarding censorship, pornography, obscenity, birth control, drug use, and homosexual rights, as Himmelfarb says, "ritualistically invoke the authority of Mill" (1974, xii). But the significance of the text to the canon of rhetoric has not been generally recognized.[8] Nonetheless, it directly addresses the classical question regarding the relationship between rhetoric and the discovery of truth. Whately's contribution to rhetorical theory was his demonstration that presumption was always on the side of established institutions and prevailing opinion, while the burden of proof must necessarily be on those who would alter those institutions or who hold opinions contrary to what "everybody knows." The Mills say in *On Liberty* that it is *only* through free and unrestrained discussion that truth can ever be approached. They successfully shift the burden of proof to the coercive society that would interfere with individual autonomy. Since we might always be wrong in our judgment, even when we are most certain of being in the right, it is in the interest of truth itself that a diversity of opinion be allowed. Freedom of thought was not a new idea by any means; what was new was the freedom of action grounded in a single inalienable right—freedom from control, "whether the means used be physical force in the form of legal penalties, or the moral coercion of public opinion" (Himmelfarb 1974, 3).

Rhetoric never provides algorithms for the discovery of truth, though it does provide heuristics for the exploration of ideas. Conservatives argue that Mill's "one simple principle" does not always guarantee a solution to the problem that exists when self-regarding behavior poses a sufficient threat to society such that "established institutions" are finally justified in interfering with an individual's autonomy. Liberals have made the same mistake about Whately, assuming that the archbishop's feelings impelled him to construct a theory of rhetoric that gave the argumentative advantage to established institutions, just as the Mills's commitment to unconventionality impelled them to construct the classic defense of individual rights. When we study them as rhetoricians, we discover a profound theoretical consistency: the archbishop who denied the possibility of knowing the truth of doctrinal pronouncements, and the unmarried couple whose principles would not condone inflicting the injury of elopement and divorce on Harriet's husband.

In his effort to explain away John's subordination of himself to Harriet, Pappé asks: "Did he not himself say that he [Mill] was merely a mediator between original thinkers and the public, and does this not mark his and Harriet's achievement as essentially weak and second-rate? . . . His analysis of his role as an interpreter of other people's thought was in reality a revolutionary description of the continuity of the human mind working within the gradually unfolding web of history" (1956, 29).

The extraordinary image of an unfolding web of history renders Harriet's authorial status relative to John more or less moot; she is one among the vast network of influences that John, who was described by Carlyle as "a reasoning machine" and "a steam-engine intellect" (qtd. in Mazlish 1988, 392; and Packe 1954, 405), took into the maw of his great intellect. Mill's most notable trait, his "willingness and ability to learn from everybody" (*Autobiography* 205), then becomes not a warrant for the proposition that a man of his extraordinary intellectual capacity might recognize genius in another person, but a warrant for the contrary proposition that someone who could learn from everyone could not be trusted to judge the intellect of anyone.

In discussing John Mill's early management of the *Westminster Review*, Bain explains the heuristic principle that characterized Mill's thinking and explains—at least on an intellectual level—his adherence to and then partial rejection of the philosophies of his father and Jeremy Bentham, Auguste Comte, and Thomas Carlyle: "The Review abounds in editorial caveats, attached to the articles: his principle of seeing partial truth on opposite sides was carried out in this form. . . . The watch-word in those days of the Review, was—Sympathize in order to learn. That doctrine, preached by Goethe and echoed by Carlyle, was in everybody's mouth, and had its fling" (1882, 57–58).

Because of the misogynist notions about female intellect as well as other personal factors, we may never know who Harriet really was or the precise nature of her contribution to *On Liberty*. It should not be necessary to cast Harriet as a paragon of virtue and intellect to credit her share in the composition of what I would propose is the most important nineteenth-century theoretic treatise in rhetoric.

Notes

I would like to acknowledge the efforts of Provost John Kozak and Dean Elizabeth Hoffman to ensure that I have some time to write and do research.

1. It is difficult not to read this as a veiled reference to Alexander Bain, who was twelve years Mill's junior and who, perhaps duplicitously, treated him as a mentor.

2. F. A. Hayek indicates that the page is torn here by the seal (306).

3. An attached page of errata changes "Their Correspondence" to "Their Friendship." I have found the text indexed under both titles.

4. Trilling never legitimizes the relationship by calling her "Mrs. Mill."

5. Martineau was hearing impaired. It was said that she heard only half of what was said and misunderstood half of that. I will note without further comment that she was an unmarried, independent woman who lived by her pen, though she was despised by John Stuart Mill. Her story, including her relationship with Bain, might be very interesting to explore.

6. Robert Young maintains that there is no record that Mill ever acknowledged the fact of its publication (1970, 132).

7. See David Stove, "The Subjection of John Stuart Mill" (1993).

8. The notable exception to this generalization is Cherwitz and Hikins (1979).

References

Anonymous. 1882. *The Nation* (11 May): 403.

Anschutz, R. P. 1955. "J. S. Mill, Carlyle, and Mr. Taylor." *Political Science* 7: 65–75.

Bain, Alexander. 1861. *On the Study of Character, Including an Estimate of Phrenology.* London: Parker, Son and Bourn.

———. 1882. *John Stuart Mill. A Criticism with Personal Recollections.* London: Longmans, Green.

———. 1904. *Autobiography.* London: Longmans.

Cherwitz, Richard A., and James W. Hikins. 1979. "John Stuart Mill's *On Liberty*: Implications for the Epistemology of the New Rhetoric." *Quarterly Journal of Speech* 65 (February): 12–24.

Connors, Robert. 1992. "The Exclusion of Women from Classical Rhetoric." In *A Rhetoric of Doing: Essays on Written Discourse in Honor of James L. Kinneavy,* edited by Stephen P. Witte et al., 65–78. Carbondale: Southern Illinois University Press.

Ede, Lisa, and Andrea Lunsford. 1990. *Singular Texts/Plural Authors: Perspectives on Collaborative Writing.* Carbondale: Southern Illinois University Press.

Diffenbaugh, Guy Linton. 1923 (30 April). "Mrs. Taylor Seen through Other Eyes than Mill's." *Sewanee Review:* 198–204.

Hayek, F. A. 1951. *John Stuart Mill and Harriet Taylor: Their Correspondence [Friendship] and Subsequent Marriage.* Chicago: University of Chicago Press.

Himmelfarb, Gertrude. 1965 (10 May). "Two Mills." *New Leader:* 26–29.

———. 1974. *On Liberty and Liberalism: The Case of John Stuart Mill.* New York: Alfred A. Knopf.

Lunsford, Andrea. 1982. "Alexander Bain's Contributions to Discourse Theory." *College English* 44.3: 290–300.

Mazlish, Bruce. 1988. *James and John Stuart Mill: Father and Son in the Nineteenth Century.* New Brunswick: Transaction Books.

Mill, John Stuart [and Harriet Taylor Mill]. [1859] 1976. *On Liberty.* Indianapolis: Hackett Publishing.

Mineka, Frances E. 1963. "The *Autobiography* and the Lady." *University of Toronto Quarterly* 32.3: 301–6.

Norton, Charles Eliot. 1974. *Letters of Charles Eliot Norton with Biographical Comment by His Daughter Sarah Norton and M. A. DeWolfe Howe.* 2 vols. Boston: Houghton Mifflin.

Packe, Michael St. John. 1954. *The Life of John Stuart Mill.* London: Secker and Warburg.

Pappé, H. O. 1956. "The Mills and Harriet Taylor." *Political Science* 8: 19–30.

———. 1960. *The John Stuart Mill and the Harriet Taylor Myth.* Melbourne: Melbourne University Press.

Robson, John M. 1966. "Harriet Taylor and John Stuart Mill: Artist and Scientist." *Queen's Quarterly* 73: 167–86.

———. 1968. *The Improvement of Mankind: The Social and Political Thought of John Stuart Mill.* London: Routledge & Kegan Paul.

Rose, Phyllis. 1983. *Parallel Lives: Five Victorian Marriages.* New York: Alfred A. Knopf.

Rossi, Alice, ed. 1970. *Essays on Sex Equality: John Stuart Mill & Harriet Taylor Mill.* Chicago: University of Chicago Press.

Semmel, Bernard. 1984. *John Stuart Mill and the Pursuit of Virtue.* New Haven: Yale University Press.

Soper, Kate, ed. 1983. *Harriet Taylor Mill and John Stuart Mill. The Enfranchisement of Women [1851] and The Subjection of Women [1869].* London: Virago Press.

Stillinger, Jack. 1961. *The Early Draft of John Stuart Mill's Autobiography.* Urbana: University of Illinois Press.

———. 1969. *John Stuart Mill: Autobiography.* Ed. with "Introduction" and "Notes." Boston: Houghton Mifflin, Riverside.

———. 1983. "Who Wrote J. S. Mill's *Autobiography?*" *Victorian Studies* 27 (Autumn): 7–23.

Stove, David. 1993. "The Subjection of John Stuart Mill." *Philosophy* 68.2: 5–13.

Trilling, Diana. 1952. "Mill's Intellectual Beacon." *Partisan Review* 19: 115–20.

[Whately, Richard.] His Grace the Archbishop of Dublin. 1854. *On the Origin of Civilization.* Dublin: Young Men's Christian Association.

———. 1963. *Elements of Rhetoric.* Ed. Douglas Ehninger. Carbondale: Southern Illinois University Press.

Young, Robert. 1970. *Brain, Mind, and Adaptation in the Nineteenth Century.* New York: Oxford University Press.

Lucie Olbrechts-Tyteca's Contribution to *The New Rhetoric*

Barbara Warnick

First published in French in 1958, Chaïm Perelman and Lucie Olbrechts-Tyteca's *Traité de l'argumentation* has contributed substantially to a revival of interest in the study of practical reasoning and argumentation during the last thirty years (Cox and Willard 1982; Perelman and Olbrechts-Tyteca 1958c; Toulmin 1958; Trapp and Schuetz 1990; van Eemeren, Grootendorst, and Kruiger 1984). Translated as *The New Rhetoric,* the treatise considered the rhetorical forms of reasoning in daily discourse and the senses in which those forms are constructed for audiences and intended to be persuasive. The work was the result of a collaboration between Perelman and Olbrechts, a collaboration that by Perelman's own reckoning lasted nearly ten years (Perelman 1990, 1083).

Yet, while Perelman has received a great deal of recognition and attention for the work, Olbrechts's contribution has been largely overlooked. In speaking of the treatise, many of my colleagues and graduate students neglect even to mention her name as co-author. In published discussions of the work, many scholars refer to Olbrechts as co-author yet attribute *The New Rhetoric*'s ideas and theory solely to Perelman (Bizzell and Herzberg 1990; Measell 1985; Walker and Sillars 1990). This phenomenon may be due in part to the fact that Olbrechts's name does not come trippingly off the tongue or pen, but it is due also to Perelman's inclination to assume ownership of the project as well as a cultural predilection to believe him. The size of his corpus, the appearance of subsequent works such as *The Realm of Rhetoric* as singly authored by him, and his own writing style have contributed to the impression that he is largely responsible for the work.[1]

While neglect of Olbrechts's contribution may be unintentional, it is all the more anomalous at a time when contemporary scholars of rhetoric seek to make women's voices heard. In this essay I will describe what I believe to be the nature of Olbrechts's contribution. The basis for my account will be Olbrechts's single-authored work that appeared after the *Traité de l'argumentation* was published.[2] This work reveals her unique interests, her style of doing research, and her theoretical and empirical contribution as subsumed within and extended beyond *The New Rhetoric*. As a preview, I can say with some confidence that Olbrechts was interested in discursive structures and in how they were culturally situated and adapted to audiences. Her work took the form of systematic and fine-grained description of discourse at work and, furthermore, discussion of the structures of discourse, their interrelations, and their effect. Since two-thirds of *The New Rhetoric* was devoted to study and exemplification of the structures of argument, we can assume that Olbrechts was a major contributor to this phase of the joint project.

The reasons why Olbrechts has been slighted are apparent. Perelman was a doctor of law; Olbrechts was a *licenciée* in social sciences (Mattis 1994). Perelman has nearly two hundred entries in his bibliography; Olbrechts probably has only a dozen or so (Olbrechts-Tyteca and Griffin-Collart 1979). Perelman was the "front man" for the project, traveling throughout Europe and the United States presenting lectures and seminars on his work; Olbrechts largely stayed home. Perelman's work was translated into English and appeared in prominent international publications: Olbrechts's single-authored work remains untranslated and is limited to European journals and publications. Therefore, Olbrechts's work is hard to find and hard to access, whereas Perelman's is readily available.

One should not assume from these facts that Olbrechts was unproductive as a scholar, however. In terms of publications, Olbrechts's vita at the end of her career would have qualified her to be appointed to the senior faculty of most major research institutions. During the period of their collaboration, Perelman and Olbrechts-Tyteca published two books and four articles together (Perelman and Olbrechts-Tyteca 1950, 1952, 1955, 1958a, 1958b, 1958c). The date of the last of these joint publications was 1958. After that time Olbrechts published at least four more articles and a book (Olbrechts-Tyteca 1960, 1963, 1974, 1977, 1979). Thus, her body of work is sizable and offers ample evidence of her talents and her emphases as a researcher.

Olbrechts's accomplishments are all the more impressive when one considers the educational and social milieu in which she worked.

She received her *license* in social sciences and economics in 1925 at the Université Libre de Bruxelles and married the statistician Raymond Olbrechts. Since it was rare for women to pursue higher studies at the time, Lucie Olbrechts-Tyteca did not undertake work toward a graduate degree. Instead she read widely in French and German literature and in sociology, social psychology, and statistics. Sometime during the 1940s she became interested in Perelman's work and began collaborating with him, and in 1947 he announced his intent to work with her on a theory of argumentation (Mattis 1994; van Eemeren et al. 1984).

The New Rhetoric has been successful in part because the respective talents of these two researchers were so well matched. He was the philosopher and provided the theoretical framework and justification for the work as a whole. She was the empiricist, providing the examples, description, and "middle level" theory that Perelman's more global theories required for application. Perelman's specialties in logic and law enabled him to identify the relations between formal logic and quasi logic and to make a significant distinction between the rational and the reasonable (Perelman 1969, 1979). Olbrechts's background in sociology and in French, German, and other literatures provided her the means to discuss the argumentative function of stylistic devices and discursive structures. His concern with legal argumentation caused him to focus on arguments adapted to courtroom exigencies such as the act/person liaison and the pragmatic argument (Perelman 1951, 1963). Her interest in literary and philosophical writings resulted in close study of the uses of values in discourse, in particular philosophical pairs, value hierarchies, and dissociation (Olbrechts-Tyteca 1979).

The remainder of this essay will focus on her work. The intention is not to diminish in any way Perelman's substantial accomplishments but to reenter Olbrechts's contribution into the record and to make her single-authored work accessible to those readers who cannot read it in French, or who would be interested in a survey of what she did. In the interest of extending and expanding *The New Rhetoric*'s contribution, I will focus on those portions of Olbrechts's single-authored work of greatest relevance to its original project. The two works to be discussed here are Olbrechts's 1974 book on comedic structures (*Le Comique du discours*) and her 1979 article on philosophical pairs ("Les Couples philosophiques"), both of which should be considered by scholars interested in the relevant sections of *The New Rhetoric*.

Le Comique du discours

In *Le Comique du discours*, a four-hundred-page book published in 1974 by the University of Brussels, Olbrechts uses the conceptual framework introduced in *The New Rhetoric* to analyze comedic discursive structures.[3] What she means by the phrase "comique du discours" only becomes clear as one reads the book. She does *not* mean "the comic *in* discourse," or overt attempts to be funny, but rather the ways in which comic structures and constructions devolve from frames and schemes recognized by the audience. That is, Olbrechts is interested in examining the comic from a rhetorical perspective. She asks, how do such phenomena as jokes, irony, parody, and the burlesque make use of values, language, quasi-logical connections, presumptions, and other aspects of "reality" tacitly recognized by the audience to make them laugh, or smile?[4] Since a specific audience reaction (amusement) is what most attempts at humor seek, comedy has much in common with argumentation, which likewise seeks a specific audience reaction (conviction or persuasion) (Perelman and Olbrechts-Tyteca 1969, 4).

Olbrechts notes that the "comique du discours," like rhetoric and dialectic, is common to all domains in the Aristotelian sense of not being field-specific or subject-specific (Aristotle 1975, 1355b; Olbrechts-Tyteca 1974, 33). As she illustrates, the comic makes use of the same sorts of schemes as argumentation, be they causal, coexistential, dissociative, analogical, or quasi-logical. Like the enthymeme, the joke or funny story often makes use of a "missing premise" or missing bit of information supplied by the audience. Making explicit a joke or punch line by explaining it kills the humor, in the same way that presenting all the premises of an enthymeme can bore an audience by belaboring the point.

Both argumentation and comedy presume and call for a certain audience attitude. Persuasion and humor rely on a sort of conspiracy of participation on the part of audience members who show a willingness to be influenced or amused and who accept and respond to the speaker's appeals. Appreciation of the comic is acquired, by virtue of one's integration into a social group (Olbrechts-Tyteca 1974, 15). Comic forms, like inference schemes, are culturally dependent and social phenomena. At the same time, the primary difference between comedy and rhetoric arises from the nature of audience response, for in comedy the audience preserves some distance or reflection; they do not take the speaker's statements seriously.

Le Comique du discours is clearly an extension and elaboration of the work done in *The New Rhetoric*. It makes use of the same organization and approach, breaking its subject down into the same categories as those described in the earlier work and examining the same schemes and aspects as they relate to humor. Here we see Olbrechts at work alone, and the nature of her method and approach are apparent. For each scheme she describes its structure; explains how it makes use of existing audience cognitions, attitudes, and expectations; identifies the features that make it comic; provides examples of the scheme; and then varies the examples to show that other, similar manifestations are not comic. The result is a painstaking, often overworked, fully elaborated explanation of the schemes. Scholars who are interested in understanding more completely how the schemes work or who would like to see further examples of the schemes in action will find much of interest here.

In this work Olbrechts's contributions and her strengths are apparent. She combines research on humor and cognitive processes from sociology and psychology with work in formal logic, analytic philosophy, speech act theory, and argumentation. For examples she draws from general interest periodicals and a wide range of literatures—French, German, English, Spanish, and Italian. The range of her background and training enables her to consider the cultural and psychological dimensions of humor and to support her discussion with appropriate examples that illustrate how the schemes work.

To exemplify the sort of work done in *Le Comique du discours*, I will treat two of the schemes she discusses—incompatibility and dissociation. Space and time constrain treatment of all the schemes, but these two, which were of particular interest to Olbrechts, are representative of the nature of her work and of her contribution. Not only do the two provide a sample, they can be conveniently linked because they often occur together, since dissociations are often used to respond to or resolve incompatibilities.

Incompatibility is an associative (connecting) liaison or argument form. It is quasi-logical because it has the *appearance* of formal logic and influences the audience because of its similarity to contradiction (a formal logical form). Like its logical counterpart, incompatibility derives its effect from the supposed impossibility of asserting a proposition and its negation, or of maintaining two mutually exclusive ideas simultaneously. Incompatibility is *associative* because it holds two views as one, and the tension or dissonance that it causes comes from this "uncomfortable" association.

Incompatibilities arise in many forms. For example, there is that between two assertions ("I hate all people who generalize"), between intention and action ("Wait a minute, you're saying that to get people to trust me, I have to deceive them into thinking I'm something I'm not?" ["Public Trust" 1989]), and between means and end (same example). Incompatibilities derive their effect from the recognition that one must choose between two mutually exclusive alternatives, and that the choice is so posed as to be difficult, if not impossible.

Incompatibilities can have a comic effect if the two alternatives themselves are incongruous or bizarre, or if there is incongruity in the interaction reported in the joke or story. Two of Olbrechts's examples illustrate this effect. One arises from a distinction between what is *said* in a situation and the set of facts to which it refers:

An explorer asks:
—Are there any cannibals in the region?
—No, we ate the last one yesterday. (Olbrechts-Tyteca 1974, 170)

Or there is the incompatibility between a rule and the consequences of applying the rule, as when a policeman climbed on the stage of a provincial theater when the audience was about to sing the national anthem to announce that anything not on the playbill was forbidden."How about you?" asked one of the audience, "are you on the play-bill?" (Perelman and Olbrechts-Tyteca 1969, 204). Olbrechts terms this sort of reaction "retort" or "autophagy"; the rule is turned back on itself in such a manner that the original argument self-destructs, often producing a comic effect in the process (Olbrechts-Tyteca 1974, 169–74).

Olbrechts notes that incompatibilities can be avoided in three ways. The first is to avoid the incompatibility in the first place by avoiding the situation that gives rise to it. Her example of this is that the son of Louis XIV entertained certain foreign sovereigns only out-of-doors in the open air so that neither one would enter the house before the other (Perelman and Olbrechts-Tyteca 1969, 198). This brings to mind such diplomatic measures as the use of a round table for treaty negotiations to avoid conflicts over seating. The second means of dealing with incompatibility is through compromise, and the third is by sacrificing one of the ideas or branches of the incompatibility. Both are illustrated in the following joke:

> A Jewish man surprised his wife in the very act with his clerk on a divan. He consulted his rabbi:
> —Repudiate your wife.
> —My business depends on her money.
> —Fire your employee.
> —Impossible. He will start a new business.
> The rabbi gave up giving advice. Some weeks later, he ran into the man who was beaming. When he questioned him, the man explained:
> —I sold the divan. (Olbrechts-Tyteca 1974, 167–68)

In argumentation one attempts to anticipate incompatibilities so as to avoid entrapping oneself in an untenable dilemma. In comedy, as in the examples above, incompatibilities are often exploited for comic effect. In any case, Olbrechts notes, many supposed "solutions" for incompatibilities are facile, superficial, and transitory (Olbrechts-Tyteca 1974, 168).

Dissociation is unique as a scheme because, unlike other schemes that bring elements together, dissociation seeks to disengage ideas or elements and to reform or reframe conceptions of them. Dissociation is a fundamentally *rhetorical* scheme because it depends on paired concepts recognized and accepted by the audience, appearance/reality being the prototype. Dissociations seek to reorder our conceptions by contrasting a Term I (appearance, the lesser concept) with a Term II (reality, the concept of greater value in terms of which the Term I is to be viewed).

One dissociative scheme preoccupying both Perelman and Olbrechts is the one between words and action, or form and substance, which forms the basis of such pairs as:

device	rhetoric	form	word
reality	substance	substance	thing

In *Le Comique du discours* Olbrechts cites another of the many examples of dissociations based on these pairs in *The New Rhetoric*:

"Laughter is the antidote to rhetoric; and rhetoric requires us to lose ourselves in an emotional orgy, to abase ourselves before some object of veneration. In freeing ourselves from the rhetorician's spell, we are surely increasing our self-esteem" (Olbrechts-Tyteca 1974, 355; Perelman and Olbrechts-Tyteca 1969, 451–55). This statement dissociates comedy from rhetoric through four pairs:

rhetoric	emotional orgy	abasemant	veneration
humor	[emotional distance]	self-esteem	freedom

Olbrechts, of course, does not neglect to mention the considerable use this author has himself made of rhetorically accepted pairs to disparage rhetoric in this dissociation!

Two comedic twists on the dissociative scheme considered by Olbrechts are reversal and paradox. In reversal, one "flips" a habitual dissociation so that the result is humorous. For example, the value hierarchy locus of the existent implies that the actual, real, and existent is to be valued over what is only contingent or possible. This common locus is "flipped," or reversed, in the following: "I can't be there in spirit, so I'm coming in person" (Olbrechts-Tyteca 1974, 328). Or one might convert something that is usually conceived in positive terms into a negative conception, as in the following:

A tiresome person once requested information from a director in a Vienna library. When the director was unable to respond, the client said furiously:
—"The emperor still pays you to know this!"
—"Excuse me," responded the director, "but the emperor pays me for what I *do* know. For if he had to pay me for what I do *not* know, the entire treasury of the empire would not suffice." (Olbrechts-Tyteca 1974, 332)

Here apparent knowledge is converted into real knowledge by being equated with what is known or actual.

Paradox is also made possible by dissociating dissociations so that the apparent and the real become so interchangeable that one cannot be discerned from the other. Here Olbrechts alludes to the *techne* of Corax cited in Aristotle's *Rhetoric* (1975, 1402a), which asserts that what is contrary to probability is nonetheless probable, so that the improbable becomes probable. Here appearance becomes reality, and reality appearance. When situations are ambiguous and interpretations of them indecisive, the potential for humor is rife. Here are two examples:

> A student confessed to his French professor that he knew of no romantic influence in seventeenth century France.
> —"You have not heard of Fénelon, a romanticist?" exclaimed the professor. "Why, only recently a bulky volume was written on the point!"
> —"The point must be very doubtful" rejoined the student, "if it takes such a bulky volume to prove it." (Olbrechts-Tyteca 1974, 350)

> The policeman signaled the driver to pull over to the side of the road.
> —"Give me your driver's license," he said in a dry tone.
> —"But," protested the driver, "I did nothing wrong."
> —"I didn't say you did," responded the policeman, "but you are driving so carefully that I said to myself that you must not yet have your driver's license." (Olbrechts-Tyteca 1974, 350)

The "better known" of the terms, the Term I concept of appearance, is always unstable and multiple and is to be known only through its relation to "reality." When the two become interchangeable, the recognition of anomaly brings about a comedic effect.

Olbrechts concludes her study of the schemes as used in comedy by noting the extent to which they are culturally dependent. "Just as we do not all speak the same language," she observes, "we are not sensitized to the same arguments, and we do not laugh at the same things" (Olbrechts-Tyteca 1974, 395). The argument schemes are a common good or property shared by the inhabitants of a culture and not necessarily recognizable outside it. Comedy itself is like a connivance or conspiracy that only remains amusing so long as its mechanisms remain implicit and tacitly recognizable. Citing M. F. Eastman, Olbrechts notes that "laughter is after speech the chief thing that holds society together" (396).

We could learn a good deal about the workings of rhetoric by observing the workings of humor. The laughter of connivance reinforces an existing and recognized communion among participants. It reveals what we know confusedly; it discloses the diversity of an audience as different groups respond to certain fictions, certain ad hominem arguments, certain allusions. The comedic plays on the ambiguity of terms, the multiplicity of audiences, and the instability of premises, thereby illustrating the specific rhetorical effects of language use. *Le Comique du discours* is thus a *techne* common to all domains that is meanwhile tied for its understanding to the existence of diverse groups, diverse cultures. Olbrechts's observations in her conclusion remind us that the term *universal audience* should be used advisedly since *The New Rhetoric*'s study of starting points and schemes assumes participation in a common culture in which the elements of argumentation, or of comedy, are inherently recognizable by those to whom discourse is addressed.

At the same time, there is an optimism in Olbrechts's work, an affirmation of the possibility that people can argue, laugh, and work together. Postmodernists who are acclimated to cynicism, paradox, and incongruity might dismiss Olbrechts's concluding thoughts on the usefulness of laughter: "The universal audience is not only this Term II, this Reason. It participates in a larger human communion, that of all beings who address one another and rejoice in understanding each other, imperfectly, but effectively all the same. . . . The laughter of the universal audience is not the laughter of the gods nor that of which Nietzsche speaks, and which would be at the very most the laughter of an elite audience. It is one of our best hopes" (Olbrechts-Tyteca 1974, 414).

Philosophical Pairs

In a 1979 article on philosophical pairs, a topic of particular interest to her, Olbrechts substantially advances *The New Rhetoric*'s discussion of paired concepts often used as value hierarchies. Close examination of the pairs in a discourse often reveals the tacit hierarchies to which a speaker or writer subscribes and of which he or she may be unaware. We have seen that these pairs, particularly the appearance/reality pair, figure prominently in comedic dissociations. But they are also quite pervasive in any discourse that has an embedded ideology, as do most discourses.

Olbrechts begins her article by expressing surprise and disappointment at the lack of subsequent attention to this topic after *The New Rhetoric* appeared. "We think that this fifty pages are among the most original of the treatise because rhetoric—ancient or modern—had never concerned itself with them. However, as far as we know, the study has hardly been developed since, and it is to it that the least critical or complementary remarks have been directed" (Olbrechts-Tyteca 1979, 81). Olbrechts later observes that the pairs have a role analogous to the common topics (89). They have only recently begun to receive attention from argumentation theorists interested in the use of values in argument, and her disappointment at their neglect seems justified.[5]

Olbrechts's article is generally devoted to explaining the nature of the relationship between Terms I and II and also the relations among the pairs themselves. Because these matters are so significant to an understanding of the pairs and their operation, it is unfortunate that this work was not originally included in *The New Rhetoric*. Olbrechts's account of the taxonomy of pairs and their potential for the study of common thought could be quite useful to rhetorical critics and to anyone who is interested in the ideological underpinnings of discourse.

Philosophical pairs are to be distinguished from classificatory pairs and antithetical pairs. While the latter two types situate both terms on the same plane and value them equally, philosophical pairs subordinate one of the two terms to the other. As I have noted above in the discussion of comedic dissociation, the Term II concept becomes the true reality which carries a superior value and functions as a norm or criterion (Olbrechts-Tyteca 1979, 82). Olbrechts begins her discussion by making this distinction, and then she turns to considering the senses in which the two terms are related to each other.

She generates a set of two-columned lists presenting a taxonomy of relations between the terms. She notes that the lists are "purely empirical" (83) and describes in turn the relations emanating from I toward II (list A) and from II toward I (list B). On the following page is a sampling of the categories and relations.

Olbrechts emphasizes that this list is specific to a given culture, that it is not exhaustive. It should be considered "a choice, an illustration, an anthology" (Olbrechts-Tyteca 1979 85). She concludes this article by calling for study of pairs in non-European cultures, a task she terms "ambitious, difficult, full of promise" (98). Indeed, it would be most interesting to consider pairs characterizing non-Western cultures, as well as whether they operate rhetorically in the same way that they do in the West.

Each of the two terms has its role. Term I is the one initially discerned, but II becomes the criterion for considering I. Those terms

A	**B**
From Term I to Term III	From Term II to Term I
dependent on II by a liaison borrowed	II toward I
from the structure of the real	
consequence	cause
effect	origin
means	end
appearance	essence
act	agent
. . . etc.	creator
	. . . etc.
I a *particularisation* of II	II toward I
application	principle
individual	type
fact	abstract
particular	general
. . . etc.	norm
	. . . etc.
I a *relativisation* of II	II toward I
multiplicity	unity
opinion	truth
relative	absolute
approximation	eternity
finitude	infinite
. . . etc.	. . . etc.
I a *fragment* of II	II toward I
point of view	totality
subjective	objective
part	universal
surface	. . . etc.
element	
. . . etc.	
I a *banalisation* of II	II toward I
quantitative	quantative
normal	unique
. . . etc.	. . . etc.
I a *representation* of II	II toward I
substitute	reality
image	archtype
copy	. . . etc.
reflection	
imitation	
. . . etc.	

classified under Term II permit us to recognize certain appearances as false, to correct their interpretation, and to realize the reasons for their insufficiency. Furthermore, while Terms I are subordinated to Terms II, they still retain a certain interest. By creating a Term I, we do not seek to annihilate it completely but rather to give it an "appropriate" meaning.

Furthermore, the elements of Terms I have hierarchies among themselves. In opinion/science the opinions can be more or less pertinent; in means/end the means can be more or less effective; in impure/pure impurity can have degrees. Thus, the Terms I themselves can be set in hierarchies as valorized by successive dissociations. Terms I generally do not become Terms II, but they approach them more and more, moving toward the End, the Truth, the Pure, the Principle (Olbrechts-Tyteca 1979, 88).

Successive dissociations of Terms I can be combined, replaced, or symbolized by the introduction of diachrony. Ultimately in this process the general value of Terms I can be augmented. For example, in hermeneutics, the couple interpretation/text is established by dissociation in such a way that one becomes aware of the multiplicity of the senses of a text. Each new interpretation bears in mind all those that preceded it and benefits from them. In the end, a radical solution consists in abandoning diachronic hermeneutics on behalf of an inverted couple: text/interpretation, in which interpretation itself becomes the Term II of the pair. Terms II can also be converted to Terms I. A prominent contemporary example, noted by Olbrechts, is the pair subjective/objective in which "objective" itself has become a Term I and the entire pair is viewed as mere appearance from a philosophical point of view, as in phenomenology, hermeneutics, and postmodernism.

Olbrechts reviews, too, the loci of the preferable discussed in *The New Rhetoric* (Perelman and Olbrechts-Tyteca 1969, 85–99). These include quantity (less/more), quality (common/unique), order (derivative/original), the existent (potential/actual), and the dignity of the person. These pervasive and prototypical pairs serve as starting points for argument and as the bases for supporting other pairs in double hierarchies. An ensemble of them forms a vision of the world, an ideology, as in Perelman and Olbrechts's study of classicism and romanticism (Perelman and Olbrechts-Tyteca 1958a). The lists of relations between pairs introduced earlier are a variation of these loci that is broader, more inclusive, and more malleable.

Olbrechts concludes her essay by speculating on the history and

future of the pairs. She wonders, "In the domain of knowledge especially, how many dissociations must have been made of which only a
trace remains. . . . The terms thus created after renewed dissatisfaction
do not disappear from our arsenal. They perform evolutions in permanent relation of some with others, but also on their own account"
(Olbrechts-Tyteca, 1979, 96). Thing, fact, event, sensation, perception,
image, idea, concept, symbol, sign reference, signifier, sense, designation, word, text, structure—one could pursue these variations
indefinitely. Indeed, are not philosophical pairs as inevitable as incompatibility itself, since their purpose is to resolve it? For example, Olbrechts
notes that the very notion of the "individual" was not indispensable so
long as the problems of the person's singularity, rights, and relative autonomy were not explicitly posed, that is, until one needed some criterion
to resolve them (97).

Conclusion

Olbrechts's contribution to *The New Rhetoric* was that of analyst and
conceptualizer.[6] By "analyst," I mean someone who spent her life considering the features of discourse, including essays, speeches, literature,
jokes, stories, and philosophical arguments. Her concern was the workings of discourse, the mechanisms that tied together concepts and ideas,
the starting points and schemes recognized by Western audiences, and
the uses of style. By "conceptualizer," I mean someone who developed
a vocabulary, a set of categories, taxonomies, and terms to describe the
structures of discourse. The salience of "audience" for both Perelman
and Olbrechts prevented their descriptions of argument from being descriptions of a static or unchanging system, however. Olbrechts, like her
co-author, was intrinsically interested in how fluid conceptions of the
audience operated recursively in the construction of messages. She was
also intrigued by the ways in which changes in time, situation, and culture played their part in the evolution of discourse.

The New Rhetoric's theoretical contributions to philosophy of law
and argument theory (such as the universal audience, the notion of presence, and the Rule of Justice) have been widely discussed, but the work's
close study of argument structures has only recently begun to receive
widespread attention (Keinpointner 1987, 1992). There is a sense in which
The New Rhetoric provided us with a phenomenology of discourse, a
fine-grained, multivalenced description of its workings, and Olbrechts
made a major contribution to this aspect of the work.

As the female half of a "philosophical pair," she served as the empiricist and analyst, while Perelman served as philosopher and theorist. Perhaps his role has been more widely recognized because of our academic proclivity to value theory and global frameworks over careful empirical work. Nonetheless, Olbrechts's untranslated, single-authored work shows her to be a middle-level theorist who teases out of close study of discursive structures their identifiable characteristics. Close description of argument structures takes up two-thirds of the treatise and provides rhetorical critics, discourse analysts, and informal logicians with a rich resource for studying situated argument (Farrell 1986; Hoover 1993; Secor 1984; Warnick and Kline 1992). Without it, Perelman's theory would remain a global conception unsupported by concrete examples. As it stands, Perelman and Olbrechts's collaboration makes clear the role of audience in argument construction. And all discourse is a composite of discursive structures so configured as to bring about a response of a certain kind. The work of Olbrechts helps us to understand these processes better, and increased consideration and use of it will inevitably repay the effort.

Notes

1. See Chaïm Perelman (1982). Of a 1984 essay by Perelman, Robert Scott observed: "In the short essay, ten of the forty paragraphs begin with the word 'I,' five others begin with a very short phrase followed by 'I.' With an occasional reference to Madame Olbrechts-Tyteca, twice in the opening pages and the use of the first person plural five times, the focus of the essay becomes *my* work . . ." (1984, 90).

2. See Lucie Olbrechts-Tyteca (1960, 1963, 1974, 1977, 1979). Her entire publication record includes two co-authored books, five co-authored journal articles, three single-authored articles, one single-authored book, and one conference paper. This list, which may not be exhaustive, results from searches in European bibliographies, the humanities and social sciences citation indices, and the catalog at the Free University of Brussels (via Internet).

3. All translations from the French in this manuscript are mine, unless otherwise noted.

4. Like nearly all notions in *The New Rhetoric*, "reality" is related to audience adherence. See Perelman and Olbrechts-Tyteca (1969, 66): "Everything in argumentation that is deemed to relate to the real is characterized by a claim to validity vis à vis the universal audience."

5. A fine discussion of value pairs can be found in Walker and Sillars (1990, 138–45).

6. George Kennedy (1980, 16) noted that a subject is "conceptualized" when it emerges into consciousness as an entity, where it is defined, develops a terminology, and is taught as such. This is what Olbrechts did for many aspects of the inference schemes and their applications.

References

Aristotle. 1975. *The "Art" of Rhetoric.* Trans. John Henry Freese. Cambridge: Harvard University Press.

Bizzell, Patricia, and Bruce Herzberg, eds. 1990. *The Rhetorical Tradition.* Boston: St. Martin's Press.

Cox, J. Robert, and Charles Arthur Willard, eds. 1982. *Advances in Argumentation Theory and Research.* Carbondale: Southern Illinois University Press.

Farrell, Thomas B. 1986. "Reason and Rhetorical Practice." In *Practical Reasoning in Human Affairs,* edited by J. L. Golden and J. J. Pilotta, 69–84. Dordrecht: D. Reidel.

Hoover, Judith D. 1993. "Reconstruction of the Rhetorical Situation in 'Letter from Birmingham Jail.'" In *Martin Luther King, Jr., and the Sermonic Power of Public Discourse,* edited by Carolyn Calloway-Thomas and John Louis Lucaites, 50–65. Tuscaloosa: University of Alabama Press.

Keinpointner, Manfred. 1987. "Toward a Typology of Argumentative Schemes." In *Argumentation: Across the Line of Discipline,* edited by Frans H. van Eemeren et al., 275–87. Dordrecht: Foris.

———. 1992. "How to Classify Arguments." In *Argumentation Illuminated,* edited by Frans H. van Eemeren et al., 178–88. Amsterdam: SICSAT.

Kennedy, George A. 1980. *Classical Rhetoric and its Christian and Secular Tradition from Ancient to Modern Times.* Chapel Hill: University of North Carolina Press.

Mattis, Noémi Perelman. 1994. "Perelman and Olbrechts-Tyteca: A Personal Recollection." An unpublished statement read by Ray Dearin at the Speech Communication Association Convention.

Measell, J. S. 1985. "Perelman on Analogy." *Journal of the American Forensic Association* 22: 65–71.

Olbrechts-Tyteca, Lucie. 1960. "Définitions des statisticiens." *Logique et analyse* 3: 49–69.

———. 1963. "Rencontre avec la rhétorique." *Logique et analyse* 6: 3–18.

———. 1974. *Le Comique du discours.* Bruxelles: Editions de l'Université de Bruxelles.

———. 1977. "Comique du discours et connaissance." In *CC77, Colloque international sur le point de vue cognitif,* 414–25. Ghent, Belgium: Communication & Cognition.

———. 1979. "Les Couples philosophiques: Une nouvelle approche." *Revue internationale de philosophie* 33: 81–98.

Olbrechts-Tyteca, Lucie, and Evelyne Griffin-Collart. 1979. "Bibliographie de Chaïm Perelman." *Revue internationale de philosophie* 33: 325–42.

Perelman, Chaïm. 1951. "Act and Person in Argument." *Ethics* 61: 251–69.

———. 1963. "Pragmatic Arguments." Trans. A. J. Ayer. In *The Idea of Justice and the Problem of Argument,* 196–207. London: Routledge.

———. 1969. *Logique et morale.* Brussels: Presses Universitaires de Bruxelles.

———. 1979. "The Rational and the Reasonable." In *The New Rhetoric and the Humanities,* 117–23. Dordrecht: D. Reidel.

———. 1982. *The Realm of Rhetoric.* Trans. W. Kluback. Notre Dame: University of Notre Dame Press.

———. 1990. "The New Rhetoric: A Theory of Practical Reasoning." In *The Rhetorical Tradition,* edited by Patricia Bizzell and Bruce Herzberg, 1077–1103. Boston: St. Martin's Press.

Perelman, Chaïm, and Lucie Olbrechts-Tyteca. 1950. "Logique et rhétorique." *Revue philosophique de la France et de l'étranger* 140: 1–35.

———. 1952. *Rhétorique et philosophie.* Paris: Bibliothèque de Philosophie Contemporaine.

———. 1955. "Les Notions et l'argumentation." *Archivio di Filosofia* 3: 249–69.

———. 1958a. "Classicisme et romantisme dans l'argumentation." *Revue internationale de philosophie* 12: 47–57.

———. 1958b. "De La temporalité comme caractère de l'argumentation." *Archivio di Filosofia* 6: 115–33.

———. 1958c. *Traité de l'argumentation.* Brussels: Université de Bruxelles.

———. 1969. *The New Rhetoric: A Treatise on Argumentation.* Trans. John Wilkinson and Purcell Weaver. Notre Dame: University of Notre Dame Press.

"Public Trust, Private Interests." 1989. *Ethics in America,* television series. Corporation for Public Broadcasting.

Scott, Robert. 1984. "Chaïm Perelman: Persona and Accommodation in the New Rhetoric." *Pre/Text* 5: 89–95.

Secor, Marie J. 1984. "Perelman's Loci in Literary Argument." *Pre/Text* 5: 97–110.

Toulmin, Stephen. 1958. *The Uses of Argument.* Cambridge: Cambridge University Press.

Trapp, Robert, and Janice Schuetz, eds. 1990. *Perspectives on Argumentation.* Prospect Heights, Ill.: Waveland.

van Eemeren, Frans H., Rob Grootendorst, and T. Kruiger. 1984. *The Study of Argumentation.* New York: Irvington.

Walker, Gregg B., and Malcolm O. Sillars. 1990. "Where is Argument? Perelman's Theory of Values." In *Perspectives on Argumentation,* 134–50. Prospect Heights, Ill.: Waveland.

Warnick, Barbara, and Susan L. Kline. 1992. "*The New Rhetoric*'s Argument Schemes." *Argumentation and Advocacy* 29: 1–15.

Part 2

A Sampler of Rhetorical Practices

But, interrupted Caesonia, still would I fain know, what ought to be the difference, there must necessarily be between a Man that speaks well, and a Woman that speaks well. For tho I know a certainty, that there ought to be a distinction, I know not accurately wherein it consists. They make use of the same words; they speak sometimes of the same things; and they have likewise pretty often thoughts in the same Livery.

Madeleine de Scudéry

The Rhetoric of Women in Pharaonic Egypt

Barbara S. Lesko

Introduction to Ancient Egyptian Rhetoric

In an article on "Ancient Egyptian Rhetoric" Michael Fox has argued for the ancient Egyptians' "rightful place in the history of rhetoric" by pointing to their theories of rhetoric expressed "both incidentally and explicitly in the context of advice about the efficacy of speech" (Fox 1983, 9–22). The "advice" Fox refers to are the so-called wisdom or didactic texts, which were copied for generations in the schools and survived for a much longer period of time than credited them by Fox; in fact they were a popular genre for at least fifteen hundred years. These texts were actually intended as helpful guides to success in life (how to gain professional and personal success, even royal and divine favor), but they were designed primarily to help the schools turn out obedient, honest, and dependable civil servants and courtiers. They do focus on "advice about the efficacy of speech" but only incidentally. However, it is possible to discern, as Fox has done, as many as five basic canons of rhetoric. All five are emphasized in the earliest of these books, attributed (as an argument from Authority) to an Old Kingdom vizier, Ptahhotep, although written in a stage of the language that was not current in his time but rather some three hundred years later. The other texts, ranging from circa 1900 B.C.E. to 500 B.C.E., mention some but not all of the five points, a feature attributed by John A. Wilson to the changing fortunes of the country and the oppressive growth of the political and theological forces resulting in the weakening individual freedom and the increase of "pietistic resignation" (Wilson 1951, 92). The following are the five basic tenets of effective speech as the Egyptians saw them:

1. Silence. When one finds oneself attacked, one holds back and lets the opponent have his say, in the likelihood the opponent or accuser will make a fool of himself, becoming enraged while you exhibit cool, detached self-possession, which in itself should win you points.
2. Finding the right moment to speak up.
3. Carefully regulated, restrained speech.
4. Fluency of speech, meaning no vacillation or evasion, having command of the facts and not getting carried away by superfluities or exaggerations; answering, not evading.
5. Truthful speech. Truth will win out; truth is effective; false words will eventually turn against their speaker.

Actually, Ptahhotep's five precepts could be said to concern deportment and behavior more than eloquence, but as Fox puts it, the Egyptians would have us believe that for them the existence of these five tenets constituted an ethos that was "itself a form of proof. The didactic wisdom literature gives no thought to argumentation as such and shows no awareness of the possibility that argumentation could operate independently of ethos. Ethos stands on its own" (Fox 1983, 16).

One important feature connecting all the known didactic texts is the fact that they were written for schoolboys who learned their precepts while they trained to be efficient, loyal civil servants in a totalitarian state. These schools did not exist to stimulate inquiring minds or independent thinking. The latest texts, from a period of political reversals for the country, are so cautious that silence seems the safest course: "Muteness is better than a hasty tongue" (Lichtheim 1980, 171). Nor was all Egyptian rhetoric characterized by such guidelines, as Fox acknowledges in citing still another literary work known as "The Eloquent Peasant" (Lichtheim 1973, 169–84). In this example hyperbole runs free. The peasant's nine petitions are long-winded speeches, full of extravagant metaphors, and by turn flattery and indignation seem to have won the hearts of the listeners (by delighting them) and the peasant his rights in the end. The author of this amusing text seems to have sought to stand the schools' teaching on its head. Fox assumes that the official class would have enjoyed the story simply because it provided a nice contrast to their own daily behavior "constantly to practice the virtues of silence and self-control" (Fox 1983, 17). But did they exercise restraint in speech and action? Has there ever been a society wherein only the virtuous succeeded or wherein every officeholder, supervisor, and secretary was the model of decorum and truth always won the day? When Fox writes that "Self-control was especially important to the strictly ordered hierarchical society of Egypt, where the social order was considered divinely ordained and ideally static and where the individual's chief duty was to bring himself into harmony with that order, certainly not to change it," he has believed the propaganda! Surely it is naive to think that Egyptians could not have "conceived of an instrumental rhetoric of deceit," for official records themselves have long been recognized as being true forms of propaganda: demeaning adversaries, skimming over political reversals, and finding victories where none existed (Wilson 1951, 246).

It is clear that the Egyptians appreciated the power of speech. Merikare, writing around 2000 B.C.E., stated: "the tongue is a sword and speaking is more powerful than any fighting" (Lichtheim 1973, 99). That is why the state tried to exercise control through their schools to discourage those who would passionately question authority and to ridicule and indeed declare irreligious the speech of the "heated man," the protester. Did they succeed? Of course not. Egyptian history had its share of political upheavals, assassinations, wars, strikes, and political persecutions, although this is not the place to enumerate them.

Of course, it would have been ideal for the king and country had the ethos explained above truly held sway in every office of the land, at every hearing, in every contact. We must give the Egyptians credit for exulting virtues such as honesty, but we must not be blinded to the fact that every human society has had its share of the ambitious and ruthless, the weak and insecure, the hot tempered, the timid, and those who would overturn the status quo. Let us turn away from the ideal and confront the reality. Fortunately, we do have original documents that can form the basis for a study of actual rhetoric from ancient Egypt. Fox is incorrect to state that trial records "only summarize the testimony of the defendants" and that no actual forensic speeches are preserved from ancient Egypt" (Fox 1983, 19, n. 7). Confronting this assertion will be the main task of my essay, even as I limit my evidence to the rhetoric of women.

Women's Rhetoric

In a society made up for the most part of men and women who were illiterate and in which many of those who were able to read rudimentary texts would not likely have been able to write well, dependence on dictation to a scribe was the norm when one wished to send a letter of some consequence. This should not preclude consideration of such secondhand messages as genuine, however, as even today courtroom testimony is recorded and regarded as an accurate and vital rendition of the testifier's intentions. The dictated messages of the ancients, whether sent by another's hand to a living correspondent or left at the tomb of the intended recipient, are genuine outpourings from the heart. More is the pity that so few letters to the living and the dead survive. The vast majority of those that do survive were written not on papyrus but on the more sturdy shards of pottery or limestone cuttings from the excavation of rock-hewn tombs. Even so, it has been estimated that only 10 percent of the original corpus remains (or has been found) of even these more durable manuscripts (Janssen 1992, 81–89).

If rhetoric is defined as the "art of persuasion," we are rewarded by the fact that surviving letters and court testimony do usually try to persuade a listener or reader to believe, to agree, or to act on the advice or command of the "speaker." Although they are in the minority of this minority of surviving letters and testimonies, women are reflected in the corpus. Surviving from particularly the Middle Kingdom (circa 1900–1600 B.C.E.) and New Kingdom (circa 1540–1000 B.C.E.) periods are letters from women—particularly women of authority—and testimonials presented before tribunals by ordinary housewives.

At the other extreme of society, we have texts, hewn in stone on monuments, which read like speeches from the throne by the great female pharaoh Hatshespsut, who reigned over Egypt from 1503 to 1482 B.C.E. Private women of means have also left us stone inscriptions from their burial sites, autobiographical in tone if not of much informative substance. We know that royal princesses were tutored by leading male courtiers, and nonroyal women of the leisure class could well have had some instruction and been able to read books of literature (Bryan 1984, 17–32). However, such educated or at least semiliterate women could, like their husbands, easily have afforded the services of a scribe when they wanted to send a letter.

If we extend the definition of rhetoric still more broadly, we can perhaps include songs or lyric poetry presented as the words of women. While more than half of the secular (romantic) poetry that survives from ancient Egypt is put into the mouths of women, scholars have doubted that any of it could have been written by women themselves. Suggestions have been made, however, that since professional women singers and musicians flourished, songs could have been heard by literate men who then committed the remembered lyrics to writing later, improving upon them in the process. However, I have pointed out elsewhere that two types of poetry represented in the corpus of some seventy love songs are easily discernible (Lesko 1986, 85–97). The more down-to-earth, those that exhibit far fewer literary devices, may well be direct renditions of a woman's words and thus comparable to our recorded letters or testimony in their validity.

In this chapter I shall give examples of the above-outlined source material and then discuss how these actual examples of rhetoric compare with the official teachings of the ancient Egyptian savants about "perfect speech." The earliest letter we shall consider is one written by a wife to her deceased husband during the Sixth Dynasty, around 2250 B.C.E. Even today letters to the dead are found in our own culture—witness the missives left at the Vietnam War Memorial in Washington, D.C. The ancient Egyptians were convinced that the "justified" dead could intervene on behalf of their living relatives to solve problems, and for this reason a number of such letters have survived from cemetery sites.

Cairo Linen CG 25975:
Your condition is like that of one who lives innumerable times. May Ha, lord of the West, and may Anubis, lord of burial, help you, as we both desire. This is a reminder of the fact that Behezti's agent came for leather while I was sitting by, your head, when Irti's (i.e. my) son Iy was caused to be summoned to vouch for Behezti's agent and when you said "Keep him hidden for fear of Iy the elder! May the wood of this my bed which bears me rot (?), should the son of a man be debarred from his household furniture."

Now, in fact, the woman Wabaut came together with Izezi, and they both have devastated your house. It was in order to enrich Izezi that she removed everything that was in it, they both wishing to impoverish our son while enriching Izezi's son. She has taken Iazet, Iti, and Anankhi away from you, and she is taking away all of your personal menials after removing all that was in your house. Will you remain calm about this? I had rather that you should fetch [me] away to yourself so that I might be there beside you than to see your son dependent upon Izezi's son.

Awaken your father Iy against Behezti! Rouse yourself and make haste against him! You know that I [have] come to you here about litigating with your fathers, your brothers, and your relations and overthrow Behezti and Aai's son Anankhi.

Recall what you said to Irti's (i.e. my) son Iy, "They are the houses of ancestors that need to be sustained," when you [also] said, "It is a son 's house and then [his] son's house." May your son maintain your house just as you maintained your father's house. (Wente 1990, 211)

Clearly the inheritance of an estate is at stake here. The rightful heir is being turned out of his father's house, perhaps because the father had been married previously and engendered children by an earlier wife. The widow hopes not only to encourage her son's father to protect his claim but to involve other deceased relatives in persecuting the other claimants who have already entered the property and carried off its furnishings. The widow emphasizes her consternation by declaring she would rather be dead than to have to witness the ruination of her son by these envious parties.

Remarkably, two letters survive, from about eight hundred years apart, in which a woman directly addresses her king. Reflecting the primary occupation of women, both letters concern weaving and reveal the senders to be in charge of weaving studios. These women with authority over others in the workplace seem to exhibit little trepidation about communicating with the all-powerful god-king of Egypt, even though in the case of the earlier letter (from the Twelfth Dynasty, circa 1900 B.C.E.) the sender uses no title that would distinguish her. The later letter, from the reign of Seti II of the Nineteenth Dynasty (circa 1215 B.C.E.), seems to be from an elderly lady who has been around the palace ateliers for many a year and is accustomed to respect. It should be understood that "l.p.h." following "the Lord" is the Egyptological abbreviation for the polite phrase "may He live, be prosperous and healthy," which invariably follows any reference to a pharaoh by his subjects.

Papyrus Kahun III.3:
What the lady of the house Irer sends: This is a communication to the lord, l.p.h., to the effect that all business affairs of the lord, l.p.h., are prosperous and flourishing wherever they are . . . a communication to the lord, l.p.h., about this neglectfulness on the part of the lord, l.p.h. Are you all safe [and sound? The women weavers(?)] are left abandoned, thinking they won't get food provisions in as much as

not any news of you has been heard. It is good if [the lord, l.p.h.] takes note. . . . This is a communication to the lord, l.p.h., about those slave-women who are here unable to weave clothes. Your presence [is demanded(?)] by those who work at(?) the warp-thread so as to be guided(?) I, your humble servant, couldn't come myself owing to the fact that I, your humble servant, entered the temple on the twentieth day of the month to serve as *wab*-priestess for the month(?). [So] may the lord, l.p.h., bring them (food supplies?) with him. . . . The lord, l.p.h., should spend some time here since [not] any clothes [have been made] while my attention is being directed to the temple, and the warp-threads are set up on the loom without its being possible to weave them. (Wente 1990, 82)

This surely is an odd letter, for even if the sender is in charge of royal weaving studios, one would not expect her to trouble her sovereign with the news that the quota is not being met, and it is surprising to find her scolding the king about his neglectfulness. However, our correspondent is presumably having difficulty getting her staff of largely foreign laborers to work due to the lack of ration deliveries, which came from the royal storehouses. Instead of appealing to an officer of the treasury or even the vizier, the king's second in command, the lady Irer, in her desperation, writes for help directly to her king!

Our second letter also concerns foreign workers in a royal weaving studio. Its opening is lost, and the reference to "Pre" is to the supreme god of that time, the sun god Re, while "One" is a polite form of address to the pharaoh.

Papyrus Gurob III, 1, recto:
. . . which I have made, for they are exactly like those which had been made for Pre. I shall have myself boasted about because of them and not let fault be found with me. It is advantageous that my Lord, l.p.h., has had people sent to me to be taught and instructed how to perform this important occupation (of weaving). It is fortunate that my Lord has found someone fit to do that the like of which had not been done for Pre (supreme god), because those who are here are senior apprentices. It is only such people as are like those people whom my Lord, l.p.h., sent who are capable of functioning and who are capable of receiving my personal instruction, since they are foreigners like those who used to be brought to us in the time of Usermare-setepenre, l.p.h., the Great God, your good [grand]father, and who would tell

us, "We were quite a number in the households of the officials," and who would receive instruction and so be able to perform whatever was told them. This is a missive for One's information. Year 2, third month of the first season, day 20. (Wente 1990, 36)

The ancient Egyptians were great record keepers, and it could be that both letters were actually reports of the kind that had to be sent in periodically by all those who were in charge of some state bureau or workshop. In the first case, the lady Irer has a problem that she must explain, and she is excusing herself by implying the problem would not exist if the king had supplied ration-pay to her workers on time. She stresses the difficulty of her situation by requesting the king to step in and solve it himself. In the second letter the, unfortunately unidentified, correspondent expresses pride in her accomplishments. Apparently she has met quotas and deadlines and wants the king to know that the products of her harem workshops are fit for the gods. She also boldly tells her royal boss that he is fortunate to have her in charge. She appreciates having "senior apprentices" who are capable of being trained by her, and she reminds the king that she has been training expert weavers since the reign of his grandfather.

Women also occupied positions of authority in temples in ancient Egypt, if not always as chief celebrants of the cult. They could, as some letters from the late Ramesside period indicate, have responsibility for looking after the storehouses from which offerings for the resident deity of the temple would be taken and for allotting the regular rations for those offerings on a daily basis. As the Chantress of Amun-Re, King of the Gods, Henuttowy wrote to the necropolis scribe Nesamenope in the Twentieth Dynasty:

Papyrus Geneva D191:
You wrote me saying, "receive the 80 *khar*-measures of grain from this transport boat of the fisherman Iotnefer," so you said [in] writing. I went [to] receive them and found only 72.5 *khar* measures with him. I asked him, "What's the meaning of only 72.5 *khar*-measures of grain," so I asked him, "whereas it is 80 *khar* measures that are stated in his letter?" The men replied, "It is three completely full withdrawals that we have measured out for ourselves, each having 2.5 *khar*-measures, thus netting 72.5 *khar*-measures of grain," so they replied. I maintained my silence thinking that until you return, Amun, United with Eternity, will have done every sort of bad thing to me.

Attend to the grain of his, which you caused to be brought in, since there is no longer even a *khar*-measure of grain for his divine offerings. It is I who have given 30 *khar*-measures of grain for his divine offerings. It is I who have given 30 *khar*-measures of emmer for his [divine offer]ings beginning [from Year] 2, second month of the first season, [day] 27, until the third month of the first season, day 2, from the grain which is stored under my supervision [. . .] for the divine offerings.

Now Amun, United with Eternity, has caused the grain to be put in a chest and has caused a seal to be affixed to it. See, you shall join up with Paseny and you two shall consult with the overseer of granaries concerning the grain for Amun, United with Eternity, because he [Amun] hasn't got even one *oipe* measure's worth for his divine offerings today. You mustn't abandon him, either of you two. (Wente 1990, 174)

Clearly the woman administrator is beside herself facing an arrears in deliveries she had expected for her temple stores. She fears the wrath of her god and is intent on impressing her correspondent with the fact that she is hard-pressed to come up with any grain for the divine offerings and has had to find it elsewhere, possibly from her own home stores. So she beseeches the men she trusts to take up the matter with the overseer of granaries and not to abandon the god to whom she is responsible.

Again from the Twentieth Dynasty comes another letter from a female temple cult leader, and probably the wife of a high priest, again revealing the possibility of female authority over temple wealth:

Papyrus Turin unnumbered:
The principal of the harem of Amun-[Re, King of] the Gods, Herere, to the troop captain Peseg: What's this about the personnel of the [great] and noble necropolis [concerning whom] I wrote to you, saying, "give them rations," that you haven't yet given them any? [As soon as my let]ter reaches you, you shall look for the grain which [I wrote you] about and give them rations from it. Don 't make [. . .] complain to me again. Have them prepared [for] people [. . .] commission them. (Wente 1990, 200)

A woman commanding much more modest wealth is encountered in the following statement, which she gave before her community's local tribunal to disinherit some of her eight children for not taking care of her in her old age. The Citizeness Naunakhte says:

> As for me, I am a free woman of the land of Pharaoh. I brought up these eight servants of yours and gave them an outfit of everything (such) as is usually made for those in their station. But look, I am grown old, and see, they are not looking after me in my turn. Who-ever of them has aided me, to him I will give (of) my property, [but] he who has not given to me, to him I will not give of my property. (Cerny 1945, 31)

Then follows a list of the four children who will inherit. Naunakhte des-ignates one son for a special reward, apparently repaying him for special consideration. But half the children would only receive the property of their father and would not share in the division of their mother's estate:

> As for these four children of mine, they shall (not) participate in the division of any of my property. And as for any property of the scribe Kenhikhopshef, my first husband, and also his landed property and this store-room of my father and also this *oipe* of emmer which I col-lected in company with my husband, they shall not share them. As for these eight children of mine, they shall participate in the division of the property of their father in one single division. (Cerny 1945, 32)

So far the examples have included orders and self-justifications. They are the responses to problems and seek to persuade others either to act or to accept the action of the speaker.

Naunakhte spoke her last will and testament before a local tribunal, and the names of her witnesses—neighbors in the small town where she lived—are also preserved on the document. So often rhetoric is associ-ated with an audience, and we wonder whether Naunakhte chose the public tribunal out of necessity or because she might have hoped to gain more sympathy there than might have been the case. Instead of allow-ing rumor or the talk of certain of her offspring to inspire the image of an "uncaring mother," by going public she had the chance to be the first to point a finger toward those who truly gave no care.

More female legal testimony survives in the court records of an in-quiry into the robbing of royal tombs during the Twentieth Dynasty, a time of some political instability and economic troubles. Cross-examinations of suspects and possible witnesses were conducted under oath and with the accompaniment of "the stick."

What follows is a woman's testimony, the beginning unfortunately lost, recorded on the British Museum Papyrus 10052:

> Now when some days had elapsed, this brother of mine came together with the foreigner Userhetnakht and the incense-roaster Shedsuknons and the incense roaster Nesamun and Perpethew, altogether 4 men. They went to this workshop, and I went after them. They reviled me, and I said to them "what am I to split with you?" This brother of mine said to me, "Go, bring me five pieces of wood." I brought them to them, and they divided a mass of treasure and made it into four (sic) parts, ten *deben* of silver and 2 *deben* of gold and 2 seals falling to each man among them. I took the share of my husband and put it aside in my store-room and I took one *deben* of silver thereof and brought *shesh*-grain with it. Now when some days had passed, Amenkhau the son of Mutemheb came with the scribe of the divine records Nesamun. They said to me, "Give up this treasure." (He was with Amenkhau my own brother). . . . But I said to them, with an air of boldness, "My brother will not let me be interfered with." So said I, and Amenkhau gave me a blow with a spear on one of my arms, and I fell (down). I got up and entered the store-room, and I brought this silver and handed it over to him together with the 2 *deben* of gold and the two seals, one of genuine lapis lazuli and one of turquoise, there was a weight of 6 *kite* of fine gold in them in mounting and setting. She said, I saw nothing else. (Peet 1930, 148–49)

Another woman was questioned by the high tribunal:

> The Citizeness Ese was brought, the wife of the gardener Ker of the funerary chapel of Ramose. There was given to her the oath of the Ruler to the effect that if she spoke falsehood she should be mutilated and placed on the stake. The vizier said to her: "what is the story of this silver which your husband brought away from the Great Tombs?" She said, I did not see it. The scribe Dhutmose said to her. "How did you buy the servants which you bought?" She said, "I bought them in exchange for the crops from my garden." The vizier said, "Let Painekh her servant be brought that he may accuse her." (Peet 1930, 152)

For the record, the servant was examined, but his testimony was incon-
clusive. Other women were brought who likewise claimed their recently
increased buying power was due to their selling of foodstuffs. One
woman claimed to have earned a considerable amount of silver "in exchange for barley in the year of the hyenas when there was a famine"
(Peet 1930, 153).

The first woman recounts with some pride the boldness of her confrontation with men, first the tomb robbers from whom she asked a
portion of their take, even though they had reviled her for following
them, and then another group of men who eventually did persuade her—
by brute force—to fetch and hand over to them her husband's portion of
the stolen property.

The alibi as defense is demonstrated again by the woman who claims
that she knows nothing about any stolen property and then claims that
her increased buying power is the result of her own clever marketing of
homegrown produce. This deceit in the face of severest punishment may
not have been convincing.

Royal Rhetoric

Now we shall move from the world of the ordinary citizens, concerned with personal and administrative problems, to the speech of a
ruler, in this case the rhetoric of the great female pharaoh Hatshepsut,
who ruled Egypt in the middle of the second millennium B.C.E. as the
fifth ruler of the glorious Eighteenth Dynasty.

Hatshepsut was surely one of the great women of history. A strong-
willed personality who carried the blood of conquerors in her veins, she
ruled Egypt successfully for almost twenty years. When faced with acting as temporary regent for the son, by a concubine, of her late husband
(with whom she had had no male child) Hatshepsut soon decided to
seize complete command herself, relegating her young nephew to the
sidelines. While she seems to have sent, and even to have led, military
campaigns into surrounding territories, her interest was more in restoring and erecting great monuments, particularly temples to the gods, and
sending forth expeditions into foreign lands to bring back luxury products, such as turquoise from the Sinai and gold and frankincense from
the southern Red Sea coast of Africa. The great inscription excerpted
here, in which Hatshepsut describes her intentions to rebuild what had
been neglected and makes her claim to divinity and awesome power,
can be seen at one of her building projects in Middle Egypt. I have num-

bered these excerpts from her inscription at the sacred grotto of Speos Artemidos for ease in referring to them later and thank Professor Leonard H. Lesko, Wilbour Professor of Egyptology at Brown University, for rendering this updated translation of Norman Davies's copy of the inscription (Davies 1946, 43–56 + double plate).

1. My divine heart is taking thought for the future. The heart of the King of Lower Egypt (herself) has planned for eternity on account of the utterance of the one who opened the Ished tree, Amun, Lord of Millions. I magnified truth which he loved, knowing that he lives on it. It is my bread that I wash down with its dew. I being of one flesh with him. It is to cause that his fame be mighty in this land that he created me.

2. I am the [heir] of Atum, the [beloved] of Kheper, the one who made that which exists, whom Re has predestined when he measured out the lands which are united under my charge, the Black Land and the Red Land being under dread of me. My power causes the foreign lands to bow down, while the uraeus on my forehead pacifies all lands for me. As for (the lands of) Reshwet and Iu, they have not been concealed from my majesty. (The land of) Punt [overflows] for me on the fields, its trees bearing fresh myrrh. The paths which were blocked on two sides have been beaten down. My army, which was unequipped, has come into possession of riches since I appeared in glory as king.

3. The temple of the Mistress of Cusae [Hathor], was fallen into ruin, and the earth had swallowed its august sanctuary while children danced on its roof. The serpent-goddess no longer gave terror, and lowly ones were counted *djadja* as perversity, and its festivals no longer appeared. I sanctified it after it had been built anew. It is in order to protect her city that I fashioned her image from gold, with a barque for a land procession. . . . The face of my majesty gives alertness to the bearers of the god. It is with limestone of Ainu that I built his great temple, its gateways with alabaster of Hatnub. Doors of Asiatic copper, the reliefs thereof of electrum, were consecrated by him who is high of plumes. . . . With a double festival I [extolled] the majesty of this god. . . . The Uniting of *Kas* and the Festival of Thoth, I established anew for him, they being in the mouth, not before its time, since the nature of the festival was unique. For him I doubled the divine offerings in excess of what they were before, in my acting for the Ogdoad and for Khnum in his forms, for Hekat, Rennutet, and

Meskhenet, who had united to fashion my body, for Nehmetawey, Nekhbet-Kau, Idjdet, Iwnespetta, and Imiutiw in Hebnw. The cities thereof are in festival, bearing witness to me, being something completely unknown. Battlements are in the plan; I have set them in order and made them festive while giving chapels to their lords. Every [god] says to himself [about] me. "One who shall spend eternity, One whom Amun has caused to appear as king of eternity on the throne of Horus." 4. Hear you, all patricians and all commoners as many as you are. I have done this by the plan of my heart. I can not sleep as a lowly one. I made to flourish what was ruined. I raised up what was cut up formerly since the Asiatics were in the fold of the Delta at Avaris, with foreigners in their midst overthrowing what had been made. Unmindful of Re they ruled, and he did not act by divine command down to (the time of) my majesty, I having been established on the thrones of Re. I was foretold for an eternity of years as "She will become a conqueror." I have come as the Sole one of Horus flaming against my enemies. I have removed the abomination of the gods, and the earth had brought away their footprints. This was the instruction of the father of my fathers who came at his appointed times, Re. "Never shall occur the destruction of what Amun had commanded." My command is firm like the mountains and the disk shines and spreads rays over the titulary of my majesty, and my falcon is high over the *serekh* forever and ever.

There is a short preamble to the royal speech, which salutes the female pharaoh as the "Good Goddess, Lady of the Two Lands, Makare, the daughter of Re Hatshepsut" and refers to the inscription itself, graven unto the cliff side above the Nile valley. Then Hatshepsut's own words begin. She stresses her piety and the fact that, in the tradition of all good Egyptian kings, she lives on *maat,* that difficult to translate concept that embodies all earthly righteousness and cosmic harmony. She also here makes her initial claim to divine birth, telling us that she is of one flesh with the great god Amun. This was crucial for her claim on the throne. In actual fact, Hatshepsut was an anomaly. Very few female pharaohs ruled during Egypt's three thousand years of ancient history. However, she was far from being a usurper. No one would have questioned her right and duty to rule the country as regent for a minor. No one seems to have opposed her consequent claim to absolute rule either, but many years after her reign her name was stricken from some of the official annals of kings, and her successor had her image and texts erased from the walls of her temples and ordered her statuary destroyed. The motivation is not clear but surely underscores the questionable claim to kingship by a woman who was not the designated heir of her husband. The claims to divine birth and thus perfect legitimacy made by Hatshepsut frequent the walls of her monuments and are sometimes graphically portrayed. Yet we know she protested too much.

In the second section Hatshepsut emphasizes her universal power and her ability to bring back the riches of lands beyond Egypt's borders, such as the Sinai and Somalia (Roshawet and Punt). Thus she works for the betterment of her country and the enrichment of its gods.

Her third point is that she has piously restored temples that had suffered depredations, particularly due to the domination of the northern part of the country by the impious Canaanite (Hyksos) dynasty, and has built new and grander monuments for the great gods of Egypt, all this with an eye toward their divine support for herself.

Her finale is a direct address to all Egyptians to take note of her unceasing energy in restoring Egypt's glories. Hatshepsut claims she is the first king since the Canaanite dynasty to give her attention to rebuilding (which is not only untrue but she is ignoring even her own father's efforts here). She claims not only to enjoy the support of the supreme god Re but actually to have been foretold. Hatshepsut stresses that she rules alone and that she is invincible against those who would oppose her—we assume all enemies both foreign and domestic. She vows to live by the god's command, and then ends with the vivid imagery of mountains and the sun and the royal falcon soaring high above the kingly ensign forever.

This is a powerful speech full of bombast and divine metaphor. We feel the queen's pride and yet still sense her insecurity with her daring undertaking, shattering precedents left and right. She attempts to persuade her subjects and us that she deserves to rule by birthright as well as by good deeds. She can protect her country effectively and bring to it riches fit for the gods. It would appear that it is the gods whom she is most concerned with impressing, as without divine sanction nothing could be accomplished. Egyptologists have regarded this text and the following as genuine oratory. Its exaggerations and stretchings of the truth are typical of royal pronouncements, at least those that have survived to our time through the medium of inscriptions on stone monuments, and should not be considered as "feminine."

The granite obelisks Hatshepsut erected at the great temple of Amun-Re, Karnak, soar higher than any in Egypt. Her pride and justification for this undertaking are expressed in the texts engraved on their surfaces, from which the following excerpts are taken:

> I declare before the folk who shall be in the future, who shall observe the monument I made for my father, who shall speak in discussion, who shall look to posterity. . . . It was when I sat in the palace and thought of my maker that my heart led me to make for him two obelisks of electrum, whose summits would reach the heavens, in the august hall of columns, between the two great portals of the King. . . . Now my heart turns to and fro, in wondering what will the people say, they who shall see my monument in later years, and shall speak of what I have done. . . . As regards these two great obelisks wrought with electrum by my majesty for my father Amun, in order that my name may endure in this temple for ever and ever. They are each of one block of hard granite, without seam, without joining together.
>
> My majesty began work on them in year 15, second month of winter, day 1, ending in year 16, fourth month of summer, last day, totaling seven months of quarry work. I did it for him out of affection, as a king for a god. It was my wish to make them for him gilded with electrum. Their foil lies on their body, is what I expect people to say. My mouth is effective in its speech; I do not go back on my word. Hear ye! I gave for them of the finest electrum. I measured it by the *hekat*-like sacks of grain. My majesty summoned a quantity beyond what the Two Lands had yet seen. The ignorant and the wise know it. (Lichtheim 1976, 27–28)

Hatshepsut obviously is proud of the accomplishments of her reign and looks forward to being remembered for them by posterity. She used, as many pharaohs did, the monumental inscription as propaganda. Clearly her aim is to impress and to cause history to remember her name. She stresses that the ideas for the great undertakings of her reign were original with her. She is boastful to the point of exaggeration, as the obelisks were not totally covered with the precious gold alloy known as electrum—as one might think from her description. Their pointed ends—still visible above the roof line of the great temple—alone were so sheathed.

Hatshepsut was by no means the only formidable female of Egypt's empire period. Later in her dynasty lived a trio of highly influential queens: Tiy, the consort of Amenhotep III; her daughter-in-law Nefertiti, and her daughter Ankhesenamum, widowed young by Tutankhamen. It is this last woman who speaks to us across time. Unfortunately, her words come to us third hand; they are preserved from a text in the royal Hittite annals far off in Anatolia that purports to quote the young queen's plea to Suppululiumas. This letter, written years after the fact, is the only record that survives from an incredible historical incident. It seems that the young widow, desperate to keep the throne of Egypt from falling to a nonroyal party, wrote to the only other powerful monarch in the ancient world of her time, the king of the Hittites. She asked Suppululiumas for one of his many sons so that she might perpetuate her own distinguished dynastic line and share with him the throne that was once her father's and her husband's. This unprecedented request so astonished the Hittite ruler that he hesitated to believe its sincerity and suspected a plot. Egypt and Hatti were not allies at this time but rather vied with one another for power and political influence in their world. So the hapless queen had to send a second letter with further assurances, losing much valuable time in the process. We know she successfully persuaded the Hittite king, who did indeed send a son forth—the thought of consolidation with the world's richest kingdom apparently winning out. However, Queen Ankhesenamum's plot was foiled as the prince died en route—whether by sickness or murder is unknown. Regardless, she disappeared from history, and a senior army officer took command of Egypt. Here are Ankhesenamum's pleas as recalled by the Hittites:

1. My husband died and I have no son. People say that you have many sons. If you were to send me one of your sons, he might become my husband. I am loath to take a servant of mine and make him my husband.
2. Why do you say "They may try to deceive me?" If I had a son, would I write to a foreign country in a manner which is humiliating to myself and to my country? You do not trust me and tell me even such a thing. He who was my husband died and I have no sons. Shall I perhaps take one of my servants and make him my husband? I have not written to any other country, I have written (only) to you. People say that you have many sons. Give me one of your sons and he is my husband and king in the land of Egypt. (Goetze 1955, 319)

Clearly the above shows a royal widow in a desperate plight. Faced with the choice between a forced marriage with one who we know was actually an aged courtier-relative, or being forced aside by an ambitious and ruthless general, Ankhesenamum reveals the same spunk, self-centered though it was, as had her ancestor Hatshepsut. Her novel approach to the Hittites was no doubt regarded as treasonous once it was discovered by the Egyptians, and she probably died for it. This assumption adds poignancy to the queen's appeal.

If we are able to judge correctly from the quoted letters, the queen probably did not go into enough detail in her first approach. If her initial message was as brief as it is reputed, it is not surprising that the Hittites did not act upon it as she had hoped. However, once she admitted that she was humiliated to be in a position of making such a request of Egypt's rival power and stressed that it was only the Hittite king to whom she had appealed, the Hittite ruler realized the sincerity and desperation of the queen and seized the opportunity to increase his political power and wealth. For him the letters presented an opportunity not to be missed. We have here a genuine case of expressed humility and of flattery of one in superior position, which is exactly the approach that the ancient rhetorician would have advised.

Later in this chapter we shall review the ancient injunctions about "perfect speech" and conduct. But first let us finish our review of female speech by examining a few examples of lyric poetry.

The Longings of Women in Love

Seventy-five percent of the Egyptian lyric poetry of romantic theme can be attributed to women, while 25 percent reflects the sentiments of men. Furthermore, two distinct traditions of love lyrics date from the Egyptian empire period: the more popular lyrics, sometimes ribald and sometimes reflecting ordinary everyday life situations, are found in women's songs; and the more refined, spiritual, and courtly compositions are generally presented as the thoughts of men (Lesko 1986, 89–97). The earliest collection of poems seems to be the twenty on Papyrus Harris 500, tentatively dated to the end of the Eighteenth Dynasty (and thus contemporary with the reign of Tutankhamen and Ankhesenamum). The anthologies of popular poetry were probably occasioned by the then recent acceptance of colloquial speech forms by the academics, who up to this time had taught Egyptian students to read and write only a long-dead classical phase of their language. Not only was literacy extended to include colloquial speech forms, but the ability to render actual speech forms facilitated the lyrical poems and allows us to hear genuine sentiments.

From Papyrus Harris 500 we hear, through these new translations by Leonard H. Lesko, how love can distract a woman from her chores, make her feel ill, and drive her to pleading and aggressive overtures of love (Fox 1985, 370–82).

Poem 1
. . . Am I not with [you]?
Where will you set your heart?
Should [you] not embrace [me]? . . .
Does my lip reach [you]?
. . . the happiness.
If you try to touch my thighs and buttocks
Is it because you remembered to eat that you go?
Is it because you are a man of his stomach?
Is it because you [are concerned] with clothes?
I am the possessor of a bed sheet!
Is it because of hunger that you go?
. . . take my breasts
that their offerings may overflow for you.
More beneficial is one day of embracing your [lover]
than a hundred thousand spent wishing.

Poem 10
The voice of the goose cries out,
caught by his worm (lure).
Love of you holds me back,
and I cannot unloosen it.
I shall take my net,
but what shall I (say) to my mother,
to whom I return each day,
(usually) loaded down with birds?
"No trap was set today!"
Love of you captured me.

These expressions of women in love are direct and honest, not coy. Their forthrightness is reminiscent of the letters of women and lends authenticity to them as genuine sentiments.

Conclusion

In this review of women's rhetoric from ancient Egypt, we have found many examples of bold speech. Indignant words were heard often—expressing impatience at the lack of a desired response—whether they concerned prompt payments, the neglectfulness of children, the failure to comprehend a desperate situation, or the lack of interest by a lover. Exaggeration was also encountered frequently, even in royal texts.

Judging from the preserved teachings of ancient Egyptians (surviving from the early Middle Kingdom and continuing as school texts for many centuries, indeed throughout Pharaonic history) as discussed by Michael Fox and others, women's rhetoric seems far from what would have then been deemed "proper" speech. The professional teachers' didactic literature, even though it survives from a long span of centuries, hardly varies in basic tenants: no chatter; silence is the wise response to the opponent. The New Kingdom scribe Any went so far as to advise: "Don't ever talk back to your attacker" (Lichtheim 1976, 140, 143). Even when not under attack by a disputant, the wise man would hold back his opinions: "Speak only when you have a solution"; "Be deliberate when you speak, so as to say things that count" (Lichtheim 1973, 75–76). Egyptian women do not seem to have been so cautious, self-effacing, or unguarded. In addition, falsehood was an abomination of the gods, and all the wise men of Egypt stressed that truth was the only way to salvation and that false words were bound to bring about a person's doom. The lack of humility and the flippant responses of the women before the state tribunal investigating the tomb robberies in the royal necropolis would not have won them points with the officials.

In this brief survey I have extended my identification of rhetoric to areas left unconsidered by Michael Fox in his study. I have included letters, which were probably dictated out loud, and I have included material from tribunals because I do not subscribe to Fox's idea that all of the court hearings have been abbreviated beyond usefulness to us. Indeed, one of my examples was quite detailed and included the asides of the woman on her bravery and on her injury. Indeed, Fox overlooks the royal oratory, cited above, even though Egyptologists, going back at least as far as the eminent James Henry Breasted, in the first decade of the twentieth century, have regarded these texts as records of speeches from the throne. Whether they are truly verbatim copies of actual speeches is not important, as they are presented as the queen's words and thus must be assumed appropriately similar to her proclamations.

As noted above, Fox's study of the ancient didactic texts—the guides to moral behavior and good social relations produced throughout Egyptian history by teachers—reveals five tenets that, he believes, must have governed all acceptable Egyptian rhetoric. These are keeping silent, waiting for the right moment to speak, restraining passionate words, speaking fluently but with great deliberation, and speaking the truth. Obviously these are ideals held out to students as a way to achieve not only social harmony and stability in the greater society but personal reputation as well. The mild-mannered, thoughtful student would win high marks and convince future employers that he would make a trusted aide. However, as we have seen, Egyptian women, perhaps because they were not as likely to be formally educated, answered their accusers back with gusto and did not hesitate to brag. The scribe Any also wrote that "A man's belly is wider than a granary and full of all kinds of answers. Choose the good one and say it while shutting the bad up in your belly" (Lichtheim 1976, 140). He would surely have paled at reading the letters our female administrators of weaving studios sent off to their kings!

While the cautious teachings may have been a significant part of the school texts copied out by advanced students, another widely read text concerns a different sort of rhetoric, the rantings of an outraged peasant who was so colorful and amusing in his retorts against his tormentors that these replies were copied down for the entertainment of his king. Perhaps Fox is correct in judging "The Eloquent Peasant" as a polemic against the tiresomely cautious dictates of Wisdom Literature. At any rate, it provides a more realistic human side to "perfect speech." Contemporaneously, or perhaps even before this text was produced, the vizier Ptah-hotep supposedly observed that "Eloquence is more hidden than greenstone, yet may be found among maids at the grindstones" (Lichtheim 1973, 63). Some of the speeches and letters of women that we have studied contain memorable passages, but we must wonder whether the reviling words and boastfulness they contain are present because these women were never exposed to the cautious teachings drummed into the schoolboys. A well-educated male would probably not have written so boldly to his royal boss that the arrears in payments were the fault of the royal government, nor would he have emphasized his own superiority in training staffs of workers. Presumably an educated man, under examination by the vizier in the serious case of royal tomb robbing, would not have spoken of his own bravery in confronting a gang of tomb robbers.

However, boastfulness in inscriptions of royal men is frequently encountered. So Hatshepsut was not out of character even though she was undoubtedly educated, as we know her daughter was—and princesses were probably exposed to the same instructional materials that were used in the schools. Nonetheless, Hatshepsut exhibits the arrogance of power, speaks in superlatives, and tries for the grand effect. Her speech preserved at Speos Artemidos is especially vivid in its metaphors and does elicit an emotional response. Indeed it is one of the most stirring compositions to survive from ancient Egypt.

Note

I wish to thank Leonard H. Lesko, Wilbour Professor of Egyptology, Brown University, for permission to quote from his unpublished translations of the *Speos Artemidos Inscription* and portions of Papyrus Harris 500, and the Scholars Press for permission to quote from Edward Wente, *Letters from Ancient Egypt* (1990).

References

Bryan, Betsy M. 1984. "Evidence for Female Literacy from Theban Tombs of the New Kingdom." *Bulletin of the Egyptological Seminar* 6: 17–32.

Cerny, Jarsolav. 1945. "The Will of Naunakhte and the Related Documents." *Journal of Egyptian Archaeology* 31: 29–53, plates VIIIa–XII.

Fox, Michael V. 1983. "Ancient Egyptian Rhetoric." *Rhetorica* 1: 9–23.

———. 1985. *The Song of Songs and the Ancient Egyptian Love Songs.* Madison: University of Wisconsin Press.

Gardiner, Alan Henderson. 1946. "Davies's Copy of the Great Speos Artemidos Inscription." *Journal of Egyptian Archaeology* 32: 43–56.

Goetze, Albrecht. 1955. "Suppiluliumas and the Egyptian Queen." In *Ancient Near Eastern Texts Relating to the Old Testament*, 2nd ed., edited by James B. Pritchard. Princeton: Princeton University Press.

Janssen, Jac. J. 1992. "Literacy and Letters at Deir El-Medina." In *Village Voices: Proceedings of the Symposium "Texts from Deir el-Medina and their Interpretations," Leiden May 31–June 1, 1991*, edited by Robert J. Demarée and Arno Egberts, 81–94. Leiden: Centre of Non-Western Studies.

Lesko, Barbara S. 1986. "True Art in Ancient Egypt." In *Egyptological Studies in Honor of Richard A. Parker*, edited by Leonard H. Lesko, 85–97. Hanover, N.H.: University Press of New England.

Lichtheim, Miriem 1973. *Ancient Egyptian Literature.* Vol. 1: *The Old and Middle Kingdoms.* Berkeley: University of California Press.

———. 1976. *Ancient Egyptian Literature.* Vol. 2: *The New Kingdom.* Berkeley: University of California Press.

———. 1980. *Ancient Egyptian Literature.* Vol. 3: *The Late Period.* Berkeley: University of California Press.

Peet, Thomas E. 1930. *The Great Tomb Robberies of the Twentieth Egyptian Dynasty.* Vol. 1: *Text.* Oxford: Clarendon Press.

Sweeny, Deborah. 1993. "Women's Correspondence from Deir el-Medineh." *Atti Congresso Internazionale di Egittologia* 2: 523–29.

Wente, Edward. 1990. *Letters from Ancient Egypt.* Society of Biblical Literature: Writings from the Ancient World. Vol. 1. Atlanta: Scholars Press.

Wilson, John A. 1951. *The Culture of Ancient Egypt.* Chicago: University of Chicago Press.

Roman Women in the History of Rhetoric and Oratory

Robert W. Cape Jr.

Histories of rhetoric are proliferating at an unprecedented rate, and the account of women's rhetoric over time is an important addition to the variety of new histories now being written. Although such studies differ widely in scope and purpose, the one historical time period almost assured of treatment is classical Greece. Thus, it is no surprise that it has become a favorite and, to some extent, privileged hunting ground for identifying women as early rhetors. Among those discovered are Arete, Aspasia, Diotima, and Sosipatra (Donawerth 1992; Glenn 1994; Sutton 1992; Swearingen 1995). Yet Greece presents challenges to this project that remain largely unaddressed, though Connors (1992) does a fair job dealing with them. The nature of the source materials, which are predominantly literary and written by men for other men, presents a major impediment. The fact that we must supplement contemporary evidence with accounts written almost half a millennium later, when women played a different role within a demonstrably different type of society, complicates our use of the sources even further (Henry 1995). Moreover, our modern preoccupation with things Greek obscures the fact that Roman rhetoric has probably contributed more to the rhetorical tradition in the West (Conley 1990).

Another major challenge to recovering women as rhetors in ancient Greece is the public and practical nature of *rhetorikê* as the Greeks defined it.[1] Respectable Greek women did not attend school and were excluded from public life—public speaking and deliberation (Cantarella 1987, 38–51; Vidal-Naquet 1986, 205–23).[2] That is not to say that no Greek women received an education or wrote. The list of famous women poets, beginning with Sappho, is deservedly well-known today (Snyder 1989). It is the public nature of rhetoric that makes the project of recovering Greek women as rhetors more difficult than recovering Greek women's voices in other, private areas such as poetry (Skinner 1993). That we have texts from Greek women poets confirms, in Skinner's words, that "patriarchal discourses evidently do not always succeed in drowning women out" (129), but their voices are still limited to the private sphere. We may concede that noncitizen women in Athens might have known the principles of *rhetorikê*, but they could not have given public speeches in the assemblies, in the courts, or in public. Public speaking was off-limits to respectable women. Only prostitutes or *hetairai* (*hetaerae*) had the opportunity to appear in public, but their status was not respectable and they could not address public meetings. A Greek man would have found it amusing at best that a woman should have something to teach him about persuading the assembly or jury.[3]

The situation in Rome was much different for women, but it has been treated less extensively. This is due partly to a tradition of cultural snobbery and preoccupation with things Greek and partly to an assumption that Roman culture is virtually the same as Greek, only later and derivative. But whereas Greece had social and legal codes that make it extremely difficult to prove that women spoke in public, much less recover aspects of their public speech, in Rome during the late republic and early empire respectable women were ubiquitous in public and were legally allowed to deliver orations in court (Fantham et al. 1994, 260 ff.). The differences were noticeable in antiquity.[4] The rise of politically important and astute women has been identified as a major social phenomenon during the first centuries B.C.E. and C.E. (Bauman 1992). Social convention still restricted women to traditional domestic roles, but the social opportunities open to Roman women were hardly imaginable during the classical period of Athens. Sarah B. Pomeroy captures the tension: "The result was that wealthy aristocratic women who played high politics and presided over literary salons were nevertheless expected to be able to spin and weave as though they were living in the days when Rome was young" (1975, 149). Public actions of Roman women were regulated by the traditional image of the woman who tended the house and spun the wool, but within that role there was the opportunity for a public persona and public voice.

The Romans also differed from the Greeks in their conception of rhetoric. A broader interest in *eloquentia*, based on the speaker's ethos, status, and contextual decorum, allowed the formation of a conceptual space in which women's speech was "naturally" appropriate. This space was not theorized as particularly feminine, but it did receive attention as a part of rhetoric in the broader context of Roman eloquentia. Thus, Rome offers us women who used traditional rhetoric in the male (public) sphere and allows us to consider elements of women's speech in the private sphere.

Roman Eloquence and the Realm of Women's Speech

In Rome the practical interest in rhetoric expressed itself as a "skill in speaking," *ars dicendi* or *ars loquendi,* or eloquentia that could naturally refer to agonistic contests, but also included the realm of conversation, *sermo,* as well as *oratio* (Kennedy 1972, 7).[5] Eloquentia stresses the aesthetic qualities of speech, particularly appropriateness of subject matter to the character of the speaker and the context, decorum, and use of a proper style for the circumstances at hand. It is hard to frame an adequate theory of eloquentia; it cannot be reduced to a series of precepts that were contained in the Hellenistic handbooks of rhetoric. In fact, the Romans took pains to define eloquentia against the Hellenistic tradition. The Elder Cato's definition of the best orator as *vir bonus, dicendi peritus* ("the good man, skilled in speaking") and his advice *rem tene, verba sequentur* ("seize the subject; the words will follow") show the Romans' preference for a socially (and culturally) appropriate manner of speaking that is not overly formalistic. Cato does not say *dicendi doctus* ("educated in speaking") but rather *peritus* ("skilled through practical application and the observance of when to use the proper elements at the proper time"). The same tension between teaching the Greek art of rhetoric by means of dry exercises and handbooks and teaching public speaking by observation, practice, and a kind of apprenticeship—*tirocinium fori*—to a man who was active in public affairs can be observed in Cicero's major rhetorical works, *De Oratore, Brutus,* and *Orator* (Kennedy 1972, 205–29, 253–58).

It was not uncommon for Roman girls to be exposed to rhetorical instruction and practice. Girls regularly received an education with boys, at least at the early stages (Bonner 1977, 27–28, 135–36), and some may even have received specific training in rhetoric.[6] A Roman woman would naturally come into contact with public oratory in the forum, and literate women would undoubtedly read history, epics, novels—literature containing speeches composed along classical rhetorical lines. Moreover, in Rome a respectable woman was entitled by law to deliver a speech in court and thus gain practical experience in judicial oratory (Gardner 1986, 262–63). We know the names of two, possibly three women who addressed juries in court cases.[7] We also know of a woman, Hortensia, who publicly addressed the triumvirs Octavian, Antony, and Lepidus on behalf of Roman women to repeal a tax imposed on them. Another woman, so-called "Turia," was praised after her death for publicly resisting the triumvir Lepidus and reciting the words of Octavian's edict "in a loud voice" (Lefkowitz and Fant 1992, 135–39). Thus, it was not unusual for women to be seen and heard in public. In a telling incident recorded by Aulus Gellius (*Attic Nights,* 10.6), the daughter of Appius Claudius Caecus was fined twenty thousand pounds of bronze for using slanderous speech (*verba tam improba et tam incivilia*) that was considered contrary to Roman *dignitas.* It is significant that there is no undue emphasis on her being a woman: the law against impudent language was meant to apply to public speech by men and women alike. The emphasis is rather on the uncivil, indecorous nature of the speech.

The Romans did not produce a handbook on women's rhetoric, since formal instruction in rhetoric was usually aimed at men. Its purpose, best characterized by Cicero's works and Quintilian's *Institutio Oratoria,* was to educate the whole man and his use of language generally. Women's speech was treated in this context insofar as it exercised a formative influence on a son's speech. In *Brutus* Cicero mentions some women who were noteworthy for their use of language:[8]

> "It makes a great difference whom one hears at home on a daily basis, with whom one speaks from infancy, and how the fathers, tutors, and even the mothers speak [*matres etiam loquantur*]. We have read the letters of Cornelia, mother of the Gracchi; it is clear that her sons were not educated so much in their mother's lap as they were by her speech [*sermone*]. We have often heard the conversation [*sermo*] of Laelia, daughter of Gaius Laelius; thus did we see that she was imbued with her father's elegance [*elegantia*], as were both of her daughters, the Muciae—whose conversation [*sermo*] was well known to me—and her grand-daughters, the Liciniae, both of whom I have heard and the one who is Scipio's wife you too, Brutus, I think, have sometimes heard speaking [*loquentem*]."
>
> "Yes, indeed, and with pleasure," said Brutus, "and all the more gladly for the fact that she was the daughter of Licinius Crassus."
>
> "What do you think about Crassus," I said, "who is that Licinia's son, the one adopted in Crassus' will?"
>
> "He is said to be a man of exceptional talent," he said, "and indeed [his brother] Scipio, my colleague, seems to me to speak [*dicere*] and to converse [*loqui*] very well." (*Brutus* 210–12)[9]

There are several things to note about this passage. The realm of a woman's speech is *sermo*, private conversation. Since a mother's conversation affects her son's speech, it is important that she speaks well. A woman's elegant speech is assumed to stem from her father's *eloquentia* or to have been passed on from mother to daughter, though still originating in a man's speech and praiseworthy if it ultimately helps form a young man's conversational style. Laelia spoke well due to her father's influence, and she passed her gift down through her daughters and granddaughters to her great-grandson. It may be that Metellus Scipio's ability to speak well in private (*loqui*) as well as in public (*dicere*) was due to his mother's influence, but the ultimate derivation from his great-great-grandfather should not be obscured. A man required the ability to speak both publicly and privately; a woman needed to speak well only in private, but her private mode of speaking (*sermo/loquor*) was the same as the man's. Thus, she could transmit at least part of her male ancestors' speech legacy.

The way Cicero introduces the importance of a woman's speech in contributing to a young man's *eloquentia* suggests that it was a novel idea: *matres etiam* ("even mothers" or "mothers too"). The idea that a mother's speech influences her son's was not new, but Cicero may have been innovative by dwelling upon women's speech. There is no indication of a similar treatment of the subjects in the rhetorical handbooks before his time. He recognizes that women's speech has an "appropriate" sphere, while admitting that a woman's own *elegantia* is derived from and productive of men's.[10] It is not a separate category of speaking but a subcategory of men's *eloquentia*. It is appropriate because it pertains to the private sphere, still the focus of women's activities in Rome.

Writing a century later, Quintilian agrees with Cicero, providing "a typically Roman view of the role of women as writers and public speakers—not so much in their own right as in relation to their capacity to educate the next generation" (Snyder 1989, 123; cf. Hallett 1984 and 1989). He also writes on the training of the young man who will study rhetoric:

> Even in the parents I would hope that there be as much learning as possible. And I don't speak only about the fathers. For we have heard that Cornelia, mother of the Gracchi, contributed much to their eloquence [*eloquentiae*], and her highly learned speech [*doctissimus sermo*] has also been handed down for posterity in her letters. And Laelia,

daughter of Gaius Laelius, is said to have reflected her father's elegant style [*elegantiam*] in her speech [*in loquendo*]. And the oration [*oratio*] of Hortensia, daughter of Quintus Hortensius, which she delivered before the Triumvirs, is read [today] not only as an honor to her sex. (*Institutio Oratoria* 1.1.6)[11]

The comments about Cornelia and Laelia are similar to Cicero's. Cornelia's sermo is called *doctissimus* ("very learned"), which suggests training, but it is still sermo. Hortensia, however, is credited with a public speech, an *oratio*. Moreover, the speech is still read in Quintilian's day, and not as an aberration but, it seems, with genuine respect for it as an oration. Since we now have mention of women's speech in both the private and public spheres we will look at each separately and then see what can be said about them together as a type of woman's *eloquentia*.

Women's Speech in the Private Sphere: *Sermo*

In his handbook *De Officiis* (On Duties) Cicero discusses the importance of decorum in a young man's manner of dressing, speaking, and living (1.132–37). When he treats speaking and the voice, Cicero divides the *vis orationis* ("power of oratory") into two parts: *contentio* ("argument") and sermo ("conversation"). He says:

> *Contentio* should be ascribed to the debates in the courts, public assemblies, the senate, and *sermo* should be involved in social circles, in philosophical debates, and in meetings of friends. It should also follow after banquets. The rhetoricians have rules for *contentio,* none for *sermo,* though I do not know why they can't apply in this case too. Teachers are found when there are students desirous for learning, but there are none who desire to learn this [*sermo*], while all the rhetorician's crowds are packed. Yet the same rules of using words and phrases also apply to *sermo.* (*De Officiis* 1.132)[12]

The rules that he lays down are as follows. The voice should be clear (*clara*) and pleasant (*suavis*) (1.133). Conversation (sermo) should be light (*lenis*), witty (*lepos*), and not obstinate (*minimeque pertinax*). A person should not exclude others from the conversation and should allow each a fair turn in the discussion. At the outset he should observe the topics of conversation; if they are important he should treat them seriously; if humorous, wittily (1.134). Conversations (*sermones*) usually concern household matters (*de domesticis negotiis*) or the state (*de re publica*) or professions (*de artium studiis*) or learning (*doctrina*). One must pay attention to the conversation to keep it on track, to make sure it is pleasant and that it has a reason for its beginning and a proper way in which to close (1.135). Finally, sermo ought to be free from extreme emotion and should not give rise to anger, covetousness, laziness, or idleness. "We ought to take the greatest care to show respect and have a special regard for those with whom we conduct our conversation" (1.136). In conversation one should never be harsh or angry, though it may be necessary to appear angry sometimes.

With this set of rules one could begin to write a rhetoric for sermo. Since this is the proper realm of women's speech[13] we have the opportunity to theorize a Roman rhetoric about women's speech. The overarching concern of sermo is to contribute to decorum and decorous behavior. That is what distinguishes it from the type of agonistic speech that had been the provenance of the rhetor. Sermo is primarily private conversation with a group of friends about domestic affairs (*de domesticis negotiis*), to be sure, but is also about politics (*de re publica*) and skills and learning. Roman women of the upper classes often knew a great deal about such subjects and could converse about them with one another or among men. The stylistic features of sermo are noted, but we cannot treat them here.[14] Finally, as is often the case in Roman rhetoric, the type of speech must suit the character of the speaker. In conversation one must be at all times polite and courteous. This was not necessary in public discourse—witness Cicero's *First Catilinarian* and *Second Philippic* orations. A sense of humor is appreciated. Like Socrates in Plato's dialogues (perhaps the supreme example of the conversational style), one should keep the conversation on track and be careful to observe its natural beginning and ending points so as not to ramble on.

Cicero's guidelines for a rhetoric of sermo should be connected with the parallel contemporary development of a theory of letter writing. Letters (*epistolae*) also belonged to the genre of sermo. Epistolary theories seem to have arisen in the first century B.C.E., and by the end of the century the practice of letter writing was connected with rhetorical education (Kennedy 1983, 70–73; Malherbe 1988). Collections of sample letters were composed and offered as models for students to imitate. The main concerns were that the style of the letter conform to the function the letter served and to the character of the sender.

We have a good example of a Roman woman's sermo in the fragments of one or two letters purportedly written by Cornelia, mother of Tiberius and Gaius Gracchus. Both fragments, found among the works of Cornelius Nepos,[15] exhibit all the features of good sermo as outlined above:

> You will say that it is gratifying to take revenge upon one's enemies. This seems neither more important nor more pleasing to anyone more than to me, but only if it can be pursued with the safety of the Roman state intact. But since that cannot happen, for a long time and in many places our enemies will not perish, and will even continue to exist, as they are now, rather than the republic should be overthrown [*profligetur*] and perish.

And:

> With words arranged in a formal oath [*verbis conceptis*] I would dare to swear that, except for those who murdered Tiberius Gracchus, no enemy has caused me as much trouble and as much work as you have in these matters. It is appropriate that you, out of all those children I had before,[16] bear their duties and take care that I have as little disturbance as possible in my old age, that at the least you should want the kinds of things you do to please me exceedingly, and that you would consider it wicked [*nefas*] to do anything contrary to my wishes on important matters, especially since only a brief space of life remains to me. Cannot even that space of time, so brief, help so you won't oppose me and overthrow [*profliges*] the state? What end will there be at last? When will our family ever [*ecquando*] cease to rage [*insanire*]? When can there ever [*ecquando*] be a limit to this affair? When will we ever [*ecquando*] cease having and offering to leave off from troubles? When will it ever [*ecquando*] cause us shame that the state is thrown into confusion and turmoil?
>
> But if it is impossible for that to happen completely, then seek the tribuneship when I am dead. As far as I am concerned, do what you want when I will not feel it. When I am dead you will honor and invoke me as your divine parent. At that time will it not shame you to seek favors of those gods whom you treated as left behind and deserted when they were alive and present? May Jupiter not allow you to continue those plans. I fear that you will undertake so much work in your life, through your own fault, that you will never be able to please yourself. (*Frag.* 59)

There is nothing in these fragments that a Roman would find unsuitable to a mother addressing her son.[17] She makes a characteristic appeal to filial pietas and urges consideration for the welfare of the state. Both are appropriate in sermo. We may note the more formal stylistic features, the four rhetorical questions, asyndeton, and anaphora of *ecquando*. They add a certain stylistic elegance which the reader would have appreciated. The questions are not particularly vehement, which is in line with the conventions of sermo. Cornelia's use of formulaic religious vocabulary at the beginning of the second fragment is consistent with, and makes an appropriate opening to, the religious appeal made shortly thereafter. Finally, her argument is a strong one according to Roman conventions, well crafted and phrased; yet it does not denigrate the addressee or seek to silence him. Following the conventions of sermo illustrated by Cicero's remarks above, Cornelia offers a compromise— "seek the tribuneship when I am dead." To a degree, then, she respects her son's wishes and expects him to respect hers.

It would be appropriate to compare Cornelia's letter to Cicero's corpus of letters to his friends and family. Therein we find illustrated in abundant detail the conventions of sermo. In terms of style, content, and argument, Cornelia's letter could have been written by Cicero, mutatis mutandis, and seems rather more typical than deserving of special notice. That, I submit, is the reason Cicero and Quintilian praise Cornelia's letters: they could have been written by men. She adopts a style that is appropriate to her as a woman but that is also completely appropriate for a man in a similar situation. She is not too emotional, she respects the person to whom she speaks, she speaks appropriately about matters of family and state, and she does not encourage laziness but rather exhorts her son to lead an active, enjoyable life. The style of her letter is one her own son could (or, as some would have thought, should) adopt in reply.[18] The greatest praise for her letter, then, is that it follows the conventions of sermo, and here the conventions are the same for men and women.

Women's Speech in the Public Sphere: *Oratio*

Since for men the boundaries between conversation and public speech were fluid, or rather the rules of both contributed to the eloquentia the Romans sought, and since women were allowed to enter and speak in public arenas (though it was not always considered proper), it would be possible for us to analyze women's public oratory according to the rules of rhetoric as applied to men. We know of three, perhaps four, women who spoke in court or before a tribunal. Hortensia, mentioned above, is the best known. We do not have the speech texts delivered by these women, but we do have brief comments about their speaking and men's judgment of them as relayed by Valerius Maximus:

> We must not be silent about even those women whom their natural condition [as women: *condicio naturae*] and the modesty of their attire [*stolae*] were not strong enough to force to be silent in the forum and in the courts.
>
> Maesia Sentinas, as a defendant, pled her own case before a great crowd of people, with Lucius Titius the Praetor presiding over the court, executing all the proper means and parts of her defense speech [*modos ac numeros defensionis*],[19] and was acquitted in the first trial by an almost universal consensus. Because she bore a male spirit under the guise of a woman, they called her *Androgyne*.[20]
>
> Gaia Afrania, wife of the senator Licinius Bucco, eager to induce lawsuits, always pled her case on her own behalf before the Praetor, not because she lacked advocates, but because she abounded in shamelessness. And so, through unwonted barking in the forum and through continual harassment of the tribunals she became the most noted example of feminine maliciousness [*muliebris calumniae*], to the point that the name of Gaia Afrania is used as a reproach for the charge of perverse morals in women. She prolonged her life until Gaius Caesar was consul a second time with Publius Servilius [48 B.C.E.], for the date when such a monster died ought to be recorded more than that when she was born.
>
> Hortensia, daughter of Quintus Hortensius, pled the women's case before the triumvirs with firm resolution and with success, when the order of matrons was burdened by a harsh tax imposed by the triumvirs and none of the men dared provide legal support for them. For the eloquence [*facundia*] of her father having come back to life succeeded in having the greater part of the money demanded waived in their case. Then Quintus Hortensius lived again in the female line and breathed through the words of his daughter. If her male descendants had wished to pursue her power [of speech], the whole inheritance of Hortensian eloquence [*eloquentiae*] would not have come to an abrupt end with the single action of a woman. (*Facta et Dicta Memorabilia* 8.3.3)[21]

Valerius indicates that two things should have prevented the women from speaking in court or in the forum: a woman's nature and her dress, the *stola* of a respectable matron. He assumes that women should not speak in such venues. According to Justinian's *Digest,* a woman might legally defend herself in court but was not expected to do so if there were male relatives to plead for her (48.2.1). She could plead on behalf of family members only if they were incapacitated (3.3.41). She was normally prohibited from initiating a prosecution (48.2.8) unless the wrong was done to her when she was attempting to obtain legal satisfaction for the death of close relatives (48.2.11.pr.). Thus, despite the legal allowances for women to speak in court, it seems that Roman men did not consider it proper for women to plead their cases in court unless special circumstances required it.

Maesia is praised for conducting her case like a man. Whether she has a family member who could plead on her behalf is not mentioned, but presumably she does not. Her success is a qualified one, for she has also earned an unflattering nickname. Afrania fares far worse, however, since she prefers to plead cases even when she has male kin who could plead them for her. Furthermore, she initiates proceedings, something a woman was not supposed to do. Thus, Afrania does not observe the proper social conventions and is labeled a *monstrum.*[22] It should be noted, however, that she is not prevented from speaking in public.

Hortensia is the only woman praised by Valerius, but again it is a qualified praise. In fact, as soon as Valerius has good things to say about Hortensia's speech, he talks not about her eloquence but about her father's *facundia.* Her success is limited to her bringing her father's eloquentia back to life. She is praised, as Cornelia was, insofar as she preserves a male mode of speech and contributes nothing herself.

We do not possess Hortensia's speech in Latin, but we do have what purports to be a version of it in Greek, rendered by Appian:

> The triumvirs addressed the people on this subject and published an edict requiring 1400 of the richest women to make a valuation of their property, and to furnish for the service of the war such portion as the triumvirs should require from each. It was provided further that if any should conceal their property or make a false valuation they should be fined, and that rewards should be given to informers, whether free persons or slaves. The women resolved to beseech the women-folk of the triumvirs. With the sister of Octavian and the

mother of Antony they did not fail, but they were repulsed from the doors of Fulvia, the wife of Antony, whose rudeness they could scarce endure. They then forced their way to the tribunal of the triumvirs in the forum, the people and the guards dividing to let them pass. There, through the mouth of Hortensia, whom they had selected to speak, they spoke as follows:

"As befitted women of our rank addressing a petition to you, we had recourse to the ladies of your households; but having been treated as did not befit us, at the hands of Fulvia, we have been driven by her to the forum. You have already deprived us of our fathers, our sons, our husbands, and our brothers, whom you accused of having wronged you; if you take away our property also, you reduce us to a condition unbecoming our birth, our manners, our sex. If we have done you wrong, as you say our husbands have, proscribe us as you do them. But if we women have not voted any of you public enemies, have not torn down your houses, destroyed your army, or led another one against you; if we have not hindered you in obtaining offices and honours,—why do we share the penalty when we did not share the guilt?

"Why should we pay taxes when we have no part in the honours, the commands, the state-craft, for which you contend against each other with such harmful results? 'Because this is a time of war,' do you say? When have there not been wars, and when have taxes ever been imposed on women, who are exempted by their sex among all mankind? Our mothers did once rise superior to their sex and made contributions when you were in danger of losing the whole empire and the city itself through the conflict with the Carthaginians. But then they contributed voluntarily, not from their landed property, their fields, their dowries, or their houses, without which life is not possible to free women, but only from their own jewelry, and even these not according to fixed valuation, not under fear of informers or accusers, not by force and violence, but what they themselves were willing to give. What alarm is there now for the empire or the country? Let war with the Gauls or the Parthians come, and we shall not be inferior to our mothers in zeal for the common safety; but for civil wars may we never contribute, nor ever assist you against each other! We did not contribute to Caesar or to Pompey. Neither Marius nor Cinna imposed taxes upon us. Nor did Sulla, who held despotic power in the state, do so, whereas you say that you are re-establishing the commonwealth."

While Hortensia thus spoke the triumvirs were angry that women should dare to hold a public meeting when the men were silent; that they should demand from magistrates the reasons for their acts, and themselves not so much as furnish money while the men were serving in the army. They ordered the lictors to drive them away from the tribunal, which they proceeded to do until cries were raised by the multitude outside, when the lictors desisted and the triumvirs said they would postpone until the next day the consideration of the matter. On the following day they reduced the number of women, who were to present a valuation of their property, from 1400 to 400. . . . (*Civil Wars* 4.32–34)

Here Appian may be presenting a version of the actual speech that was somehow transmitted in written form and translated into Greek. Or he may be presenting a completely fabricated speech, which the conventions of ancient historiography allowed and Appian does elsewhere with speeches of men. In either case we see an example of good oratory by a woman. The "rules" of sermo can be applied, and so can the rules of contentio, since this is a speech delivered in the public sphere and designed to persuade under the same formal requirements imposed on a man.

Hortensia opens with a justification of her action: she and the other women tried to act properly by appealing through the wives of the triumvirs but were repulsed by Fulvia and treated with disrespect. Since no men would plead their case for them, Hortensia was forced to present it. Arguably, their case was analogous to a court case, and so Hortensia's actions could be viewed as justified. A woman was allowed to make a public defense of her actions when the customary forms of redress were unavailable. She then offers a qualitative argument, that the triumvirs have already taken the most important things and they want even more. She points to the social inequity that women are punished despite their having no formal power in the state. A well-chosen historical exemplum from the Second Punic War illustrates her point that women have helped the state in times of crisis, but in times of crisis against legitimate enemies. Her argument calls into question the status of the crisis as the basis for this unprecedented action. Her argument is reasoned and compelling; it is appropriate to her social position and gender; it makes appropriate use of culturally specific arguments involving tradition (*mos maiorum*), innovation, gender roles, and devotion to the res publica; its tone is appropriate as an address to the triumvirs. In fact, it fulfills all the requirements of decorum. Its success can also be measured in the audience's support of the women when the triumvirs try to use physical violence to expel them from the forum. It stands as a reasoned speech against brute force.

Conclusions

What I have been suggesting in these brief remarks is that it may be possible to recover ancient women's voices and to understand how contemporary men (and women?) judged them as rhetoric. In this project I think Rome offers more possibilities than Greece. Histories of rhetoric usually omit serious consideration of Rome as part of our past, but they have also omitted women: perhaps there is a connection. To explore this further I can see several possible avenues for further research. An important one would be examining the differences between Roman and Greek rhetorics in a positive, productive way. Not all differences arise from a Roman "misunderstanding" of some Greek precept, nor are they all signs of ingenuity and genius. The traditional grouping of the two as though they belonged to the same society erases important differences of nationality, personality, language, and chronology. Granted, this is a feature of older criticism, but the traces still linger.

Part of my argument in this essay is that Roman rhetoric opens up a conceptual space in which women's rhetoric has a part. Further research on sermo as feminine speech would help us understand the limitations and opportunities of this expression. The connection between women's conversation and the epistolary genre suggests a link to the origin and development of women's letter-writing practice and instruction in the West. It also provides the natural setting for Ovid's creation of a new literary genre—women's amorous epistles—in the *Heroides*. Ovid claims to have invented it (*Ars Amatoria* 3.345–6), and no direct models can be found in previous Greek literature. Its later development has provided a major vehicle for women's voices (Kauffman 1986).

The second part of my argument is that Roman culture and Roman rhetoric allow for women's public speech that can be set side by side with men's. This is also, I believe, the first time the possibility arises in the West. Further research in this area might show how Roman women exploited their opportunities for public expression despite the fact that their traditional role encouraged them to confine their voices to the private sphere. This would tie the experiences of Roman women to those of their female descendants up to the present day.

A rhetoric based on eloquentia and decorum can have few hard and fast rules. It must be able to adapt to ever changing conditions. Such a rhetoric compels a thoroughly contextualized understanding of the historical setting. If Roman women shared an interest in this kind of rhetoric with Roman men, analysis of their speech must be equally rigorous. To do this well we must analyze all the material in the original languages and pay close attention to context—social, political, intellectual, cultural, and so forth. We may be able to see the possibility of a women's rhetoric in Rome, but we shall have to be extremely careful and diligent to uncover it.

Notes

Different parts of this essay were presented at meetings of the Classical Association of the Middle West and South and the Speech Communication Association, Fall 1994. I am grateful to the audiences for useful observations and greatly indebted to John Kirby and Molly Meijer Wertheimer for detailed, critical, yet sympathetic comments which have improved the written version.

1. Plato broadens the scope of *rhetorikê* to private as well as public speech at *Phaedrus* 261A7ff. His concern is not, however, to encompass all conversation, but to include philosophic discourse (261D6ff.) in order to claim that true rhetoric must follow the method of philosophy, i.e., dialectic (266C6 ff.).

2. Sarah B. Pomeroy captures well the historical facts: "Direct participation in the affairs of government—including holding public office, voting, and serving as jurors and as soldiers—was possible only for male citizens. The advanced education of a boy concentrated on the art of rhetoric, with the aim of delivering persuasive speeches at public meetings and winning a fine reputation among men. . . . The qualities admired in girls were the opposite from those admired in boys: silence, submissiveness, and abstinence from men's pleasures" (1975, 74) The literary uses of women in Plato's dialogues do not alter those facts.

3. A hetaera knew about love and was properly a teacher in that sphere, as Diotima is in Plato's *Symposium* (Swearingen 1995). Similarly, Aspasia is represented as giving good advice typical of a women who acts as matchmaker or marital go-between (*promnêstria*) in a private, not a public, context (Xenophon, *Memorabilia*, 2.6.36; cf. *Oeconomicus*, 3.15). Plato is being ironic when he discusses Aspasia's rhetorical talents in *Menexenus*, for he values neither the political position of Pericles nor the purported contribution funeral oratory makes to the state (Loraux 1986, 321–27; Coventry 1989; Tyrrell and Brown 1991, 191–94).

The literary accounts of women taking part in civic affairs are from comedy, such as Aristophanes' *Lysistrata* and *Thesmophoriazusai.*

4. The historian-biographer Cornelius Nepos notes that "the same things are not honorable and shameful to all peoples," and "many of our customs are proper according to our own way of thinking, which are considered shameful among them [Greeks]. For what Roman is ashamed to take his wife to a dinner party? Whose lady of the house [*mater familias*] does not hold the first place in the household and is not among the crowd? This is very different in Greece, for she is not admitted to dinner parties, unless she is a close relative, nor does she sit [to eat], except in an interior part of the house which is called 'the women's quarters,' where no man goes unless he is a close relative" (1991, 6–7).

5. To Kennedy's discussion add Cicero *De Officiis* 1.115 and *Partitiones Oratoriae* 79.

6. See Bonner (1977) and also the scholiast on Juvenal's *Satire* 6.434 in Courtney (1980, 289). It is significant, however, that there are no women grammarians or rhetoricians (i.e., teachers of grammar or rhetoric) in the historical sources (see the prosopography in Kaster 1988, 237–440).

7. They are Maesia and Afrania, but the law codes mention a Carfania who may or may not be Afrania; see Gardner (1986, 263).

8. All translations are my own, unless otherwise indicated. Most Greek and Latin works are found by the English or Latin titles under their authors in the volumes of the Loeb Classical Library (Heinemann and Harvard University Press). The translations should always be checked against the Greek or Latin text on the facing page. Many of the translations are more elegant than my own, but I am trying to stay close to each author's own language. Since it is important to use texts with a full *apparatus criticus* (which the Loeb volumes do not possess), I generally cite in the notes the preferable Greek or Latin text to use. Many of the sources here are also given in translation, with an abundance of other pertinent material, in Lefkowitz and Fant (1992).

9. Douglas (1966, 154) points out the differences between *loqui* and *dicere:* "to speak good Latin and to be an orator," with an apt reference to Cicero's *de Oratore* 3.38: "neque enim conamur docere eum dicere [to be an orator] qui loqui nesciat [who cannot talk good Latin]."

10. I think there is evidence here for a tension between the desire of Roman men to educate their daughters and wives and the practical social problems such a male-oriented, rhetorical education entailed. See Jardine (1987) for a discussion of similar (but not exactly equivalent) problems in the Renaissance. The function of the woman as a "speech vessel" which nourishes but does not actually generate good speech is, perhaps, similar to the role assigned to women by medical writers in the process of conception and gestation (Lefkowitz and Fant 1992, 82–85).

11. Latin text edited in two volumes by Michael Winterbottom (1970).

12. Latin text edited by Michael Winterbottom (1994).

13. The epitaph of Claudia, from the second century B.C.E., which is often taken to represent the traditional virtues of a Roman matron, praises her *sermone lepido*, "charming speech" (Lefkowitz and Fant 1992, 16). Sempronia, described by Sallust at *Bellum Catilinum* 25, knew how to use speech that was proper to a respectable woman and speech that was improper (*sermone uti vel modesto vel molli vel procaci*).

14. Part of the difficulty with regarding style is that we are not certain we have the actual words a woman spoke or wrote. In the case of Hortensia, a summary of her Latin speech is preserved only in Greek, and by a much later Greek historian, Appian (*Bella Civilia* 4.32–34). We are in a better position with Cornelia's letter, since the language is consistent with late-second-century B.C.E. usage and is "appropriate" to a woman of her position, but it is not necessarily a direct quote from Cornelia (Horsfall 1987; Fantham et al. 1994, 264–65).

15. Latin text edited by P. K. Marshall (1991).

16. Cornelia gave birth to twelve children, three of whom survived to adulthood: Tiberius (killed 133 B.C.E.), Sempronia (still alive at the time of this letter, circa 124), and Gaius (killed 122), who was about to be murdered. As the only remaining son, Gaius had certain obligations for preserving the family household religion and seeing to the cult of the ancestors, to which Cornelia would belong after her death. The religious obligations she wishes to foist upon Gaius account for her careful phrasing of her argument in religious terms.

17. The genuineness of Cornelia's letter is in dispute (see Horsfall 1987; Fantham et al. 1994, 264–65). For the purpose of this paper it does not matter whether the fragments represent the exact words Cornelia wrote, her words at some remove, or, as I believe, a rhetorical exercise in how to write a letter like a woman would. It is more important that the language follows the conventions of the *sermo* genre and be appropriate to a woman writer. I agree with Fantham et al., who note that whether Cornelia could have written the letters or not is not the issue: the existence of just these fragments, on one of the most important political decisions in the late Republic, is simply too opportune and politically useful for the dominant conservative party to be accepted at face value. Given the importance of rhetorical compositions in propria persona and the existence of several from the late Republic, it is difficult not to see Cornelia's letters as part of the trend.

18. Closely associated with the style is the politics she exemplifies in this letter. Cicero would have preferred the Gracchi to pursue the political position Cornelia puts forward here.

19. *Modos* could refer to the manner of her speaking but has a strong element of "proper bounds" or "proper limits," with the idea of "proper" referring to a man's forensic speech. Likewise, *numeros* is difficult, for it can apply to prose rhythm (= style), but it also refers to the successive parts of a speech in correct

order. The whole phrase indicates she delivered a defense speech which a man could have delivered.

20. Some of the Latin expressions in this section are similar to those Jardine (1987) finds used by the humanists.

21. Latin text edited by Carl Kempf (1888). There is no Loeb volume for Valerius Maximus, but this passage is translated in Lefkowitz and Fant (1992, 151–52).

22. *Monstrum* cannot be translated easily into English. It is often translated as "portent," "wonder," and "supernatural event," but these English words do not capture the whole meaning. Roughly translated *monstrum* means "something so strange that it is probably a sign from the gods that something bad is going to happen."

23. Translation by Horace White.

References

Appian. 1913. *Civil Wars.* In *Appian's Roman History,* trans. Horace White, 195–99. Cambridge: Harvard University Press.

Aristophanes. 1987. *Lysistrata.* Ed. J. Henderson, with commentary. Oxford: Clarendon Press.

———. 1994. *Thesmophoriazusae.* Ed. A. Sommerstein, with commentary. Warminster: Aris and Phillips.

Bailey, David Roy Shackleton, ed. 1986. *The Second Philippic.* In *Cicero: Philippics,* 31–105. Chapel Hill: University of North Carolina Press.

Bauman, Richard A. 1992. *Women and Politics in Ancient Rome.* New York: Routledge.

Bonner, Stanley F. 1977. *Education in Ancient Rome.* Berkeley: University of California Press.

Cantarella, Eva. 1987. *Pandora's Daughters: The Role and Status of Women in Greek and Roman Antiquity.* Trans. Maureen B. Fant. Baltimore: Johns Hopkins University Press.

Cicero. 1903. *Partitiones Oratoriae.* In *Rhetorica,* Vol. 2, edited by A. S. Wilkins. Oxford: Clarendon Press.

———. 1905. *Orationes,* Vol. 1, edited by Albert C. Clark. Oxford: Clarendon Press.

———.1966. *Brutus.* Ed. Alan E. Douglas, with commentary. Oxford: Clarendon Press.

———. 1969. *De Oratore.* Ed. K. Kumaniecki. Teuber: Leipzig.

———. 1986. *The Second Philippic.* In *Cicero: Philippics,* edited by David Roy Shacketon Bailey, 31–105. Chapel Hill: University of North Carolina Press.

———. 1994. *De Officiis.* Ed. Michael Winterbottom. Oxford: Clarendon Press.

Cole, Susan G. 1981. "Could Greek Women Read and Write?" In *Reflections of Women in Antiquity,* edited by Helene P. Foley, 219–45. New York: Gordon and Breach.

Cole, Thomas. 1991. *The Origins of Rhetoric in Ancient Greece.* Baltimore: Johns Hopkins University Press.

Conley, Thomas M. 1990. *Rhetoric in the European Tradition.* Chicago: University of Chicago Press.

Conners, Robert J. 1992. "The Exclusion of Women from Classical Rhetoric." In *A Rhetoric of Doing: Essays on Written Discourse in Honor of James L. Kinneavy,* edited by Stephen P. Witte et al., 65–78. Carbondale: Southern Illinois University Press.

Courtney, Edward. 1980. *A Commentary on the Satires of Juvenal.* London: Athlone.

Coventry, Lucinda J. 1989. "Philosophy and Rhetoric in the *Menexenus.*" *Journal of Hellenic Studies* 109: 1–15.

Donawerth, Jane. 1992. "Transforming the History of Rhetorical Theory." *Feminist Teacher* 7.1: 35–39.

Fantham, Elaine. 1986. "Women in Antiquity: A Selective (and Subjective) Survey 1979–84." *Echos du monde classique/Classical Views* 30.1: 1–24.

Fantham, Elaine, Helene P. Foley, Natalie B. Kampen, Sarah B. Pomeroy, and H. Alan Shapiro, 1994. *Women in the Classical World.* New York: Oxford University Press.

Gardner, Jane F. 1986. *Women in Roman Law and Society.* Bloomington: Indiana University Press.

Glenn, Cheryl. 1994. "Sex, Lies, and the Manuscript: Refiguring Aspasia in the History of Rhetoric." *College Composition and Communication* 54.2: 180–99.

Hallett, Judith P. 1984. *Fathers and Daughters in Roman Society: Women and the Elite Family.* Princeton: Princeton University Press.

———. 1989. "Women as *Same* and *Other* in Classical Roman Elite." *Helios* 16.1: 59–78.

———. 1993. "Feminist Theory, Historical Periods, Literary Canons, and the Study of Greco-Roman Antiquity." In *Feminist Theory and the Classics,* edited by Nancy S. Rabinowitz and Amy Richlin, 44–72. New York: Routledge.

Henry, Madaline. 1995. *Prisoner of History: Aspasia of Miletus and Her Biographical Tradition.* New York: Oxford University Press.

Horsfall, Nicholas. 1987. "The 'Letter of Cornelia': Yet More Problems." *Athenaeum* 65: 231–34.

Jardine, Lisa. 1987. "Cultural Confusion and Shakespeare's Learned Heroines: 'These are Old Paradoxes.'" *Shakespeare Quarterly* 38.1: 1–18.

Justinian. 1985. *The Digest of Justinian.* 4 vols. Eds. Theodor Mommsen, Paul Kreger, and Alan Watson. Philadelphia: University of Pennsylvania Press.

Kaster, Robert A. 1988. *Guardians of Language: The Grammarian and Society in Late Antiquity.* Berkeley: University of California Press.

Kauffman, Linda S. 1986. *Discourses of Desire: Gender, Genre, and Epistolary Fictions.* Ithaca: Cornell University Press.

Kennedy, George A. 1972. *The Art of Rhetoric in the Roman World, 300 B.C.–A.D. 300.* Princeton: Princeton University Press.

———. 1983. *Greek Rhetoric Under Christian Emperors.* Princeton: Princeton University Press.

Lefkowitz, Mary R., and Maureen B. Fant. 1992. *Women's Life in Greece and Rome.* 2nd ed. Baltimore: Johns Hopkins University Press.

Loraux, Nicole. 1986. *The Invention of Athens: The Funeral Oration in the Classical City.* Trans. Alan Sheridan. Cambridge: Harvard University Press.

Malherbe, Abraham J. 1988. *Ancient Epistolary Theorists.* Atlanta: Scholars Press.

Marshall, Anthony J. 1989. "Ladies at Law: the Role of Women in the Roman Civil Courts." In *Studies in Latin Literature and Roman History,* Vol. 5, edited by Carl Deroux, 35–54. Brussels: Latomus Revue d'Études Latines.

Nepos, Cornelius. 1991a.*Vitae cum Fragmentis.* 3rd ed. Ed. P. K. Marshall. Teubner: Leipzig.

Plato. 1915, 1903. *Phaedrus. Menexenus.* In *Opera,* Vols. 2 and 3, edited by John Burnet. Oxford: Clarendon Press.

Pomeroy, Sarah B. 1975. *Goddesses, Whores, Wives, and Slaves: Women in Classical Antiquity.* New York: Shocken.

Quintilian. 1970. *Institutio Oratoria.* 2 vols. Ed. Michael Winterbottom. Oxford: Clarendon Press.

Richlin, Amy. 1993. "The Ethnographer's Dilemma and the Dream of a Lost Golden Age." In *Feminist Theory and the Classics,* edited by Nancy S. Rabinowitz and Amy Richlin, 272–303. New York: Routledge.

Sallust. 1991. *Bellum Catilinum.* In *Opera,* edited by L. D. Reynolds. Oxford: Clarendon Press.

Skinner, Marilyn B. 1993. "Woman and Language in Archaic Greece, or, Why Is Sappho a Woman?" In *Feminist Theory and the Classics,* edited by Nancy S. Rabinowitz and Amy Richlin, 125–44. New York: Routledge.

Snyder, Jane McIntosh. 1989. *The Woman and the Lyre: Women Writers in Classical Greece and Rome.* Carbondale: Southern Illinois University Press.

Sutton, Jane. 1992. "The Taming of the *Polos/Polis:* Rhetoric as an Achievement without Woman." *Southern Communication Journal* 57.2: 97–119.

Swearingen, C. Jan. 1995. "A Lover's Discourse: Diotima, Logos, and Desire." In *Reclaiming Rhetorica,* edited by Andrea A. Lunsford, 25–51. Pittsburgh: University of Pittsburgh Press.

Tyrrell, William Blake, and Frieda S. Brown. 1991. *Athenian Myths & Institutions: Words in Action.* New York: Oxford University Press.

Valerius Maximus. 1988. *Facta et Dicta Memorabilia.* Ed. Carl Kempf. Stuttgart: Teubner.

Vidal-Naquet, Pierre. 1986. *The Black Hunter: Forms of Thought and Forms of Society in the Greek World.* Trans. Andrew Szegedy-Maszak. Baltimore: Johns Hopkins University Press.

Vitanza, Victor. 1994. *Writing Histories of Rhetoric.* Carbondale: Southern Illinois University Press.

Xenophon. 1920–1922. *Memorabilia. Oeconomicus.* In *Opera*, Vols. 2 and 4, edited by E. C. Marchant. Oxford: Clarendon Press.

Women, Commerce, and Rhetoric in Medieval England

Malcolm Richardson

As women's history moves from being an addendum to "real" history toward assuming its correct place in mainstream studies of the past, historians are gradually uncovering the lost story of women as active participants in the economic history of the West. As in other areas in which women's contributions have been obscured, uncovering their economic importance comes in part from learning to reinterpret traditionally male-centered primary and secondary sources, as well as discovering other female-centered primary material. Another part, however, comes from relearning to see the economic value of the kinds of commerce in which women were once likely to participate (chiefly home-based industries) but which after the Industrial Revolution dropped from the consciousness of most historians. Despite the pioneering work of scholars such as Eileen Power, only in the past fifteen years have academics been seriously studying women's work for the thousand years of the medieval period (Hanawalt 1986; Herlihy 1990; Howell 1986; Shahar 1983).

The historians of rhetoric, even feminist historians, have likewise passed over these women, while rhetoricians in general have done little research in the history of applied rhetorics such as business writing. Our ignorance or indifference has made it unnecessary to rewrite a male-centered history. Fortunately, some good beginnings have been made in the last decade (for example, Locker 1985; Tebeaux 1993; Tebeaux and Killingsworth 1992), including studies of medieval women's epistolary rhetoric of a more literary kind (Cherewatuk and Wiethaus 1993; Classen 1988).

The following essay surveys and classifies the rhetoric of English women writers of business-related correspondence of the late Middle Ages, 1401–circa 1500. Such a study, preliminary though it might be, is especially appropriate since recent gender studies about modern business writing suggest that today men and women write their business documents in the same style (Lay 1994, 66–67). It shows some disturbing if not surprising continuities with problems noted by feminist scholars about women in professional environments today, some five hundred years later.

Medieval Women and Commerce

Because literacy was for so long the exclusive property of the largely antifeminist clergy and because well-known secular writers (Chaucer, Malory) mined clerical writing for their own creations, the late-medieval period seems grotesquely, savagely antiwoman. Leaving aside inequities in private relations, women were rigorously excluded from any of the official decision-making processes of public life. With few exceptions, the many women in the largest and most powerful body in Western society, the Church, played no part in its governance; nor were secular women allowed to play the slightest role in secular governance (Shahar 1983, 11–14).

In trade and commerce, however, at least three circumstances mitigated these harsh conditions. First, most European women became legally independent when they became widows; with the high mortality rates of the time, many of them did, often at comparatively young ages. More fundamentally, the bleak realities of both urban and rural life made it imperative in all but the wealthiest households that all family members work at the family business. The women of the family of necessity labored alongside the men in many aspects of the family trade. In addition, wives and daughters had to be able to manage the business alone in the absence of the husband, who might well be away from home for weeks or months (Howell 1986).

Consequently, whether as wives, widows, or maids (the medieval classification of women's states of being), women permeated European commerce. Among the gentry and nobility, whose wealth depended on what is today called "agribusiness," women leased land, collected rents, received reports from bailiffs, sent surplus crops to market, maintained buildings, and were active managers of large, varied, and sometimes widely spread estates (Archer 1992; Shahar 1983, 150). In towns women's economic life was astonishingly varied. There were, for example, guilds that were exclusively female and some mixed guilds in which women drew up the statutes (Herlihy 1990, 143–44; Shahar 1983, 190–93).

The above information may make the late Middle Ages sound like the "Golden Age of Women's Work," but some sobering qualifications make the picture considerably less rosy. Most women worked under men's supervision and in the less lucrative professions (Graham 1992; Shahar 1983, 195). Most followed their husbands' occupations, and then chiefly in occupations compatible with child care. Finally, at the end of the Middle Ages most women were gradually being forced out of organized trades to make room for men, much like the situation in the United States after the two World Wars (Herlihy 1990, 180).

Medieval Commerce, Rhetoric, and Women Writers

If the past is a foreign country, the medieval past often seems like another planet. The issues we are dealing with here (commerce, rhetoric, and women commercial writers) all require special definitions and qualifications to separate them from modern conceptions of apparently similar phenomena. To begin with commerce, the separation of work from the home characteristic of modern life was, as noted, largely unknown to medieval practice. Not only did all members of the family beyond infancy contribute to the family economy, but traditional "women's work" often generated scarce hard cash through the sale of surplus products such as milk, eggs, and beer.

In rural areas, where nearly all medieval English people lived, commerce was defined by the acquisition and use of agriculturally productive land and its products. This was very much the "business" of practically all persons above the subsistence farming level. Land was the economic and social foundation of the nobility and gentry, for cultivatable land remained until this century the rock upon which family fortunes (and titles) were built. Thus, as we shall see, successful lawyers such as William Paston and his son John left their wives managing the family estates and practiced law in London with the sole aim of protecting and expanding those estates. There was no question of moving the family to London, for a family fortune which could not be translated into land was considered unstable and a social dead end under the feudal assumptions of the time. The wives were thus obligated to administer the estates in person, often a more contentious and stressful job than those the husbands faced.

It is from this group of middle- to upper-class estate-managing women, rather than from the guildswomen or female artisans, that most written documents survive. Often distanced from their husbands, stewards, and other allies, they needed the written word more strongly and embraced it much earlier. For example, some very early English-language letters of Elizabeth, Lady Zouche, were once printed by the eminent Chaucerian scholar Edith Rickert chiefly because they were "of a character highly personal for their early date" (Rickert 1932, 257). The letters actually illustrate the mixing of what we would consider personal with business: hiring a new, respectful butler; ordering ribbon and cloth; examining indentures and bonds; buying white wine and black velvet; dealing with the tailor and other creditors. A gift for Lady Zouche's mother, for example, seems designed to soften her mother up to helping Lady Zouche with her mismanaged estate; the new butler would be the new manager of her multiple households, much more like Chaucer's Reeve than like Jeeves. In the long era of European feudal agriculture when nearly everyone lived in the country, the manor house was the focal point of local business. Indeed, it combined the modern economic and social functions of state government, city center, industrial park, licensing offices, church administrative center, and shopping mall. If Lady Zouche were living today, most of the "personal" expenses in her letters would be written off on her income taxes as business expenses, the medieval equivalent of the businessperson's three-martini lunch and the academic's tax-deductible computers and trips to London—and with justification: many people depended on the success of her manor for their daily bread.

The rhetoric of medieval business writers was, at the base, the same as that used by all other writers of nonliterary prose: the *dictamen*, or that part of medieval rhetoric that governed letter writing (Camargo 1991, 17–28; Murphy 1974, 194–268). (There were, of course, also lists of merchandise, inventories, guild regulations, etc.) As virtually all public documents were cast in the form of letters—a royal proclamation was theoretically a letter from the king to his subjects, for example—it is not surprising that the dictamen was universally accepted for public and private correspondence. People then as now learned from imitation, and it was the socially prestigious model to imitate.

There were essentially two chief types of dictamen in use in private English letters at the end of the Middle Ages: Type 1 was a terse, tightly structured, single-subject style used for all types of business; and Type 2 was a more chatty, improvisational, looser version found in letters such as Lady Zouche's and in the family letters discussed below. As an example of Type 1, here is a letter to the Foresters of Blackmore from

Elizabeth Woodville, Edward IV's queen and Shakespeare's "care-crazed mother to many sons":

> By the Queen
> We will and charge you that you deliver or do to be delivered unto our trusty and right well-beloved Sir William Stonor, knight, or unto the bringer hereof in his name one buck of this season, to be taken of our gift within our forest of Blakmore, any restraint or command-ment to you directed to the contrary hereof notwithstanding. And this our letter shall be your sufficient warrant anent ["on behalf of," (*Middle English Dictionary*)] us in that behalf. Given under our signet at my lord's castle of Windsor the nineteenth day of August the twenty-first year of my said lord's reign [1481]. (Public Record Of-fice, London, PRO SC1/44/64)

Its brisk, direct, and authoritative style matches that of the English-language Signet letters of Henry V and the French Signet letters of his predecessors.

Here, however, I am focusing on commercial documents, that is, correspondence between at least two persons seeking to carry out a com-mercial action. The dictamen as a business form I have dealt with elsewhere in detail (see Richardson 1985; Richardson and Liggett 1993, 116–20), but essentially Type 1 was a somewhat less florid version of the style and format used by the high-born to issue commands or the less-born to petition humbly. The chief parts of the English professional and familiar letters were usually:

1. A formulaic greeting, sometimes followed by information about the reader or writer's health (*salutatio*);
2. A description of the occasion of the letter (*narratio*);
3. A request or demand (*petitio* or *dispositio*);
4. A formulaic ending, usually something like "and God have you in his keeping," followed by the place and date of writing (*conclusio*). (Davis 1967)

Many letters by women follow this structure combined with the wording and logic used often in the Signet letters: "Trusty and welbeloved, I greet you well/recommend myself to you . . . whereas [this is the case], . . . wherefore [I ask or request you to do something].

And God have you in his keeping. Written at [place], the [date]." Consequently, the rhetorical structure of most of the surviving Type 1 and Type 2 letters will be strikingly similar. The only significant variant may be found in letters based on the structure of the formal petition.

Type 1, a high feudal rhetoric, marks one end of a continuum of the dictamen use; at the other end of the continuum, and less frequently found, is the Type 2 style, illustrated later in this chapter by the Paston family letters. It is marked by the usual dictamenal openings, closings, and formulas but with a greatly expanded middle section consisting of unorganized bits of news and queries, as if taken down by dictation over several days.

The rhetoric used by medieval English businesswomen was affected by two other crucial factors. First, framing the correct rhetorical format and wording was the responsibility of the person who physically wrote the letters. This person was only rarely the sender or signatory of the letter, for most correspondence was actually penned by scriveners, scribes, or attorneys. Since physically writing out a document in its final form was a technical skill separate from composing the content of the letter (Clanchy 1979, 88–105), the relationship between a medieval document's author and its writer was roughly that of the modern computer programmer and a technical writer.

A second rhetorical influence was the use of a messenger not only to deliver letters but to supplement them with information. In the days before a regular government postal service, mail delivery depended on hired messengers or household servants. The disadvantages were legion, of course, but the advantage was that information too extensive, complicated, or delicate to put in a message could be delivered by word of mouth through the messenger. In a letter printed in full below, Lady Sudeley urges her agent to examine the "deeds the bearer of this shall show unto you, as my full trust is and hath been unto you, like as the bearer hereof shall inform you, to whom I pray you give credence." Messengers would sometimes carry tokens as a sign of their trustworthiness, as shown below in one of Elizabeth Stonor's letters (Kingsford 1919, 2:22). The inclusion of a messenger in the letter-writing process forms an "epistolary quadrangle" quite different from modern correspondence practices (Richardson 1989). These letters underscore the oral-written interdependence that has been largely ignored by rhetoricians and writing theorists, despite being an important part of daily professional relations to this day (Cross 1994). It would be interesting in the case of women's letters to know if women sometimes employed female messengers.

Sources of Women's Commercial Writing

No printed or archival collection devoted to women's commercial correspondence exists from medieval England. For sources we must rely on other collections put together for quite different purposes than to illustrate women's writing. These sources are invariably letter collections, usually letter collections of one family. Numerically, most examples of women's writing in print actually come from one collection, the famous Paston family letters. Other collections of historical letters include women's correspondence, although these are usually of queens and great ladies and tell us little about less exalted personages.

To balance the printed material—neither queens nor duchesses being typical of women in commerce—we have a sizable number of unpublished documents from the later Middles Ages by a fairly wide spectrum of women. The documents are predictably weighted toward women from the gentry; equally predictable is the absence of women from the lower end of the social ranks, women brewers or bakers, for example. (The same is generally true of men, however.) Of particular interest are the collections in the Public Record Office, Chancery Lane, London, known as Ancient Correspondence. These are bound volumes of loose letters from the Middle Ages arranged more or less chronologically. Most of them were originally part of lawsuits or petitions, and many are in poor condition. Even when the letters are perfectly readable, they all too often refer vaguely to events well-known to both letter writer and letter receiver half a millennium ago but wholly obscure even to the most assiduous historian. But they are our best surviving record of how people carried out their business in writing. For women's writing, they are virtually unique.

The Family Letter Collections

The printed family letters have achieved the most attention, and with good reason: they tell a continuing, often compelling story of struggle, betrayal, civil war, and love. The four great family letter collections from England's later Middle Ages—those of the Paston, Stonor, Plumpton, and Cely families—give an incomparably rich picture of life among the middle to middle-high classes of the fifteenth and early sixteenth centuries. The three families under consideration (the Cely letters are nearly all by males) were all of the gentry class, were all on speaking terms with those prominent names of the age notorious to us through Shakespeare's history plays, and all possessed considerable farmland, manors, and villages. Nevertheless, their letters, taken together, go a long way toward dispelling any Hollywood-inspired images of the medieval leisured class. Their daily lives plainly had more to do with buying and selling and dealing with lawyers than with tournaments and troubadours. The families were never far from financial disaster at any moment. Some of their members were dispossessed under questionable circumstances, sometimes by a corrupt legal system and sometimes by violence. All spent their lives embroiled in ruinous, protracted lawsuits. All were short of ready cash most of the time, and in one case the head of a titled family and his wife were thrown into debtor's prison. The gentry had their joys, of course, but their letters show lives haunted by fear of penury, exhausted by legal chicanery, and often blighted by greed.

The famous "Paston Letters" are actually a miscellany of letters, deeds, wills, indentures, memorandums, inventories, and other documents extending in time from 1425 to the late seventeenth century, although printed versions cover only the considerable fifteenth-century material, about twelve hundred pages worth in the standard Norman Davis edition (Davis 1971). Taken together they form a vivid picture of life in fifteenth-century England. The mixture of the personal and political upheavals most closely resembles a historical novel in epistolary form, except that, as in real life, events often end confusingly or undramatically.

The Pastons were a prominent although not aristocratic Norfolk family. Indeed, some of their seemingly endless problems detailed in their letters stemmed from the fact that they were perpetually taken as nouveaux riches and had to fight for survival in a class-bound society. The family was pulled rapidly out of the mud of a medieval farm by William Paston (1378–1444), who rose to become sergeant at law, justice of the Common Bench, and owner of considerable if spread-out property in his home county. William's holdings were both physically and legally defended by his son John Paston I (1421–1466), another attorney, and then his grandsons, both named John. Especially after the death of the astute William, family members were involved in countless lawsuits and intrigues about their lands and legal rights and were never far from the personal violence endemic to fifteenth-century England.

Of the Paston women, four left correspondence: William's wife Agnes, his daughter Elizabeth, John Paston I's wife Margaret, and John Paston III's wife Margery. Elizabeth, who lost two husbands to the bloodiness of the times (one to Richard III), and Margery each left a handful of newsy but unremarkable letters. More letters survive from Agnes, a woman toughened by her marriage to a much older man and by the family's relentless struggles to stay ahead (Thomsen 1989). She was especially hard on the long-unmarried daughter Elizabeth and once urged her son's tutor to beat him to make him "amend" poor study habits. Like the letters of Elizabeth and Margery, Agnes's letters are more like local news bulletins, in her case to her son John in London. In one letter she urges John to follow his late father's advice and learn the law, for "he should so ever dwell at Paston should have need to defend himself" (no. 14).

Such advice in modern times might well be given to her daughter-in-law Margaret, for Margaret handled the tumultuous affairs in Norfolk while her husband handled his lawsuits in London. Over a hundred of her letters survive. Margaret was sometimes in real physical danger from the many powerful men seeking to eject the Pastons from their property. At one point she was besieged, captured, and expelled from her own manor of Gresham (no. 131). Another time her husband was thrown into Fleet Prison while her manor of Hellesdon was destroyed and the village and its church ravaged. She and Agnes were called "strong whores" in front of her own church at Oxnead while Mass was being said inside (no. 129). Often hard-pressed for cash, from 1459 until 1476 she conducted much of the local business in a devastating lawsuit over lands inherited from Sir John Fastolf. These problems and many more went on during a protracted civil war in which her sons were sometimes fighting. In the midst of all this her husband died at age forty-five, leaving her five sons and two daughters of only fair abilities. No wonder she had earlier written to her husband that "this is too weary a life to abide for you and yours" (no. 180). Later she wrote to her son about the Fastolf lawsuit, "Remember, it was the destruction of your father" (no. 213). But as Diane Watt notes in her study of the Paston women's correspondence, Margaret was a powerful, stubborn woman.

The Stonor family letters, chiefly from 1420 to 1483, record similar if less dramatic problems (Kingsford 1919, 1923). Most of them center around Sir William Stonor, who married three times to successively wealthier wives. After his death there were the usual nasty lawsuits along with (in the suitably archaic words of the letters' editor) "great expenses and divers and sundry riots, assaults, and affrays" lasting over forty years.

The Stonor papers contain a wider variety of women correspondents than the Paston papers and record increasing female literacy in the upper class as the fifteenth century drew to a close. Whereas none of the Paston women could write beyond signing their names in a "tremulous, totally unformed hand," most of the Stonor women could write their own letters if they chose to (Davis 1955; Kingsford 1919, xlvii). William Stonor's sister Jane was writing letters in her own hand as early as 1463.

Of the Stonor women, Elizabeth was the most active correspondent. Unlike her husband, Sir William, she did not come from the gentry but from a London mercantile background. As the editor of her letters says, "she was a masterful women, who took an active interest in her husband's affairs" (xxviii). Her letters are perhaps less directly concerned with business affairs than Margaret Paston's, but it is clear from them that she was an inveterate networker who introduced her husband to many important London merchants and traders. She worked as hard in her family's interests as any ambitious modern professional. In a revealing gender-role reversal, she reports to her ailing husband that, although she worries about him, she cannot come to him because she must wait to finish some legal business (no. 208). In another letter she says, "I would I were at Stonor, for truly I am weary of London," but nevertheless she chooses to stay in the city and handle money affairs (no. 229).

The correspondence of the Plumpton family of Yorkshire chiefly comes from the early Tudor period and is of somewhat less interest (Stapleton 1839). It largely derives, predictably, from yet another extended lawsuit. This one was caused by Sir William Plumpton (d. 1487), an unattractive man whose attempts to dispossess his female heirs by his first marriage in favor of his son by his second wreaked havoc on the family for generations. This son, Sir Robert, was despite all odds a decent man, but eventually the legal complications of his late father's doing threw him and his wife into debtor's prison during Henry VIII's reign.

The Plumpton letters contain a number of business letters by women, most from Sir Robert's long-suffering first wife, Agnes. Chiefly in her directions for their son to carry out, her letters movingly reveal her attempts to handle an estate fatally encumbered by lawsuits. Dame Agnes was obviously competent and painstaking, so her death in the middle of the lawsuit cost Sir Robert dearly. A year after Agnes's death he married Isabella, daughter of Lord Neville. Within a short time this granddaughter of the powerful earl of Westmoreland would write to her husband:

> Sir, I have set to Wright of Idell for the money that he promised you, and he saith he hath not it to lend, and makes excuses, and I can get nowhere. As for [selling our] wood, there is none that will buy [it], for they know you want money. . . . Sir, for God's sake take an end, for we are brought to the beggar's staff. (Stapleton 1839, 198)

The Plumpton letters often make pitiful reading. Like the women in some of Shakespeare's history plays, the Plumpton women often seem to have spent their lives as victims of someone else's greed and ambition. To their credit, however, they took a more active role in shaping their destinies (Kirby 1991).

In fact, the letters of the Paston, Stonor, and Plumpton women show most of them as active participants in the family business affairs, fully capable of carrying out transactions on their own. There is nothing in these letters particularly feminine in the traditional sense. If frequent mention is made of personal items such as gowns, fabrics, jewels, shirts, and foodstuffs, the same is true of letters from men (as in Paston letter no. 275). Margaret Paston's letters, for example, show her as a shrewd businesswoman. While she asks business advice of her husband on many occasions, he, after all, was an Inns of Court attorney. She is not afraid to throw herself into his business: "Gerrard's wife is dead, and there is a fair place of hers to sell in St. Gregory's parish, as it is told to me. I suppose if you like to buy it you should have it worth the money" (no. 144); or this hastily added postscript, "I pray you trust not to the sheriff for no fair language" (no. 141).

The Rhetoric of Women's Correspondence

While most other surviving letters from the fifteenth century are Type 1—relatively short and tightly controlled by the rules of the dictamen—the family letters, especially those of the Pastons, are loosely constructed, even rambling, and usually long. One subject follows another with little relationship, frequently set off by the word *Item*. Often, however, subjects are run together with no separation, a practice made more jarring to modern readers because medieval letters lacked any paragraphing, as the Paston reproductions at the end of both volumes of the Davis edition show clearly. Although the Paston letters are almost always written in a single hand and are probably based on drafts (as with no. 209), they give the impression of being put together from earlier notes or (more likely) being dictated over a long evening or so to a secretary and sent out without much revision of form. Postscripts are frequent. On the other hand, the most important news generally comes first, especially if it concerns a topic previously written about.

Rhetorically, the jumble of information in the family letters illustrates again the medieval lack of division between public and private, home and business. Modern readers may be amused or horrified, for example, at Margaret Paston's bits of gossip:

> Heydon's wife had a child on St. Peter's Day. I heard said that her husband will [have] nought of her, or of her child that she had last neither. I heard say that he said if she come in his presence to make her excuse that he should cut off her nose to make her to be known what she is [i.e., a punished adulteress], and if her child come in his presence he said he would kill [it]. (no. 127)

But John Heydon was an ally of the Pastons' deadly enemy Lord Moleyns; every aspect of his personal life could be used against him in court. If Heydon won some Paston property in a lawsuit, the paternity of his children could figure powerfully if the Pastons tried to get it back later. Similarly, the many local disputes and private conversations she reports so vividly form part of a tight web of local power relations, some of which is still discernible.

The family letters often have a novel-like vivacity and gripping narrative style rare even in fiction. In this they are unique and hence misleading. Practically no other letters from the period, either by male or female writers, in any way resemble them except superficially.

The typical Type 1 commercial letter found in Ancient Correspondence, by contrast, follows closely the dictamen formulas discussed earlier. The results may be illustrated most readily by a letter from Alice Butler, Lady Sudeley, to her agent Nicholas Wendover:

> Trusty and welbeloved, I greet you well. And whereas I of singular trust in you have before that enfeoffed you with other of my manors,

lands, and tenements within diverse others [therefore I] will and herewith pray you for great considerations and causes touching my worship and great profit that you seal the deeds made in your name and other of the said manors to such persons as be named in the same, which said deeds the bearer of this shall show unto you, as my full trust is and hath been unto you, like as the bearer hereof shall inform you, to whom I pray you give credence. And God have you in his keeping. Written at Sudeley the iiii day of April [1462]. (PRO SC1/ 51/50, unpublished)

If we can ignore the oddness of some of the phrasing and the stringy, paratactic sentence construction, both wholly typical of writing of this period, two characteristics stand out. First, the letter is short. Like most of the king's own Signet office letters, Queen Elizabeth Woodville's letter quoted above, and Aristotle's well-made play, the letter sticks to one topic and one topic only. Second, this conciseness enables them to work out the well-wrought logic of the dictamen format: either "since X has happened, therefore you must do Y for me" or "since X has happened, therefore I ask you to do Y for me." The format was clearly designed for the feudal system of carefully graduated, hierarchical social roles whereby one is either commanding an inferior or begging a superior (Richardson and Liggett 1993, 117). It is obviously less well suited for commerce, where relationships are usually more subtle, or at least different. Nevertheless, this is the voice of commercial woman as well.

The *Dictamen* and Female Rhetoric

The great unasked question in this essay so far must be this: "Does the writing of medieval women in commerce differ from that of men?" On the limited basis of this study, the answer, it should be clear by now, is "no." If a sizable number of these letters by both sexes were mixed together and the writers' identities concealed, it would be difficult to detect any difference. Although the Type 2 business letter, with its somewhat more personal, nonlinear rhetoric, might seem to be closer to what some feminist theorists consider "feminine," in practice most Type 2 letters are by men and numerically most women chose the rigid Type 1. Yet while the medieval business letter is no place to look for the origins of *écriture féminine*, there are at least two things of importance in the history of women's rhetoric that explain the lack of a distinctive female voice and women's favoring of the more patriarchal Type 1 letter. Most obviously, the letters were almost always physically written by male secretaries or professional scribes. While the inability to write was not a sign of poor education or low social status in the Middle Ages, there is little question that we would have a different view of the medieval world had more women's thoughts been written down by women.

Second and equally important, even if all secretaries had been female, it might have made little difference. The notarial form of the dictamen cast its hand over everything. A letter that did not at least make gestures toward following the dictamenal formulas had no authority. It would have violated the medieval sense of rhetorical decorum and, however serious its purpose, risked being taken lightly, as would a modern attorney appearing in court without a tie. The looser Type 2 letters offer more structural opportunities for individualism and intimacy, but these women did not take them.

Certainly most should find it curious that although women have been shown to have distinctly different problem-solving styles than men, business letters designed to solve problems show no significant rhetorical differences. Although some scholars have argued that women's rhetoric and "voice" are essentially different from men's, recent studies in the *Journal of Business Communication* suggest that in everyday business rhetoric women's writing is no different from men's (Smeltzer and Werbel 1986; Sterkel 1988). It might be hypothesized, then, that women's adoption of universal, authoritative voice and rhetoric appears to be a constant in commercial rhetoric.

To end on a fairly positive note, however, we can with justice claim that the chief virtue for women of following the standard commercial rhetoric was (and is) that it rendered them rhetorically equal to men. The voice of the medieval letter is an even more patriarchal voice than that in modern commercial letters: it is always oratorical, tersely logical, hierarchical. It was created by the papacy and the church based on Roman models, then spread throughout the royal and ducal administrations by clerics, and finally theorized by Italian academic churchmen—about as male a lineage as any institution except perhaps boxing. It was certainly not created for intimacy; in the Paston family letters, for example, the second-person pronoun was always "you" or "ye," in Middle English grammar more formal than "thou" or "thee" (Davis 1955, 61). When it was handed to lesser mortals writing in the vernacular toward the end of the Middle Ages it had no rival. Consequently, when women began using correspondence to do business, they (and their secretaries) had no real option but to adopt the patriarchal voice. There was, after all, no feminine dictamen.

Consequently, a perhaps surprising number of brisk, commanding letters from women to men have survived. The much-put-upon Agnes Plumpton could write to her husband:

> Sir, I marvel greatly that you let the matter rest so long, and labor no better for yourself, and you would labor it diligently. But it is said that you be less forward, and that [your enemy] underworketh falsely; and it is seen and known by them. . . . Sir, I beseech you to remember the great costs and charges, and mine, and labor the matter that it might have an end. . . . (Stapleton 1839, 186–87)

Whether these were really the strong, business-savvy women the letters show them to be is not the point. What is worth observing is that the rhetoric of the letters makes them strong. Whether the rhetorical strength gained was worth the price is a question to be answered today, when little seems to have changed after five hundred years of "Dear Sir."

Note

Support for research for this essay came in part from grants by the National Endowment for the Humanities, the American Council of Learned Societies, and a 1994 Louisiana State University Summer Grant.

References

Archer, Rowena E. 1992. "'How Ladies . . . Who Live on Their Manors Ought to Manage Their Households and Estates': Women as Landholders and Administrators in the Later Middle Ages." In *Woman is a Worthy Wight: Women in English Society, c. 1200–1500*, edited by P. J. P. Goldberg, 149–81. Phoenix Mill, Gloucestershire: Alan Sutton.

Camargo, Martin. 1991. *Ars dictaminis, ars dictandi*. Turnhout, Belgium: Brepols.

Cherewatuk, Karen, and Ulrike Wiethaus, eds. 1993. *Dear Sister: Medieval Women and the Epistolary Genre*. Philadelphia: University of Pennsylvania Press.

Clanchy, M. T. 1979. *From Memory to Written Record*. Cambridge: Harvard University Press.

Classen, Albrecht. 1988. "Female Epistolary Literature from Antiquity to the Present: an Introduction." *Studia Neuphilologica* 60: 3–13.

Cross, Geoffrey. 1994. "Recontextualizing Writing: Roles of Written Texts in Multiple Media Communications." *Journal of Business Communication* 8: 217–18.

Davis, Norman. 1955. "The Language of the Pastons." *Proceedings of the British Academy* 40: 119–44.

———. 1967. "Style and Stereotype in Early English Letters." *Leeds Studies in English* 1: 7–17.

———, ed. 1971, 1976. *Paston Letters and Papers of the Fifteenth-Century.* 2 vols. Oxford: Clarendon Press.

Goldberg, P. J. P., ed. 1992. *Woman is a Worthy Wight: Women in English Society, c. 1200–1500.* Phoenix Mill, Gloucestershire: Alan Sutton.

Graham, Helena. 1992. "'A Woman's Work . . . ': Labour and Gender in the Late Medieval Countryside." In *Woman is a Worthy Wight: Women in English Society, c. 1200–1500,* edited by P. J. P. Goldberg, 126–48. Phoenix Mill, Gloucestershire: Alan Sutton.

Hanawalt, Barbara A., ed. 1986. *Women and Work in Preindustrial Europe.* Bloomington: Indiana University Press.

Herlihy, David. 1990. *Opera Muliebria: Women and Work in Medieval Europe.* Philadelphia: Temple University Press.

Howell, Martha C. 1986. *Women, Production and Patriarchy in Late Medieval Cities.* Chicago: University Press.

Kingsford, C. L. 1919, 1923. *Stonor Letters and Papers, 1290–1483.* 2 vols. 3rd ser., nos. 29, 30. London: Camden Society.

Kirby, Joan W. 1991. "Women in the Plumpton Correspondence: Fiction and Reality." In *Church and State in the Middle Ages: Essays Presented to John Taylor,* edited by Ian Wood and G. A. Loud, 219–32. London: Hambledon Press.

Lay, Mary. 1994. "The Value of Gender Studies to Professional Communication Research." *Journal of Business and Technical Communication* 8: 58–90.

Locker, Kitty O. 1985. "The Earliest Correspondence of the British East India Company; and 'Sir, This Will Never Do': Model Dunning Letters, 1592–1873." In *Studies in the History of Business Writing,* edited by George Douglas, 69–86, 179–200. Urbana: University of Illinois / Association for Business Communication.

Murphy, James J. 1974. *Rhetoric in the Middle Ages.* Berkeley: University of California Press.

Richardson, Malcolm. 1985. "The First-Century of English Business Writing; Researching Early English Business Writing: a Methodology; and Business Writing and the Development of English Prose." In *Studies in the History of Business Writing,* edited by George Douglas. Urbana: University of Illinois / Association for Business Communication.

———. 1989. "Medieval English Vernacular Correspondence: Notes Toward an Alternative Rhetoric." *Allegorica* 10: 95–118.

Richardson, Malcolm, and Sarah Liggett. 1993. "Power Relations, Technical Writing Theory, and Workplace Writing." *Journal of Business and Technical Writing* 7: 112–37.

Rickert, Edith. 1932. "Some English Personal Letters of 1402." *Review of English Studies* 8: 257–63.

Shahar, Shulamith. 1983. *The Fourth Estate: A History of Women in the Middle Ages.* Trans. Chaya Galai. New York: Methuen.

Smeltzer, Larry R., and James D. Werbel. 1986. "Gender Differences in Managerial Communication." *Journal of Business Communication* 23: 41–50.

Stapleton, Thomas, ed. 1839. *Plumpton Correspondence.* 1st ser., no. 4. London: Camden Society.

Sterkel, Karen S. 1988. "The Relationship Between Gender and Writing Style in Business Communication." *Journal of Business Communication* 25: 17–38.

Tebeaux, Elizabeth. 1993. "Technical Writing for Women of the English Renaissance: Technology, Literacy, and the Emergence of a Genre." *Written Communication* 10: 164–99.

Tebeaux, Elizabeth, and M. Jimmie Killingsworth. 1992. "Expanding and Redirecting Historical Research in Technical Writing." *Technical Communication Quarterly* 1: 5–32.

Thomsen, Lis Hygum. 1989. "Agnes Paston." In *Female Power in the Middle Ages,* edited by Karen Glente and Lise Winther-Jensen, 143–47. Copenhagen: C. A. Reitzel.

Watt, Diane. 1993. "'No Writing for Writing's Sake': the Language of Service and Household Rhetoric in the Letters of the Paston Women." In *Dear Sister: Medieval Women and the Epistolary Genre,* edited by Karen Cherewatuk and Ulrike Wiethaus, 122–38. Philadelphia: University of Pennsylvania Press.

Black Women on the Speaker's Platform (1832–1899)

Shirley Wilson Logan

To speak of the rhetorical activities of African American women in the nineteenth century is to speak of their advocacy for change. The term *rhetorical activities* in this discussion includes those occasions when black women delivered persuasive public speeches. Such a discussion could develop around the oratorical careers of the most vocal and prominent women rhetors of the century, beginning in 1832 with Maria Stewart in Boston and ending at the close of the century with the speeches of Nannie Helen Burroughs or Victoria Matthews. It could also focus on varying tactics of delivery, arrangement, invention, and style, from the strongly religious and self-referencing appeals of Sojourner Truth or Stewart to the factual, disengaged approach of Ida Wells and the traditional grand style of Frances Ellen Watkins Harper or Anna Julia Haywood Cooper. Literary societies, such as the Bethel Literary and Historical Association, founded in 1881 by Washington, D.C.'s black elite, provided opportunities for black women to develop skills in oratory.

But perhaps one can acquire a better sense of the extent of black women's public involvement in nineteenth-century political life by considering their rhetorical responses to the panoply of issues challenging peoples of African descent throughout America at the time. In addition to the oppressive defining issue of slavery, these concerns included employment, civil rights, woman's rights, emigration, and self-improvement. After the Civil War mob violence, racial uplift, and support for the southern black woman were added to the list of concerns demanding articulation. Nineteenth-century black women articulated them all. They spoke out at church conferences, political gatherings, woman's rights conventions, and antislavery meetings. Not limiting themselves to mere participation in public forums, black women also created, organized, and publicized a large number of them. Maria Stewart, the first American-born woman to speak publicly to a mixed group of women and men, was African American. She delivered her first address in 1832, six years before Angelina Grimké's appearance at Pennsylvania Hall, and her speeches were published in William Lloyd Garrison's *Liberator*. Mary Ann Shadd Cary, after considerable discussion, was reluctantly seated at the 1855 Colored National Convention in Philadelphia, becoming the first woman to address that body by a vote of 38 yeas and 23 nays (*Minutes* 1855, 10). An article in the 26 October 1855 edition of *Frederick Douglass' Paper* describes that performance: "She at first had ten minutes granted her as had the other members. At their expiration, ten more were granted, and by this time came the hour of adjournment; but so interested was the House, that it granted additional time to her to finish, at the commencement of the afternoon session; and the House was crowded and breathless in its attention to her masterly exposition of our present condition, and the advantages open to colored men of enterprise" (Sterling 1984, 171).

Frances Harper was employed as a lecturer for the Maine Anti-Slavery Society in 1854, becoming possibly the first black woman to earn a living as a traveling lecturer. She was certainly the most prolific. The black women's club movement also sparked extensive issue-oriented public discussion, as any edition of the *Woman's Era* demonstrates. The pages of this periodical, published by the Woman's Era Club of Boston from 1894 to 1897, were filled with reports from the various black women's clubs around the country relating their very public presence in current affairs. For example, the April 1895 issue carried an article by Mary Church Terrell, editor of the Washington, D.C., column, in which she condemned T. Thomas Fortune, editor of the *New York Age*, for criticizing "the race with which he is identified for whining." In the same issue, the column from Georgia, edited by Alice Woodby McKane, reported on the club's interest in the emigration of two hundred blacks to Liberia. In the 1 June 1894 issue Ednah Cheney commended the *Woman's Era* for its involvement in opening the medical profession to women. Later issues teemed with support for a national gathering of women, which did occur in 1895. This conference of black women held in Boston was an occasion for black women publicly to address urgent race concerns. These intersecting concerns and occasions have been classified here for discussion into the following necessarily overlapping categories: the abolition of slavery, women's rights, lynching, and racial uplift. They represent some of the interwoven consequences of African existence in America.

Abolition of Slavery

It should be clear that the abolition of slavery dominated discourse among black women during the first half of the century. Of the 750,000 blacks living in the United States at the time of the census of 1790, approximately 92 percent, or 691,000, were enslaved, and most lived in the South Atlantic states. In 1808 legislation finally made the African slave trade illegal, although it continued underground for many years. In the 1790 census Boston was the only city that listed no slaves, with approximately 27,000 free blacks living in the North and 32,000 free blacks in the South (Franklin and Moss 1988, 80–81).

This discussion of black women's abolitionist rhetoric centers on the public discourse of three speakers who migrated to new locales, delivering their antislavery messages to audiences in England, Canada, and across the United States. Sarah Parker Remond, a member of a prominent abolitionist family in Massachusetts, lectured in England and Scotland. Mary Ann Shadd Cary, whose father was a leader in the Underground Railroad movement in Delaware, fled with her family to Canada to avoid the consequences of the Fugitive Slave Act of 1850 and developed into an outspoken presence in the antislavery movement there. Frances Harper, whose uncle William Watkins was active in the abolitionist movement, left Baltimore in about 1850, also in response to the Fugitive Slave Act, eventually traveling across the country with her antislavery message.

Although slavery was abolished in the British Empire in 1833, antislavery activities against its American version continued throughout the first half of the century, at which time a number of black abolitionists traveled to the British Isles to generate support for their cause. Some were freeborn blacks, like Charles Lenox Remond, and others were, like Frederick Douglass and William Wells Brown, formerly enslaved. Sarah Remond (1815–1894) was one of eight children born to Nancy and John Remond, a native of Curaçao. Her family was part of the abolitionist society of Salem, Massachusetts. In 1856 she was appointed agent for the American Anti-Slavery Society and, as an associate of Garrison, became one of the first black women to lecture regularly before antislavery audiences. Initially a reluctant speaker, Remond toured throughout New England, New York, and Ohio between 1856 and 1858 and developed into an accomplished orator. She traveled to England in 1859 to deliver a series of lectures. From 1859 to 1861 she delivered more than forty-five lectures in eighteen cities in England, three cities in Scotland, and four cities in Ireland (Wesley 1994, 974). She was received enthusiastically wherever she spoke. In 1866 she returned to the United States and applied her oratorical skills to the task of racial uplift, in the manner of her brother Charles Remond and of Douglass. In 1867 she returned to England and subsequently settled in Florence, Italy, to practice medicine. It was said that she spoke in a "well-toned" and "pleasing style" and "demonstrated an unerring sensitivity to the political and social concerns of her listeners—particularly women reform activists" (Ripley 1985, 441).

Although most male lecturers were reluctant to speak about the exploitation of enslaved black women, Sarah Parker Remond, probably the most prominent woman abolitionist to travel and speak in the British Isles, was not. In a one-and-a-quarter-hour lecture delivered to an overflowing crowd at the Music Hall in Warrington, England, on 24 January 1859, Remond relentlessly detailed the treatment of the enslaved black woman, using as a case in point the story of Kentucky slave mother Margaret Garner. Garner, who "had suffered in her own person the degradation that a woman could not mention," escaped with her children to Cincinnati. Rather than allow her to be recaptured, Garner killed her three-year-old daughter, but she was prevented from killing her other children. Remond stated that "above all sufferers in America, American women who were slaves lived in the most pitiable condition. They could not protect themselves from the licentiousness which met them on every hand—they could not protect their honour from the tyrant" (Remond [1859] 1985a, 437). She also criticized the Dred Scott Decision of 1857, denying blacks the right to citizenship, and the heinous Fugitive Slave Act, which sent many blacks fleeing to northern states, Canada, and the British Isles.

Remond drew support for her arguments from contemporary events. She chronicled current and widely publicized incidents with significant impact on American slavery, showing how such events—for example, the trial of Margaret Garner and the Dred Scott Decision—mirrored the sad conditions of a slave society. Stressing the hypocrisy of the Christian church, in this same speech Remond cited the shooting of a black man for insubordination by a clergyman in Louisiana and the dismissal of a minister in Philadelphia after he preached an antislavery sermon. From her English audiences she wanted public outcry. In a 14 September 1859 speech delivered at the Athenaeum in Manchester, England, she asked them to exert their influence to abolish slavery in America: "Give us the power of your public opinion, it has great weight in America. Words spoken here are read there as no words written in America are read. . . . I ask you, raise the moral public opinion until its voice reaches the American shores. Aid us thus until the shackles of the American slave melt like dew before the morning sun" (Remond [1859] 1985b, 459).

Mary Ann Shadd Cary (1823–1893), the first black female newspaper editor, published the *Provincial Freeman,* a weekly Canadian newspaper for fugitive slaves and others who had fled to Canada in the wake of the Fugitive Slave Act during the 1850s. From 1852 to 1853 she was the only black missionary in the field for the American Missionary Association (AMA), the largest abolitionist organization in America (DeBoer 1994, xi). Cary taught fugitive slaves recently arrived who, in her view, lacked motivation and self-discipline. She, along with Samuel Ward and Alexander McArthur, established the *Provincial Freeman* in March 1853, after the AMA informed her that it would no longer support her school. The *Freeman* soon became Cary's vehicle for promoting industry among former slaves and exposing the misconduct of unscrupulous antislavery agents. In 1863 Cary returned to the United States, eventually settling in Washington, D.C., where she taught and ultimately practiced law.

In her historic 1855 address to the Colored National Convention, she advocated for the emigration of blacks from America to Canada and for their total integration into Canadian society. Cary's intense speaking style left its impression, as noted by the eyewitness quoted here: "Miss Shadd's eyes are small and penetrating and fairly flush when she is speaking. Her ideas seem to flow so fast that she, at times hesitates for words; yet she overcomes any apparent imperfections in her speaking by the earnestness of her manner and the quality of her thoughts. She is a superior woman; and it is useless to deny it; however much we may differ with her on the subject of emigration" (Sterling 1984, 170–71).

All accounts of the works and days of the strong-willed Cary suggest that she rarely held her tongue or backed down from a position. She opposed the growing popularity of evangelical, better-life-in-the-afterworld preachers who neglected contemporary issues, with "their gross ignorance and insolent bearing, together with their sanctimonious garb," and who hung "tenaciously to exploded customs," giving some the impression that "money, and not the good of the people" motivated them (Cary 1986a, 32–33). One biographer describes her style as follows: "By nineteenth-century norms, Cary's caustic, jolting language seemed ill-suited to a woman. She used phrases such as 'gall and wormwood,' 'moral pest,' 'petty despot,' 'superannuated minister,' 'nest of unclean birds,' 'moral monsters,' and 'priest-ridden people,' in order to keep her ideas before the public" (Calloway-Thomas 1994, 225).

Most of Cary's extant writings are letters and scathing editorials from the *Provincial Freeman* railing against intemperance, "addled brained young people," and any number of other displeasing states of affairs. Texts of her speeches are scarce, but the following excerpt, reprinted with limited editorial intervention, comes from a sermon "apparently delivered before a Chatham [Canada West] audience on 6 April 1858" (Ripley 1986, 388) and suggests the fervor of her biblically based and feminist antislavery rhetoric: "We cannot successfully Evade duty because the Suffering fellow . . . is only a woman! She too is a neighbor. The good Samaritan of this generation must not take for their Exemplars the priest and the Levite when a fellow woman is among thieves—neither will they find excuse in the custom as barbarous and anti-Christian as any promulgated by pious Brahmin that . . . they may be only females. The spirit of true philanthropy knows no sex" (Cary 1986b, 389).

As William Still's history of the Underground Railroad documents, Frances Ellen Watkins Harper (1825–1911) joined the abolitionist movement largely because of an incident that occurred in the slave state of Maryland, her home state. In 1853 a law was passed prohibiting free blacks from entering Maryland. When a man unintentionally violated that law, he was arrested and sent to Georgia as a slave. He escaped but was recaptured and soon died. Hearing of this sequence of events, Harper remarked, "Upon that grave I pledge myself to the Anti-Slavery cause" (Still 1872, 786). In 1854 Harper gave up teaching to become a lecturer for the Maine Anti-Slavery Society.

Harper delivered what was probably her first antislavery speech at a meeting in New Bedford, Massachusetts, in 1854; it was possibly titled "Education and Elevation of the Colored Race" (Still 1872). She continued to speak out against slavery and its consequences, traveling throughout the New England area, southern Canada, and west to Michigan and Ohio. During one six-week period in 1854 she gave at least thirty-three lectures in twenty-one New England towns (Foster 1990).

Because of her articulate and reserved manner, many who heard her found it difficult to believe that she was of African descent. Grace Greenwood, a journalist, labeled her "the bronze muse" and bemoaned the fact that a woman of such stature could possibly have been a slave, as if to suggest that slavery was more acceptable for some human beings than for others. For such observers she was considered a fascinating aberration, as this account by a Maine abolitionist suggests: "Miss W. is slightly tinged with African blood, but the color only serves to add a charm to the occasion which nothing else could give, while at the same time it disarms the fastidious of that so common prejudice which denies to white ladies the right to give public lectures" (Sterling 1984, 161). This commentary also highlights the perception that white women were different and that, while they were yet denied the right to give public lectures, black women were not always frowned upon in this role.

Harper frequently focused on the economic aspects of slavery and the irony of owning "property that can walk." In a lecture titled "Could We Trace the Record," delivered during the 1857 meeting of the New York City Anti-Slavery Society, she argued that slavery's financial benefits would make its abolishment more difficult: "A hundred thousand new-born babes are annually added to the victims of slavery; twenty thousand lives are annually sacrificed on the plantations of the South. Such a sight should send a thrill of horror, through the nerves of civilization and impel the heart of humanity to lofty deeds. So it might, if men had not found a fearful alchemy by which this blood can be transformed into gold. Instead of listening to the cry of agony, they listen to the ring of dollars and stoop down to pick up the coin" (Harper 1990a, 101).

Her commitment to the abolition of slavery led her to do more than lecture. Harper was active in the Philadelphia Underground Railroad, giving time, money, and talents to its efforts. She never refused an opportunity to engage in activities designed to promote emancipation. Without exception, those who reviewed Harper's lectures commented as much on her platform presence and her ethos as upon the content of her speeches. Such phrases as "splendid articulation," "pure language," "pleasant voice," "thought flowed in eloquent and poetic expression," "never assuming, never theatrical," "spoke feelingly and eloquently," and "a nature most femininely sensitive" characterize the lasting impression she left on her audiences. Even her contemporary Mary Ann Shadd Cary acknowledged Harper's superiority as an orator. In an 1858 letter to her husband Cary wrote, "She is the greatest female speaker ever was here, so wisdom obliges me to keep out of the way as with her prepared lectures there would just be no chance of a favorable comparison" (Sterling 1984, 174). These reactions add credence to the claim that a speaker's personality may be her most persuasive appeal.

Harper's magnetic personality should not, however, overshadow the powerful substance of her antislavery messages. One of her strongest messages, "Our Greatest Want," appeared in an 1859 issue of the *Anglo-African Magazine,* addressed not to whites but to northern blacks, in response to a growing interest in material wealth: "The respect that is bought by gold is not worth much. It is no honor to shake hands politically with men who whip women and steal babies. If this government has no call for our services, no aim for your children, we have the greater need of them to build up a true manhood and womanhood for ourselves (Harper [1859] 1990b, 103).

Women's Rights

Prominent black women abolitionists such as Remond and Cary, as well as Maria W. Stewart and Sojourner Truth, frequently combined antislavery discussions with discussions of feminist issues, framing their antislavery arguments in feminist terms. By the same token, white free antislavery feminists, as Jean Fagan Yellin puts it, conflated the oppression of enslaved and free women by equating the literal enslavement of black women to their own figurative enslavement. Yellin goes on to point out, however, that the speeches of black women testify to no confusion between the two experiences. "Nor," she writes, "did they confuse the free women's struggle for self-liberation from a metaphorical slavery with their own struggle for self-liberation from slavery. For them, the discourse of antislavery feminism became not liberating but confining when it colored the self-liberated Woman and Sister white and reassigned the role of the passive victim, which the patriarchy traditionally had reserved for white women, to women who were black" (Yellin 1989, 78–79).

Remond often cited the abuses of enslaved black women to bolster her abolitionist appeals. In her 1859 speech in Manchester she made a special appeal to the women of England, pointing out that "women are the worst victims of the slave power." Cary, in addition to her abolitionist activities in Canada, addressed groups on behalf of woman's rights, assigning the emancipation of slaves and the liberation of women equal importance. In her 1858 Chatham sermon, quoted from above, she makes appeals for "the Slave mother as well as the Slave father" and places in the same "pit" the "colored people of this country" and "the women of the land," invoking Christ as the supreme example of one who implied "an Equal inheritance" for the sexes. When in 1869 Cary, under pressure from black women delegates, was allowed to address the National Colored Labor Union, she spoke on woman's rights and suffrage. As a result, the union voted to include women workers in its organizations (Giddings 1984).

Black women had been defending their rights well before these and other more organized events occurred. A religious abolitionist who justified social activism with biblical scriptures, Maria W. Stewart (1803–1879) addressed the Afric-American Female Intelligence Society of Boston in 1832, exhorting the women to exert their influence: "O woman, woman! Your example is powerful, your influence great; it extends over your husbands and your children, and throughout the circle of your acquaintance" (Stewart [1832] 1995a, 16). In a speech at Franklin Hall she commented on the lack of employment opportunities for young black women in Boston as a consequence of "the powerful force of prejudice," a force which prevented them from becoming more than domestic workers (Stewart [1832] 1995b, 6).

Born in Connecticut, Maria Miller moved to Boston and married James W. Stewart, a ship's outfitter, in 1826. They were members of Boston's black middle class and friends of David Walker, the fiery, outspoken abolitionist and author of *Walker's Appeal, in Four Articles, Together With a Preamble, to The Coloured Citizens of the World, But in Particular And Very Expressly, To Those of the United States of America* in 1829. In this pamphlet Walker urged the slaves to revolt, slay their masters, if necessary, and escape to freedom. Incorporating much of Walker's style, Stewart delivered her Franklin Hall address in 1832, shortly after her husband's death. Stewart spoke on several other occasions between 1832 and 1833, but because of strong criticism she retired from public speaking, delivering her farewell address on 21 September 1833. In her 1833 "Farewell Address" Stewart lamented the fact that she was not well received as a public speaker, declaring, "I am about to leave you, perhaps never more to return. For I find it is no use for me as an individual to try to make myself useful among my color in this city. It was contempt for my moral and religious opinions in private that drove me thus before a public. Had experience more plainly shown me that it was the nature of man to crush his fellow, I should not have thought it so hard" (Stewart [1833] 1987, 70). Marilyn Richardson points out the irony that, although Stewart's speeches called for the liberation of all men and women, when published in William Lloyd Garrison's abolitionist newspaper, the *Liberator*, they were "for the sake of editorial propriety" relegated to the "Ladies' Department" (1987, 11).

After leaving slavery Isabella Baumfree (1797–1883) moved to New York City, became a domestic worker, and joined a religious commune. In 1843, at that time about forty-six years old, Baumfree declared herself to be Sojourner Truth, called by God to travel and preach. In this manner she began her career as a lecturer. She told her story across Long Island and entered Connecticut and then Massachusetts, where she joined the Northampton Association of Education and Industry. While in Massachusetts she met some of the leading abolitionists, including William Lloyd Garrison, Frederick Douglass, David Ruggles, Parker Pillsbury, and Wendell Phillips. It was during her affiliation with the association that she sharpened her speaking skills.

At the Akron, Ohio, Woman's Rights Convention in 1851, Sojourner Truth publicly validated all women when she contradicted previous speakers who had claimed women weak and helpless. Truth, after observing convention proceedings for one day, asked for permission to speak. Permission was granted even though many of the women feared that Truth's appearance would damage their cause by association with the slavery issue. It was on this occasion that she delivered her well-known "Ain't I a Woman" speech. Interestingly, the speech, quite popular among women activists today, received little attention at the time it was delivered. No mention of it was made in the conference proceedings. In this speech she pointed to contradictions exemplified in her ability to perform physical tasks as well as any man and reminded her audience that Jesus was the product of God and a woman, without the help of a man. Several years later, at the 9 May 1867 meeting of the American Equal Rights Association (AERA), Truth entered the debate over the proposed Fifteenth Amendment to grant black men but not women the right to vote. There she estimated the consequence of such a change on black women in particular: "There is a great stir about colored men getting their rights, but not a word about the colored woman; and if colored men get their rights, and not colored women get theirs, you see the colored men will be masters over the women, and it will be just as bad as it was before. . . . I want women to have their rights. In the courts women have no right, no voice; nobody speaks for them. I wish woman to have her voice there among the pettifoggers. If it is not a fit place for women, it is unfit for me to be there (Truth [1867] 1995, 28). A former slave, Truth, perhaps more than any of the other black women activists discussed in this chapter, embodied the arguments she made in support of women and abolition. She spoke not of weakness but of power, "the lack of power that men ascribe to womankind and the presence of her own power and the power of all women" (Yellin 1989, 80).

After emancipation black women speakers concentrated on the newly freed women in the South, who needed training and protection. They addressed women's rights conventions and church conferences, and they organized their own gatherings to defend their honor and claim their place in public life. Frances Harper continued to lecture on convergence in the plights of black and white women. In her 1866 address to the Eleventh National Woman's Right's Convention, "We Are All Bound up Together," she described her shabby treatment by the state of Ohio two years earlier upon the death of her husband Fenton Harper. She acknowledged that "justice is not fulfilled so long as woman is unequal before the law." Later in that same speech, however, she expressed doubt that all white women could be counted on to look out for the best interests of black women: "I do not believe that white women are dewdrops just exhaled from the skies. I think that like men they may be divided into three classes, the good, the bad, and the indifferent. The good would vote according to their convictions and principles; the bad, as dictated by prejudice or malice; and the indifferent will vote on the strongest side of the question, with the winning party" (Harper [1866] 1990c, 217–18). Harper's words here indicate black women's awareness that although there were common interests among black and white women, there were also major differences.

The black church provided a number of rhetorical opportunities for black preaching women and black women advocates of such secular causes as woman's rights and abolitionism. As C. Eric Lincoln and Lawrence H. Mamiya point out, "many of these community service and political activities stemmed from a moral concern to uplift the race that was deeply rooted in religious motivation" (1990, 281). In fact, nearly all the women discussed in this essay were active members of black churches. It is not surprising, then, that much of the discourse on women's rights emerged from church women such as those associated with the Black Baptist Convention.

Lucy Wilmot Smith (1861–1890) spoke of black women's needs to a largely male audience at the 1886 meeting of the American National Baptist Convention. At the time of her address she was historian of the association and, along with two other Baptist churchwomen, Mary Cook and Virginia Broughton, led the challenge against this predominantly male organization (Higginbotham 1993). Smith opened her address, "The Future Colored Girl," by decrying the lack of adequate professional training for all women through the ages, and she closed by describing in particular the black woman's condition. She cataloged employment options for black women, among them raising poultry, small fruit or flowers; bee farming; dairying; lecturing; newspaper work; photography; medicine; teaching; and practicing elocution. Her point was that black women needed to explore a range of work opportunities in order to move beyond domestic labor toward some independence: "It is one of the evils of the day that from babyhood girls are taught to look forward to the time when they will be supported by a father, a brother or somebody's [sic] else brother. In teaching her that in whatever field of labor she enters she will abandon after a few years is teaching her to despise the true dignity of labor. The boy is taught to fill this life with as many hard strokes as possible. The girl should receive the same lesson" (Smith 1887, 74). She spoke uncompromisingly of the lack of training and employment opportunities for black women. A close friend and colleague, Mary Cook, eulogized her as follows: "She was connected with all the leading interest of her race and denomination. Her pen and voice always designated her position so clearly that no one need mistake her motive" (Higginbotham 1993, 126). Cook, in an essay prepared for an 1890 work titled *The Negro Baptist Pulpit: A Collection of Sermons and Papers,* encouraged the church to give women more responsibilities for "the salvation of the world" and to enlist them "to labor by the side of the men" so that "it will not be many years before a revolution will be felt all over this broad land, and the heathen will no longer walk in darkness, but will praise God, the light of their salvation" (Brawley [1890] 1971, 285).

In the 1890s black women organized themselves nationally, in part as a result of the powerful rhetorical activities of Ida B. Wells. In 1895 Josephine St. Pierre Ruffin, a Boston woman's activist, issued a call for a conference of black women. One concern was an open letter from John W. Jacks, president of the Missouri Press Association. The letter attacked Wells's character and by implication the morality of all black women in an attempt to rebut Ida Wells's accounts of southern lynching. As a result of Ruffin's call, the First Congress of Colored Women convened on 29 July 1895 in Boston. On the program at the 1895 conference were the names of several prominent black women who spoke on issues affecting all black women.

One of the most provocative addresses, "The Value of Race Literature," was delivered by Victoria Earle Matthews (1861–1907). Matthews, born in Fort Valley, Georgia, moved to New York in 1873. She became a journalist and helped to organize the Women's Loyal Union of New York and Brooklyn. In the speech Matthews paraded before her elite audience the range of stereotypical black characters portrayed in literature by whites, and she called for those present to take the lead in creating more literature of their own. But the speech more specifically focused on women's rights was "The Awakening of the Afro-American Woman," delivered in 1897 at the San Francisco meeting of the Society of Christian Endeavor. A former slave, Matthews recalled slavery's past horrors: "As I stand here to-day clothed in the garments of Christian womanhood, the horrible days of slavery, out of which I came, seem as a dream that is told, some horror incredible. Indeed, could they have been, and are not?" (Matthews [1897] 1995, 150). Matthews also protested the laws forbidding mixed marriages, laws which, she claimed, disgraced black women most: "As long as the affections are controlled by legislation in defiance of Christian law, making infamous the union of black and white, we shall have unions without the sanction of the law, and children without legal parentage, to the degradation of black womanhood and the disgrace of white manhood" (154).

At the World's Congress of Representative Women race activists addressed white women about black women. The congress, part of the Columbian Exposition, was held 15–22 May 1893 in Chicago. The women's exhibit was to illuminate the accomplishments of American women, but only after much political maneuvering were a few prominent black women invited to participate. Fannie Williams, well-known in Chicago women's circles, presented one of the major addresses, "The Intellectual Progress of the Colored Women of the United States since the Emancipation Proclamation."

Fannie Barrier Williams (1855–1944) was born to a prominent New York family and attended the Collegiate Institute of Brockport, the New England Conservatory of Music, and the School of Fine Arts in Washington, D.C., where she taught for almost ten years. Williams eventually settled in Chicago and gained a solid reputation as a speaker. In her speech to the Congress Williams spoke of common womanhood shared by all those present. Given the constraints under which she spoke, Williams wisely emphasized similarities rather than differences. She argued that many black women were rapidly becoming social and intellectual equals to white women and that those who were not needed their support. Such support, she claimed, would be in the best interest of all women: "The fixed policy of persecutions and injustice against a class of women who are weak and defenseless will be necessarily hurtful to the cause of all women. Colored women are becoming more and more a part of the social forces that must help to determine the questions that so concern women generally. . . . If it be the high purpose of these deliberations to lessen the resistance to woman's progress, you can not fail to be interested in our struggles against the many oppositions that harass us" (Williams [1893] 1995, 118).

Anna Julia Cooper (1858–1964), present at both the National Conference of Colored Women and the Congress of Representative Women, delivered her most challenging defense of black women at the 1886 Convocation of Colored Clergy in Washington, D.C. She criticized the clergy and the Episcopalian Church for discriminating against women. Cooper taught at Wilberforce College in Xenia, Ohio, from 1884 to 1885, then returned to St. Augustine's College in Raleigh, North Carolina, where she began her education, and remained there until 1887. Cooper then moved to Washington, D.C., where she held several teaching positions. She was also in the vanguard of the black women's club movement, helping to organize the Washington Colored Women's League.

In her speech "Womanhood A Vital Element in the Regeneration and Progress of a Race," she rehearsed the history of women in general and the future prospects for the southern black woman in particular. Like Frances Harper twenty years earlier, Cooper employed the "same but different" argument directed to audiences throughout the century. Appealing, on the one hand, to a common womanhood, Cooper highlighted, on the other, those differences resulting from slavery and color prejudice: "With all the wrongs and neglects of her past, with all the weakness, the debasement, the moral thralldom of her present, the black woman of to-day stands mute and wondering at the Herculean task devolving upon her. But the cycles wait for her. No other hand can move the lever. She must be loosed from her bands and set to work" (Cooper [1892] 1995, 63).

Lynching

That the entry "antilynching movement" in *Black Women in America: An Historical Encyclopedia* (1994) is essentially an article about Ida Wells indicates clearly the extent of her campaign against mob violence. Although most of the speakers discussed in this chapter spoke out against lynching, none did it more effectively and more consistently than Ida B. Wells. This discussion of antilynching discourse also centers on this forceful speaker.

In manner of speaking and reputation, Wells can be compared to Cary. Both were bold, straightforward, and hard-hitting. Wells also attended the 1893 World's Congress of Representative Women, but unlike her contemporaries Frances Harper and Fannie Barrier Williams, Wells had no official slot on the program of speakers. Instead, she positioned herself near the Haitian Pavilion, where Frederick Douglass was presiding, and distributed copies of an eighty-one-page protest pamphlet, *The Reason Why the Colored American Is Not in the World's Columbian Exposition.* The pamphlet contained pieces by Douglass; Ferdinand Barnett, a prominent Chicago attorney who later married Wells; I. Garland Penn, a newspaperman; and Wells herself. Over ten thousand copies were circulated during the fair. But this was only one of many causes Wells espoused. Wells the social activist spoke out over a period of almost forty years, until her death in 1931, against the denial of women's rights, against racism generally, and, of course, against the practice of lynching.

Ida B. Wells (1862–1931), born in Holly Springs, Mississippi, was the child of former slaves. Both parents died of yellow fever in 1878, leaving Wells, at sixteen the oldest, in charge of five siblings. Taking two sisters with her, she eventually moved to Memphis to teach. However, she soon discovered that she did not adapt well to the profession's constraints, and she confesses in her autobiography, "I never cared for teaching" (Wells 1970, 31). In 1889 Wells became editor and part owner of the *Memphis Free Speech and Headlight.* Her editorials protested racial injustice in education, voting rights, and public transportation. Eager to get her newspaper into the homes of those who could not read, Wells printed several editions on easily identified pink paper. Not until 1892, after three of her friends had been lynched in Memphis and her newspaper office had been burned down by an angry mob, did Wells launch a verbal war against lynching that continued into the twentieth century. In response to the events in Memphis, a group of prominent black women from New York and Brooklyn organized a testimonial in her honor at Lyric Hall on 5 October 1892. On this occasion Wells delivered her first public speech, "Southern Horrors: Lynch Law in All Its Phases," in which she proposed corrective action against lynching: "Nothing is more definitely settled than [that] he must act for himself. I have shown how he may employ the boycott, emigration, and the press, and I feel that by a combination of all these agencies can be effectually stamped out lynch law, that last relic of barbarism and slavery" (Wells [1892] 1989, 419). Many prominent blacks, including Wells, had convinced themselves that those being lynched were indeed guilty and deserved to die. But after incidents such as the one in Memphis, they began to recognize lynching as an attempt to suppress black progress. Wells stressed this point in her first public speech.

Not limiting herself to this country, she took her antilynching campaign to Europe and found favor there, in the face of disparagement by the southern press in the United States. Wells traveled to England and Scotland in April 1893 to deliver a series of antilynching lectures. She returned to England for a six-month stay in 1894, serving as paid correspondent for the *Chicago Inter-Ocean*. On 13 February 1893, before leaving for her first tour of England, Wells addressed the Boston Monday Lectureship. In this speech, "Lynch Law in All Its Phases," Wells rehearsed in detail the Memphis incident and appealed to her audience with gruesome details of a lynching in Paris, Texas, only two weeks earlier. She appealed to this predominantly white audience for public outcry, advancing her belief that their failure to act was a result of ignorance rather than apathy and drawing on their concern for America's reputation:

> I am before the American people to-day . . . because of a deep-seated conviction that the country at large does not know the extent to which lynch law prevails in parts of the Republic, nor the conditions which force into exile those who speak the truth. I cannot believe that the apathy and indifference which so largely obtains regarding mob rule is other than the result of ignorance of the true situation. . . . Repeated attacks on the life, liberty and happiness of any citizen or class of citizens are attacks on distinctive American institutions; such attacks imperiling as they do the foundation of government, law and order, merit the thoughtful consideration of far-sighted Americans; not from a standpoint of

sentiment, not even so much from a standpoint of justice to a weak race, as from a desire to preserve our institutions. (Wells [1893] 1995, 80)

Racial Uplift

In the midst of the struggle for freedom and equality, black women pressed their people toward self-help, self-improvement, and racial uplift. Racial uplift was emphasized from two perspectives: encouraging those who were in need to take initiative; and challenging those who had accomplished to "lift" those who had not. Although public address focused specifically on improving the working and living conditions of black women is considered above in the section called "Women's Rights," the speeches of three activist educators who argued for general assistance to southern blacks after the Civil War are considered under the heading of "Racial Uplift." Frances Harper made a point of addressing directly those in need of social and emotional uplift in the post–Civil War South. Edmonia G. Highgate spent her brief life teaching the newly freed in the South and lecturing for financial support in the North. Lucy Craft Laney in 1893 organized a day and boarding school in Augusta, Georgia; developed the city's first kindergarten; and stressed in her speeches to educated blacks their crucial role in the work of racial advancement.

Frances Harper, who spoke on all the issues discussed in this essay, adopted the first perspective—encouraging self-help. She availed herself of every opportunity to speak directly to the people for whom she fought, traveling throughout the Midwest before the war and in the deep South after the war. In a biographical sketch William Still writes, "For the best part of several years, since the war, she has traveled very extensively through the Southern States, going on the plantations and amongst the lowly, as well as to the cities and towns, addressing schools, Churches, meetings in Court Houses, Legislative Halls, &c., and, sometimes, under the most trying and hazardous circumstances" (1872, 767). According to one story, during an appearance in Darlington, South Carolina, instead of standing in the pulpit of the church in which she spoke, she stood near the door where those outside as well as those inside could hear her.

In a 21 September 1860 letter to Jane E. Hitchcock Jones, a Quaker abolitionist from Ohio, she expresses her view that such lectures among free and formerly enslaved blacks help to lift morale and develop self-esteem:

There are a number of colored settlements in the West, where a few words of advice and encouragement among our people might act as a stimulant and charm; and if they would change the public opinion of the country, they should not find it, I hope, a useless work to strive to elevate the character of the colored people, not merely by influencing the public *around* them but *among* them; for after all, this prejudice of which such complaint has been made, if I understand it aright, is simply a great protest of human minds rising up against slavery, and so hating it for themselves that they learn not only to despise it, but the people that submit to it, and those identified with them by race. (Harper 1992, 82)

Harper must have recognized the opportunity for instruction that public speaking afforded to those who did not read and did not subscribe to newspapers. She also wrote of giving lectures privately to women at no charge. Her speeches to such audiences were usually impromptu, and generally journalists were not present; consequently, no extant texts of these spontaneous orations remain.

Born to former slaves in Syracuse, New York, Edmonia Highgate (1844–1870) lived for only twenty-six years, but during those years she did all she could for racial uplift, alternately teaching the newly freed in the South and lecturing for their support in the North. At the age of twenty Highgate was sent to Norfolk, Virginia, by the American Missionary Association to teach. After three months of intense work, she had a mental breakdown and returned to Syracuse. Shortly after her return Highgate addressed the 1864 National Convention of Colored Men, held in Syracuse. Highgate and Frances Harper were the only women to address the exclusively male organization. When Frederick Douglass introduced her he said, "You have your Anna Dickinsons; and we have ours. We wish to meet you at every point" (*Minutes* 1969, 14). Douglass was referring here to the orator Anna Dickinson, who had achieved fame after her 1861 Philadelphia address on "The Rights and Wrongs of Women" at the age of nineteen. Although the convention minutes do not include the text of Highgate's speech, a summary in the 26 October 1864 *New Orleans Tribune* demonstrates the tenor of her political activism and astuteness: "Miss Highgate said she would not be quite in her place, perhaps, if a girl as she is, she should tell the Convention what they ought to do; but she had, with others *thought* about what had been proposed and those thoughts she would tell them. Miss Highgate was evidently a strong *Lincoln* Man; so much so, that she felt that Gen. Fremont ought not to be a candidate. . . . Miss Highgate urged the Convention to press on, to not abate hope until the glorious time spoken of to-night, shall come" (Sterling 1984, 296).

While back in New York, Highgate lectured to raise funds for freedmen's relief. She returned to the South in 1865, teaching for a while in Maryland, Louisiana, and Mississippi. After four years she resumed lecturing in New York, New England, and Canada. In February 1879 she spoke at the Thirty-sixth Annual Meeting of the Massachusetts Anti-Slavery Society. Following a lengthy address by John M. Langston, a prominent black activist from Ohio, Highgate warned against hasty optimism. A paraphrase in the *National Anti-Slavery Standard* stated the following:

> Miss Highgate said that, after laboring five years as a teacher in the South, it was perhaps appropriate for her to give a report on the state of things there. In her opinion, even if the Fifteenth Amendment should now be ratified, it would be only a paper ratification. Even in the instruction given to the ignorant there lacks some of the main essentials of right instruction. The teachers sent out by the evangelical organizations do very little to remove caste-prejudice, the twin sister of slavery. . . . President Lincoln was accustomed to take credit to himself for moving forward no faster than the people demanded. The Republicans in the South do no better. We need *Anti-Slavery* teachers there; teachers who will show that it is safe to do right. The Anti-Slavery Society must not disband, because its work in the South is not yet half done; and if not now thoroughly done, it will have to be done over again. (*National Anti-Slavery Standard* 1870)

In a June 1870 letter to the abolitionists Gerrit and Ann Smith, Highgate mentions the advice of Theodore Tilton, famous speaker and friend, who, impressed with her speaking skills, urged her "to write a lecture to interest the general public, deliver it as other lecturers do and you will then be on your way to secure the funds necessary to aid the cause to which you are so devoted" (Sterling 1984, 301). Highgate implied in the letter that she might like to visit the Smiths to gain the privacy needed to write such a lecture. But she never did so. A month later she requested instead that the AMA send her south again to Jackson, Mississippi, for another teaching tour. She never returned to the South, however. Edmonia Highgate died in Syracuse in October 1870.

As the title of Lucy Laney's 1899 speech, "The Burden of the Educated Colored Woman," indicates, the lecture centered on racial
uplift. During the post-Reconstruction period, those who had acquired education and prosperity felt a duty to educate those less
fortunate. This education extended to morality and economy as well
as reading and writing, for as Paula Giddings, at one point quoting
Laney, writes, "Whatever their views about social sanctions, one reason for the emphasis on morality was that lack of it could be
impoverishing. . . . a good part of the philosophy of racial uplift had
to do with lifting the burdens of 'ignorance and immorality' with
'true culture and character, linked with—cash'" (1984, 102). Although
Laney called this challenge a "burden," she was not resentful but
despairing that the times had created this triple burden of "shame
and crime and prejudice." The "shame" Laney saw as a consequence
of nonlegalized slave marriages, poor parenting skills, and ignorance
of hygiene. The large numbers of young men and women incarcer-
ated provided evidence of the "crime." The "prejudice" came from
those in power, who made it difficult to overcome the other two
burdens. This speech was delivered in 1899 at the third Hampton
Negro Conference on the Virginia campus of Hampton University,
one of the black schools formed after the Civil War. At these annual
conferences Hampton graduates and other prominent race leaders
discussed strategies toward racial improvement. As was the case at
many such conferences, the men and women met separately, under
the unfortunate assumption that women operated in a separate
sphere and had no need to address issues that were, in fact, of collective importance.

Lucy Craft Laney (1854–1933) was born in Macon, Georgia, to free,
literate parents. Her father, an ordained Presbyterian minister, earned
enough money while enslaved to purchase freedom for himself and his
wife. Laney was graduated from Atlanta University in 1873, a member
of the first graduating class. After teaching for ten years, Laney established a school in Augusta, Georgia, which eventually became the Haines
Normal and Industrial Institute. Near the end of the century Laney, one
of several black women who founded their own schools, offered a curriculum in liberal arts as well as vocational training and was especially
interested in the education of girls. By the time she spoke to the Hampton Negro Conference in 1899, Laney's school was on its way to becoming

an established success. In "The Burden of the Educated Colored Woman" she called specifically on "the educated Negro woman" not only to teach but to speak. Laney argued that "as a public lecturer she may give advice, helpful suggestions, and important knowledge that will change a whole community and start its people on the upward way." She cited the example of Frances Harper (as well as four other women). She closed her speech with a story about a group of male laborers who successfully lifted "a heavy piece of timber to the top of a building" only when they asked the women to help them, rein-forcing her message that women as well as men were needed to ensure successful racial uplift: "Today not only the men on top call, but a needy race,—the whole world, calls loudly to the cultured Negro women to come to the rescue. Do they hear? Are they com-ing? Will they push?" (Laney [1899] 1992, 174).

Summary

The rhetorical activities of numerous other nineteenth-century black women speakers have not been mentioned here. These women spoke their minds from platform and pulpit and went to work cor-recting the wrongs they saw before them. They left no records, wrote no books, organized no conferences; but they helped to establish a tradition of political activism among black women. The activities of the women discussed merely illustrate the ranges of issues brought to public attention by women using oratory to effect change. The general response of white audiences to the very presence of intelli-gent, articulate black women was often much stronger than their response to anything the women had to say. These speakers were the embodiment of their messages—whether the message was anti-slavery, feminist, or an appeal for racial dignity. They authenticated their arguments; the messengers were their messages. African Ameri-can women of the nineteenth century participated in history largely through their rhetorical activities. The pages of the *Woman's Era* pro-vide ample evidence of their participation in the political discourse of their time. On the front page of its 24 March 1894 inaugural edi-tion can be found a photograph and tribute to Lucy Stone, pioneer women's rights advocate and anti-slavery lecturer, known for her moving oratory. The Women's Era Club members chose as their motto a phrase from her last message, "Make the world better." (*The Women's Era*, Vol. 1, No. 1, 24 March 1894, p. 1).

Note

I wrote most of this essay during the spring of 1995, while on leave from the Department of English at the University of Maryland, College Park. I thank the department and the College of Arts and Humanities for the research time.

References

Brawley, Edward M. [1890] 1971. *The Negro Baptist Pulpit: A Collection of Sermons and Papers*. Freeport, N.Y.: Books for Libraries Press.

Calloway-Thomas, Carolyn. 1994. "Cary, Mary Ann Shadd." In *Black Women in America: An Historical Encyclopedia*, Vol. 2, edited by Darlene Clark Hine et al., 224–26. Bloomington: Indiana University Press.

Cary, Mary Ann Shadd. 1986a. "Mary Ann Shadd Cary to Frederick Douglass, 25 January 1849." In *The Black Abolitionist Papers*, Vol. 4: *The United States 1847–1858*, edited by C. Peter Ripley, 31–34. Chapel Hill: University of North Carolina Press.

———. 1986b. "Sermon" [6 April 1858]. In *The Black Abolitionist Papers*, Vol. 2: *Canada, 1830–1865*, edited by C. Peter Ripley, 388–91. Chapel Hill: University of North Carolina Press.

Cooper, Anna Julia. [1892] 1995. "Womanhood a Vital Element in the Regeneration and Progress of a Race." In *With Pen and Voice: A Critical Anthology of Nineteenth-Century African-American Women*, edited by Shirley Wilson Logan, 53–74. Carbondale: Southern Illinois University Press.

DeBoer, Clara Merritt. 1994. *Be Jubilant My Feet: African American Abolitionists in the American Missionary Association 1839–1861*. New York: Garland.

Foster, Frances Smith, ed. 1990. *A Brighter Coming Day: A Frances Ellen Watkins Harper Reader*. New York: Feminist Press.

Franklin, John Hope, and Alfred Moss. 1988. *From Slavery to Freedom: A History of Negro Americans*. New York: McGraw-Hill.

Giddings, Paula. 1984. *When and Where I Enter: The Impact of Black Women on Race and Sex in America*. New York: William Morrow.

Harper, Frances E. W. 1990a. "Could We Trace the Record of Every Human Heart." In *A Brighter Coming Day: A Frances Ellen Watkins Harper Reader*, edited by Frances Smith Foster, 100–102. New York: Feminist Press.

———. [1859] 1990b. "Our Greatest Want." In *A Brighter Coming Day: A Frances Ellen Watkins Harper Reader*, edited by Frances Smith Foster, 102–4. New York: Feminist Press.

———. [1866] 1990c. "We Are All Bound up Together." In *A Brighter Coming Day: A Frances Ellen Watkins Harper Reader*, edited by Frances Smith Foster, 217–19. New York: Feminist Press.

———. 1992. "Letter to Jane E. Hitchcock Jones, 21 September 1860." In *The Black Abolitionist Papers*, Vol. 5: *The United States, 1859–1865*, edited by C. Peter Ripley, 81–83. Chapel Hill: University of North Carolina Press.

Higginbotham, Evelyn Brooks. 1993. *Righteous Discontent: The Women's Movement in the Black Baptist Church, 1880–1920.* Cambridge: Harvard University Press.

Laney, Lucy. [1899] 1992. "The Burden of the Educated Colored Woman." In *The Rhetoric of Struggle: Public Address by African American Women,* edited by Robbie Walker, 167–74. New York: Garland Publishing.

Lincoln, C. Eric, and Lawrence H. Mamiya. 1990. *The Black Church in the African American Experience.* Durham: Duke University Press.

Matthews, Victoria Earle. [1897] 1995. "The Awakening of the Afro-American Woman." In *With Pen and Voice: A Critical Anthology of Nineteenth-Century African-American Women,* edited by Shirley Wilson Logan, 149–55. Carbondale: Southern Illinois University Press.

Minutes of the Proceedings of the National Negro Conventions 1830–1864. 1969. Ed. Howard Holman Bell. New York: Arno Press.

National Anti-Slavery Standard. 1870 (5 February).

Remond, Sarah Parker. [1859] 1985a. "Speech at the Music Hall." In *The Black Abolitionist Papers,* Vol. 1: *The British Isles 1830–1865,* edited by C. Peter Ripley, 435–44. Chapel Hill: University of North Carolina Press.

———. [1859] 1985b. "Speech at the Athenauem." In *The Black Abolitionist Papers,* Vol. 1: *The British Isles, 1830–1865,* edited by C. Peter Ripley, 457–61. Chapel Hill: University of North Carolina Press.

Richardson, Marilyn, ed. 1987. *Maria W. Stewart, America's First Black Woman Political Writer: Essays and Speeches.* Bloomington: Indiana University Press.

Ripley, C. Peter, ed. 1985. *The Black Abolitionist Papers.* Vol. 1: *The British Isles 1830–1865.* Chapel Hill: University of North Carolina Press.

———. 1986. *The Black Abolitionist Papers.* Vol. 2: *Canada, 1830–1865.* Chapel Hill: University of North Carolina Press.

Smith, Lucy Wilmot. 1887. "The Future Colored Girl." In *Minutes and Addresses of the American National Baptist Convention,* Saint Louis, Mo., 25–29 August 1886, 68–74. Jackson, Miss.: J. J. Spelman.

Sterling, Dorothy, ed. 1984. *We Are Your Sisters: Black Women in the Nineteenth Century.* New York: Norton.

Stewart, Maria W. [1833] 1987. "Mrs. Stewart's Farewell Address to her Friends in the City of Boston." In *Maria W. Stewart, America's First Black Woman Political Writer: Essays and Speeches,* edited by Marilyn Richardson, 65–74. Bloomington: Indiana University Press.

———. [1832] 1995a. "An Address Delivered before the Afric-American Female Intelligence Society of Boston." In *With Pen and Voice: A Critical Anthology of Nineteenth-Century African-American Women,* edited by Shirley Wilson Logan, 11–16. Carbondale: Southern Illinois University Press.

———. [1832] 1995b. "Lecture Delivered at the Franklin Hall." In *With Pen and Voice: A Critical Anthology of Nineteenth-Century African-American Women,* edited by Shirley Wilson Logan, 6–10. Carbondale: Southern Illinois University Press.

Still, William. 1872. *The Underground Rail Road*. Philadelphia: Porter & Coates.

Truth, Sojourner. [1867] 1995. "Speech Delivered to the First Annual Meeting of the American Equal Rights Association." In *With Pen and Voice: A Critical Anthology of Nineteenth-Century African-American Women*, edited by Shirley Wilson Logan, 28–29. Carbondale: Southern Illinois University Press.

Wells, Ida B. 1970. *Crusade for Justice: The Autobiography of Ida B. Wells*. Chicago: University of Chicago Press.

———. [1892] 1989. "Southern Horrors: Lynch Law in All Its Phases." In *Man Cannot Speak for Her*, Vol. 2: *Key Texts of the Earliest Feminists*, edited by Karlyn Kohrs Campbell, 385–419. Westport, Conn.: Greenwood Press.

———. [1893] 1995. "Lynch Law in All Its Phases." In *With Pen and Voice: A Critical Anthology of Nineteenth-Century African-American Women*, edited by Shirley Wilson Logan, 80–99. Carbondale: Southern Illinois University Press.

Wesley, Dorothy Porter. 1994. "Remond, Sarah Parker." In *Black Women in America: An Historical Encyclopedia*, Vol. 2, edited by Darlene Clark Hine et al., 972–74. Bloomington: Indiana University Press.

Williams, Fannie Barrier. [1893] 1995. "The Intellectual Progress of the Colored Women of the United States since the Emancipation Proclamation." In *With Pen and Voice: A Critical Anthology of Nineteenth-Century African-American Women*, edited by Shirley Wilson Logan, 106–19. Carbondale: Southern Illinois University Press.

The Woman's Era (Boston, Mass.). 24 March 1894, 1 June 1894, April 1895.

Yellin, Jean Fagan. 1989. *Women & Sisters: The Antislavery Feminists in American Culture*. New Haven: Yale University Press.

Part 3

Authorized by Faith

There is a feminine as well as a masculine side to truth; and . . . these are related not as inferior and superior, not as better or worse, not as weaker or stronger, but as complements—complements in one necessary and symmetric whole.

Anna Julia Haywood Cooper

Dhuoda's *Handbook for William* and the Mother's Manual Tradition

Clella I. Jaffe

The noblewoman Dhuoda, who lived in the Frankish kingdom of Charlemagne's heirs, wrote a manual of moral instructions to guide her son, William (826–850), who had been sent to the court of Charlemagne's grandson, Charles the Bald. Her work survives in nine fragments of a late-tenth- or early-eleventh-century manuscript; in a complete, comparatively accurate manuscript from the fourteenth century; and in an error-filled seventeenth-century copy. Recent scholarly work collating these texts has resulted in three contemporary versions (Bowers 1977; Neel 1991; Riché 1975)[1] that make this work accessible in both French and English. Dhuoda's text stands as the lone woman author's voice from the ninth century. Moreover, it is the first surviving mother's manual—a genre that King (1991) calls the principal genre of laywomen in the ensuing centuries.

In its broadest definition, a genre is "any group of works selected on the basis of some shared features" (Reichert 1978, 57). Genres are cultural creations that operate within a social code of behavior established between the rhetor and the audience (Dubrow 1982); that is, a genre provides a set of "frames" or "fixes"—mental forms or schemata—that the rhetor uses to compose a work and the audience uses to take it in (Colie 1973). Genres can be transformed by varying the speaker or the addressee in ways that "loosen" or change the genre (Fowler 1982). This chapter will argue that a group of rhetor mothers created a unique "frame" within the broader genre of courtesy literature when they penned advice to their children. This led to a new type of rhetor-audience relationship, one influenced by both biological and socially legitimized role expectations.

Although nearly five centuries elapsed before Christine de Pisan wrote the next known mother's manual, Karen Cherewatuk and Ulrike

Wiethaus (1993) contend that existing examples of women's literature are only a fraction of the total output of their rhetorical endeavors. Marie Ann Mayeski concurs, suggesting, "Dhuoda's Handbook . . . teases us with the possibility that she is not an extraordinary phenomena of the early Middle Ages but an example of a larger tradition that was subsequently lost" (1988, 32).

In contrast, Dale Spender (1980) argues that we cannot assume that female authors, scattered as they were in time and space, knew of each other's work. Women, as a muted group, do not necessarily pass on their rhetorical traditions, and new writers in their own generations must discover afresh the forms necessary to fit their rhetorical situations (Bitzer 1968). Alastair Fowler terms this "polygenesis" (1982, 154). However, whether they were part of a tradition largely lost or whether individual women created similar works arising from similar exigencies, these mother-rhetors produced advice manuals for their offspring that are enough alike to merit study as a group.

The purpose of this chapter is to examine the mother's manual as a "frame" or "fix" within women's rhetorical traditions. Since Dhuoda's book is the earliest extant manual, it deserves to be analyzed in detail as a rhetorical act as well as a representative of implicit theories mother-rhetors held regarding the art of persuasion. Her text demonstrates the practical use of rhetorical forms as means of "describing and directing life" (Neel 1991, xiv) in the private realm of mothers, rather than the public world of fathers.

This chapter contains a survey of the broader category of courtesy literature. This is followed by a look at Dhuoda and the circumstances that compelled her to write. Next her manual is examined as a paradigm of the genre. And finally mother's manuals in general will be discussed, and the chapter will conclude by returning to the larger issues regarding women's rhetorical traditions raised by Cherewatuk and Wiethaus (1993) and Spender (1980).

Courtesy Literature

Courtesy literature is defined as "didactic literature meant to serve as a guide for secular life" (Bornstein 1983, 11). It is especially suited to female voices because its advisory and didactic purposes intersect with traditional social expectations in which women bear and socialize children, advise husbands, and counsel female friends and relatives in the private settings of their homes. Etiquette books fall broadly into this category—as do modern-day advice columns, a territory in rhetoric generally reserved for women (Regnier-Bohler 1992). Three historical genres are related to mother's manuals: the *speculum* (or mirror), the *enchiridion* (handbook or manual), and the epistle.

The didactic genre called speculum was so common that a journal devoted to medieval topics is named *Speculum*. Medieval readers saw *specula* as mirrors in which they could "gaze at themselves and other folks—mirrors of history and doctrine and morals, mirrors of princes and lovers and fools" (Rand, qtd. in Bradley 1954, 101). Through attentive reading they could learn moral truths and Christian doctrines and, as a result, purify their souls.[2]

In addition, there was a long tradition of manuals or handbooks (Greek: *enchiridion*)—summaries of philosophical or religious moral teachings. Widely circulated examples include the Stoic philosopher Epictetus's *Enchiridion* ([138] 1948) and Saint Augustine's *Enchiridion on Faith, Hope, and Love* ([421] 1955, 339). Augustine explains its purpose, "You [Laurentius] have asked for an *enchiridion*, something you could carry around, not just baggage for your bookshelf. . . . It is not enough just to put an *enchiridion* in the hand. It is also necessary that a great zeal be kindled in the heart."

Finally, epistles (*epistula*) are technically almost any written document with a salutation (Cherewatuk and Wiethaus 1993). Originally orality was closely connected to literacy, and ancient rhetoricians did not clearly distinguish between writing and speaking. Authors often dictated epistles, and recipients read them aloud—witness Saint Paul's epistles to the early churches. As early as the fourth century C. Julius Victor in *Ars Rhetorica* linked *epistola* with *sermo* (informal discourse) and virtually declared a letter to be "a type of conversation" (Murphy 1974, 196). Cassiodorus (480–575) applied rhetorical principles to *dictamen,* documents that were originally dictated aloud, resulting in a dialogical quality that seems direct and immediate (Murphy 1974). Since letters are often informal, direct, and flexible as to author, topic, audience, and purpose, they are especially suited for women's self-expression (Cherewatuk and Wiethaus 1993).

Although John Rodden characterizes rhetoric as "a tradition that has emphasized the historically feminine, caregiving, and concrete activities of teaching and advising" (1993, 125), most scholarly studies have examined the rhetoric of men speaking in judicial, legislative, and epideictic settings to adult audiences, predominantly male. While it is probably true that women did not produce as many rhetorical works as men, even when they did write or speak, few of their works were preserved. In addition, the extant creations have been excluded from the canon largely because of the content, audience, and situation in which the rhetoric occurred (Wilson 1984), and mother's manuals are a good example of this. Whereas manuals written by and for adult males are widely available, mother's manuals, written by women for children and young people, are difficult to locate. We now look at the author of the first surviving mother's manual.

The Carolingian Noblewoman, Dhuoda

Dhuoda was born into a wealthy family near the end of Charlemagne's reign. After an excellent liberal arts education—possibly at Charlemagne's palace where noble daughters as well as his sons were schooled (Labarge 1986)—she married Bernard, Count of Septimania (prol.) in 824 in a palace wedding. Bernard—whose father was later canonized as Saint William, the patron saint of knights—was godson of Louis the Pious, Charlemagne's heir. The couple's first son, William, was born on 29 November 826. The next fourteen years were a time of "struggles and disruptions" in the kingdom (prol.) and in Dhuoda's personal life.

Louis's reign was a time of jockeying for power and control of the Carolingian empire. Before he was widowed, he legally divided his lands among his three heirs. However, his second wife, Judith of Bavaria, produced a fourth son, Charles. Judith was determined that young Charles would inherit a portion of the kingdom, and the necessity of reconfiguring the realm to include an additional heir was a source of political maneuvering throughout much of the second quarter of the ninth century.

Dhuoda's personal troubles were related to these events. The ambitious Bernard was in the middle of court intrigues. Because of his royal connections and his military victories, Louis appointed him to be chamberlain—second in command—a post he held for only one winter. That was long enough for Bernard's enemies to portray him as a villain who committed adultery with the empress (Radbertus [836? 851?] 1967). Amid scandalous accusations, Bernard fled; the king was stripped of power; and Judith entered a convent. Both Bernard and Judith maintained their innocence, but he never regained his title even though the king and the empress were eventually restored to power. During this period one of Bernard's brothers was blinded and his sister was drowned as a witch.

Any dreams Dhuoda had for happiness as the wife of a prominent man seem to have been simply that. The couple probably lived separately much of the time. While Bernard participated in public events, his humble Christian spouse retired to Uzès on the Rhone River where she managed both of their estates and interests. This was sometimes difficult; she indicates that she borrowed from both Christians and Jews to maintain their properties and to keep Bernard from abandoning her and William (X.4). Moreover, she probably heard rumors of the alleged affair spread by her husband's enemies. Contemporaries whispered that Charles was really Bernard's son; indeed, there was a marked physical resemblance between the two (Duckett 1972).

In addition to these troubles, Dhuoda alludes to physical problems. She calls herself "a fragile vessel" (I.6) whose "continual illnesses" (X.4) lead her to observe, "the time of my parting hastens, and the suffering of pains everywhere wears my body down" (X.1). The cause of her suffering is unknown. According to Suzanne F. Wemple (1981), the average Carolingian woman lived only thirty-six years, largely due to childbearing problems, inadequate health care, and dietary deficiencies.

After Louis's death in 840, Bernard returned to Uzès where Dhuoda bore their second son on 22 March 841. Unfortunately, her powerful husband linked his fortunes with the wrong Carolingian heir, and as a result his family was separated. Bernard sent William to Charles's court where the young man may have been a virtual hostage to guarantee his father's loyalty (Labarge 1986). Bernard himself left for Aquitaine where he mustered an army. To insure that at least one heir would survive, he had the bishop bring the yet-unnamed baby to him (prol.). In his thoughtlessness he neglected to inform Dhuoda of the baby's name. In her loneliness and anxiety this grieving mother began her manual on 30 November 841, the day after William turned fifteen, the age of majority. She completed her text in February 843.

Tragedy followed. In 844 Charles executed Bernard for treason. A few years later William unsuccessfully attempted to avenge his father's death. Charles captured and beheaded him in 850; he left no heirs. The career of the infant, also named Bernard, is obscure because of the ninth-century "problem of the Bernards" (Bouchard 1986). According to Allen Cabaniss (1974), he tried to avenge the deaths of both his father and brother and was killed in a riot, ending the family line. In contrast, Bouchard (1986) concludes that Dhuoda's younger son was Bernard Plantagenet, who attempted to murder Charles but was pardoned, married, and became Marquis of Aquitaine. He fathered William the Pious, who endowed the preeminent Benedictine abbey Cluny. If this account is true, Dhuoda's grandson, the original handbook owner's namesake, was the one who put into practice his grandmother's advice.

Dhuoda's Handbook

Dhuoda's manual has received some scholarly attention. All her translators wrote extended introductions. Carol Neel (1991) summarizes Dhuoda's life and the contents of the manual. Myra E. Bowers's (1977) introduction is especially useful for its discussion of Dhuoda's style. Pierre Riché (1975) collates the three manuscripts and provides invaluable background information on the manuscript tradition. In addition, other scholars have discussed Dhuoda in larger works. Allen Cabaniss (1974) is quite negative about her style and the personal tone of her work. In contrast, James Marchand (1984) sees Dhuoda's work as valuable for its revelations about the intellectual and spiritual life of her age. Peter Dronke (1984) is similarly appreciative. He describes her manual as holding out the Christian-aristocratic goals in a unique fashion, one that could not be written by a male cleric. Finally, Marie Ann Mayeski (1988) focuses on Dhuoda as a self-confident "model of liberation."

The overriding purposes of Dhuoda's manual are pragmatic. First, she wants William to know how to live in this world and how to prepare for the next. To these ends, Dhuoda prays that William, with God's help, will be able to accept her "helpful words" and understand to his own "profit" (prol.). She articulates her twofold intent in the prologue: "Also from the beginning of this little book until the end, . . . in every way, and in all cases [it] has been written for the salvation of your soul and body . . . for it is necessary for you in everything, my son William, to show yourself in your two tasks as one able to succeed in the world and always able to please God above all" (Bowers 1977, 4, 14).

Dhuoda's roles as a rhetor parallel her socially legitimated maternal roles, and she variously presents herself as mother, teacher, adviser, and spiritual director. Since she is unable to "mother" her younger son, she instructs William to assume her duties when his baby brother is older, using the manual "to teach him, educate him, love him, and call him to progress from good to better" (I.7). Her handbook, in short, is a didactic tool in which she is "instructing" (VII.1) and "shaping" (prol.) her sons' thoughts regarding both spiritual and temporal matters.

Dhuoda also writes as much for herself as for her children. Since the family is separated through circumstances she did not choose, rhetoric is her only means to continue a didactic and advisory relationship with her sons. Were the circumstances different, she would almost certainly not choose this medium; however, the exigency of the situation compels her to apply the implicit theories of rhetoric she has formulated. She sees writing as action, a way of doing what she can no longer do in person. Her prologue continues: "Seeing myself, Dhuoda, living far away from you, my dear son William, filled with anxiety because of this and with the desire to be of aid to you, I am sending you this little manual, written by me, for your scrutiny and education, rejoicing in the fact that, though I am absent in body, this little book will recall to your mind, as you read it, the things you are required to do for my sake" (Marchand 1984, 12).

Her direct and immediate prose makes it apparent that she intends the manual to substitute for her presence. For example, she says, "Dhuoda, your orator is always here . . . [through] this little moral book . . . you may be able to behold me, body and mind, as in a mirror" (Mayeski 1988, 49). She indicates that she is dictating at least parts of the manual; thus, in a very real way, she is speaking directly to her audience. Early in the manual she says, "I ask of you . . . just as if I were with you in person" (I.1) and "Hear me as I direct you and listen carefully" (III.1). She tells William to share the book with his baby brother: "I, your mother Dhuoda, urge you, as if I even now spoke to both of you" (I.7).

In several places Dhuoda protests her inability to write. Some of her statements may reflect her real hesitancy to enter the world of authors, almost exclusively populated by men, and clerics at that. Other protestations may simply be medieval commonplaces of affected modesty—used by speakers or writers to put their hearers in a receptive state of mind (Curtius 1953). Rhetors typically confessed to a general inadequacy, a lack of education, poor language, or poverty of mind, as Dhuoda demonstrates: "Things that are obvious to many people often escape me. Those who are like me lack understanding and have dim insight, but I am even less capable than they" (prol.).

She does seem to approach certain topics hesitantly. For instance, she characterizes didactic writing on the topic of God as *agonizatrio acumine laboris* (I.1)—translated as an "extremely challenging task" (Bowers 1977, 19), "a lofty and perilous task" (Neel 1991, 7), or a "perilous public contest" (Mayeski, 1988, 34). In speaking of the Trinity and other theological abstractions, she will "neither presume or is able" (II.1) to exposit them in full, and her "mind is wrapped in shadows" (I.2); consequently, she refers William to the teachings of experts (male clerics) on the topics. Finally, when she speaks about priests, her spirit "shrinks from the task" (III.11).

In contrast, in her instruction regarding interpersonal behaviors—everyday relationships with such people as peers, counselors, and the poor—her voice is clear and strong. She "instructs," "beseeches," and "counsels" her sons to live worthy secular lives. Similarly, she expresses confidence when she gives practical advice on maintaining a personal relationship with God through prayer and worship, for then she speaks from experience. By the time she writes the practical advice in Book IV, which she terms her *sermone* (homily), she is at her most directive, using phrases such as "I pray you, direct you, and ask of you" (IV.4, 5, 9). Further, she even offers her interpretation of a biblical text, saying, "Here I think he means" (IV.4) rather than quoting or paraphrasing the opinions of scholars, which is her usual custom.

Dhuoda justifies her decision to write in several ways. First, her relationship with her audience is socially sanctioned; indeed, it is her maternal duty to remind her sons of their moral obligations. She takes as exemplars praiseworthy women who were spiritual as well as biological mothers (VII.3)—specifically, Celsus's mother and Augusta, the mother of Saint Symphorian.

Her second justification relates to the manner in which she presents her material. Since she is writing to children, she must simplify the great truths and make them understandable to the young, thus keeping them within her own intellectual capabilities (prol.). She adapts a biblical metaphor (Heb. 5:12) to explain this simplification: "I have seen fit to address myself to you, who are only a boy, in the childish terms appropriate to my own understanding. I have done so as if you were unable to eat solid food but could take in something only like milk . . . I who am but as a child myself have given you milk rather than solid food, for you are also a little one in Christ" (VI.1). She explains that if he were older, she would write of more difficult things in more complex language (I.1).

A number of biblical passages also give her confidence. Since she has asked for God's guidance, she believes that he who enabled the dumb to speak (Isa. 35:6) and made children eloquent (Ps. 8:2) is at her side. If he can make an ass talk (Num. 22:28–30), he can certainly give her insight (I.2). Further, she somewhat playfully depicts herself as an "insistent little bitch" (*catulla*) scrambling under the table with the male puppies (*catulli*) for crumbs from the Lord's table (Matt. 15:21–28). As a female, she must observe from afar the priest "puppies" who minister at the holy altar, but she can gather and pass on worthy words from their intellectual and spiritual crumbs (I.2).

Dhuoda declares her work to be a manual or handbook, and she may have used Augustine's *Enchiridion on Faith, Hope, and Love* (1955) as a model for organization. The saint divides his treatise into books and chapters. Throughout, the Apostles' Creed and the Lord's Prayer undergird his discussion. Dhuoda similarly divides her work into seventy-three chapters with the beatitudes and the Lord's Prayer as the framework. Riché (1975) arranges her chapters into eleven books, presented here. Dhuoda's organizational pattern is topical; she begins and ends with spiritual topics; the material in the middle section consists of practical advice for secular living.

Dhuoda opens with an etymology of the word *manualis*, an acrostic poem—a common device throughout the Middle Ages (Godman 1990)—another prologue, and an autobiographical preface. Then she turns to her first subject, and the most important in her worldview: God. Books 1 and 2 describe God's attributes; explain the virtues of faith, hope, and charity; and instruct her readers in effective praying. In spite of her frailty and unworthiness, she directs her readers to accept her words. Her role is that of a teacher defending the doctrine of the Trinity, which was under attack in the ninth century.

In books 3–5 Dhuoda turns to earthly matters. Acting as his adviser, she reminds William of his responsibilities toward his father and other men—the powerful as well as the humble. She exhorts her son to arm himself with the gifts of the Holy Spirit, remain sexually pure, control his emotions, help the poor, strive for justice, and be generous with his wealth. In a perilous, changing world William is to submit to God's chastening and face difficulties bravely.

In books 6–9 Dhuoda returns to spiritual matters. She wants her son to be able to choose calmly, confidently, and honorably either the active or contemplative life. In either choice he needs to experience daily rebirth in Christ, so her purpose here is to be his spiritual as well as his physical mother (VII.1). She counsels him to use "holy reading" and to learn how to pray. Finally, she presents fifteen steps designed to lead both boys to spiritual perfection (IX.1).

In books 10 and 11 Dhuoda concludes several times. After summarizing her major ideas, she "finishes" with "This handbook ends here. Amen. Thanks be to God" (X.4). However, in the face of her weakness and her fear of imminent death, she appends two additional chapters and then an extra book. Finally she bids him farewell and concludes with Christ's final words, "It is finished" (*Consu[m]matum est*).

Dhuoda employs many medieval rhetorical devices, including a technique called *florilegia*—literally, "cullings." Authors "culled" through the Bible, the classics, and texts of the patristic fathers and other well-known authors to weave together mosaics constructed of excerpts, paraphrases, verbal echoes, and direct copying. The ability to weave phrases from a number of sources seamlessly, and generally without acknowledgment into the text, illustrated an author's learning and skill (Howell 1941; McKitterick 1989). Wallace-Hadrill (1983) broadly classifies Dhuoda's manual in this genre. Dhuoda herself admits, "The knowledge in this little book is partly derived from several other books, but my loving intent here has been to refashion their content in a matter appropriate to your age" (IX.1).

Culling from well-known texts particularly suits Dhuoda's strategies, for she grounds her arguments in appeals to authority. That is, instead of presenting the wisdom in the manual as her own, she commonly cites scriptures and the opinions of others to back her ideas. The majority of her illustrations, quotations, and paraphrases come from the Vulgate Bible. The Rule of Saint Benedict and other Benedictine writings are her second most important sources (Bowers 1977). She also directly quotes or paraphrases such authors as Augustine, Isidore of Seville, Gregory the Great, and her contemporary Alcuin of York.

Forms of reasoning evident in Dhuoda's ninth-century work are consistent with claims made by contemporary feminist philosophers (Griffiths and Whitford 1988; Jaggar 1989); they argue that women often ground their conclusions in personal experiences, narratives, and examples. Dhuoda regularly uses examples of biblical heroes, historical characters, and even animal behaviors to make her points persuasive. For instance, she urges William, "Seek out, respect, and faithfully observe the examples of the great worthies in the past, present, and future" (Bowers 1977, 142). Her longest narrative details the life of Joseph, a model of chastity who endured servitude and imprisonment before he became a ruler. More commonly, she simply names the characters whose feats she has undoubtedly been instilling in William since babyhood.

Dhuoda's reasoning sometimes seems peculiarly medieval, quaint, forced, even tiresome to a modern reader. However, her use of etymology provides clues to her theories regarding words and meaning. Drawing from Isidore of Seville, who believed that knowing the origin of a word enables one to comprehend it and recognize its force (Curtius 1953), Dhuoda divides the word *manualis* into two parts: *manus* and *alis*. She links *manus* (hand) with the power of God; consequently, *hand* means "action carried out" (prol.). Her discussion of *alis* is more complex. Since it resembles *ales* (wings), she compares the suffix to a cock—the messenger of morning who signals the end of the night; consequently, she reasons that a manual can be thought of as an end to the night of ignorance. Furthermore, as a messenger, the cock is like Christ whose words call followers from night into day—something she hopes her manual will accomplish. Words, to Dhuoda, are instruments that skillful rhetors can use to call their audiences to knowledge and action.

In addition to reasoning through authority, examples, and etymology, a great deal of Dhuoda's persuasive appeal comes from her ethos—both from her righteous character and from her relationship with her audience. In regard to character, she can speak of humility, for, although she does not say it outright, her manual indicates that she is humble; similarly, she can encourage her sons to persevere under hardship, for her own life is beset with difficulties. Her advice on prayer is likewise persuasive, for young William has undoubtedly observed his mother in prayer.

The socially sanctioned mother-son relationship calls for good intentions on the part of the mother and respect and obedience on the part of the son. As a result, Dhuoda can uniquely appeal to William and his brother, who will never know her, because she is their mother and her "watchful heart" (prol.) and the "sweetness of her great love" for them (X.4) virtually guarantees that all her advice is only given for their best interests. Furthermore, she indicates her motivation: "You will have many teachers, my son, who will offer you instructions that are lengthier and of greater usefulness, but none like mine in character nor given with such a burning heart as I, your mother, give you, my firstborn son" (Mayeski 1988, 49). In addition, since William is used to taking advice and orders from his mother, the manual poses no major change in his expectations regarding filial obedience.

The messages he has heard all his life now come through the medium of print rather than from face-to-face interactions.

One device that clearly illustrates both the personal tone of Dhuoda's work and her understanding of her authoritative relationship with her audience is her use of what might be called "matriarchal blessings." Using the biblical mother Rebekah as her example, Dhuoda takes authority to pray for her sons. She probably models her prayers on the patriarchal blessings in the Old Testament[3] and the apostolic blessings that Saint Paul commonly inserts at the end of a major section of an epistle.[4] Here is one such blessing: "May your God and Lord be favorable and kind to you in all things, your defender, your gracious director, and protector, and in all your actions may he be at hand as helper and constant defender. As his will is in heaven, so may it be done. Amen" (Bowers 1977, 83). Seventeen matriarchal blessings are found in the manual, commonly at the ends of chapters. Typically, they function to summarize the preceding material.[5]

Throughout the text Dhuoda creates a number of emotional proofs. She judiciously uses fear of the devil (IV.5), his angel (IV.6), the ultimate burning of evil things (V.1), and the punishment that befell characters such as Absalom (III.1) to warn her sons not to engage in vices. However, she more commonly appeals to positive values and emotions such as loyalty (III.2, 4), love (III.10), and family pride (III.2; VIII.14) as reasons for her sons to act nobly. For instance, she holds out the hope of heaven as a motivation for her sons to live humbly, asserting, "the humble Lord . . . causes those who share his humility to climb up step by step to find peace in heaven" (IV.3).

Finally, the fact that she is near death undoubtedly exerts emotional pressure on her sons to act in accordance with her wishes. By the end of the text she has lost hope for a reunion in this life; however, there is hope that family members will see each other in the next, *if* the two boys put her words into practice (VIII.17; X.2).

So far, we have examined Dhuoda's purpose, her rationale for authorship, her organizational pattern, and her reasoning strategies. Now we turn to a brief discussion of Dhuoda's style. Much has been made of the nonstandard forms of Latin displayed in the text (Cabaniss 1974; Dronke 1984; Neel 1991). Her first English translator concedes that Dhuoda's Latin "presents unexplainable vagaries" (Bowers 1977, lxi). However, Marchand (1984) argues that we should judge her style by standards of lay forms of Carolingian Latin rather than those of classical

Latin. Rosamond McKitterick (1989) contends that in the ninth century there was a great deal of language diversity. Carolingians spoke a form of late Latin, but they had restored the classical rules for writing, spelling, and grammar. Two registers or levels of the same language may have been used—one for oral and another for written communication. While the "higher" text language was used in the government and the church, Dhuoda's linguistic choices may have been closer to the Latin used in daily discourse.

Putting aside issues of grammar and syntax, an examination of linguistic pragmatics is more important for this study. That is, how is language actually used? What forms of language are appropriate in which settings? Is Dhuoda writing in the men's language as J. M. Wallace-Hadrill (1983) says, and is her knowledge of learned Latin faulty? Or is she writing in a colloquial form, one common in normal conversation? Ursula Le Guin (1989) would call this the "mother tongue," a language comprised of everyday forms used to discuss mundane, practical issues. This code of mothers contrasts with the language of public discourse—the political, powerful language of the fathers. Le Guin describes the mother tongue in this way: "It's vulgar . . . common speech, colloquial, low, ordinary, plebeian, like the work ordinary people do, the lives common people live. The mother tongue, spoken or written, expects an answer. It is conversation, a word the root of which means 'turning together.' The mother tongue is . . . relationship. It connects. It goes two ways, many ways, an exchange, a network. Its power is not in dividing but in binding, not in distancing but in uniting" (149).

Dhuoda's manual is arguably written in the mother tongue. Her advice is practical, dealing with everyday situations. Her words emphasize connections: help the poor; have faith in God; pray every day; treat women well; seek wise advisers; speak gently. In short, Dhuoda writes in conversational language that shows young William how to have an effective relationship with his God, his father, and his contemporaries.

In summary, Dhuoda's manual reveals her use of rhetoric to communicate practical advice in the private realm of her family. She draws from contemporary genres, but her work is uniquely her own. Her justification for writing and many of her persuasive appeals are grounded in the biological and socially sanctioned relationship that exists between rhetor and audience. Dhuoda summarizes great theological truths with some apology, and she uses authority extensively to support her ideas.

However, when she deals with practical affairs, she seems surer of herself because of her personal experiences in living out the Christian virtues that she encourages her sons to embody. She writes in the immediate, direct, conversational style of the mother tongue that emphasizes relationships.

Mother's Manuals

Extant mother's manuals span both temporal and geographical boundaries (Bornstein 1983; King 1991). Four and a half centuries after Dhuoda, Christine de Pisan wrote two books for her son: *Les Enseignements Moraux* (Moral Teachings) and *Les Proverbes Moraux* (Moral Proverbs). Perhaps following her example, Anne of France presented her betrothed daughter Suzanne with a manual in 1504 or 1505. The sixteenth-century German reformer and ruler Elisabeth of Braunschweig continued the tradition in a manual on marriage for her daughter and another on government for her son. A century later two Englishwomen added to this body of literature. Elizabeth Grymeston advised her son on education, marriage, devotions, and death. Elizabeth Joceline left a small, unfinished treatise, *Legacie to My Unborne Childe,* for the daughter whose birth would subsequently result in her own death. In the eighteenth century Sarah Pennington wrote *A Golden Legacy to Daughters or Advice to Young Ladies* when she was separated from her young daughters.

In addition to these texts whose authorship is quite certain, there are a number of works ostensibly written or dictated by women for their daughters. One thirteenth-century poem is a dialogue between a Bavarian lady and her daughter. In the 1300s an Italian mother purportedly wrote twelve precepts for her betrothed daughter. *The Good Wife Taught Her Daughter* (oldest manuscript, 1350) is another treatise that gives religious, moral, and practical advice, this time from the point of view of a lower-middle-class woman (Bornstein 1983).

Although each woman's work is unique, mother's manuals share several important similarities. First, they are alike in purpose. All mother-rhetors intend to pass on "vital knowledge . . . communicable only through words and replicable only in ink" (King 1991, 23). All summarize briefly the important beliefs, behaviors, and values that it takes ten to twelve years to inculcate. Their topics involve everyday living, and mothers typically write to emphasize practical information their inexperienced and unsophisticated children need in order to survive in an often deceitful world (Pennington 1857). Arguably, mothers saw their manuals more as conversations with their children than as polished rhetorical works (Donawerth 1994).

Often good advice is all mothers can offer; for instance, Christine de Pisan's manual opens with these lines:

> Son, I have here no great treasure
> To make you rich, but a measure
> Of good advice which you may need;
> I give it hoping you'll take heed. (qtd. in Willard 1984, 173–74)

However, mothers do not want their children simply to understand the concepts and know how to behave; they intend that their children put these principles into practice and live effectively in this life while preparing for the next. This dialectical tension between the spiritual and the temporal worlds is a recurring theme of these works. Just as Dhuoda begins with religious matters, Pennington urges her daughters first to consider their duty to God and establish a daily pattern of Bible reading and prayer. Anne of France similarly begins with religious instruction, and Joceline's initial charge is to honor God first.

In addition, the manuals are similar in that they are directed to private rather than public audiences, recipients who are bound to the rhetor by the most personal of biological and social ties. Although Joceline is "ashamed" and feels she "durst not undertake" the task of writing, she "can find no other means to express [her] motherly zeale." Three justifications compel her: the advice is for a child as a foundation for a better life; it is her own offspring who will excuse the mother's errors; it is for a good purpose that God will prosper.

Mothers all assume specific, socially acceptable roles in their manuals. They continue their roles of advice givers, authoritative disciplinarians, teachers, and trainers. Within societies that support obedience to parental authority, Joceline's words are typical, "If God takes mee from thee, be obedient to these instructions, as thou oughtest to be unto mee" (p. 11). She "charges" her child to serve God, pray, live carefully, and avoid sin; however, on less important topics her words are more advisory than authoritative, and she assumes the role of counselor, saying, "I do not direct, but deliver my opinion" (p. 11).

The manuals reveal similar types of arguments. Each mother commonly appeals to authority. Just as Dhuoda quotes scriptures and scholarly sources, Christine de Pisan offers her son proverbs that contain the wisdom of the culture. Similarly, other mothers cite the Bible and other literary sources to support their ideas. In addition, all these mothers rely on their own ethos—and this is their distinctive appeal. Their credibility lies in being the child's first teacher and model. They also depend on the persuasive power of maternal love and goodwill as a convincing strategy. The manuals are permeated with the sense that their authors only intend to be helpful.

Separation is the exigency that commonly compels mothers to compose their texts. Often this separation occurs when the children come of age. Christine de Pisan's works and those of Elizabeth of Braunschweig, Elizabeth Gandymere, and Anne of France are written to children who are making the transition to adulthood. Other separations are less natural. Joceline expects to die, and she writes out of love, anxiety, and grief the things she would teach, were she to live. Dhuoda's and Pennington's children were taken from them—William and the infant for political reasons, Pennington's daughters amid hints of scandal.

As Dhuoda's manual illustrates, not only do the audiences need reminders of their moral obligations, the mother-rhetors have personal needs that rhetoric helps to meet. All take up their pens to communicate not only a message but also the relationship that the message implies (McGuire and Slembek 1987). Dhuoda needs to maintain contact with someone who loves her at a time when she is lonely, dying, and deserted by a thoughtless husband. Since Joceline's child will never know her, the manual stands as a testimony of its author's love. Other mothers are anxious as their children leave the home, and rhetoric provides a means for them to perpetuate their influence. In addition, a mother-rhetor may hope to influence her own future. In the event of her husband's death, a woman often relied on her children for care, protection, and assurance of her place in society (Stafford 1978). Finally, some writers may hope to vindicate their reputations or those of their families. Dhuoda, knowing the rumors about Bernard, insists (perhaps for other readers) that disloyalty "has not been seen among [your ancestors], it is not seen now, and it will not be seen in the future" (III.4). Pennington sees rhetoric as a way to rescue her own reputation and prove that she is a fit mother. While she admits that her public behavior as a young woman may have appeared "wild," she swears she was privately chaste.

In short, examination of a number of manuals reveals that mother-rhetors have similar didactic and advisory purposes, and they are commonly prompted to write by the exigency of separation. Typically, they deal with practical topics from the private realm in which one must work out relationships with God and with others. Ethos—the unique love and commitment that comes from the mother-child bond—is their most powerful persuasive tool. Finally, the manuals function to meet the mothers' needs as well as the needs of their children.

Conclusion

This examination of a number of surviving mothers' manuals has increased our knowledge of women's rhetorical activities and traditions. The mother's manual can be considered a genre or "kind" (Colie 1973) of rhetorical production, for a genre has shared features that "persist among works vastly separated chronologically and culturally" (Reichert 1978). All these manuals demonstrate that women, compelled to write by similar circumstances, transformed existing genres such as epistles or the enchiridion to meet their rhetorical needs. They justified their decisions to address audiences consisting of their own children, over whom society had legitimated their moral and didactic influence. While it is true that all the mothers used rhetoric to influence the actions of their children, their rhetoric was also—and perhaps predominantly—a means of maintaining the mother-child bond. The rhetor-audience relationship thus provides the "frame" in which the recipients understand how to interpret the work. This relationship provides a compelling reason—the mother's zeal for her offspring—for the child to put these principles into action.

At the beginning of this chapter we looked at two theories regarding women's writing that apply to mother's manuals. One proposed that existing works represent a tradition largely lost (Cherewatuk and Wiethaus 1993; Mayeski 1988). The other posited that individual rhetors did not know of one another's work, and each one invented afresh the forms she needed to create her rhetorical act (Spender 1980). Perhaps in the case of mother's manuals the two positions coalesce. It is arguable that early authors did not know of one another's work and each rhetor created her manual by adapting rhetorical strategies of male authors. However, as literacy became widespread among the privileged classes more mothers produced advice manuals, and while some may have been circulated, the majority vanished.

What arguments can be made to support the contention that the two positions coalesce? First, it seems that Dhuoda's work is not part of a larger body of literature produced by women in the early medieval period. In fact, she most probably created the genre. She had the good fortune to live in Charlemagne's kingdom when noble children, both male and female, were educated. Furthermore, she could afford a book, a luxury item that required up to nineteen processed animal skins to construct (McKitterick 1989). However, her era was followed by years of widespread illiteracy in the West, and few mothers produced manuals during that period. Exceptions may include women such as the Bavarian poet, the Italian mother, and the lower-middle-class "Good Wife" who dictated works to their daughters.

Unlike Dhuoda and the others, the professional writer Christine de Pisan might have been expected to write to her son, for she had frequently been commissioned by kings and others of high rank to advise young people in print. No evidence indicates that de Pisan read Dhuoda's manual, although that would not have been impossible. Preserved manuscripts reveal that Dhuoda's work was copied and distributed as a pedagogical text in both France and Spain. Because of Christine de Pisan's interest in education, she may have seen it. Similarly, she may or may not have been familiar with the other texts. More probably, she constructed her work, as did Dhuoda, by adapting existing rhetorical forms to meet her purposes.

By Christine de Pisan's time literacy was somewhat more common for privileged women, and in the ensuing centuries, with the advent of the printing press and the availability of writing materials, a tradition of sorts may have begun. Many unknown mother-rhetors may have, in fact, known of one another's work and used existing manuals—including Christine de Pisan's—as models for their own. Since only a few remain, it seems reasonable to conclude that few were published and distributed publicly; most remained in the private realm, possibly in the form of long letters, poems, or handwritten books, loosely fastened together.

Our understanding of women in rhetoric would be furthered by a study that contrasts mother's manuals with other politeness or courtesy literature. For instance, Christine de Pisan wrote advice manuals for young women who would later find themselves in positions of authority. One text, *A Medieval Woman's Mirror of Honor: The Treasury of the City of Ladies*, was a well-received treatise addressed to young women from the highest rank to those in common occupations. In content it is similar to mother's manuals. However, it relies on different appeals, for the author is now a mentor rather than a mother. That is, author and audience are bound by social rather than biological-sociological ties. In addition, Lady Sarah Pennington's manual might be considered a forerunner of the modern etiquette book, for she provides specific instructions for running a home and living with servants. Including later etiquette manuals in a subsequent study would further increase our understanding of laywomen's authorship in rhetorical territories largely reserved for them.

Notes

I would like to thank Sharon Downey, who provided useful comments on an earlier draft of this essay.

1. Myra Ellen Bowers's translation is faithful to the Latin text, and Dhuoda's sometimes confusing style and occasional verbosity show through. Carol Neel translated into contemporary English. Unless noted otherwise, her translations are used throughout this paper. Pierre Riché collated the three manuscripts, noting textual discrepancies in footnotes to the Latin text—placed side-by-side with his French translation. Additional excerpts were translated by Mary Ann Mayeski and James Marchand.

2. Two widely disseminated Carolingian specula included Jonas of Orleans's *De Institutione Laicali* for Matfrid, count of Orleans, and Alcuin's *De Virtutibus et Vitiis*, written for Count Wido.

3. For example, Isaac blessed Jacob and Esau in Gen. 27:26–40; Jacob (Israel), in turn, blessed his twelve sons in Gen. 49.

4. See Phil. 1:9–11; Col. 1:9–13; Eph. 3:14–20; 1 Thess. 3:11–13.

5. Matriarchal blessings occur in Books I.7; II.2, 3; III.3, 4, 5, 6, 8, 9, 10, 11; VI.3; VIII.17; IX.4, 5, 6; and X.3.

References

Augustine. 1955. "Enchiridion." In *Augustine: Confessions and Enchiridion*, translated and edited by A. C. Outler, 335–416. Philadelphia: Westminster Press.

Bitzer, Lloyd F. 1968. "The Rhetorical Situation." *Philosophy and Rhetoric* 1.1: 1–14.

Bornstein, Diane. 1983. *The Lady in the Tower: Medieval Courtesy Literature for Women*. Hamden, Conn.: Archon Books.

Bouchard, Constance B. 1986. "Family Structure and Family Consciousness among the Aristocracy in the Ninth to Eleventh Centuries." *Francia* 14: 639–58.

Bowers, Myra E. 1977. "Introduction." In "The Liber Manualis of Dhuoda: Advice of a Ninth-Century Mother for Her Sons," i–lxvi. Ph.D. diss., Catholic University of America.

Bradley, Ritamary. 1954. "Backgrounds of the Title *Speculum* in Medieval Literature." *Speculum* 29: 100–109.

Cabaniss, Allen. 1967. *Charlemagne's Cousins: Contemporary Lives of Adalard and Wala.* Syracuse, N.Y.: Syracuse University Press.

———. 1974. *Judith Augusta: A Daughter-in-Law of Charlemagne and Other Essays.* New York: Vantage.

Cherewatuk, Karen, and Ulrike Wiethaus, eds. 1993. "Introduction: Women Writing Letters in the Middle Ages." In *Dear Sister: Medieval Women and the Epistolary Genre,* 1–19. Philadelphia: University of Pennsylvania Press.

Christine de Pisan. 1989. *A Medieval Woman's Mirror of Honor: The Treasury of the City of Ladies.* Trans. C. C. Willard. Ed. M. P. Cosman. Tenafly, N.J.: Bard Hall Press/Persea Books.

Colie, Rosalie L. 1973. *The Resources of Kind: Genre-Theory in the Renaissance.* Berkeley: University of California Press.

Curtius, Ernst R. 1953. *European Literature and the Latin Middle Ages.* Bollingen Series. Trans. W. R. Trask. New York: Pantheon.

Dhuoda. 1975. *Manuel Pour Mon Fils.* French trans. Pierre Riché. Paris: Les Éditions du Cerf.

———. 1977. "The Liber Manualis of Dhuoda: Advice of a Ninth-Century Mother for Her Sons." Trans and ed. M. E. Bowers. Ph.D. diss., Catholic University of America.

———. 1991. *Handbook for William: A Carolingian Woman's Counsel for Her Son, by Dhuoda.* Trans. C. Neel. Lincoln: University of Nebraska Press.

Donawerth, Jane. 1994. "Madeleine de Scudéry and Renaissance Rhetorical Theory." Unpublished paper, Eastern Communication Association. Washington, D.C.

Dronke, Peter. 1984. *Women Writers and the Middle Ages: A Critical Study of Texts from Perpetua to Marguerite Porete.* Cambridge: Cambridge University Press.

Dubrow, Heather. 1982. *Genre.* New York: Methuen.

Duckett, Eleanor. 1972. *Medieval Portraits from East and West.* Ann Arbor: University of Michigan Press.

Epictetus. 1948. *The Enchiridion.* Trans. T. W. Higginson. Indianapolis: Bobbs-Merrill.

Fowler, Alastair. 1982. *Kinds of Literature: An Introduction to the Theory of Genres and Modes.* Cambridge: Harvard University Press.

Godman, Peter. 1990. *Poets and Emperors: Frankish Politics and Carolingian Poetry.* Oxford: Oxford University Press.

Griffiths, Margaret, and Margaret Whitford, eds. 1988. *Feminist Perspectives in Philosophy.* Bloomington: Indiana University Press.

Howell, W. S. 1941. "Introduction and Notes." In *Alcuin. The Rhetoric of Alcuin and Charlemagne,* edited by W. S. Howell. Princeton: Princeton University Press.

Jaggar, Alison M. 1989. "Love and Knowledge: Motion in Feminist Epistemology." In *Women, Knowledge, and Reality: Explorations in Feminist Philosophy,* edited by A. Garry and M. Pearsall, 129–55. London: Unwin.

Joceline, Elizabeth. [1625] 1975. *The Mother's Legacie to her Unborne Childe.* Reprinted [1852], London: W. Blackwood. Reel 271, no. 1821. New Haven: Research Pub. Inc.

King, Margaret. 1991. *Women of the Renaissance.* Chicago: University of Chicago Press.

Labarge, Margaret Wade. 1986. *A Small Sound of the Trumpet: Women in Medieval Life.* Boston: Beacon Press.

Le Guin, Ursula. 1989. *Dancing at the Edge of the World: Thoughts on Words, Women, Places.* New York: Grove Press.

Marchand, James. 1984. "The Frankish Mother Dhuoda." In *Medieval Women Writers,* edited by Katharina M. Wilson, 1–29. Athens: University of Georgia Press.

Mayeski, Marie Ann. 1988. *Women: Models of Liberation.* Kansas City: Sheed & Ward.

McGuire, M., and E. Slembek. 1987. "An Emerging Critical Rhetoric: Hellmut Geissner's Sprechwissenschaft." *Quarterly Journal of Speech* 73.3: 349–400.

McKitterick, Rosamond. 1989. *The Carolingians and the Written Word.* Cambridge: Cambridge University Press.

Murphy, James J. 1974. *Rhetoric in the Middle Ages: A History of Rhetorical Theory from Saint Augustine to the Renaissance.* Berkeley: University of California Press.

Neel, Carol. 1991. "Introduction." In *Handbook for William: A Carolingian Woman's Counsel for Her Son by Dhuoda,* ix–xxviii. Lincoln: University of Nebraska Press.

Pennington, Sarah. 1857. *A Golden Legacy to Daughters or Advice to Young Ladies.* Boston: Higgins, Bradley, and Dayton.

Radbertus, Paschasius. [836? 851?] 1967. "The Life of Saint Adalard. The Life of Wala: Or an Epitaph for Arsenius" (Books I & II). In *Charlemagne's Cousins: Contemporary Lives of Adalard and Wala,* translated by A. Cabaniss. Syracuse, N.Y.: Syracuse University Press.

Regnier-Bohler, Danielle. 1992. "Literary and Mystical Voices." Trans. Arthur Goldhammer. In *A History of Women in the West,* Vol. 2: *Silences of the Middle Ages,* edited by C. Kalpisch-Zuber, 427–82. Cambridge: Belknap / Harvard University Press.

Reichert, John. 1978. "More Than Kin and Less Than Kind: The Limits of Genre Theory." In *Theories of Literary Genre,* edited by J. P. Strelka, 57–79. University Park: Pennsylvania State University Press.

Riché, Pierre. 1975. "Introduction, Texte Critique, Notes." In *Manuel pour Mon Fils, Dhuoda,* translated by P. Riché, 9–59. Paris: Les Éditions du Cerf.

Rodden, John. 1993. "Field of Dreams." *Western Journal of Communication* 57.2: 111–38.

Spender, Dale. 1980. *Man Made Language*. London: Routledge and Kegan Paul.

Stafford, P. 1978. "Sons and Mothers: Family Politics in the Middle Ages." In *Medieval Women*, edited by Derek Baker, 79–109. Oxford: Basil Blackwell.

Wallace-Hadrill, J. M. 1983. *The Frankish Church*. Oxford: Oxford University Press.

Ward, Elizabeth. 1990. "Caesar's Wife: The Career of Empress Judith, 819–829." In *Charlemagne's Heir: New Perspectives on the Reign of Louis the Pious (814–840)*, edited by P. Godman and R. Collins, 205–27. Oxford: Oxford University Press.

Wemple, Suzanne F. 1981. *Women in Frankish Society: Marriage and the Cloister 500–900*. Philadelphia: University of Pennsylvania Press.

Willard, Charity C. 1984. *Christine de Pizan: Her Life and Works*. New York: Persea Books.

Wilson, Katharina M. 1984. "Introduction." In *Medieval Women Writers*, edited by Wilson, vii–xxix. Athens: University of Georgia Press.

The Visionary Rhetoric of Hildegard of Bingen

Julia Dietrich

As scholars have brought feminist questions to medieval studies, particularly in the last twenty years, we have been drawn time and again to Hildegard, the abbess of the Benedictine house of Rupertsberg, near Bingen. Hildegard was adviser to Frederick Barbarossa; correspondent of Bernard of Clairvaux; and writer of visionary tracts, the first morality play, a medical handbook, and Latin hymns that have been recorded with increasing frequency in recent years. But our interest in Hildegard forces us to confront the contradiction between her personal self-assertion and her repetition of the traditional arguments for the weakness and necessary submissiveness of women. In the *Scivias,* the most famous and influential of her writings, she resolved this contradiction through recourse to Neoplatonism and the literary genre of allegory. In doing so, she created a rhetoric that allowed her to write with the authority of the divine, to use marginalization as a source of credibility, to support her arguments with the warrant of (visionary) experience, and to figure forth a cosmos in which authority and salvific activity are in female hands.

Born in 1098 to a wealthy noble family of Bermersheim, Hildegard inherited an aristocratic outlook and joined the circle that expected to exercise power in the secular world and in the Church. At the age of eight she was given by her parents to join Jutta, a daughter of the count of Sponheim, who had chosen to live as an anchoress. We do not know whether she too was intended to live all her life as an anchoress or whether this entry into religious life was a form of oblation to the Benedictine order (Flanagan 1994), but we do know that Jutta taught her to read the Bible in Latin and to chant the Benedictine office. At Jutta's death in 1136, Hildegard was elected abbess of the small community that had formed around Jutta. In the late 1140s a vision instructed her to separate her group from the male monastic foundation of Saint Disibod with which they had been associated. The abbot of Saint Disibod was reluctant to release the nuns from his authority over their spiritual lives, their property, and the daily life of their convent, but Hildegard persisted in spite of his opposition and that of the local nobility and some of her own nuns (Flanagan 1989, 5–6). To establish her new monastery, the Rupertsberg, she used all of her considerable force of will and good family connections.

Visions had offered themselves to Hildegard from earliest youth, but only in 1141, after the death of Jutta and her own elevation to abbess, did she come to see in them a prophetic dimension.[1] In that year, she records, light from heaven filled her heart and her mind and compelled her to convey to the wider world the truth with which she had been entrusted. The *Scivias,* a reduction of the full title, *Scito vias Domini,* or *Know the Ways of the Lord,* written over the years 1141 to 1151, is composed of three books, focusing on, respectively, creation, redemption, and sanctification (Newman 1990, 22). Each book is a progressive series of visions, and each vision begins with a description of what Hildegard saw and is followed by an interpretation presented as if coming from the mouth of God. Book 1 takes up the seamless order of the universe, in which the eternal and the mundane are united by a series of analogies. Book 2 centers on Ecclesia (Holy Mother Church) and the sacraments through which she reunites the faithful to God. And book 3 deals with the building up, throughout history, of the "edifice of salvation," an allegorical architectural project that showcases the moral virtues, generally personified as women. In the winter of 1147–48, when the *Scivias* was nearing final form, Pope Eugenius III attended a synod of bishops at Trier and was persuaded by Bishop Henry of Mainz and by Bernard of Clairvaux to read the unfinished manuscript, which he read aloud to the bishops and endorsed (Newman 1990, 13). Such direct papal approbation brought Hildegard authority, a wide audience, and a good deal of leverage. It was shortly after this gesture of papal approval that she initiated the separation from the monastery of Saint Disibod.

At the Rupertsberg she had a scriptorium to copy and illuminate the *Scivias* manuscript, thus giving her an access to publication that was rare for women in the Middle Ages. Between 1158 and 1163 she undertook three preaching tours that took her to monasteries and cathedral towns across Germany. She also completed the *Liber vitae meritorum* (Book of Life's Merits), a visionary allegory of virtues, vices, cosmology, and penance. In 1164 she joined the German ecclesiastics who condemned Frederick Barbarossa, her patron, for naming and supporting the antipopes set up against Alexander III. In the 1170s she finished the *Liber divinorum operum* (Book of Divine Works), her final visionary work, and in 1178, a year before her own death, she refused the orders of the bishop of Mainz to have exhumed a once-excommunicated nobleman who had been buried in her convent's cemetery. She insisted that he had repented and thus deserved Christian burial, and she continued her refusal to comply even when an interdict was placed on the Rupertsberg, denying it all access to the sacraments and to Mass and denying the nuns the right to sing the Divine Office for six months. As Barbara Newman has suggested, it seems likely that the conflict between Hildegard and the bishopric stemmed from something more than the one unfortunate nobleman, but we do not know what that might have been (1990, 16).

The overwhelming impression that arises from Hildegard's biography is that of a woman who was far from submissive, who struggled to establish, in the Rupertsberg, a sphere of influence literally beyond the reach of the male authority at Saint Disibod, and who did not avoid conflict with the secular or ecclesiastical authorities who had control over her. It is with some surprise, therefore, that late-twentieth-century readers come to her reference to women as "an infirm and weak habitation appointed to bear children and diligently nurture them" and thus unworthy to be priests (Hart and Bishop 1990, II, vi, sec. 76) or to her saying, "A man should never put on feminine dress or a woman use masculine attire, so that their roles may remain distinct, the man displaying manly strength and the woman womanly weakness; for this was so ordered by Me [she is recounting the words of God] when the human race began" (Hart and Bishop 1990, II, vi, sec. 77).

How did this believer in "womanly weakness" take it upon herself to become the first great female preacher and theologian of western Christendom? Before dismissing Hildegard as one of the sort who breaks the rules and then compensates by insisting that others observe them, we ought to keep in mind that the terms in which gender roles were defined were vastly different in the twelfth century from what they are in the late twentieth. Another two hundred years would pass before Christine de Pisan could use secular and humanistic arguments to upbraid Jean de Meung for his portrayal of women in the *Roman de la Rose*. The material conditions of the twelfth-century Rhineland and the religious culture that had formed Hildegard from earliest childhood set the parameters within which she could consider gender definitions. To ask retroactively whether she was a feminist is to ask a question she could not have asked herself and to confuse the picture with categories very different from those in which she was trained to think. As Barbara Newman demonstrates in *Sister of Wisdom,* Hildegard saw herself as continuing traditions of spirituality that no one would term feminist. What we can usefully do, however, is to examine the rhetorical strategies by which Hildegard authorized herself as a theologian in spite of the deutero-Pauline proscription against women preaching, and the rhetorical means by which she created a space for her particular vision within the religious tradition. Then we might usefully ask whether those strategies altered or amplified the rhetorical tradition on which later writers could draw. In addressing such questions, this study will concentrate on the *Scivias,* with occasional reference to the later works.

The phrase "to create a space" recommends itself to anyone writing about Hildegard because it describes her activity literally when she founded the Rupertsberg; because she herself favored architectural metaphors, such as the "edifice of salvation"; and because her rhetorical project was to make room within orthodox religious doctrine for her vision and for her preaching. Hildegard was no radical. She defended orthodox Catholic teaching against the Cathar heresy and defended the papal succession against Barbarossa's tampering. She defended secular and ecclesiastical hierarchies and accepted only noblewomen into the novitiate. She was most influenced by the oldest intellectual traditions and models within the western Christian tradition, Neoplatonism and the Book of Revelation. A strong proponent of the Gregorian reform, she preached against careless or sinful clerics, whose corruption invited divine retribution. Calling the Church, and particularly the clergy, to become what it was meant to be, she argued not for innovation but for a return to purity, for a clear perception of the true nature of things.

Thus situated rhetorically, Hildegard used as her primary trope that of *reversal.* This trope is foundational to Christian rhetoric, with roots in scriptural passages such as "That stone which was rejected by the builders has become the cornerstone," "The last shall be made first," and "He who would save his life must lose it." In the hands of early Christian ascetics and Neoplationists, it came to express the condition in which the true nature of things is obscured by the grossness of the fallen world. The first step to correct action, therefore, is *to see* correctly, *to see* the spiritual truth behind the misleading mundane appearance. It would be difficult to overstress the importance and the prevalence of this mode of thinking in early medieval Christianity. It carried virtually unassailable authority by its association with Jerome and Augustine; it underpinned the Benedictine conviction of monastic men and women as no longer "in the world" as well as the even more foundational assumption that what distinguishes Christians from others is their knowledge that the material world is one of misleading appearances. The anonymous patristic letter written to Diognetus around the year 200 exemplifies this ascetic tradition which third-century Neoplatonism magnified: "[Christians] live in their own countries as though they were only passing through. . . . To speak in general terms, we may say that the Christian is to the world what the soul is to the body. . . . The body hates the soul and wars against it. . . . The soul, though immortal, has a mortal dwelling place; and Christians also live for a time amidst perishable things, while awaiting the freedom from change and decay that will be theirs in heaven" (*Liturgy* 1976, 2: 841–42). A rhetoric that grounds its arguments in the distinction between the illusory material world and the true eternal reality is therefore enlisting the most unassailable authority, that of Christian self-definition in the early medieval period.

Allegory, both as literary genre and rhetorical device, is ideally suited to serve this philosophical position. It takes its characters, settings, and action from the world of unchanging reality, and it presumes to make visible the invisible truths obscured by the material world. Its rhetorical raison d'être in the early Middle Ages was its implicit claim to *show* the human experience in its true light. As Carolynn Van Dyke has noted, "Allegory, the narrative of universals, envisions human life as a continual interchange between temporal event and eternal pattern" (1985, 63). Ironically, the Church-promoted understanding of an ultimate reality that differed from earthly appearances created a rupture, a space in which Hildegard could authorize herself as a preacher and envision a world of female authority.

The *Scivias* is visionary in two senses of the term: it came directly from God in a vision to Hildegard; and it makes visible the hidden reality. The benefit of a visionary claim in authorizing a woman's writing is obvious. As Hildegard insists, God and not she is the author of the work. The *Scivias* opens with this insistence, as she reports the voice of God, telling her:

O fragile human, ashes of ashes, and filth of filth! Say and write what you see and hear. But since you are timid in speaking, and simple in expounding, and untaught in writing, speak and write these things not by a human mouth, and not by the understanding of human invention, and not by the requirements of human composition, but as you see and hear them on high in the heavenly places in the wonders of God. Explain these things in such a way that the hearer, receiving the words of his instructor, may expound them in those words, according to that will, vision and instruction. Thus, therefore, O human, speak these things that you see and hear. And write them not by yourself or any other human being, but by the will of Him Who knows, sees, and disposes all things in the secrets of His mysteries. (Hart and Bishop 1990, 59)

The conviction of having received a divine commission to write was critically important not only in securing an audience for a medieval woman but also in helping her overcome the internalized strictures against women preaching (Petroff 1986, 6). "Filth of filth" sounds harsh and gratuitously insulting to modern ears, but it is worth noting that it is just the sort of formula used by many of the early Church fathers in describing women. Collections of these derogatory writings on women were circulated again, with the blessing of the Church, during the twelfth century to support the Gregorian campaign against married clergy. Hildegard chooses to steal the fire from her detractors by declaring at the very outset that she is unworthy and that the message is not hers but God's. Further, he has determined even the form that it should take (lest anyone attack the theology or Hildegard's awkward, sometimes cryptic, Latin style). Behind the unworthy human writer stands the Divine Author.

The second sense in which the *Scivias* is a visionary work is in its creation of pictures. It sets out to reveal spiritual truth—what the later author of *Everyman* will call "ghostly sight." Here too the trope of reversal is apparent. In her visual, memorable allegories earthly realities are transmuted—and implicitly superseded—in interesting ways. Most notable is the series of gender transmutations. Recalling the ancient Christian tradition in which a virginal woman, having overcome the flesh through celibacy, becomes in the words of Saint Jerome a "spiritual man" (Brown 1988, 3–24), Hildegard separates gender from biological sex. She does so not by demonstrating the cultural construction of gender, as modern feminist theorists have done, but by taking up the patristic idea that moral virtue is constitutive of one's true, spiritual nature. If the baptized Christian "enters unto a new life," and if the sacraments, a favorite theme of Hildegard, effect unseen spiritual changes, then in the realm of the spirit we are what we make of ourselves. She does not go as far as John Wycliffe[2] will later go in exploiting the radical potential in extreme philosophical realism; aristocratic background and conservative temperament make her a supporter, not an attacker, of sacred and secular institutional authority. She supports the class and gender hierarchies as they exist on earth but reiterates throughout the *Scivias* that humble woman, as weaker vessel, has been exalted over sinful men. In the first vision of book 1, she writes, as if in the voice of God: "'Burst forth into a fountain of abundance and overflow with mystical knowledge, until they who now think you contemptible because of Eve's transgression are stirred up by the flood of your irrigation. For you have received your profound insight not from humans, but from the lofty and tremendous Judge on high, where this calmness will shine strongly with glorious light among the shining ones'" (Hart and Bishop 1990).

In book 2, vision 5, we note again the rhetorical reversal, as Hildegard writes in a section called "On the Noble and Joyous State of Perfect Virginity": "There arose the noblest perfection of churchly religion, which tasted heavenly sweetness with burning ardor and stringently restrained itself in order to gird itself with secret power; rejecting the union of human coupling, it avoided the division caused by the bitterness of the flesh" (Hart and Bishop 1990, 204). Burning ardor leads to restraint, which leads to secret power, and unity arises from the refusal of union.

In the visual adjunct to such reversals in which the weak are made strong, the allegory enables Hildegard to present a visionary world that is overwhelmingly female. The institutional Church was, of course, entirely in male hands, but book 2, the longest of the books, is dominated by Ecclesia, or Holy Mother Church, and thus envisioned as female. Speaking authority throughout the *Scivias* is given to the Virtues, personified as women. Allegory is a medium in which spiritual reality is given visual form, and spiritual authority is female in the *Scivias*. Nuptual imagery is very much downplayed in Hildegard's work, compared to its role in the writings of later female visionaries and mystics, because she is emphatically not a unitive mystic but also because even the male God has a maternal aspect, named as Charity in book 2, vision 2 (Newman 1987, 64).

The "edifice of salvation," which dominates book 3, includes another of Hildegard's reversals, as she explains why human beings are stronger than the never-fallen angels:

Therefore people work more strongly in soul and body than if they
had no difficulty in doing it, since they struggle against themselves
in many perils; and, waging these fierce wars together with the Lord
God Who fights faithfully for them, they conquer themselves, chas-
tising their bodies, and so know themselves to be in His army. But an
angel, lacking the hardships or an earthly body, is a soldier of Heaven
only in its harmonious, lucid and pure constancy in seeing God; while
a human, handicapped by the filth of his body, is a strong, glorious,
and holy soldier. (Hart and Bishop 1990, III, ii, sec. 19)

In that reasoning, it is not difficult to see the parallel argument that
women, struggling against greater weakness, exemplify a more impressive spiritual triumph than do men.[3]

Hildegard provides no grounds for challenging the strictures that
constrained women's lives. Reading with an interest in her rhetoric,
however, one is struck by the fact that she did open up some space,
create a path that could be followed by other women writers. Using the
reversal trope, arguing that those who struggle against the greatest barriers exemplify the greatest triumphs, she provides the grounds for
women's claim to authority. Such grounds do not throw open the door
but merely edge it open: women who claim authority using
Hildegard's logic must "earn" it by virginity and conspicuous sanctity, and the authority they thus achieve is limited to the moral sphere.
The fourteenth-century mystic Margery Kempe, for example, encountered particular resistance to her visionary claims because she was
not virginal and cloistered (Glenn 1992, 551). Nothing in Hildegard's
writings authorizes women to go into the construction trades. And
yet it is imaginable that the example of Hildegard herself establishing the Rupertsberg and her allegorical picture of virgin-stonemasons
building the Tower of the Savior's humanity (III, viii) were not entirely
lost on later female readers.

Before anything can be done, it must be imagined. Hildegard up-
held the rightness and immutability of the sex role segregation of her
time, but in her allegorical vision narratives she figured forth a world of
female authority, female power, female achievement. As her allegory
represents, or visualizes, for us an ideal spiritual reality, it shares with
later utopian narratives the power to let us see a desired reality not yet
discernible in our mundane lives.

To write, as Hildegard did, through an explication of visions is an ancient device. The Book of Revelation, her ultimate literary model, keeps its hold on the human imagination even in our own time. Over centuries when most of the population was illiterate and books scarce even for those who could make use of them, preaching through highly visual, symbolic, and memorable narratives made splendid sense. Hildegard's architectural analogies have much in common with the "houses of memory" used as mnemonic devices. As she preached, both in monastic houses and in the public squares of cities such as Mainz and Cologne, her hearers could use the well-known plan of a castle or monastic building, with foundation, walls, and towers, to follow and to remember her moral vision. Just as later Franciscan preachers realized that exempla would give a concrete reality to the morals of their sermons, so Hildegard used the vivid concreteness of her allegorical vision to reach her listeners. Indeed, it would be difficult to think of a more haunting vision than "The New Heaven and the New Earth," which comes at the end of the *Scivias* just before the "Symphony of Praise": "Fire no longer had its raging heat, or air density, or water turbulence, or earth shakiness. And the sun, moon and stars sparkled in the firmament like great ornaments, remaining fixed and not moving in orbit, so that they no longer distinguished day from night. And there was no night, but day. And it was finished" (Hart and Bishop 1990, III, xii).

This eschatological vision of the end of time reminds us that the *Scivias* is in part an apocalyptic vision, and the apocalyptic element looms yet larger in her later work, particularly the *Liber divinorum operum*. Kathryn Kerby-Fulton, in *Reformist Apocalypticism and 'Piers Plowman,'* has demonstrated convincingly that Hildegard was consciously locating herself within the visionary Reformist tradition, that she knew and used *The Shepherd of Hermas,* an allegorical apocalypse written in the first or second century and available in numerous medieval manuscripts in northern Europe (1990, 85). Kerby-Fulton has claimed for Hildegard the distinction of being "probably the single most influential figure in the development of a Northern European apocalyptic visionary tradition, [who] was consciously imitated by later visionary writers" (1990, 76).

Hildegard insisted on being seen not as a unitive mystic, one whose experience of the divine is ineffable and non-noetic,[4] but rather as a visionary, whose experience was fully communicable. As Peter Dronke has pointed out, her experience corresponds to the third level of vision as described by her contemporary Richard of Saint Victor, because God communicated with her through pictures, rather than the fourth and highest level, in which experience of the divine is direct and unmediated by pictures of any material thing (1984, 146). The communicability of her message was of the essence, because her intentions were Reformist.

Writing in the years when the nobility and the clergy were contending for power—a contest played out most dramatically in the Rhineland—with the large monastic foundations at the center of the controversy (Southern 1970, 100ff.), she viewed the struggle in apocalyptic terms, warning that the continued corruption of the clergy would invite despoliation of the clerical endowments by the nobility. In the *Scivias* (III, ii) she pictures Ecclesia giving birth to Antichrist, but, interestingly, she does not imagine the despoliation of the earthly Church as a signal of the end of time, but rather as the end of one age and the beginning of a new age in which the Church will return to its apostolic purity. Such a hopeful expectation was extremely rare among apocalyptic writers and at odds with the Augustinian understanding of history as devolution (Kerby-Fulton 1990, 41). Her view thus parallels that of her contemporary Joachim de Fiore, the leading light of the southern visionary tradition, who foresaw the dawning of an enlightened third age, the age of the Holy Spirit (Kerby-Fulton 1990, 44).

The coming period of retribution for Church corruption came to loom larger in Hildegard's writings as she grew older and the political tensions in the Rhineland heightened. Apocalyptic themes and visions dominate the *Liber divinorum operum,* and the manuscript illuminations in that text, prepared under her own direction, give an interesting clue to the tradition in which she saw herself acting. There she is represented seated and writing on a double tablet such as that associated with Moses and the Ten Commandments; she had earlier explicitly compared herself to Moses when writing about the resistance to her move from Disibodenberg (Lerner 1993, 64, 58). By the last years of her life she appears to have seen herself as a Mosaic figure, one who proclaims the end of one era and the beginning of another epoch, and to have regarded her writings not merely as a visionary call to reform but as pronouncements of a new era of morality and changed divine-human relations.

The apocalyptic visionary tradition, given new life by Hildegard and Joachim de Fiore in response to the ferment of the twelfth century, continued to flourish into the late Middle Ages as a dominant form of protest literature. The continuing struggle between Church and state, the charges of corruption made against the friars in the fourteenth century, and the protests against Church authoritarianism leading into the Reformation all created a climate in which reformers would choose a visionary literature—either as a literary form or with a claim actually to have had a visionary experience—in order to claim an authority outside that of the institutional Church. The importance of Hildegard in creating the rhetorical space for such critiques cannot be overestimated. In 1220 Gebeno of Eberbach prepared a widely circulated redaction of Hildegard's apocalyptic writings for the purpose of countering "the end is upon us" apocalyptic writers of his own time with Hildegard's vision of an era peace and morality preceding the Last Days; Gebeno's *Pentachronon* was widely circulated in northern Europe in the late Middle Ages (Kerby-Fulton 1990, 28). In 1513 Jacques Lefevre D'Etaples published the *Liber trium virorum & trium spiritualium virginum*, excerpts from visionary works including *The Shepherd of Hermas* and the writings of Hildegard, Elizabeth of Schonau, and Robert of Uzes, making clear that he regarded them as forming a single tradition (Dronke 1981, 221). Kerby-Fulton argues for the further influence of Hildegard on Bridget of Sweden and, at least indirectly and possibly directly, on William Langland, the author of *Piers Plowman* (1990, 96). This tradition, however, has been less obvious to historians of rhetoric than the tradition running from Aristotle to the scholastics into modern practice.

In the two decades before Hildegard began writing the *Scivias* Peter Abelard had been attempting to resolve contradictions in Christian teaching by using dialectic, the great new intellectual tool acquired when the West discovered the Arab commentaries on Aristotle and encountered Aristotelian thought in an un-Platonized form. Scholastic argumentation, based in dialectic and reliant on *quaestio, disputatio,* and *sententia,* would dominate theological discourse for centuries to come, and the western rhetorical tradition would associate argumentation almost entirely with logic and dialectics. Further, the Neoplatonic underpinnings of Hildegard's rhetoric were challenged by the Aristotelian formulation termed "moderate realism," which made universal categories dependent on particular manifestations, in effect tying the invisible reality much more closely to the material world. By emphasizing the connections between the material and the spiritual and deemphasizing the differences, moderate realism undercut the power of the reversal trope. Indeed, one of the ironies is that her Neoplatonic views were unassailable by the Church at the time she wrote precisely because they had just begun to come under attack from Aristotelian renegades such as Abelard and the Arab philosopher Averroës, followed in the next century by Thomas Aquinas.

The lively northern European visionary tradition, stemming from Hildegard, bears in its rhetoric the marks of its social positioning and its apocalyptic antecedents. Though orthodox and vetted by the pope, Hildegard's work was highly critical of contemporary clerical abuses. Her writing persona, therefore, is constructed as an "outsider" to the greatest degree possible. Like the author of *The Shepherd of Hermas*, she exaggerates her own smallness in order to stress that she is not a political player but a simple vessel of the Lord. It is in this light that we should read her characterization of herself as a poor, weak woman within the text of *Scivias* (as opposed to letters or illuminations). Her insistence on the weakness of women not only bolsters her claim to divine inspiration and thus her authority but also enhances her status as a outsider, one free to criticize from a personally disinterested position. Kerby-Fulton notes that Hildegard cites only the Bible, even though her work shows the influence of her considerable extrabiblical reading (1990, 68). When power, strength, and learning are corrupted, then authority accrues to the simple, unlearned woman. Though the modesty topos is a staple of Reformist apocalyptic writing, Hildegard is the first to use gender in the construction of an authoritative outsider persona. Such a use of gender goes some way in explaining the apparent contradictions in her characterizations of women.

Gender, in fact, seems the key to a number of contradictions in Hildegard's writings. Whereas Neoplatonism, with its insistence on the distinction between reality and the material world, naturally fosters dichotomies and oppositions, her cosmos is one of complementarity between male and female, with Sophia, Mary, and Ecclesia as female principles within salvation history and Eve presented as blamelessly cooperating with God's eternal plan to send a redeemer (Lerner 1993, 61–62). Likewise, Hildegard is unwilling to follow Neoplatonic logic to the conclusion of derogating the material world and the body (Dronke 1984, 171). Although it is the spirit that is important (and virgins are spiritual men), the body is seen as its complement, not its enemy. Perhaps because she received her visions during periods of great bodily sickness and suffering, she recognized the body as one source of her authority (Lerner 1993, 57). Although a phrase such as "embodied knowledge" would have meant nothing to her, one suspects that her strong opposition to the Cathars, or Albigensians, a radically ascetic heretical movement that viewed the body as evil, might have owed something to an unconscious recognition that her visions of the spiritual world were the products of bodily experience.

The fact that virgins became spiritual men but also remained bodily women is likely to have steered her toward complementarity and images of wholeness and away from dichotomous and oppositional thinking. *Viriditas,* or "greenness," was Hildegard's term for the life force as it ran through all of the natural world and the spiritual world, and the illuminations of the Rupertsberg Codex prefer waves, circles, and mandalas over more hierarchical designs (Lerner 1993, 63). The unity of the temporal and spiritual worlds, in contravention of the reversal trope, is further insisted on by the correspondence between Hildegard herself, as abbess, and Ecclesia, the maternal figure of Church. Indeed, the choir of virgins described in *Scivias* (II, v) is dressed just as Hildegard allowed the virgins of Rupertsberg to dress for communion on feast days, and, as Newman notes, "it is even possible to identify the nun whom the abbess imagined as Virginitas herself. . . . The correspondence is complete. On the plane of allegory we see the stark, imposing figure of Mater Ecclesia sheltering a throng of virgins in her bosom, with the Virgin Mary at her heart. But the historical record shows us Hildegard, mother of her own flock of virgins decked in their bridal veils, with her favorite daughter in the midst of them" (1987, 222–24). *Scivias* is a vision of truth, a chronicle of cosmic history, a Reformist apocalyptic narrative, and also a discursive embodiment of Hildegard's own experience.[5]

The conservative, aristocratic abbess of the Rupertsberg was thoroughly trained in the intellectual tradition of Benedictine spirituality. With Augustine's belief in the "divine illumination of the intellect," she was trained to meditate upon a text until it revealed its many truths. Her rhetoric is one of vision and interpretation, and it speaks the truth of her experience, seeking to persuade her hearers and readers without the use of dialectic argumentation. She warrants her arguments not with the logic of a claims-reasons sequence but with the authority of revelation and the ethos of an outsider persona. Her writings are in the style of the Reformist visionary tradition, with personifications who abruptly appear and disappear according to an elliptical allegorical logic and with pronouncements that are, as Kerby-Fulton says, "terse, aphoristic, *unreasoning*" (1990, 58, my emphasis).

Beyond breathing new life into this tradition, Hildegard has given it her own stamp most notably in her handling of gender. Allegory and the reversal trope enable her to represent Virtue and Authority as female, even as she uses the cultural assumption of women's weakness to enhance her persona of the inspired, uncorrupted outsider. Writing as a woman and as a "spiritual man" appears to have predisposed her to seek the ideal in complementarity rather than dichotomy. Rhetorically doubly gendered, she took naturally to the allegorical rhetoric in which truth is personified in one form and then another, and characters replace one another as the narrative requires. And out of Neoplatonism and reformism she envisioned a cosmos of greenness—a vision which has endeared her to the environmental and creation theology movements, which in recent decades have reprinted her writings.

After Hildegard, the number of religious women writers increased, so that in the thirteenth century we have Marie of Oignies, Hadewijch of Brabant, Mechtilde of Magdeburg, and the school of Helfta; in the fourteenth century we recognize such lights as Julian of Norwich and Marguerite Porete among many others. Hildegard, by the very fact of her having written authoritatively, preached publicly, and been listened to by Churchmen, must inevitably have been an important example to many of these women. As the culture of western Europe became more prosperous and more complex in the thirteenth and fourteenth centuries, some women found themselves with time and the prompting to write. As they were excluded from university training, the dialectical tradition was not available to them. Instead, they positioned themselves within the mystical discourse, speaking from their own experiences of the divine. As Peter Dronke has noted, however, the women who follow Hildegard do not write apocalyptically and prophetically, as she did, but rather "in their own name" (1984, 206). The shift is conspicuous: Hildegard wrote the voice of God speaking through her as if through an amanuensis.

As we reexamine western cultural history, looking beyond the obvious exemplars for a fuller history of rhetoric, the privileged but marginalized Hildegard shows us how much innovation was possible within traditional materials, in service of traditional ideas, but in a woman's hands. She did much to accustom northern Europe to hear a woman's voice speaking authoritatively, and she revivified the polemical protest tradition through which those marginalized by gender or class (as with Langland) could use their marginalization as a position from which to speak truth to power.

Notes

1. For scientific efforts to explain Hildegard's visions, see Singer (1917) and Sachs (1985).

2. Arguing from an extreme realist position that the Church was composed of the faithful of all ages and could not be the flawed and mutable institutional Church on earth, Wycliffe then argued that we can distinguish a true member of the Church by his or her virtue, not by institutional position. The argument was easily extended to the secular realm where it supported the idea that, as the Wyf of Bath put it, "noble is as noble does." For an examination of Wycliffe's philosophical grounding for this argument, see Leff (1966).

3. See Petroff (1986) for discussion of the "weak woman raised to greatest strength" idea as it recurs throughout the writings of late medieval mystics.

4. For a discussion of noetic and non-noetic mystical traditions, cross-culturally, see Smart (1983).

5. Newman's reference to "her favorite daughter" recalls one of the more famous incidents in Hildegard's life, when she vehemently opposed the appointment of Richardis von Stade as abbess of the Benedictine convent at Bassum in 1151. Richardis had been her confidant and probably her amanuensis in the writing of the *Scivias*. Hildegard fought hard, even against Richardis's well-positioned noble family, to keep her at the Rupertsberg.

References

Brown, Peter. 1988. *The Body and Society: Men, Women, and Sexual Renunciation in Early Christianity.* New York: Columbia University Press.

Dronke, Peter. 1981. *Arbor Caritatis.* In *Medieval Studies for J. A. W. Bennett,* edited by P. L. Heyworth, 207–53. Oxford: Oxford University Press.

———. 1984. *Women Writers of the Middle Ages.* Cambridge: Cambridge University Press.

Flanagan, Sabina. 1989. *Hildegard of Bingen: A Visionary Life.* London: Routledge.

———. 1994. "Sts. Hildegard, Elizabeth, Ursula, and the 11,000 Virgins." Unpublished paper, International Congress of Medieval Studies. Kalamazoo, Mich.

Glenn, Cheryl. 1992. "Author, Audience, and Autobiography: Rhetorical Technique in *The Book of Margery Kempe.*" *College English* 54: 540–51.

Hart, Mother Columba, and Jane Bishop, trans. 1990. *Hildegard of Bingen: Scivias.* New York: Paulist Press.

Kerby-Fulton, Kathryn. 1990. *Reformist Apocalypticism and 'Piers Plowman.'* Cambridge: Cambridge University Press.

Leff, Gordon. 1966. "John Wycliffe: The Path to Dissent." *Proceedings of the British Academy,* 52.

Lerner, Gerda. 1993. *The Creation of Feminist Consciousness: From the Middle Ages to Eighteen-seventy.* New York: Oxford University Press.

The Liturgy of the Hours. Vol. 2. 1976. New York: Catholic Book Publishing Co.

Newman, Barbara. 1987. *Sister of Wisdom: St. Hildegard's Theology of the Feminine.* Berkeley: University of California Press.

————. 1990. "Introduction." In *Hildegard of Bingen: Scivias,* translated by Mother Columba Hart and Jane Bishop, 9–48. New York: Paulist Press.

Petroff, Elizabeth Alvilda. 1986. *Medieval Women's Visionary Literature.* New York: Oxford University Press.

Sachs, Oliver. 1985. *Migraine: Understanding a Common Disorder,* 106–8. Berkeley: University of California Press.

Singer, Charles. 1917. "The Scientific Views and Visions of Saint Hildegard." *Studies in the History and Method of Science,* 1: 1–55.

Smart, Ninian. 1983. "The Purification of Consciousness and the Negative Path." In *Mysticism and Religious Traditions,* edited by Steven T. Katz, 117–29. Oxford: Oxford University Press.

Southern, R. W. 1970. *Western Society and the Church in the Middle Ages.* Harmondsworth, U.K.: Penguin.

Van Dyke, Carolynn. 1985. *The Fiction of Truth.* Ithaca: Cornell University Press.

Women, Rhetoric, and Letter Writing
Marguerite d'Alençon's Correspondence with Bishop Briçonnet of Meaux

Laurel Carrington

Marguerite d'Alençon (1492–1549), sister to France's king Francis I and after 1527 Queen of Navarre, lived during a period of significant change in European history. She was raised on her family's estate in Angoulême, where along with her brother she received an education unusually rich in both spiritual and secular literature.[1] She became famous as a poet and as the writer of the *Heptameron,* as well as for her patronage of other writers and for her support of the French evangelical reform. In this last capacity she conducted during the early 1520s an extensive correspondence with Bishop Guillaume Briçonnet of Meaux, around whom were gathered leading figures calling for reform in the French church.

We tend today to see private letter writing as an entirely personal form of communication, not to be shared with third parties and not governed by rules of decorum beyond those limits that may obtain in the friendship itself. Such was not the case during the sixteenth century, when letters between friends were routinely circulated and even published, and were structured carefully to reflect the status of writer and reader, the linguistic competency of the writer, and the respective needs and concerns of both parties. These observations notwithstanding, letters were not orations; the major rhetorical works of antiquity classified written correspondence as an example of *sermo,* everyday speech, not as the sort of formal oratory that was the subject of such works (Henderson 1983, 334). The particular exchange discussed in this chapter was preserved by Marguerite to be copied and assembled as a unit. The letters come to us in the form of a single manuscript text in the handwriting of two separate copyists, the latter of whom broke off literally in the middle of a sentence, leaving the last of Briçonnet's letters unfinished (Martineau and Vessière 1975, 1: 2–3). While we can speculate that there were more letters, the correspondence seems to have dropped off soon after November 1524.

To see how these letters might contribute to an understanding of the participation of women in the history of rhetoric, we should first look more closely at the traditions governing letter writing. During the medieval period epistolary practice drew upon models that were preserved from Roman antiquity and thus demanded some familiarity with ancient sources. By the twelfth century the practice of letter writing came increasingly to be regulated by manuals known as *artes dictaminis*, written by teachers of rhetoric, *dictatores*. The rules for division of the oration were adapted to the letter, and as time went on the genre became more formalized. A letter written according to the formula would incorporate five elements: the *salutatio*, which was the initial greeting; the *benevolentiae captatio*, a quotation of a commonplace or proverb to establish the theme; the *narratio*, or statement of purpose; the *petitio*, a request (which would be based on the terms of the narratio), and finally the *conclusio* (Cherewatuk and Wiethaus 1993, 5; Constable 1976, 16, 17). Giles Constable (1976, 40, 41) documents an increasing rigidity throughout the twelfth and thirteenth centuries, followed in the fourteenth century by a new flowering brought about by humanist writers and by an increasing acceptance of writing in the vernacular. While the humanists encouraged greater freedom than the dictatores would allow, they also placed a stronger emphasis on imitating ancient writers. Thus they were not necessarily innovative in their approach to letter writing. Real innovation came with the increase in letters written in the vernacular, which in turn led to the involvement of different kinds of writers with different kinds of agendas.

The correspondence between Marguerite and Briçonnet occurred at a turning point, one that expanded opportunities for all sorts of people who had been excluded from the earlier literary culture that had been carried out exclusively in Latin. Women constituted one of the groups able to benefit from these changes. Neither the schools of the medieval dictatores nor those of the Renaissance humanists had been open to women; indeed, the rhetorical tradition itself was in many ways deliberately constructed to exclude women (Donawerth 1992, 35–39; King 1980). Yet in spite of these obstacles, women found that letter writing, on the boundary between public and private, formal and informal communication, was a form of written expression that was more open to them than others, and throughout the Middle Ages they made active use of it (Cherewatuk and Wiethaus 1993, 1).

What might have been the norms governing letter writing in the 1520s with which these two would have been familiar? Europe's most celebrated humanist, Erasmus of Rotterdam, wrote in his 1522 treatise *De conscribendis epistolis*, "if there is something that can be said to be characteristic of this genre, I think that I cannot define it more concisely than by saying that the wording of a letter should resemble a conversation between friends" (*CWE* 1974, 25: 20).[2] Erasmus gives advice concerning appropriate ways of addressing one's correspondent. Flattery must be rigorously avoided, and epithets and titles should be appropriate to the person addressed ("father" would be appropriate for churchmen, for example). As for adoptive names, Erasmus approves of them "as when we call the powerful, by whose influence we are supported and by whose kindness assisted, 'patrons,' 'fathers,' and 'instructors'; the women 'patronesses' and 'mothers' . . . " (60).

While at least one commentator feels that Marguerite does not seem in her correspondence to have been strongly influenced by the models of Roman antiquity (Neubert 1963, 118), in her use of French she shows a familiarity with certain of the standards of classical Latin, and we will also note that her letters maintain some continuity with the demands of the dictatores. Both Margaret King and Lisa Jardine, focusing on the Italian Renaissance, have emphasized that learned women were in a difficult position during this period (King 1980; Grafton and Jardine 1986). Humanist learning in particular served political ends, and those associated with it were either important leaders in their communities or the servants of those who were. A woman skilled in rhetoric, therefore, was an anomalous being, someone qualified by her education to occupy a role that was forbidden by her gender. However, in contrast to the subjects of King's and Jardine's researches, a female member of the royal family in France, a kingdom that was becoming consolidated under the single house of the ruling family, could consider literary accomplishment as a valued attribute. Francis himself was heralded for his support of literary arts, yet he was no Latinist.[3] Being perceived as a supporter of the arts enhanced his prestige as a ruler, and for that reason he was willing to patronize artists and writers and to support his sister in her own patronage of such figures. Furthermore, while King and Jardine both give examples of humanist men who showed signs of discomfort in their responses to educated women, we have examples of letters in which Erasmus praised unstintingly the learning of a number of women, some of them of royal rank such as Marguerite herself (*CWE* 1974, 11: 285) and others the daughters of humanist friends such as Thomas More. In his letter to Margaret Roper (10: 133–35), Erasmus indicates that a mother well versed in good literature will be in a good position to conduct her child's early education, which to Erasmus is a highly important stage in a child's development.

Marguerite's relationship to humanistic writing is ambiguous, however. When Erasmus made his own epistolary overtures to her she did not trouble herself to reply, although she was doubtless a better Latinist than her brother and was friendly to French scholars who shared Erasmus's interest in ancient languages and literature. Yet her own commitments were to the mystical theology of preachers such as Briçonnet, and as a writer she pursued poetry and storytelling in her native French, as opposed to the classical oratory or philological interests of humanist scholars such as Erasmus. Still, in her letters to Briçonnet, Marguerite's French displays a suppleness and complexity that speak to a familiarity with the Latin classics.

At the point of this correspondence, what is now called the Reformation had not yet developed into a decisive split with Rome, and possibilities still existed for reform from within the Roman church. In a short time positions on either side would harden, and Marguerite's brother would eventually join in persecuting reformers in France as a threat to his royal authority. Marguerite's correspondence with Briçonnet took place well before this, during a period of fluidity and promise when a segment of the French reform party looked to the court as a source of support against their deadly enemies, the conservative theologians of the Sorbonne in Paris.

Guillaume Briçonnet, who entered into his diocese at Meaux in 1518, had quickly established himself as a reforming bishop who emphasized sermons over ceremonies and who supported the expansion of biblical literacy among the population (Imbart de la Tour 1914, 3: 110–15). He relied on Scripture as the basis for a theological perspective that was both personal and deeply mystical, strongly influenced by Dionysius the Psuedo-Areopagite.[4] His theology and ecclesiology were well within the scope of traditional Catholicism, yet in the immediate wake of the upheaval brought on by Luther's critique of the sacraments and clerical hierarchy, his perspective was feared by the conservative faction of Paris theologians as being too individualistic and doctrinally too close to Luther's belief in justification by faith alone. As he carried out the reform of his own diocese in an atmosphere of danger and opposition, he would have been eager to welcome the support of a woman such as Marguerite, in the hope that her influence with the king could help him prevail against his enemies.

It is obvious from a reading of the first few letters between Briçonnet and Marguerite that the king's sister had known the bishop prior to writing her initial letter to him and that she was sympathetic to his approach. Marguerite's relationship with Briçonnet was motivated on her side by a desire for spiritual direction. A woman of intense religious feeling, she sought guidance from the bishop's mystical perspective to help her meet the challenges of her own spiritual life. Their exchange of letters is thus also an exchange of one sort of support and counsel for another, spiritual direction for political advocacy (Febvre 1944, 88). At the same time, each claimed to value the fulfillment of the other's need as well as his or her own: Briçonnet writes again and again of the spiritual sustenance he receives from the exchange; and Marguerite shares his concern that the healthy functioning of the Church be restored along patterns that he favors.

In reading selections of the correspondence between Marguerite and Briçonnet, we will find that the two writers make their own peculiar use of the advice in Erasmus's treatise. Their letters may be a kind of conversation, but at the same time they go well beyond this, developing a pattern of verbal exchange that unites epistolary convention with mystical theology, in the process of which otherworldly goals are intertwined with the earthly reality of Church politics. We will examine three aspects of this curious union: first, the manner in which spiritual metaphors and biblical motifs, always introduced by Marguerite, are repeated and developed by both writers through several exchanges; second, how Marguerite's writing communicates simultaneously her exalted social status and her sense of spiritual emptiness; and finally, the theological and gender-related messages that are embedded in the correspondents' manners of addressing each other.

It was Marguerite who initiated the exchange with Briçonnet at a time when she was feeling in need of spiritual assistance and consolation. In her first letter she addresses the bishop as follows: "Monsieur de Meaulx, recognizing that one thing is necessary" (Martineau and Vessière 1975, 1: 25), a reference to the episode in Luke 10:38–42 in which Jesus is visiting the two sisters Martha and Mary. Martha busies herself preparing the food, while her sister sits rapt in contemplation at Jesus' feet.

When Martha says to Jesus, "Tell my sister to get up and help me!" he replies, "Martha, you are anxious about many things, and yet there is only one thing that is necessary."

We see combined in this simple statement the salutatio and benevolentiae captatio from the formula of the dictatores. Marguerite's beginning point will provide a frame, to which both writers will return again and again. In this, her first letter, Marguerite's concession that she recognizes *ung seul necessaire* is the preface to a brief recital (the narratio) of the anxieties that persist in distracting her from this transcendent concern: her worry for her husband's safety in his new position of command; hope for a military victory; her loneliness and isolation in the wake of the recent departure of her aunt and friend Philiberte de Savoie—all summarized in the words "for I must deal with many things that are bound to give me anxiety."[5] The woman of the world wants to be shown how to sit at the feet of her Lord, and thus she demands of Briçonnet spiritual aid (the petitio). She signs the letter "yours entirely, Marguerite."

Briçonnet begins his response with a gesture that he will repeat throughout the exchange: he turns around Marguerite's recommendation of herself to him by recommending her to the Lord, beginning: "Madame, the gentle and noble Lord who is and who alone is the source of all things" (1: 28). In so doing he adopts Marguerite's initial reference to "ung seul" from the benevolentiae captatio and uses it to show how the very thing she requests is implicit in her own words that she has offered to him. Briçonnet's task as Marguerite's adviser will become that of expanding again and again on the language she offers him, unfolding the spiritual aid that she already has embedded in her words—which in turn are the words of Scripture.[6] "I have been overjoyed, Madame, to see from the letter that you have pleased to write me that you recognize one thing is necessary, or, to say it more appropriately, that he has brought about that knowledge in you, for he is the knowledge of himself and can only by means of himself be known, who communicates himself to his creatures by his infinite bounty."[7]

While Briçonnet's adoption of Marguerite's language represents in a significant way his deference to her, his self-correction at the same time aims to emphasize his belief in a total reliance on God, such that even the recognition of God as "ung seul necessaire" must come from God's illumination, not from one's own understanding. Marguerite in her reply indicates that she is pleased with what Briçonnet has given her and that she wants more: "Believing that your opinions come from the Holy Spirit, I pray you that you at least by your writing see to it that you visit and move my heart to the love of God" (1: 30).[8] This passage creates a play on words between *esperit* (spirit) and *escript* (writing). The Holy Spirit is the advocate that Christ promises will come to visit his disciples after he is gone, to give them the strength to maintain their ardor in his absence (John 14:16). Like the Holy Spirit, Briçonnet's writing is able to move Marguerite's heart in the absence of Christ and, of course, of the bishop himself. Thus she asks that he complete his verbal meditations on *ung seul bien necessaire*.

Briçonnet's reply begins in the same manner as his previous letter, turning the request over to Christ: "May the sweet and gentle Lord, who wishes and who alone is able and whose wishing is efficacious, visit by means of his infinite bounty your heart, in moving it to loving him from your very depths, with all your self" (1: 30).[9] Christ *seul* (alone) is both willing and able to effect the inward stimulus that Marguerite demands of Briçonnet's language. Marguerite's complaint that she is alone (*seulle*) becomes a further opportunity for Briçonnet to recommend le seul necessaire, which she will find only when she is alone.

Marguerite's next letter, while continuing to speak of le seul bien necessaire, introduces a new motif: that of sight and blindness. God has been pleased to open her eyes, even though we are by nature blind, and by means of Briçonnet has turned her toward the light. But now, "I pray you, in honor of Him, that you not by failing to continue your salutary letters, allow my eye to close again out of sloth" (1: 33).[10] Marguerite needs Briçonnet's continuous ministrations in order to achieve perseverance in the light she is only beginning to see. Briçonnet's answer begins by adopting her metaphor, invoking "the heavenly, infinite, gentle, noble, true and only light" (1: 34),[11] which both blinds and illuminates every creature capable of receiving it, asking that it may both blind and illuminate Marguerite.

The correspondence is thus built on a paradox: Marguerite begs Briçonnet repeatedly for the one thing that only God can give her. Briçonnet's response is always to redirect her to the only source of satisfaction for her request, thus using her language as a beginning point to cancel his own agency, replacing it with God's. Each request Marguerite issues to him is an occasion for Briçonnet to cancel himself anew, taking his cue from whatever motif she offers him. In so doing, however, he pours out language of his own, expanding on hers, to describe to her the one thing she needs or to direct her gaze to the light, and in this way he brings her at least some satisfaction, as her letters to him testify. However, she must continually repeat the exercise and ask him for more.

What is it that Marguerite wants? One answer that is readily apparent is that she wants him to pray for her, to intercede with the all-powerful God to effect the changes in her soul that will make it possible for her to know God. This is something Briçonnet willingly accommodates: his opening passages, in addition to turning Marguerite's attention to God, also invoke God's aid in giving her what she asks, and prayers to God are repeated throughout his letters. Another wish on Marguerite's part is to be instructed, not just in the tenets of belief but in the means by which she can be inspired to love. Briçonnet accommodates her in two ways: by direct discussion and interpretation of Scripture; and by example. While he steadfastly maintains that only God can truly instruct her, Briçonnet utilizes his self-annihilating language as a means through which she learns to annihilate herself, thus making her receptive to God.

There is one thing remaining that he offers her, however, the most important of all. Briçonnet's language provides her not only with instruction or illumination but with spiritual refreshment to nourish her parched and famished spirit. He accomplishes this with a language that revels in paradox, one that Marguerite will utilize herself in framing her requests to him. Both writers employ subordinate clauses piled one on another, playing on words in a discourse that twists and turns in unexpected directions, to seek the appropriate linguistic vestment for a reality that must always escape expression. Thus Briçonnet's language draws Marguerite into the contemplation of paradox in an attempt to help her create in herself the conditions necessary to receptivity. The language of love, describing the joys of union with God, alternates with the language of self-annihilation, urging Marguerite's withdrawal from the joys of the world. Marguerite meanwhile writes to Briçonnet with new variations on the theme of her spiritual wretchedness, describing herself as alone, blind, wandering, chilled, famished, parched, and sick. Briçonnet's words, she hopes, will console her loneliness, illuminate her, lead her home, warm her heart, fill her emptiness, satisfy her thirst, and cure her sickness. Thus Marguerite's rhetoric aims to persuade Briçonnet to take on the task of using his rhetoric to instruct, please, and, above all, move her. One commentator has remarked on the likelihood that Marguerite made use of Briçonnet's letters in her practice of daily meditation (Martineau and Vessière 1975, 2: 261, n. 2).

It may seem that Briçonnet is the dominant partner in the exchange; after all, it is his language that Marguerite craves, and the space accorded to his writing far surpasses hers. Yet while requests to Marguerite may be inserted at various points, their main purpose is to provide what she has requested in her letters, often seeming to take the form of tracts written for her exclusive benefit. Thus this expansiveness on his part is the very substance of his deference to her, as her servant. Her power is well understood between the two of them, reflected not only in Briçonnet's deference but also in Marguerite's rhetorical approach, as it reveals itself in her brief petitionary letters.

An excellent example occurs in letter 10, written in late October 1521. The entire letter consists of two sentences, which together comprise a substantial paragraph. Marguerite combines motifs of self-abasement with elements of the "grand style," the features of which are expansiveness, magnificence of vocabulary, richness of rhetorical figures (particularly metaphor), and an exalted rather than a familiar tone (Hendrickson 1905). While such a style would be appropriate to a formal oration, for a person to use it in a conversational form such as a letter is a signal of one of two things: the grandeur of the subject matter or the high social rank of at least one of the correspondents. Indeed, when one of Erasmus's humanist friends, Guillaume Budé, attempted such an approach in his letters to Erasmus, his correspondent replied with an accusation that Budé's writing was inappropriate, reflecting personal vanity (Carrington 1990, 81–82). It is, however, a variation on the grand style that Erasmus will adopt when he himself addresses Marguerite by letter (*CWE* 1974, 11: 285–87), and it is her own approach in all of her letters to Briçonnet, as well as his responses to her. We will examine here the first of the two sentences in the October 1521 letter:

Because the response to your greatly consoling letter is beyond my power, and because there can be no grasp of it without further association and special grace in my poor understanding, the small sense of it which the frozen heart has received, as if filled beyond itself (whence the quantity given, exceeding its strength for receiving, brings about blinded ignorance), has commanded the sheep to close its mouth at the representation of the one perfect lamb, confessing by its silence the incomprehensibility of so lofty, spiritual, and devout a discourse to which, by means neither of understanding nor of feeling, neither can it respond nor can it return for the pains which, on behalf of my salvation, you have undertaken (revealing yourself to be the true father and minister of the great shepherd), a thousand thanks; but seeing that in no part can it bring satisfaction in this, it supplicates the All-Powerful (to whom is all glory) to provide for my deficiency and give to you that which He wishes to be demanded of Him in His regard (for no one more than myself feels held to this), begging you not to attribute to ungrateful idleness that I have not written sooner, but consider that after such unknown clarity the eyes of the sheep did not for a long time know to be reassured, seeing neither within nor around itself anything but the confusion of darkness. (1: 49)[12]

At this point in the correspondence Marguerite has dispensed with the formula of the dictatores with which she began, and yet many of the elements are there in truncated form. There is no salutatio, but Marguerite picks up several of the motifs, or benevolentiae captationes, that have been exchanged in the correspondence thus far. There is first of all a reference to the motif of le seul in the mentioning of the one perfect lamb. The letter also draws on an earlier discussion of the various kinds of sheep over which Christ acts as shepherd, a motif which Marguerite introduced by asking Briçonnet to write to her about how Christ's sheep might be categorized (1: 37). Here Marguerite describes herself as a sheep that, in the presence of such a portrayal of Christ the Lamb as Briçonnet has given in his most recent letter, cannot do justice with her own expressions of thanks to the spiritual illumination her mentor has brought about. Briçonnet's words make Christ a presence for her (as the Holy Spirit will do for the Apostles and the Church) by virtue of his capability in representing the ineffable mysteries, but neither her understanding nor her capacity for feeling can contain such loftiness. Two other motifs from earlier letters appear here as well: the blinded eye or vision that must be illuminated, symbolizing her limited understanding; and the frozen heart that must be moved to feeling, indicating her insufficiency of will.

There is also in evidence the classical pose of affected modesty, which would be familiar to all persons educated in the Latin epistolary tradition (Curtius 1953, 83–85). In this case it is merged with a mystical pose of personal inadequacy and even nullity in the presence of the divine. Marguerite's paradoxically articulate protest that she cannot speak does in fact succeed in demonstrating her speechlessness; this is effected by means of one parenthetical statement after another, many of which form pincer constructions at various points in the sentence, functioning to defer closure to the point that the reader is threatened with losing the thread altogether. She may not be capable of doing verbal justice to Briçonnet's teaching, but she proves herself of a capacity equal to his in her expressions of mystical paradox.

In Briçonnet's replies to her, however, it is her spiritual fecundity, not the quality of her writing, that he praises. In adopting a mystical approach, Marguerite, like her predecessors Hildegard of Bingen and Julian of Norwich (and her near-contemporary Theresa of Avila), is availing herself of a medium that had in the past allowed women to cut through traditional lines of authority and attain their own spiritual authority in writing. In many of Briçonnet's letters the bishop lauds Marguerite as his spiritual superior, one whose sophisticated understanding is beyond his own. Yet it is neither spiritual nor temporal authority that Marguerite attempts to claim in her bid for direction from Briçonnet, but rather discipleship. The bishop, in turn, does not willingly accommodate himself to the role she has chosen for him, but rather tries to claim a role of dependency on her.

While Briçonnet in his letters to Marguerite goes to great pains to satisfy her need for spiritual direction, Marguerite, although she is strongly supportive of his theology and patterns of reform, gives only allusions to his need for political advocacy in her letters. At several points she indicates that she is assigning a verbal postscript to the letter carrier, evidently not wishing to commit to writing whatever she has to tell him (2: 71, 76–77). At other times she will make a remark to provide him with the reassurance he is seeking; for example, in a letter written in November 1521 she attaches a postscript saying, "it appears to me that it is best to close the mouths of ignorant people most quickly, assuring you that the king and Madame [the queen mother, Louise of Savoy] have well considered to let it be known that the truth of God is not heresy" (1: 71).[13] This comment is indicative of the derivative nature of Marguerite's power, depending on the goodwill of the king and their mother; however, it also demonstrates that Marguerite is in a relationship with the king that is sufficiently intimate that she may presume to inform Briçonnet of the king's intentions.

The titles that the bishop and the princess assign to themselves and each other reflect their respective attempts at defining their relationship. Marguerite signs several letters as la vostre fille (your own daughter), for which she is rebuked by Briçonnet: only God is her true father (1: 32).

However, Briçonnet attempts something similar by claiming in the letter of 24 October 1521 that he is a son to Marguerite; he begins by saying, "Madame, the fruitfulness of your letters is so great that I could not satisfy it, by means of one or of many, coming out of my ignorance" (1: 41).[14] Marguerite's letters, brief and compressed as they are, carry within them spiritual profundities that Briçonnet in his own letters must struggle to bring to realization. He continues several pages later, in closing: "As a mother, you have awakened your discerning son, in providing rich meat which hardly benefits him, for he is feverish, and because of this unable to taste it" (1: 48).[15] She has awakened his understanding but not his capability, his awareness but not his power; and thus, he beseeches her further help. Within the framework of the spiritual danger of blasphemy against what is sacred, Briçonnet requests help from a powerful woman in facing a dangerous political situation: "In regards to which, Madame, I beg you humbly to be helpful to me and to extend your maternal charity."[16] Marguerite's motherhood has two implications, political and spiritual. She moves Briçonnet to contemplate the mysteries in words, thus nurturing his spiritual understanding; she also by her maternal care can help him in his dangerous role as reformer.

Marguerite's reply, the letter of 24 October 1521 cited above, is, as we have seen, a protestation of her own weakness and incapacity, an appeal to God to provide the bishop what she cannot, and a further request for Briçonnet's ministrations. She signs her letter as "vostre bonne fille, Marguerite" (1: 49), ignoring his earlier admonition that she not call herself his daughter. Briçonnet in his reply once again corrects her: Marguerite belongs to herself, so that she may be the spouse of Christ (1: 60).

Erasmus's recommendations for adoptive names allow for referring to a patroness as a mother; however, the exchange that develops between Marguerite and Briçonnet eventually goes well beyond any such convention. When Briçonnet introduces the mother-son terminology, he is indirectly asking Marguerite for help in promoting the very truth she is seeking from him. Marguerite appears at first to be unwilling to accept this designation of power, signing subsequent letters to him as "la foieble Marguerite," "l'indiscrete Marguerite," or, signifying a spiritual as well as physical illness, "la doublement malade, Marguerite" (1: 63–64, 71). The next significant use of the term *mère* does not occur until about four months later, without further development. Finally, however, at the end of 1522, Briçonnet openly expresses his wish that Marguerite consider both him and his brother Denis, also a bishop and an ally in his efforts for reform, as her own adopted sons, "thanking you humbly and with all my heart for the grace that it has pleased him to give you in adopting [your son]. . . . If you wish, the two of us will always be whole-heartedly commended to you" (1: 229).[17] Marguerite in her reply accepts the designation by referring to herself as "vostre vielle mere" (your old mother) (2: 11), and from that point on the pattern is established.

The two thus carry on a competition in which each attempts to rep-resent himself or herself as being weaker than the other and thereby in need of the other's ministrations. By calling herself *fille* toward the be-ginning of the correspondence, Marguerite places a special kind of claim on Briçonnet, one which he refuses in his answer. He continuously pro-tests his incapacity, even unwillingness, to give her what she asks. Marguerite nevertheless presses her claims relentlessly, saying at one point, "I well know that my demand is great, but just as great is the necessity that prevents me from thinking of your pains for the good that they will bring to the honor of the Master and only Lord" (1: 215).[18] At this time in the correspondence, Briçonnet has just finished a long com-mentary on the escape of the Hebrew people from Egypt and their wanderings in the desert; Marguerite now wants him to take her fur-ther, for she indicates that for her own salvation she needs his help and instruction, gifted as he is by the Holy Spirit. Her demands in this case are pressed not only on the basis of Briçonnet's capabilities and her manifest need, but in the name of the sovereign Lord himself.

One might surmise, then, that in offering himself and his brother to Marguerite as adoptive sons, Briçonnet is attempting to reverse their relationship and place himself in a position to ask Marguerite for her support and strength. Marguerite's acceptance of the title of mother might seem to be her acceptance of a reversal of their roles. However, her as-sumption of motherhood turns out not to be an assumption of strength but a new basis for expressing her weakness: for she describes herself as his *aged* mother and describes him as the one who has the things she desires, the one who knows the taste of the restorative, heavenly food and who can at least provide his poor old mother with crumbs ("les myettes") (2: 10–11). Briçonnet's reply tries to turn Marguerite's language of poverty and weakness back on itself by expressing the paradoxical inversion between poverty and wealth: with your poverty of spirit you can renew Jesus' presence in your soul; in the meanwhile, your son with his many riches cannot taste the delicate, royal food, for only beggars can enter into the kingdom of heaven (2: 13). For many letters to come, "les myettes" will occupy a place comparable to that of "le seul" in the earliest letters.

For certain readers these metaphors and modes of address appear to be insufferably precious, casting doubt on the sincerity of the correspondents' intentions (Becker 1900, 426–27). Yet to dismiss such language as a mere conceit is to overlook evidence that proves that Marguerite and Briçonnet themselves treated it with the utmost seriousness. The months that were to follow saw the serious illness of Louise of Savoy and the illnesses and deaths of Marguerite's sister-in-law, Queen Claude, and of her beloved niece Charlotte, all of which enter into the correspondence. Throughout these calamities the two will continue to name themselves and each other according to their adoptive family relationship. Most poignantly, Marguerite will refer to herself at one point as "vestre sterile mere," an indirect reference to her own childlessness in her marriage to Charles d'Alençon (2: 67). Briçonnet will meditate on the spiritual sterility that is ultimately the source of fruitfulness, a paradox that transforms Marguerite's spiritual and personal barrenness into its opposite (2: 67).[19]

In the end, one could say that both Marguerite and Briçonnet won their competition, for both of them found their power to affect earthly events (of which church reform is unfortunately a part) to be seriously limited by their weakness. In 1525, following Francis I's defeat at Pavia and capture by his archrival Charles V, Marguerite would journey to Spain to negotiate the terms of his release. In the absence of both Marguerite and her brother, Briçonnet would come under severe pressure from the Parlemente in Paris, eventually issuing a testimonial to his orthodoxy that would destroy his credibility among the reform party. Yet the effects of his influence on Marguerite would persist, and she would draw on his insights and his language in her later mystic poetry (Cottrell 1986; Sommers 1989).

Marguerite, for her part, would become increasingly marginalized and alienated from the royal court after 1534, when her brother decided to act aggressively against the reform (Jourda 1930, 1: 181–97). She eventually withdrew to a monastery on the border between France and Spain, and her stories in the *Heptameron* reflect more and more an attitude of world-weariness. During the period of her exchange of letters with Briçonnet, however, each correspondent gained strength from the other. Marguerite became a prominent figure at court whose prestige drew on her renowned piety and on the prestige and boldness of the movement with which she became associated. Under her protection Briçonnet and his circle were able to fend off the attacks of their enemies for at least a few years and carry on with their work of scholarship and reform.

In the meantime, however, the letters themselves present a valuable opportunity to explore the ways in which a man and a woman attempted to sort out rhetorically issues of power, gender, and spirituality in an epistolary exchange at a time when the rules of language and writing were changing. While the wordplay in which they engaged may seem puzzling to modern readers, it expanded the boundaries of the conventions of the period in which Marguerite and Briçonnet lived. As Marguerite and Briçonnet worked through the mysteries of the spiritual life, they engaged in wordplay based on Scripture, they engaged in the play of outbidding one another in their protestations of weakness, and they engaged in the playful assumption of gender-based roles of deepest intimacy.

Notes

All translations are my own unless otherwise noted.

1. Knecht (1982, 4–5) describes the education the children received under the guidance of their mother, Louise of Savoy. See also Jourda (1930, 1: 21–27) regarding the unusually expansive nature of Marguerite's education.

2. For discussions of the significance of this treatise in terms of the traditional practice of letter-writing see Henderson (1983) and Gerlo (1971, 1978).

3. Knecht (1982, 4) points out that Guillaume Budé wrote his treatise on the education of a prince in French, knowing that if he had written it in Latin the king would not have bothered to read it.

4. In the Medieval and Renaissance periods it was widely believed that a set of mystical writings compiled in the sixth century was the work of the Dionysius whom Paul converted in Athens (Acts 17:34). For the influence of these texts on Briçonnet, see Heller (1971).

5. "Monsieur de Meaulx, congnoissant que ung seul est necessaire . . . car il me fault mesler de beaucoup de choses qui me doivent bien donner crainte."

6. Saulnier (1977, 457–58) suggests that Marguerite introduces scriptural motifs according to the lessons that occur in the liturgy each week.

7. "Moult joieulx ay esté, Madame veoir par les lettres qu'il vous a pleu m'escripre que congnoissez ung seul necessaire, ou, pour mieulx parler, qu'il se face congnoistre en vous, car il est sa congnoissance et ne se peult que en luy mesme estre congneu, qui se communique par sa bonté infinie à ses creatures."

8. "Pensant que voz oppinions procedent du Sainct-Esperit, au moings je vous prie que par escript vueillez visiter et exciter à l'amour de Dieu mon cueur."

9. "Le doulx et debonnaire Seigneur, qui veult et seul peult et lequel puissamment veult, . . . visite par son infinie bonte vostre coeur, en l'excitant a visceralement de tout soy l'aymer."

10. "Je vous prie, en l'honneur de luy, que, par faulte de continuer voz tant salutaires lettres ne le laisser en paresse recloure."

11. "Le superceleste, infinie, doulce, debonnaire, vraie et seulle lumiere."

12. "Pour ce que la responce de vostre tant consolable lettre est hors de ma puissance et que l'intelligence n'en peult estre sans plus grant frequentation et grace specialle en mon pauvre entendement, le petit sentiment que en a receu le refroidy coeur, comme par sus soy remply, dont la quantité donnée excedant la force du recepvoir, cause aveuglée ignorance, a commandé à la brebis clourre sa bouche à l'exemple de l'aigneau seul parfaict, confessant par son taire l'incomprehensibilité d'un sy hault, spirituel et devot propos, dont, par ne l'entendre ne sentir, ne puis respondre ne vous rendre de la poene que, pour mon salut, en avez prinse, vous monstrant le vray pere et ministre du grand pasteur, mil mercis, mais voiant que en nulle partie n'y puis satisffaire, supplie le Tout-Puissant, à qui la glore de tout est, subvenir à ma defaulte et vous donner ce qu'il veult que, envers luy, pour vous luy soit demandé, car nulle plus que moy ne s'y sent tenue, vous priant n'estimer à ingrate paresse sy plus tost n'ay escript, mais pensez que après telle incongneue clarté les yeulx de la brebis ne se sont sceu de long temps rassurer, ne voiant en soy ni autour que confusion de tenebres."

13. "Il me semble que le plus tost clorre la bouche aux ygnorans est le meilleur, vous asseurant que le Roy et Madame i ont bien deliberé de donner à congnoistre que la verité de Dieu n'est point heresie."

14. "Madame, la fecundité de voz lettres est sy grande que par une ne pourrois, ne par plusieurs, venans de mon ignorance, y satisfaire."

15. "Comme mere, avez reveillé vostre subtille filz, en luy subministrant viande fecunde laquelle ne luy profitte guere, car il est febricitant et, par ce, sans goust."

16. "A quoy, Madame, vous supplie très-humblement me estre aydant et que estendez vostre charité maternelle."

17. "Vous merciant très-humblement et de tout mon coeur de la grace qu'il vous a pleu faire d'en adopter ung. . . . Tous deux vous seront, s'il vous plaist, à jamais viscerallement recommandés." It is important to note that Briçonnet was more than twenty years older than Marguerite, a woman in her early thirties at the time of the correspondence.

18. "Je sçay bien que grande est ma demande, mais aussy bien grande est la necessité qui me garde de penser à vostre peine pour le bien qui en vient à l'honneur de Maistre et seul Seigneur."

19. "It is good to desire the fruitful sterility and the sterile fecundity." See Heller (1971, 289–90) for a discussion of this letter and its continuing influence on Marguerite.

References

Becker, Ph. 1900. "Marguerite, Duchesse d'Alençon et Guillaume Briçonnet, Évêque de Meaux d'après leur Correspondance Manuscrite 1521–1524." *Bulletin de la Société de l'Histoire de Protestantisme Française* 49: 393–477, 661–67.

Carrington, Laurel. 1990. "The Writer and His Style: Erasmus' Clash with Guillaume Budé." *Erasmus of Rotterdam Society Yearbook Ten*, 61–84.

Cherewatuk, Karen, and Ulrike Wiethaus. 1993. "Introduction: Women Writing Letters in the Middle Ages." In *Dear Sister: Medieval Women and the Epistolary Genre*, edited by Cherewatuk and Wiethaus, 1–19. Philadelphia: University of Pennsylvania Press.

Collected Works of Erasmus (CWE). 1974. Toronto: University of Toronto Press.

Constable, Giles. 1976. *Letters and Letter Collections*. Typologie des sources du Moyen Âge occidental, fasc. 17. Turnhout: Brepols.

Cottrell, Robert D. 1986. *The Grammar of Silence: A Reading of Marguerite de Navarre's Poetry*. Washington, D.C.: Catholic University of America Press.

Curtius, E. R. 1953. *European Literature in the Latin Middle Ages*. Trans. William R. Trask. New York: Pantheon.

Donawerth, Jane. 1992. "Transforming the History of Rhetorical Theory." *Feminist Teacher* 7: 1, 35–39.

Febvre, Lucien. 1944. *Autour de L'Heptaméron: Amour Sacré, Amour Profane*. Paris: Gallimard.

Gerlo, A. 1971. "The *Opus de Conscribendis Epistolis* of Erasmus and the Tradition of the *Ars Epistolica*." In *Classical Influences on European Culture a.d. 500–1500*, edited by R. R. Bolgar, 103–14. Cambridge: Cambridge University Press.

———. 1978. "Genèse de l'Épistolographie Classique: Rhétorique Humaniste de la Lettre, de Pétrarque à Juste Lipse." *Revue d'Histoire Littéraire de la France* 78: 6, 886–905.

Grafton, Anthony, and Lisa Jardine. 1986. *From Humanism to the Humanities*. Cambridge: Harvard University Press.

Heller, Henry. 1971. "Marguerite of Navarre and the Reformers of Meaux." *Bibliothèque d'Humanisme et Renaissance* 33: 271–310.

Henderson, Judith Rice. 1983. "Erasmus on the Art of Letter-Writing." In *Renaissance Eloquence: Studies in the Theory and Practice of Renaissance Rhetoric*, edited by James J. Murphy, 331–55. Berkeley: University of California Press.

Hendrickson, G. L. 1905. "The Origin and Meaning of the Ancient Characters of Style." *American Journal of Philology* 26: 249–90.

Imbart de la Tour, P. 1914. *Les Origines de la Réforme*. Vol. 3: *L'Évangélisme (1521–1538)*. Paris: Librairie Hachette.

Jourda, P. 1930. *Marguerite d'Angoulême, Duchesse d'Alençon, Reine de Navarre (1492–1549)*. Vol. 1. Paris: Librairie Ancienne Honoré Champion.

King, Margaret L. 1980. "Book-Lined Cells: Women and Humanism in the Early Italian Renaissance." In *Beyond Their Sex: Learned Women of the European Past*, edited by Patricia H. Labalme, 66–90. New York: New York University Press.

Knecht, R. J. 1982. *Francis I.* Cambridge: Cambridge University Press.

Martineau, Christine, and Michel Vessière, eds., with Henry Heller. 1975. *Guillaume Briçonnet-Marguerite Angoulême Correspondance (1521–1524).* Geneva: Librairie Droz.

Neubert, Fritz. 1963. "Zür Problematic der Briefe der Margarete von Navarre." *Zeitschrift für Römanische Philologie* 79: 117–72.

Saulnier, V. L. 1977. "Marguerite de Navarre aux Temps de Briçonnet." *Bibliothèque d'Humanisme et Renaissance* 39: 437–78.

Sommers, Paula. 1989. *Celestial Ladders: Readings in Marguerite de Navarre's Poetry of Spiritual Ascent.* Geneva: Librairie Droz.

Women's Voices and Women's Silence in the Tradition of Early Methodism

Vicki Tolar Collins

While scholarship such as Susan C. Jarratt's on Sappho (1993) has made space for women rhetors in the classical period, Cheryl Glenn's work on Margery Kempe (1992) has opened exploration of medieval women's religious discourse, and Patricia Bizzell's work (1992) has addressed the problem of women rhetors in the Renaissance, female figures have largely been absent from the history of eighteenth-century rhetoric. One remedy for this absence is a shift of focus from "the rhetorical tradition" to what Thomas P. Miller (1993) has called "the rhetoric of traditions," for in the tradition of eighteenth-century British Methodism women rhetors operated in a rich discourse community with remarkable courage and effectiveness.

This essay will examine the dynamics of discourse practices and the politics of public rhetoric in early Methodism, revealing how Methodist women found rhetorical spaces from which they could speak, preach, and declare their faith, with the support and protection of their leader John Wesley. This study will also chronicle and analyze the fate of women speakers after Wesley's death, noting how his successors used discursive and literacy practices to silence the speaking women and give limited voice to the silent. An important part of this project is to identify historical Methodist women leaders who enacted rhetoric through their preaching, their public speaking, and their written texts, thus inviting women such as Sarah Crosby, Mary Bosanquet Fletcher, and Hester Rogers to take their places in the history of rhetoric. As Miller argues, "Instead of just the rhetorical tradition, we need to study the rhetoric of traditions—the ways that political parties, ethnic groups, social movements, and other discourse communities constitute and maintain the shared values and assumptions that authorize discourse" (1993, 26).

A Rhetorical Space for Women: Sarah Crosby, Mary Bosanquet, and the Female Brethren

Prior to the advent of Methodism as a spiritual movement within the Anglican Church in the mid–eighteenth century, few Christian sects had allowed women to speak in the church. Traditionally men were the priests, the pastors, and the theologians. Women were the listeners, the followers, the quiet, faithful laborers in the spiritual vineyards. John Wesley, an ordained Anglican priest, transformed those roles and relationships in Methodism through his new "method" of religion, new material practices, and new institutional forms. Wesley's frustration with the lack of spiritual vigor in the Church of England led him to travel the English countryside preaching at dawn to the lower and middle classes, offering them personal salvation through faith, passionate interpretation of scripture, and a socioreligious organization that attracted new members at an astounding pace.[1] These religious innovations created spaces, sanctions, and support for women to speak in public and write for publication.

Among the organizational practices that made space for women to speak before groups, the itinerancy of Methodist preachers was particularly important. The Methodist system was set up so that a town might not have its own pastor but rather be visited periodically by an itinerant Methodist preacher traveling "the circuit." The preacher's long absences created a leadership vacuum in the church community. Who would gather and lead the faithful? Wesley sought to fill the void by organizing Methodists into bands and classes devoted to spiritual growth. Bands were single-sex groups of about ten or twelve persons more experienced in the faith, with women's bands being led by women and men's bands by men. Classes were attended by men and women together, some being advanced in the faith and some new "seekers." These groups might be led by either men or women. While classes usually began small (ten or twelve members), a strong teacher might quickly attract scores of people to his or her class, at which point, according to Wesley's directive, the class would be subdivided and new leaders identified. Because women were strong in numbers in early Methodist groups, many classes had female leadership, and many of the most successful class leaders were women.

In fact, in Methodist communities women spoke publicly in a number of roles, according to the historian of Methodism Earl Kent Brown

(1983). The most informal level of public utterance was casual conversation on religious subjects, which was expected of all Methodist women. Within classes and bands some women led discussions, while others prayed publicly and gave testimony concerning their religious experiences. Exhortation, the fervent urging of an audience to embrace the gospel message, was practiced by women, as was expounding, which involved explaining a passage from the Bible or from another spiritual text. A few Methodist women preached, which involved "taking a text" from scripture, interpreting it, and proclaiming a message (Brown 1983, 15–31).

One of the first Methodist women to speak publicly was Sarah Crosby (1729–1804), who began by addressing other women in bands; her meetings became so popular that she was called upon to address large groups of men and women as early as the 1760s. Elizabeth Ritchie often traveled the circuit with John Wesley but usually did not preach. Other traveling women preachers, according to Paul Wesley Chilcote's *John Wesley and the Women Preachers of Early Methodism* (1991), included Mary Bosanquet (later Mrs. John Fletcher), the blind Margaret Davidson, Elizabeth Harrell, and "Praying Nanny" Cutler, among others. Hester Ann Rogers, while not a preacher, was well known for the large number of converts she brought into the church in Ireland and England through her classes and spiritual conversations.[2]

Methodist women who spoke in public frequently had to defend themselves from public attack. Women who prayed, testified, exhorted, and expounded often claimed that their authority to speak had come from the voice of God. Women preachers justified their public address through four main arguments. First, they claimed the power of their own inner witness, i.e., they had experienced a call from God to speak out. They pointed pragmatically to the success they were having with conversions, cited scripture that supported women's speaking, and reinterpreted scripture that seemed to forbid it. But none of these justifications would have succeeded without the powerful, if initially reluctant, support of John Wesley for their preaching (Brown 1983, 28–30).

Correspondence between Wesley and Methodist women leaders (correspondence that is often cited as causing the end of his marriage) not only reveals Wesley's centrality in allowing, supporting, and controlling women's public speech, but also manifests the conflicts and anxiety women speakers experienced regarding their speaking.

Early in the growth of Methodism, Wesley drew a distinction between Quakerism and Methodism in that Quaker women addressed
large gatherings, while Methodist women addressed only small classes
and bands. Wesley's early opposition to women preaching was based
on scriptural prohibitions of women's speech (1 Cor. 14:34, 1 Tim. 2:12).
However, Wesley was ever the pragmatist, and his views on women's
speech became more generous as Methodist women led larger and larger
classes and brought more and more souls to Jesus. When some women
preachers expressed concern about the appropriateness of their own
speeches, Wesley guided them. For example, when Sarah Crosby wrote
to Wesley that her class had expanded to over two hundred members,
he advised her to open her remarks by saying: "'You lay me under a
great difficulty. The Methodists do not allow of women preachers; neither do I take upon me any such character. But I will just nakedly tell
you what is in my heart.' This [wrote Wesley] will in great measure ob-
viate their grand objection. . . . I do not see that you have broken any
law" (qtd. in Brown 1983, 26). Wesley believed, erroneously, that the
modesty of this introduction would provide a positive beginning for
Crosby's speech and quiet her critics.

Mary Bosanquet constructed her own strong defense of women's
public speech in a 1776 letter to Wesley, stating each common objection
to women's speech and then answering it. She refuted Saint Paul's admonition against women speaking or teaching mixed groups by pointing
out the specific political environment in the Corinthian church to which
Paul's letter was addressed. In an "Objection and Answer" format she
answered with this response to literalists who argued that women should
not speak at all in church:

> Then why is it said, Let the woman prophesy with her head covered,
> or can she prophesy without speaking? or ought she to speak but not
> to edification?
>
>   Ob:—She may now and then, if under a peculiar impulse, but never
> else.
>
>   An:—But how often is she to feel this impulse? Perhaps you will
> say, two or three times in her life; perhaps *God* will say, two or three
> times in a week, or day—and where shall we find the Rule for this?
> But the consequences (here I acknowledge is my own objection, that
> all I do is *lawful*, I have not doubt, but is it expedient? that, my dear
> Sir, I want your light in) but what are the consequences feared?

Making a powerful parallel case argument from Scripture, Bosanquet continued:

> Now I do not apprehend Mary sinned . . . or could in the least be accused of immodesty, when she carried the joyful news of her Lord's Resurrection and in that sense taught the Teachers of Mankind. Neither was the woman of Samaria to be accused of immodesty when she invited the whole city to come to Christ. Neither do I think the woman mentioned in the 20th chapter of the 2nd Samuel could be said to sin against modesty, tho' she called the General of the opposite army to converse with her, and then . . . went to all the people, both Heads and others, to give them her advice and by it the City was Saved. (Davies and Rupp 1988, 4: 168–71)

Bosanquet defended her own call as "extraordinary" and refused to take responsibility for the danger that other less able women who lacked a call might seek to preach as she had done.

Wesley responded to her:

> My dear sister,
> I think the strength of the cause rests there, on your having an *Extraordinary Call*. So, I am persuaded, has every one of our Lay Preachers: otherwise I could not countenance his preaching at all. It is plain to me that the whole Work of God termed Methodism is an extraordinary dispensation of his Providence. Therefore I do not wonder if several things occur therein which do not fall under ordinary rules of discipline. St. Paul's ordinary rule was, "I permit not a woman to speak in the congregation." Yet in extraordinary cases he made a few exceptions; at Corinth, in particular. (qtd. in Chilcote 1991, 143)

Supported by their leader and justified by apostolic precedent, the women preachers and speakers of early Methodism became gradually more active and visible in the 1770s and 1780s, with an influential group led by Sarah Crosby and Ann Tripp calling themselves, with what we can assume is intentional irony, the "Female Brethren." This group of women not only supported each other's preaching but also took public stands regarding church politics, on at least one occasion opposing the assignment of a certain male itinerant preacher to their circuit (Chilcote 1991, 200–201).

Although women had been preaching since the 1760s, the first official Methodist document sanctioning a woman's preaching was addressed in 1787 to Sarah Mallet of Long Stratton. Chilcote calls this note "probably the single most important piece of documentary evidence concerning the women preachers of early Methodism" (1991, 195). It is a simply worded authorization to preach by the Manchester Conference of 1787 that states: "We give the right hand of fellowship to Sarah Mallet, and have not objection to her being a preacher in our connexion, so long as she preaches the Methodist doctrines, and attends to our discipline" (qtd. in Taft 1825, 1: 84). Sarah Mallet's journal records her reaction: "When I first travelled I followed Mr. Wesley's counsel, which was, to let the voice of the people be to me the voice of God;—and where I was sent for, to go, for the Lord had called me thither. To this counsel I have attended to this day. But the voice of the people was not the voice of some preachers. But Mr. Wesley soon made this easy by sending me a note from the Conference, by Mr. Joseph Harper, who was that year appointed for Norwich" (qtd. in Taft 1825, 1: 84).

Sarah Mallet was an interesting choice to receive the first official authorization to preach, for she was a young woman who resisted the call to preach and only began the practice while in the midst of seizures that lasted many hours at a time. She would fall senseless into a stupor and then begin to preach, speaking as if she were addressing some particular congregation. She would take a text and preach from it while in a trance. Says Taft, "She continued to preach in every following fit, speaking clear and loud, though she was utterly senseless" (*Arminian Magazine* 1788, 11: 92). Up to two hundred people would gather in her uncle's home to hear her preaching during a seizure. She was finally persuaded to embrace her call to preach and began to answer calls from many churches. Wesley was supportive of her call but cautioned her about her preaching style, writing in 1789 that she should guard her health by not accepting every invitation to preach. He further advised: "Never continue the service above an hour at once, singing, preaching, prayer, and all. You are not to judge by your own feelings, but by the word of God. Never scream. Never speak above the natural pitch of your voice; it is disgustful to the hearers. It gives them pain, not pleasure. And it is destroying yourself" (Wesley 1931, 7: 190).

Ever aware that the Methodists were accused of "enthusiasm" (a pejorative label that Wesley denied), Wesley was concerned that Sarah

Mallet's emotional fervor be moderated. In retrospect, it is interesting to speculate whether the Manchester Conference intentionally chose as the approved female preacher a woman whom some might call mad or ill. While her call might have been strong, her ethos was surely suspect. Psychoanalytic critics might speculate that the fits provided evidence of the depth of the social prohibition against women's public speech. But fervent or moderate, sane or mad, she had the official approval of the Methodist Conference to preach.

Hester Rogers and the Rhetoric of the Spiritual Journal

While Sarah Crosby, Mary Bosanquet, and Sarah Mallet were daring to "take a text" and preach the gospel to Wesley's flock gathered in fields, barns, and preaching houses, Hester Rogers was following a less public spiritual path as a class leader, visitor to the sick, writer, helpmate to her husband (the Methodist preacher James Rogers), and soulmate to John Wesley. Her role in early Methodism illustrates not only the importance of literacy to Wesley's spiritual project, but also the way the institutional church after Wesley's death strategically used literacy to limit the public roles of women in the church.

Hester Rogers's rhetorical project was not played out in the pulpit but rather on the written page. Her spiritual journal, compiled and edited for publication at the urging of John Wesley, became one of the most widely published texts among the thousands published by the early Methodist presses, being issued first in 1793 and going into over fifty British and American editions during the nineteenth century. While texts by other Methodist women might see one or two printings if they were published at all, the *Account of the Experience of Hester Ann Rogers* became a best-seller among American Methodists. Examining the institutional context that shaped and controlled this woman's voice, her life choices, her text, and her popularity in an institutional context sheds considerable light on the development of early Methodism and the place of women therein.

The fact that Hester Rogers did not preach has resulted in her rhetorical importance in Methodism being overlooked by current historians of early Methodism. Chilcote mentions her only on the first page of the preface of his study of Methodist preachers, recalling that Rogers's manuscript journal was the first document by a Methodist woman that he read. He quickly moves on to focus on the more intriguing preaching women. Earl Kent Brown's study (1983) includes a substantial section on Hester Rogers, but she is cast as important primarily because she represents two common female types in the early movement: before her marriage, the woman in the pew; after her marriage, the faithful wife of the itinerant preacher. "She was an unusual woman, and she doubtless did the things we are about to describe unusually well. But the activities themselves are the typical behavior of a Methodist woman in a local society," writes Brown (208).

While her roles in the spiritual community might be typical, her relationship with John Wesley was not. Wesley believed that Hester Rogers was one of the few persons to have experienced spiritual perfection in the midst of life rather than at the moment of death. Rogers and Wesley corresponded regularly from the time they met in 1776, when she was just twenty and had already raised the wrath of her Anglican family by becoming a Methodist. They continued to meet and correspond regularly for the rest of Wesley's life. When Wesley became too ill to travel the circuit any longer, he transferred Hester's husband to London so that Hester might care for Wesley and his household during his final illness. Even though she had just given birth to her fifth child, Hester was at Wesley's bedside when he died. She was also entrusted with the sensitive task of cataloging Wesley's papers after his death.

Wesley encouraged Hester Rogers to assume rhetorical authority during their first conversation in 1776. When she cautiously told him of her recent experience of ecstatic union with the Godhead, he urged her to reveal her experience publicly and "declare what the Lord has wrought" (Rogers 1837, 50). She does not record whether she publicly revealed her experience immediately, but Wesley promptly initiated a correspondence with her seeking to establish similarities between her experience and that of his favorite French Quietist mystic, the Marquis deRenty.

Hester Rogers was also important in the history of Methodism because of the quality and intensity of her relationship with God and because of her ability to capture that intensity in the lines of her spiritual journal. Her ultimate declaration of what God had wrought in her life was the publication of a version of her spiritual journal in 1793, one year before she died of causes related to childbirth.

Rogers's journal is spiritually significant because of the process by which it was composed, because of its popularity with readers, and because of the favored institutional position it held in nineteenth-century Methodism. Hester was already keeping a spiritual journal when she first met John Wesley. Her earliest journal-keeping dates to an adolescent discipline at about age thirteen in which she carried with her a running list of the good and evil that she did. At that time she believed, "we are all to be judged according to our works": if good works exceeded evil ones, she would be saved; if evil exceeded good, she would be damned. She wrote: "I thought I would impartially examine myself by this rule, and see what hope I should have for my own soul. . . . I therefore made a little day book, in which I put down every good and bad action with great sincerity. . . . I went on resolving to be better, and still keeping the account, till being at a dance, I pulled out my day book with my pocket handkerchief, and it was found, and made the jest of the company. I was then so ashamed, that I resolved to follow this method no more" (12). This type of journal writing involves a kind of self-rhetoric, or persuasion of the self, in which the mere cataloging of sins might act as a deterrent to further misdeeds.

Several years later at about the time of her justification by faith, Hester Rogers began a journal that was not a tally of good works but a passionate expression of her relationship with God. The entries from this period seem to be a kind of exploratory writing in which the journal writer probes the meaning of her own faith and doubt, describing the tension between her love for God and her frequent temptation by Satan. (The Satan with whom Hester converses appears to be the voice of cynical reason within her own mind.) To the discipline of journal writing Rogers adds the practice of severe fasting, which leads to the speculation that she may have practiced holy anorexia common among medieval mystics of the Catholic Church (Collins 1995).

According to her account, Hester Roe was the serious and pious child of an Anglican vicar. Her father died when she was nine, leaving her to be raised by her controlling and difficult mother. After her father's death, Hester's relatives tried to "cure" her of her seriousness by introducing her to dancing, novels, plays, and card games. She recalls her early adolescence as a crazy quilt of flagrant frivolity alternating with intense self-chastisement. At one point Hester was so determined to forgo the superficial social whirl in which she was living that she ripped her fine dresses to shreds and cut off her hair so that she could no longer be admired.

On another occasion she was equally determined not to let religion ruin her pleasure in dancing. Having reasoned that dancing was spiritually harmful, she wrote: "But then, if this is really true (said I to myself,)

I ought not to follow this amusement any longer. And can I give it up? My vile heart replied, I cannot, I will not. The Spirit of God whispered, Will you then indulge yourself in what you know to be sin? Would you wish to be struck dead in the ball room? My conflict was great, yet I was resolved to run all hazards rather than give up this pleasure . . . and after this ran more eagerly than ever into all pleasurable follies" (Rogers 1837, 17–18).

Her approach/avoidance relationship with the spiritual continued until her late teens when she embraced the disciplines of Methodism as the answer to her struggles. So adamantly did her mother oppose Hester's association with Methodism that she threatened to expel Hester from the family. Hester bargained for the privilege of staying in her mother's home, promising that she would live as her mother's servant if she were permitted to associate with the Methodists.

Although we know from other sources that, after her marriage to the itinerant preacher James Rogers at age twenty-eight and subsequent relocation to Ireland, Hester Rogers brought hundreds of new converts into Methodism through her class leadership, her spiritual journal focuses almost exclusively on her personal relationship to God. Day by day she records in intimate detail the ebb and flow of her soul, barely mentioning her marriage, her children, or her work among the Methodists.

Women and Wesley's Literacy Project

The rhetorical importance of Hester Rogers's journal becomes clear when placed in the larger context of John Wesley's literacy practices. Simply put, the Methodist women needed something to read. Wesley himself was a tireless reader and writer; as he traveled throughout England and Ireland, he read constantly and wrote daily, including a private diary, a more formally developed journal, sermons, and other spiritual texts for publication. He also founded and edited *The Arminian Magazine* and edited abridged versions of classic texts, both sacred and secular, for the enlightenment of his flock. He was a reader of universal taste and amazing memory, which helps account for the diversity of literary allusions in his prolific writings.

Having published his journals serially as a model, Wesley encouraged his followers, particularly the preachers, to read extensively and regularly examine their own souls in spiritual journals. The journal-keeping was part of the spiritual discipline or method of Methodism. Wesley had a particular interest in spiritual autobiography. The reading lists he compiled for the itinerant preachers (Wesley suggested they should read at least five hours each day) were largely composed of spiritual autobiographies of past Christian leaders. Most texts were abridged by Wesley. The preachers were not only to read such texts but also to compose their own accounts, with each preacher writing the story of his call and his life as a minister of God. Wesley saw spiritual benefit in both the self-examination of composing such a document and in the rhetorical effect these stories might have on others who read them (Rivers 1978).

While there is a democratic spirit in the general call for and publication of these accounts, Wesley tightly controlled their publication, editing them himself and forbidding self-publishing by the preachers. He urged the writers not to be concerned about inelegance of expression, assuring them that he would make their texts presentable. Thus Wesley controlled the ethos of the Methodist itinerants in print and insured that their texts would present a consistent and uplifting model for other Methodists.

Short accounts appeared in *The Arminian Magazine,* which functioned as a sort of early Methodist *People Magazine.* Longer accounts were published cheaply as separate tracts. Wesley encouraged Methodists who could read and write to educate the illiterate in their midst. (Even into the nineteenth century many working-class children and adults learned to read and write in Methodist Sunday schools.)

That Wesley would encourage reading, journal-keeping, and autobiography among the men who preached on the circuit is not surprising. What is more surprising is that he encouraged similar literacy of the spirit among women and men of the laity. He believed that the regularity of journal-keeping and self-reflection would keep the Methodists progressing in the faith.

While Wesley's own diaries are full of imperatives and self-rhetoric ("Avoid" this or "Remember" that), his published journals are clearly for the edification of his readers, recording not only his rigorous daily schedule but also sermons, letters, testimonies, and so on. Felicity Nussbaum, a scholar of eighteenth-century British literature, suggests that Wesley's journals offer a revision of the usual conversion narrative; rather than offering the old paradigm of "I once was lost but now am found," Wesley presents "the description and continual revising of the converted self" (1989, 91). Wesley believed that Methodist readers would learn more from the story of a whole life well lived than from the account of a moment's conversion. Wesley's willingness to publish his journals as a testament of faith and model of life "is a reassurance that each individual's interiority may not be so dangerous, for it may be purchased and consumed" as a published text (94). The serialization of Wesley's journals, as Isabel Rivers points out, "effectively emphasized that Wesley's quest was never complete" (1978, 194).

In the issues of *The Arminian Magazine* that Wesley edited and published from 1778 to 1791, a gradual but clear increase in the number of women's entries is noticeable. There were no women in the first volume of 1778, but more were added each year. By 1791, when Wesley died, male and female accounts were about equal in number. Also in that period a few women's accounts were published as separate tracts, specifically those by Margaret Davidson and Jane Newland. Sarah Grubb's account was published one year after Wesley's death (Chilcote 1991, 253–87).

Through the systematic publication and distribution of life stories, John Wesley challenged the hold that popular secular texts had over the general reading public. Methodists who might be tempted and titillated by novels such as *Clarissa* or *Tom Jones* could instead find edification in the accounts of "real" experiences of fellow Methodists found in *The Arminian Magazine* or in novelistic accounts such as *The Life of Mr. Silas Told*, which by 1790 was in a third edition. While novelists such as Frances Burney portrayed women characters who were molded and controlled by social constraints of polite British society, John Wesley welcomed stories, such as those of Sarah Mallet's "preaching fits," that suggested aspects of body and spirit that are ineffable, marginal, and beyond human understanding. Even in the case of Hester Rogers, what seemed to attract Wesley was not her ordinary piety, as Brown suggests, but the possibility of the mystical in her dealings with God.

Thus Hester Rogers's practice of keeping a spiritual journal and Wesley's urging that she edit it for publication are part of a rich context of literacy, rhetoric, and religion that flourished in the Methodist community during Wesley's lifetime.

Silencing the Methodist Women: The Committee of One Hundred

That many current studies of women in early Methodism limit themselves to the period of John Wesley's life is not coincidental. With Wesley's death church roles open to women were limited and the rhetorical space denied. An examination of what happened to Methodist women rhetorically and politically after Wesley's death demonstrates a transformation and silencing that have often been ignored or glossed over in Methodist scholarship.

Certain that a struggle for power in the church would ensue after his death, Wesley devised a plan that would transfer the power from one individual, himself, to the Committee of One Hundred, which was composed of the leading male preachers of the Church. Just twelve years after Wesley's death this group led the Annual Conference to rule women's preaching "unnecessary." The male leaders of post-Wesley Methodism reverted to the more conservative, traditional view of women: they should not speak in public. In 1802 Joseph Entwisle wrote concerning his circuit at Macclesfield:

> We have *no female preachers* in this part of the country. I think women might with propriety exercise their gifts in a private way, or amongst their own sex; but I never could see the propriety of their being public teachers. Under the Patriarchal dispensation, the oldest male was the priest of the family. Under the Law, all the priests were men. The seventy preachers sent out by our Lord were all men. So were the twelve Apostles. Nor do we ever read of a woman preaching, in the Acts of the Apostles. Hence I conclude, women are not designed for public teachers. (qtd. in Chilcote 1991, 232)

In 1803 the Manchester Conference passed a resolution that drastically limited the public speech of women. They argued that because most Methodists opposed women preaching and because God had currently supplied them with an ample number of male preachers, women should not preach. The resolution stated: "But if any woman among us think she has an extraordinary call from God to speak in public, (and we are sure it must be an *extraordinary* call that can authorize it,) we are of the opinion she should, in general, address her *own sex, and those only.*" A woman's preaching to her own sex was further limited by a ruling that women could not preach in their own circuit without approval or in any other circuit without a written invitation from the Superintendent of the circuit (*Minutes* 2: 188–89). A few men, such as Zechariah Taft, fought vigorously for the right of women to preach and speak in public, but the majority of men in power in British Methodism favored silencing the women.

It appears that Methodist women in America may have fared even worse, for the historian George Coles, writing in 1857, felt it necessary to apologize for even having included certain women in his work *Heroines of Methodism.* He writes: "It will be seen that many of those women whose religious experience is here related were class-leaders and leaders of bands, and as the practice of appointing females to the office of leaders does not obtain in this country, and band meetings are obsolete; and as the practice of praying in prayer-meetings by our gifted sisters is nearly so in most places, some apology for the practice, as it existed among Methodists in the mother country, may not be out of place" (13).

Coles leaves it to a Reverend Jobson to explain why a woman should not speak in public: "Her constitution and sympathies entirely unfit her for that [public speech]; but she has, nevertheless, a sphere of her own. She cannot speak in loud, clarion tones; her voice is rather that of the soft lute, soothing and alluring; but it is not less powerful for its gentleness. . . . Mothers, next to ministers, have been the chief instruments of God in building up the Church" (qtd. in Coles 1857, 17). This relocation of women to the private sphere parallels the rise in America of what has been called the "cult of domesticity" (Welter 1976).

It is not surprising, therefore, that when the burgeoning Methodist publishing establishment, controlled by the Committee of One Hundred, decided to publish widely a woman's spiritual account, the chosen text was not one by a preaching woman, but rather the *Account of the Experience of Hester Ann Rogers*—better a mystic than a female preacher. Although thirty-seven of the eighteenth-century Methodist women preachers left no known publications, several did write accounts of their lives that were never published. These women, including Alice Cambridge, Ann Gilbert, Mary Gilbert, Hannah Harrison, and Sarah Mallet, were silenced not only as preachers by the Conference order of 1803 but also as writers by the Methodist publishing establishment. A number of women preachers had short accounts published in *The Arminian Magazine,* and several, including Mary Bosanquet Fletcher, Dorothy Ripley, Mary Stokes, and Mary Taft, did have their writings published. Mary Bosanquet Fletcher did not publish her own account. Her journal was edited and compiled, with a mixture of admiration and condescension, by Henry Moore, who, by the way, minimized the fact that she had ever preached. The following chart indicates the number of entries listed for several women leaders of early Methodism as they appear in *The British Museum Catalog* (BMC), *the National Union Catalog* (NUC), and *OCLC,* an online catalog.

Existing Narratives by Early Methodist Women

Name	Preacher?	BMC	NUC	OCLC
Hannah Ball	no	2	0	1
Mrs. Grace Bennet	no	0	0	1
Ann Cutler	yes	2	0	2
Margaret Davidson	yes	1	0	0
Mary Bosanquet Fletcher	yes	6	0	7
Mary Holder	yes	0	0	0
Hannah Kilham	yes	3	1	0
Elizabeth R. Mortimer	yes	4	3	4
Frances Pawson	no	0	1	0
Dorothy Ripley	yes	0	0	0
Hester Ann Rogers	no	8	46	71
Mary Stokes	yes	0	0	1
Mary Barritt Taft	yes	0	0	1

Paradoxically, the women preachers of early Methodism were silenced, both in voice and in written word, and the silent woman, the pious and sanctified Hester Rogers, was published, promoted, and praised. In 1878 the American historian Thomas O. Summers called Hester Rogers "a household name in every home."

While the *Account of the Experience of Hester Ann Rogers* was certainly a tool used by Methodist leaders after her death to repress the speech of other women, Hester's text contains no condemnation of her preaching sisters. Her text was also somewhat problematic in that it was so personal, so focused on her relationship to God, that it did not adequately promote the roles of wife, mother, and woman in the pew that the Methodist men desired. They felt that if Methodist women took Hester's model literally, they might be too busy with their inner lives to perform such roles as cooking dinner or raising children. The production authorities solved this problem by the material practice of accreting other descriptive texts onto Hester Rogers's journal, texts written by men that praise Hester for her wifely devotion and maternal virtues.[3]

Values, Assumptions, and Social Practice

This study enables us to begin to identify the shared values and assumptions that authorized and controlled women's discourse in early Methodism. The fact that women, with Wesley's support, were able to preach and attract large audiences assumes that extraordinary call from God to speak takes precedence over normal social controls of discourse, even those scripturally based; that in matters of spiritual enlightenment God deals directly with women as well as men; and that success with conversions is more important than purity of process, and, in fact, that numerical success could be read as a sign of divine favor toward a female speaker.

Implicit in the literacy practices of early Methodism and the success of Hester Rogers's journal are notions that each believer's experience of the spirit is important and valuable and can be instructive for others, i.e., is rhetorical. This is clearly a community in which personal narratives embody rhetorical and ethical value both for the writer and for the reader, a community in which the experiences of women as well as men provide valuable leading of the spirit, and in which literacy is, in fact, a location of spiritual practice.

The post-Wesley silencing of women preachers constituted a return to the traditional beliefs that males were the exclusive members of the priestly class, that women should not exercise authority over men, and that women's speaking should be limited to the private domain or to members of their own sex. The reshaping and promotion of Hester Rogers's journal by the Church establishment enforced and enacted the valuing of the pious woman and good preacher's wife who devoted herself to family and supported her husband's work without complaint. It took the women of Methodism nearly two hundred years to reclaim rhetorical space they lost when John Wesley died.

The women of early Methodism add to the history of rhetoric spiritual pioneers—Sarah Crosby, Mary Bosanquet, Sarah Mallet, Hester Rogers, to name a few—whose courageous staking out of rhetorical territory and telling of their own stories shaped and enacted rhetoric that transformed the ways women might relate to the discourse of a spiritual community. Through scholarship that reveals the social praxis of women's speech and women's silence in early Methodism we can join historians of women in rhetoric such as Susan Jarrett, Cheryl Glenn, and Patricia Bizzell as we accept Thomas Miller's invitation to make "the discursive practices of marginalized traditions a central part of the history of rhetoric" and help the history of rhetoric "become more central to our interest in rhetoric as a social praxis" (1993, 26). Speaking and silenced, spiritual and spirited, pious and pragmatic, the women rhetors of historical traditions await us.

Notes

I want to gratefully acknowledge research grant support from the Commission on Archives and History of the United Methodist Church and from the Oregon State University Faculty Women's Network. I also wish to thank Dennis Rygiel, Martha Solomon Watson, and Harry M. Solomon for their wise guidance in the early stages of this project.

1. See Rack (1989) for a full discussion of the rise of Methodism.

2. Conducting scholarly research on the speaking and preaching of early Methodist women leaders can be challenging because there are few extant texts of women's sermons or other forms of address. Scholars rely on contemporary accounts of their preaching, references made in letters (especially those exchanged among Methodist women in various towns), references to women in John Wesley's papers, articles in Wesley's publication *The Arminian Magazine,* and in a few cases published autobiographies or spiritual journals written by the women themselves. An appendix in Chilcote (1991) lists known writings by early women preachers of Methodism.

3. In a work in progress I examine the rhetorical importance of the documents published with the *Account of the Experience of Hester Rogers* during the nineteenth century.

References

The Arminian Magazine. 1778–1796.

Bizzell, Patricia. 1992. "'The Praise of Folly': The Woman Rhetor, and Postmodern Skepticism." *Rhetoric Society Quarterly* 22 (Winter): 7–17.

Bramwell, William. 1798. *A Short Account of the Life and Death of Ann Cutler: a Pious Character, and Useful Instrument in the Work of God.* Leeds: Newsom.

British Museum. 1960–1966+. *Catalog of Printed Books and Supplements.* London.

Brown, Earl Kent. 1983. *Women of Mr. Wesley's Methodism.* New York: Mellen.

Chilcote, Paul Wesley. 1991. *John Wesley and the Women Preachers of Early Methodism.* Metuchen, N.J. & London: American Theological Library Association and Scarecrow Press.

Coles, George. 1857. *Heroines of Methodism.* New York: Carlton and Porter.

Collins, Vicki Tolar. 1993. "Perfecting a Woman's Life: Methodist Rhetoric and Politics in *The Account of Hester Ann Rogers.*" Ph.D. diss., Auburn University.

———. 1995. "*The Account of Hester Rogers:* The Rhetoric of an Early Methodist Mystic." Unpublished paper, Modern Language Association, Chicago.

Cumbers, Frank. 1956. *The Book Room.* London: Epworth Press.

Davies, Rupert, and E. Gordon Rupp, eds. 1965–1988. *A History of the Methodist Church in Great Britain.* 4 vols. London: Epworth Press.

Enos, Theresa, ed. 1993. *Learning from the Histories of Rhetoric: Essays in Honor of Winifred Bryan Horner.* Carbondale: Southern Illinois University Press.

Glenn, Cheryl. 1992. "Author, Audience, and Autobiography: Rhetorical Technique in *The Book of Margery Kempe.*" *College English* 54: 540–59.

Jarratt, Susan C. 1993. "Sapphic Pedagogy: Searching for Women's Difference in History and in the Classroom." In *Learning from the Histories of Rhetoric: Essays in Honor of Winifred Bryan Horner,* edited by Theresa Enos, 75–90. Carbondale: Southern Illinois University Press.

Miller, Thomas P. 1993. "Reinventing Rhetorical Traditions." In *Learning from the Histories of Rhetoric: Essays in Honor of Winifred Bryan Horner,* edited by Theresa Enos, 26–41. Carbondale: Southern Illinois University Press.

Minutes of the Methodist Conferences, from the First, Held in London; by the Late Rev. *John Wesley, A.M. in the Year 1744.* 1812– . London: Printed at the Conference Office.

Moore, Henry. 1835. "Afterword." In *The Life of Mrs. Mary Fletcher: Consort and Relict of the Rev. John Fletcher, Vicar of Madely, Salop, Compiled from her Journal and Other Authentic Documents.* New York.

National Union Catalog and Supplements. 1968+. London.

Nussbaum, Felicity. 1989. *The Autobiographical Subject.* Baltimore: Johns Hopkins University Press.

OCLC. 1978–1993. Dublin, Ohio: Online Computer Library Center.

Rack, H. D. 1989. *Reasonable Enthusiast: John Wesley and the Rise of Methodism.* Philadelphia: Trinity Press International.

Rivers, Isabel. 1978. "'Strangers and Pilgrims': Sources and Patterns of Methodist Narrative." In *Augustan Worlds,* edited by J. C. Hilson et al., 189–203. New York: Barnes and Noble.

Rogers, Hester Ann. 1837. *Account of the Experience of Hester Ann Rogers; and Her Funeral Sermon, by Rev. T. Coke, LL.D. to Which is Added Her Spiritual Letters.* New York: Mason and Lane.

Summers, Thomas O. 1878. "Introduction." In *The Life and Correspondence of Mrs. Hester Ann Rogers with Corrections and Additions Comprising an Introduction by Thos. O. Summers.* Nashville: Southern Methodist Publishing House.

Taft, Zechariah. 1825. *Biographical Sketches of the Lives and Public Ministry of Various Holy Women.* 2 vols. London: Published for the author, and sold in London by Mr. Kershaw; Leeds: Printed for the author by H. Cullingworth, and sold in London by J. Stephens, 1828.

Told, Silas. 1786. *An Account of the Life and Dealings of God with Silas Told, Later Preacher of the Gospel.* 3rd ed., corrected. London: George Whitfield.

Welter, Barbara. 1976. *Dimity Convictions: The American Woman in the Nineteenth Century.* Athens, Ohio: Ohio University Press.

Wesley, John. 1931. *The Letters of the Rev. John Wesley, A.M.* 8 vols. Ed. John Telford. London: Epworth Press.

Part 4

Women's Intellectual Desires

It is because we feel we have powers which are crushed, responsibilities which we are not permitted to exercise . . . rights vested in us as moral and intellectual beings which are utterly ignored and trampled upon . . . it is because we feel this so keenly we now demand an equal education with man.

Sarah Grimké

Aspiring to the Rhetorical Tradition
A Study of Margaret Cavendish

Christine Mason Sutherland

Those who study the role of women in the history of rhetoric are faced with a problem: for almost the entire period of its history rhetoric has excluded women. Historians of women's rhetoric have addressed the problem in various ways. Some have decided that wherever there is writing there is rhetoric—defining rhetoric broadly, as does Plato in the *Phaedrus*. Some, as Jane Donawerth has noted, have concentrated on the debate itself, treating as rhetoric the complaints of women that they were not allowed to engage in it (1992, 35–39). Though I do not necessarily disagree with these approaches, my own in this essay is somewhat different.

First, I see Margaret Cavendish as a practitioner of rhetoric rather than as a theorist. She certainly had ideas about it, but she never developed a coherent theory as did, for example, Mary Astell. Second, I perceive Margaret Cavendish as a practitioner of rhetoric in two distinct ways. In the narrower and more conventional sense she engaged in rhetoric by writing in the specifically rhetorical genre of oratory. But there is another, broader but less conventional sense in which Cavendish may be said to have practiced rhetoric: the whole of her output may legitimately be seen as an exercise in persuasion. By her own admission, she was using her abilities as a writer to force both her contemporaries and posterity to recognize her. That was why she not only wrote—as many women did—but also published, and published under her own name. "A glorious fame" was what she aimed at, and she was consistent in her pursuit of it. She wrote in many different genres: poetry, drama, letters, romances. But two in particular she chose, I believe, because they traditionally belonged exclusively to men: one was the oldest form of rhetoric, the public speech; the other was then the newest, scientific discussion and debate. What they had in common was their exclusion of women, and part of their attraction for her lay, I believe, precisely in this exclusion: a woman writing in these genres would be certain to draw comment, and this may well have been what she had in mind. Her *Orations of Divers Sorts* is a conscious and deliberate attempt to join the rhetorical tradition by writing in a genre of the most traditional (masculine) sort. I shall discuss this work at some length. I will also discuss *The Description of a New Blazing World*. Before writing this work, Cavendish had published a number of books on philosophy—that is, science—without much success, owing to her lack of education. *Blazing World*, the most unusual of her works, represents her ingenious way of circumventing the problem of her deficiencies as a philosopher.

Cavendish's Life

In order to reach an understanding of her work, we must know something of her life. Margaret Lucas was born in 1623 just outside Colchester, an ancient town in eastern England. Margaret was the youngest of eight children. Her father died when she was only two years old; but her mother was left well provided for and, as she was an astute manager, was well able to handle the running of the estate. Margaret grew up in easy circumstances, surrounded by a family of unusual closeness and affection. Her mother was generous and indulgent to her children—perhaps too indulgent: Margaret grew up almost without education of any kind. She hated the sort of domestic training girls of the time were supposed to receive, and her mother did not insist upon it. Nor did she insist upon any other kind of teaching except in morality and good behavior, and this she was strict about. For the rest, Margaret informs her readers in *A True Relation of My Birth and Breeding:* "As for tutors, although we had for all sorts of Vertues, as singing, dancing, playing on Musick, reading, writing, working and the like, yet we were not kept strictly thereto" (371). *Sociable Letters* provides a little more information: "I . . . know no Rules in Rhetorick, nor never went to School, but only Learn'd to Read and Write at Home, Taught by an Antient Decayed Gentlewoman whom my Mother kept for that Purpose" (367). By her own admission, she did not really have the scholarly temperament, certainly not as a young girl. In many ways her indulgent mother and her close-knit family gave Margaret the great advantage of knowing herself to be loved and esteemed. On the other hand, her upbringing also promoted a debilitating bashfulness that she never overcame, for the Lucases conducted their social life almost entirely within the family circle.

This social isolation was exacerbated, if not caused, by their estrangement from their neighbors, who were mostly Puritan whereas the Lucases were Royalist. When the political and religious unrest finally erupted into civil war, in 1641, the Lucases' house was vandalized by a rioting mob. Worse riots followed the next year, and Margaret and her mother took refuge in Oxford, where the king now held his court (Jones 1990, 19). Margaret Lucas never saw her home again. In 1643, at the age of twenty, she became a maid of honor to Queen Henrietta Maria; and when in 1644 Oxford could no longer provide a safe refuge for the queen, Margaret accompanied her first to the West Country and later to France. After a dangerous and terrifying journey, the royal party was eventually housed, uncomfortably, in the Louvre. It was here that, in April 1645, Margaret met her future husband.

William Cavendish, Marquis of Newcastle, was some thirty years Margaret's senior, a widower with grown-up children. He had been a prominent general in the royal army and had indeed been a companion in arms of Margaret's brother Sir Charles Lucas. After the disastrous defeat at York, he went into voluntary exile. Newcastle and Margaret Lucas seem to have been attracted to one another from the first. It was in many ways a strange match and one that did not at first have the unqualified approval of the queen. Nevertheless, Newcastle and Margaret were married in November 1645. Margaret's marriage to Newcastle was the great good fortune of her life—a judgment in which she would have wholeheartedly concurred. Without it, it is unlikely that she would have written and almost certain that she would never have been published. Her husband nurtured her in several important ways. First, and perhaps most important, he was supportive. In spite of what sometimes appears to be arrogance, Margaret was fundamentally insecure. Newcastle's belief in her was a necessary condition of her attempt to be a writer in the first place. Second, he provided a model. Himself a virtuoso, he opened up for her the whole world of the arts and sciences. Third, he acted as her tutor and mentor. Perhaps he was rather too indulgent in this role: Margaret would have profited from a more rigorous discipline. Nonetheless, he did encourage her to learn, providing the necessary resources and sharing with her his interest in the newly developing study of natural philosophy. His collection of telescopes and microscopes must have helped and encouraged her study, even though her opinion of them was not always favorable. Newcastle was also a patron of artists and philosophers. He and Margaret entertained, among others, Pierre Gassendi and René Descartes. Owing to her bashfulness and her ignorance of foreign languages, Margaret did not profit from these acquaintances as much as she might have. Nonetheless, she was, through her husband, part of the community of supporters of the new scientists, which included her brother-in-law, the eminent scholar Sir Charles Cavendish. Finally, it was Newcastle who paid for the publication of her books and encouraged her to publish them under her own name. In all these ways, but most particularly in this last, he was a most unusual husband for his times. Most men would have felt publicly disgraced by a wife who wrote and published. Newcastle, on the contrary, was proud of her. He collaborated with her on some of her works and for all of them wrote extravagant and laudatory prefaces.

The Cavendishes remained in Europe, first in France and later in Holland, until the Restoration of the Stuarts in the person of Charles II in 1660. They were, of course, overjoyed by the return of the monarchy and by their own deliverance from sixteen years in exile. Newcastle himself hastened to England with all speed, leaving Margaret behind in Antwerp as security for his debts. Before long she joined him in England. But in spite of their initial relief and joy, in the long term the Restoration was a disappointment to the Newcastles. They did not fit the style of the new court, and they were not among those closest to the king, in spite of all their sacrifices. Before long they retired to their country estates, visiting London seldom. (It was on one of these visits to the capital that Margaret Cavendish was invited to attend a meeting of the Royal Society.) During her last years Cavendish devoted herself to helping her husband in the management of his large estates. These years were clouded by false accusations from jealous servants and by arguments with Newcastle's children about her jointure (Jones 1990, 166 ff.). She died suddenly in 1673 at the age of fifty and was buried in Westminster Abbey.

Rhetoric in the Seventeenth Century

Just as it is important to an understanding of her work to know something of Margaret Cavendish's life, it is also necessary to understand, at least in general outline, the history of rhetoric in her time. The life of Margaret Cavendish spans a great transition in the history of rhetoric. Her ideas, and those of her closest associates, her brothers, and later, her husband and her brother-in-law, were formed by the traditions of the high Renaissance. Before she died, those traditions had become outdated. The plain style was in vogue, and the values of the Enlightenment prevailed. Had she been born, like Mary Astell, in the 1660s, her relationship with the rhetorical tradition might have been simpler and easier, as Astell's was. But her ideas about rhetoric were formed in her youth; they were transmitted to her, moreover, by men much older than herself—first her brothers and later her husband and her brother-in-law, whose education had begun during the previous century. Most important of all, she had been a maid of honor to Queen Henrietta Maria, at whose court, even in the reduced grandeur of its residence at Oxford, masques were still put on as regular entertainments. The masque is the richest expression of the rhetoric of the Renaissance, which values the grand style for its ability to move the emotions. It combines all the arts in the great moral project of impressing upon the audience the beauty of the moral order. Sophie Tomlinson recognizes the importance of Cavendish's familiarity with the masque in the formation of her artistic values: "At Oxford she would have witnessed the plays and other entertainments which continued to be staged in modified form. The masque appeared in her early work, such as her prose fiction "The Contract" (1992, 139). It not only influenced her selection of material in her writing, but at a deeper level it formed her ideas about the power of rhetoric. In letter 28 of *Sociable Letters*, Cavendish has this to say about Eloquence: "The truth is, it can make Men like Gods or Devils, as having a Power beyond Nature, Custom and Force, for many times the Tongue hath been too Strong for the Sword, and often Carried away the Victory" (54).

Unfortunately, the more highly Margaret Cavendish regarded rhetoric, the more daunted she became. The ability to use rhetoric, so understood, took years to acquire. It involved, among other skills, an intimate knowledge of the Latin language and literature and a thorough grounding in classical culture and history. This was the kind of education traditionally provided for boys at the time; only rarely was it offered to girls. Cavendish never ceased to lament her lack of proper training in rhetoric. It is interesting to speculate what her career as a writer might have been had she lived a generation later. By the end of the seventeenth century, the plain style had taken hold. The new philosophers effectively campaigned against the grand rhetorical style and its (to them) useless ornamentation. As Catherine Hobbs Peaden (1992) has argued, the idea that rhetoric is social and public, in all its manifestations a moral force for good, is displaced in the philosophy of John Locke by the notion that language is private and chiefly concerned with transmitting the single speaker's meaning with the utmost clarity and the least fuss.

Margaret Cavendish was aware, to some extent at least, of what was going on. Following, perhaps, the example of Joseph Glanvill, she modified her original style, stripping it down, as was becoming the fashion. According to Douglas Grant, "responding as immediately as she did to the spirit of the age, she grew sensitive to the general change in style, and in the preliminaries to *Philosophical Letters*, she stated portentously that she thought 'it best to avoid metaphorical, similizing and improper expression in natural philosophy as much as one can; for they do rather obscure than explain the nature of truth'" (1957, 210). But her ideas about rhetoric had long been set, and she was never really convinced of the adequacy of the plain style. Her ambivalence is clearly demonstrated in an epistle, "To My Readers," at the beginning of *Nature's Pictures*, in which she proclaims: "I have not endeavoured so much for the eloquence, and elegancy of speech, as the naturall and most usuall way of speaking, in severall Discourses, and ordinary Phrases; but perchance my Readers will say, or at least think I have dressed the severall subjects of my Discourses too vulgar, or that the Garments, which is the language, is too thread-bare" (n.p.). The truth is that Margaret Cavendish lived at an exceedingly awkward time. Even experienced men, who had the full benefit of a Renaissance education, were sometimes at a loss to cope with the changes demanded by the values of the new age. Cavendish never seems quite sure whether her stated preference for the simpler style is genuine or a mere excuse for her ignorance of the intricacies of the grand style. Mary Astell, some forty years her junior, had no such exaggerated respect for an eloquence beyond her educational resources: she genuinely took the Cartesian position that the ability to think and to write is inborn. But Cavendish was too old when the changes became apparent ever really to believe in her own adequacy.

Orations of Divers Sorts

It is her anomalous position vis-à-vis the rhetorical tradition that in part explains the curious nature of *Orations of Divers Sorts*. This book was not among the earliest of her works to be published. It came out in 1662, when the Cavendishes were back in England after their long exile abroad. However, we cannot assume that it was written after their return. It is probable that the work was at least begun much earlier. We know something about its inception from letter 175 in the collection *So-*

ciable Letters. This work was published even later than the *Orations*, in 1664, but most of the letters were written during the years in exile. Although Cavendish always addresses herself to a correspondent, it is probable that many of them were fictitious. She was simply using the genre of letter writing to express her opinions:

> In your last letter you Advised me to write a Book of Orations, But how should I write Orations who know no Rules in Rhetorick, nor never went to School, but only Learn'd to Read and Write at Home, Taught by an Antient Decayed Gentlewoman whom my Mother kept for that Purpose which my ill hand (as the Phrase is) may sufficiently Witness; yet howsoever, to follow your Advice, I did try to Write Orations, but I find I want Wit, Eloquence and Learning for such a Work, and though I had Wit, Eloquence and Learning I should not find so many Subjects to Write so many Orations as will Fill a Book, for Orations for the most part, are concerning War, Peace and Matters of State, and Business in the Commonwealth, all of which I am not Capable of, as being a Woman, who hath neither Knowledg, Ability, nor Capacity in State Affairs and to Speak in Writing of that I Understand not, will not be Acceptable to my Reading Auditors: Nevertheless, to let you see how Powerful your Perswasions are with me, I will send you those two or three Orations I have Written for a Trial, if you Approve them, I will Write as many as I can find Subjects to make Orations of, and if I can get so many as will make a Book, I will set them forth in Print, although I have no Hopes nor Confidence in that Work, for I fear it will be Lost Labour and Wast Time. (367)

In spite of her fears that she would not "find so many Subjects to Write so many Orations as will Fill a Book," she found enough material to fill over three hundred pages. It is hard to know how to read the *Orations*. When I first read them, I was inclined to take them as ironic: their defects are so gross that it is tempting to interpret them as deliberately concocted in order to hold up oratory as a matter for scorn. Let me quote one of the orations to demonstrate what I mean:

An Oration Against Liberty of Conscience

Fellow Citizens, I am not of the former Orator's opinion; for if you give Liberty in the Church, you must give Liberty in the State, and so let everyone do what they will, which will be a Strange Government, or rather I may say, no Government: for if there be no Rules their [*sic*] can be no Laws, and if ther be no Laws, there can be no Justice, no Safety, and if no Safety, no Propriety, neither of Goods, Wives, Children, nor Lives, and if ther be no Propriety, there will be no Husbandry, and Lands will lie Unmanured, also there will be neither Trade nor Traffick, all which will cause Famine, Warr and Ruine, and such Confusion as the Kingdome will be like a Chaos, which the Gods keep us from. (Part III, 70)

The above quotation comprises the whole speech. Though this is one of the shortest of the orations, it is by no means unusually short, and few orations are significantly longer. This whole speech can be read in something under thirty seconds; the average speech would take about a minute, and the longest no more than five. The effect of such violent abbreviation is, of course, to undermine the seriousness of the project. What is remarkable, and almost inexplicable except under an ironic reading, is that Margaret Cavendish herself knew how such brevity might compromise the persuasive capacity of a speech: here is a quotation from the letter "To the Readers of my Works," which introduces the collection: "Some of them [the speeches] are so short, that had they been shorter, they would not have been of Force to Perswade, whereas the intention of an Orator, or Use of Orations, is to Perswade the Auditors to be of the Orators Opinion or Belief, and it is not Probable, that Forcible Arguments or Perswasions can be Contain'd in two or three Lines of Words" (n.p.). But it is not only the brevity of the speech in relation to the importance of its theme that suggests irony: notice too the serious gaps in the argument, the non sequiturs, the begging of the question, the lack of appropriate argumentation or support and even of illustration or example. What better way to ridicule oratory than to offer such a travesty of speeches and speech making? Is she, perhaps, disvaluing the rhetorical tradition that excludes her?

What makes such a reading difficult to justify, however, is her manifest regard for rhetoric expressed in *Sociable Letters*. Letter 27 makes it abundantly clear that, far from wishing to ridicule rhetoric, she longs to be able to practice it: she desperately wants to "Speak Rationally, Movingly, Timely and Properly, as to the purpose . . . which I fear Women are not Capable of, and the Despair thereof makes me Envy or Emulate Men. . . . I Admire Eloquence, and would choose Wit for my Pastime. Indeed Natural Orators that can speak on a Sudden and Extempore upon any Subject, are Nature's Musicians, moving the Passions to Harmony, making Concords out of Discords, Playing on the Soul with Delight" (52). Letter 28 she devotes entirely to the praise of eloquence. It is not, she protests, the words themselves that she loves "before all other Musick," but "the Sense, Reason and Wit that is Exprest and made Known by Words" (53). What she chiefly covets, it becomes apparent, is its power: She cannot but "Wonder at the Power of Eloquence, for there is a strange hidden Mystery in Eloquence, it hath a Magical Power over mankind, for it Charms the Senses, and Inchants the Mind, and is of such a Commanding Power, as it Forces the Will to Command the Actions of the Body and Soul, to Do, or to Suffer, beyond their Natural Abilities, makes the Souls of men the Tongue's Slaves" (54).

If, then, the defects in the *Orations* are not deliberate and ironic, how are we to explain them? Why, in spite of her (fully justified) reservations, did Cavendish go ahead with the project? What was she trying to do? There is no simple answer to these questions, but I think we can find clues in her prefaces and letters that cast some light upon the matter and help us gain a more just appreciation of the work than a simple reading of it might provide. First, the matter of brevity: I think it is possible that Margaret Cavendish was simply confused by the conflicting opinions and advice she may have heard from her husband and his circle of friends—which included many of the "new philosophers," the promoters of the new science. These new men, in particular, were inclined to make a virtue of brevity, in reaction against the diffuseness and verbosity of the old high rhetorical style. Joseph Glanvill, for example, with whom Cavendish corresponded, twice rewrote his *The Vanity of Dogmatizing*, stripping it down and significantly reducing its length each time. Brevity was the passion of the time, not only among the scientists but also among other scholars who were trying to promote an Attic prose style (Croll 1966, 87 ff.). I think that Margaret Cavendish misunderstood what she heard about it and misapplied it to her *Orations*. "Had I been a Learned Scholar," she writes in her letter to the readers, which serves as a preface to the *Orations*, "I might have Written my Orations more Short than I have done." She goes on to object, in the passage already quoted above, that they are already so short as to be only minimally persuasive. Further on in the same paragraph she adds: "Also had I been a Learned Scholar, I might have Written them more Compendiously, and not so Loose, but I affect Freedome and Ease, even in my Works of Writings; Besides, I have Observ'd, that whatsoever is Bound or Knit Close, is difficult to Disclose, and for Writings, whatsoever is very Compendious, requires some Study to Conceive and Understand the Sense and Design of the Authors Meaning" (n.p.). What Cavendish is referring to here is the tendency among writers of the Attic style to "brevities, suppressions, and contortions of style which are in fact inconsistent with a primary devotion to the virtue of perspicuity" (Croll 1966, 86).

Untrained in writing as she was, Margaret Cavendish was understandably confused, I believe, by the contradictory voices in the debate about style that was going on in her time. I do not suppose that any of the debaters would seriously have considered such brevity to be appropriate in speeches; but Cavendish may well not have fully understood the demands of the genre, as the men would have, though her objections show that she had her doubts. She is well aware of the problems set by her own ignorance: "I hope that Defect or want of Learning, will not Blemish my Work, nor Obstruct the Sense of my Orations, nor Puzzle the Understanding of the Reader" ("To the Readers," n.p.). Cavendish's want of learning probably explains most of the anomalies in the *Orations*. As we have seen, she was well aware of her lack of education and bitterly regretted it. She picked up the crumbs of learning from her husband, whom she calls in the dedicatory letter which prefaces her biography of him "my onely Tutor" (1667, n.p.). The brief account she gives there makes clear that trying to remedy the deficiencies of her education was a lifelong project. She knew very well that she was unusually inventive; but she also knew that she was lacking in "good method and order." "Truly, my lord," she continues to her husband, "I confess that for want of Scholarship, I could not express myself so well as otherwise I might have done, in those Philosophical Writings I publish't first; but after I was returned with your Lordship into my Native Country, and led a retired Country life, I applied my self to the reading of Philosophical Authors, of purpose to learn those names and words of Art that are used in Schools."

It is, in fact, as an exercise in self-education that *Orations of Divers Sorts* is best understood. The preface to *Sociable Letters* illuminates for us the author's intentions in the earlier work: "As for my Orations, I have heard, that some do Censure me for speaking too Freely, and Patronizing Vice too much, but . . . it is not out of Love to Vice that I plead for it, but only to Exercise my Fancy, for surely the Wisest and Eloquentest Orators, have not been Ashamed to Defend Vices upon such Accounts, and why may not I do the like? for my Orations for the most part are

Declamations, wherein I speak Pro and Con, and Determine nothing" (n.p.). What she is doing is practicing *declamatio,* an advanced exercise in rhetoric sometimes written by senior students in grammar schools but more usually by undergraduates at Oxford and Cambridge (Clark 1964, 129). Their purpose was to train the young men for the learned professions and public life that they were expected to enter as lawyers, clergymen, diplomats, and statesmen. It is significant that she wished to educate herself in such a specifically masculine art. Not only is the form the masculine one of the public speech, but the content of the *Orations* is typical of the issues addressed by men in public life: the very topics about which she confesses she knows nothing (in her letter 175, quoted above) hold a strong attraction for her, simply because they *are* public matters and therefore lead more probably to that fame which she so much covets. She did not succeed very well in this masculine genre, but it is to her credit that she tried.

But although she was, in the *Orations,* attempting to train herself in the techniques and topics of a masculine education, there is one part in which she addresses issues of particular interest to women. The last two orations of Part X ("Orations to Citizens in the Market Place") are on the subject of the liberty of women. The first takes the position against it. In this the speaker makes the standard arguments so often set forth in the moral literature of the time: women should be restrained in the interests of making them moderate, sober, and silent. The next oration, the last in Part X, takes a dissenting position and argues for the liberty of women; but the arguments are not of a kind to appeal to twentieth-century feminists: they present women as "Goddesses on Earth . . . to be Beloved, Admired, Desir'd, Ador'd, and Worshipp'd, Sued and Praised to by our Sex" (224). The use of "our" in the last sentence makes it clear that Cavendish is here adopting the persona of a man. Immediately after this speech comes the first oration in Part XI, titled "Femal Orations." There are seven of them; all the speakers are women, and the audience is exclusively female. But any attempt (and attempts have been made) to assume that these female orators speak for Cavendish herself is defeated by the variety of contradictory positions taken. The first speaker represents women as the slaves of men; the second incites the audience to revolt; the third reverses the position of the first and argues that men are the willing servants of women, who themselves are "Witless, Strengthless, and Unprofitable." The fourth speaker attributes this weakness to nurture, not nature, and suggests that in order to strengthen themselves women should adopt a masculine way of life, practicing men's sports and conversing in "Camps, Courts, and Cities, in Schools, Colleges, and Courts of Judicature, in Taverns, Brothels, and Gaming Houses." The fifth speaker takes the contrary position: "We cannot change the Nature of our Sex," she says, and to try to do so would be to make ourselves "like as the Defects of Nature" (229). The sixth speaker disagrees with the fifth: "Women ought to Imitate Men, as being a Degree in Nature more Perfect, than they Themselves" (230). But the seventh speaker denies that men are superior; they are simply different: "if Men are More Eloquent in Speech, Women are more Harmonious in Voice; if Men be more Active, Women are more Gracefull" (231).

What Cavendish is doing here cannot, I think, be interpreted as feminist activity; she is simply joining in the *Querelle des Femmes,* described by Linda Woodbridge in *Women and the English Renaissance.* The participants in this discussion were principally, if not exclusively, men, and Cavendish typically joins in. This is not to say that she did not have a particular and personal interest in the question. But I do not think we can get much light on the subject of her own views from a form that deliberately avoids commitment to one position over another.

The Description of a New Blazing World

If Cavendish was attracted to the genre of orations because it was a specifically masculine one, the same may be said about her scientific writings. As Kathleen Jones says, she was "driven on by the knowledge that she was the only woman working in an exclusively masculine field" (1990, 118). In all, Cavendish wrote five philosophical or, as we would say, scientific works. Their value in terms of the science of their time has been usefully discussed by Londa Schiebinger, Gerald Meyer, Sylvia Bowerbank, and Lisa Sarasohn, among others. I am concerned with these works primarily as rhetoric: that is, as part of Cavendish's lifelong project of making herself famous. And from this point of view, the most interesting of them is *The Description of a New Blazing World.* Uncomfortable with nearly all the genres in which she attempted to write, for this work Cavendish creates her own. It has been hailed as the first work of science fiction; it has also been included in the list of female utopias (Schiebinger 1989). But in fact, it is sui generis, combining romance and scientific speculation with what can only be called wish fulfillment; it cannot really be compared with any other work, ancient or modern.

Cavendish published it together with *Observations Upon Experimental Philosophy*, both in 1666 and 1668.

The story concerns a young lady who is kidnapped by a would-be lover. Their boat is caught in a storm and blown to the pole of their world, where the lover, together with everyone else on board except the lady, is frozen to death. The boat passes from their own world to another joined to it at the pole. The lady is rescued by the inhabitants, who admire her great beauty, and taken to their emperor, who is so captivated by her loveliness that he not only marries her but gives her power over the whole of his world to govern as she likes. Toward the end of this work Cavendish introduces herself as a character (this is part of the wish fulfillment). She has herself declare to the Empress of the Blazing World that she has a great ambition to be empress of a world of her own, so that she may achieve "a glorious fame." Thereupon, the obliging Empress summons her immaterial spirits to see if such a world is to be had. The spirits reply: "We wonder . . . that you desire to be Empress on a terrestrial world, whenas you can create yourself a celestial world if you please. . . . By creating a world within yourself, you may enjoy all both in whole and in parts, without control or opposition, and may make what world you please, and alter it when you please" ([1666] 1992, 186).

There is an obvious analogy between the fictional world the Duchess is recommended to create for herself in the romance and her creation of the romance itself. Indeed, Cavendish herself makes the connection at the end of the letter to the reader that prefaces the work: "although I have neither power, time, nor occasion to conquer the world as Alexander and Caesar did, yet rather than not to be mistress of one, since Fortune and the Fates would give me none, I have made a world of my own" (n.p.). Both here in the letter and in the story, the power referred to is political: Cavendish compares herself with Alexander and Caesar, not with God; but much of the attraction of writing this romance must have been in the philosophical freedom it gave her, for a great deal of it is taken up with scientific speculation of the kind that she had made in her earlier philosophical works. Enlightening here is a letter she received from Glanvill: she must, if she is to be true to the spirit of science, be willing "to tie down the mind in Physical things, to consider Nature as it is, to lay a Foundation in sensible collections, and from thence to proceed to general Propositions and Discourses" (*Collection* 1678, 111–12). Tying herself down to facts was something Cavendish was deeply unwilling to do. As Bowerbank points out in her illuminating essay,

Cavendish's lack of method was disastrous to her scientific ambitions. By her own admission, Cavendish was anything but methodical; she disliked the constraint of following a set program, particularly one not designed by herself. As Bowerbank says, what dominated her work was fancy. By inventing her own world, she was free to indulge in the quasi-scientific speculation she so much enjoyed and at the same time avert criticism and contradiction. It is her world; she determines its scientific principles; and therefore no one can contradict her.

Nor is this the only freedom that she can enjoy within this new world. This particular fictional form sets her free to indulge in all kinds of wish fulfillment. As Bowerbank says: "In her own world Cavendish can refuse to moderate her desires to accessible goals and can create her women free from the restrictions which hampered Cavendish in both the social and intellectual realms" (1988, 200). Debarred from the scientific community in Europe by her sex, the Duchess finds compensation in creating a world in which a woman (the Empress) is in charge of the whole of scientific research. Disabled, too, in the sphere of military activity, Cavendish includes in the romance a successful invasion by sea, directed by the Empress, which involves the use of something very like a submarine.

Another sphere in which Cavendish as a woman had no authority was the Church: the Empress in the Blazing World finds the religion of the inhabitants "very defective," and therefore resolves to convert them to her own. Interestingly, Cavendish stops short of instituting a woman in the Church as having spiritual authority over men, even in fiction. Perhaps she knew the controversy that such a suggestion might arouse. Her Empress decides to "make up a congregation of women, whereof she intended to be the head herself" ([1666] 1992, 162). Since she possesses "an excellent gift of preaching," she is soon able to convert them.

Not only did the romance form thus modified allow Cavendish vicariously to fulfill some of her more impossible ambitions, it also allowed her to criticize and even lampoon with impunity some of the institutions of her own day in her own country. For example, she takes an obvious pleasure in satirizing the logicians and rhetoricians: the Empress's magpie-parrot and jackdaw-men are her professional orators and logicians: "One of the parrot-men rose with great formality, and endeavoured to make an eloquent speech before her Majesty; but before he had half ended, his arguments and divisions being so many, that they caused a great confusion in his brain, he could not go forward, but was forced to retire backward, with the greatest disgrace both to himself, and the whole society" ([1666] 1992, 160). As for the logicians, the Empress tells them: "[Y]our art of logic . . . consists only in contradicting each other, in making sophisms, and obscuring truth, instead of clearing it" ([1666] 1992, 162).

The romance form, then, allowed Cavendish the power and freedom that were denied her in real life. In strong and ironic contrast to the power and adulation enjoyed by her fictional Empress is the almost complete rejection of Margaret Cavendish by the scientific community of her time. It is true that she was invited to attend a meeting of the Royal Society, but the invitation was extended reluctantly and only because of her position as wife of the duke of Newcastle, a Founder member. Furthermore, the visit was not a success. The duchess was so late in arriving that the proceedings had to begin without her; and when finally she did arrive, she was apparently afflicted with her usual bashfulness and could do nothing but gushingly admire the various experiments prepared for her to view by Robert Boyle. Although Cavendish wrote critiques of the philosophy of Descartes, Thomas Hobbes, Jean Baptiste Van Helmont, and Henry More, her own work was not seriously regarded, and only Glanvill is known to have corresponded with her. She sent copies of *Philosophical and Physical Opinions* to Oxford and Cambridge, and received fulsome letters of patently insincere flattery in return. The scientific community almost unanimously denied her the "glorious fame" she aspired to.

Conclusion

Margaret Cavendish was a pioneer, and like many pioneers she apparently failed: neither the literary nor the scientific community has been inclined to adopt her, and though she has achieved fame, that fame has certainly not been glorious. She proclaimed insistently her ambition to be taken seriously not just as a woman but as a human being. She was shameless in proclaiming the kind of ambition that was thought proper and even praiseworthy in a man but inappropriate and immodest in a woman. She wanted to go public in an age that was determined to restrict women to a shrinking private sphere. Neither men (except her husband) nor women applauded her ambition. But in publicizing it remorselessly and insistently throughout her numerous works and in her prefaces and letters, she performed an essential service for the women who succeeded her. At least the idea that women might wish to publish their work was not unknown after her time. She got the issue, as it were, on the table. Most of her claims and protestations lay dormant for many years, generations even, and it is hard to trace her influence, however sure we may be that it is there. Nonetheless, she did what a pioneer must do: she broke the ground. Women writers of today have good reason to be grateful to Margaret Cavendish, Duchess of Newcastle.

References

Bowerbank, Sylvia. 1988. "The Spider's Delight: Margaret Cavendish and the Female Imagination." In *Women in the Renaissance*, edited by Kirby Farrell et al., 392–408. Amherst: University of Massachusetts Press.

Cavendish, Margaret. 1656. *Nature's Pictures, including "A True Relation of My Birth and Breeding."* London: J. Martin and J. Allestyre.

———. 1662. *Orations of Divers Sorts.* London.

———. 1666. *Observation upon Experimental Philosophy. To which is added The Description of a New Blazing World.* London: A. Maxwell..

———. 1663. *Philosophical and Physical Opinions.* London: J. Martin and J. Allestyre.

———. 1664. *Philosophical Letters.* London.

———. 1664. *Sociable Letters.* London: William Wilson.

———. 1667. *The Life of the Thrice Noble, High and Puissant Prince William Cavendishe, Duke, Marquess and Earl of Newcastle.* London: A. Maxwell.

———. 1992. *Margaret Cavendish Duchess of Newcastle. The Description of a New World called The Blazing World and Other Writings.* Ed. Kate Lilley. New York: New York University Press.

Clark, Donald Lemen. 1964. *John Milton at St Paul's School.* New York: Archon Books.

A Collection of Letters and Poems. Written By Several Persons of Honour and Learning, Upon Divers Important Subjects, to the Late Duke and Duchess of Newcastle. 1678. London: Langly Curtis.

Croll, Morris W. 1966. *Style, Rhetoric and Rhythm.* Princeton: Princeton University Press.

Donawerth, Jane. 1992. "Transforming the History of Rhetorical Theory." *Feminist Teacher* 7.1: 35–39.

Glanvill, Joseph. [1661] 1970. *The Vanity of Dogmatizing.* Hove, Sussex, England: Harvester Press.

Grant, Douglas. 1957. *Margaret the First: A Biography of Margaret Cavendish, Duchess of Newcastle.* London: Rupert Hart-Davis.

Jones, Kathleen. 1990. *A Glorious Fame: The Life of Margaret Cavendish, Duchess of Newcastle, 1623–1673.* London: Bloomsbury.

Lilley, Kate, editor. 1992. *Margaret Cavendish Duchess of Newcastle. The Description of a New World called the Blazing World and Other Writings.* New York: New York University Press.

Meyer, Gerald Dennis. 1955. *The Scientific Lady in England 1650–1760.* Berkeley: University of California Press.

Peaden, Catherine Hobbs. 1992. "Understanding Differently: Re-reading Locke's Essay Concerning Human Understanding." *Rhetoric Society Quarterly,* 22: 75–90.

Plato. 1973. *Phaedrus.* Trans. Walter Hamilton. Harmondsworth, U.K.: Penguin.

Sarasohn, Lisa. 1984. "A Science Turned Upside Down: Feminism and the Natural Philosophy of Margaret Cavendish." *Huntington Library Quarterly* 47: 289–307.

Schiebinger, Londa. 1989. *The Mind Has No Sex.* Cambridge: Harvard University Press.

Tomlinson, Sophie. 1992. "My Brain the Stage: Margaret Cavendish and the Fantasy of Female Performance." In *Women, Texts and Histories, 1575–1660,* edited by Clare Brant and Diane Purkiss. London: Routledge.

Woodbridge, Linda. 1986. *Women and the English Renaissance: Literature and the Nature of Womankind, 1540–1620.* Urbana: University of Illinois Press.

Ethos, Authority, and Virtue for Seventeenth-century Women Writers

The Case of Bathsua Makin's *Essay to Revive the Antient Education of Gentlewomen* (1673)

Nancy Weitz Miller

In recent years scholars have begun the difficult but exhilarating task of excavating the deeply buried and long-neglected textual remains of seventeenth-century women to discover hundreds, maybe thousands, of extant works.[1] The discovery of these works raises questions about their reception, and to draw assumptions only from the statistical data may lead one to imagine erroneously the typical seventeenth-century woman as happily publishing her thoughts for an accepting or at least tolerant readership. On the contrary, seventeenth-century English society was at best ambivalent toward women who attempted to enter what was perceived to be a thoroughly male arena of public life. At worst, women writers, who often lacked the benefit of a classical education, were ridiculed, condemned, and threatened with ruined reputations if their works were judged poorly written. Well-written works were often falsely attributed to male authors despite evidence of female authorship.[2] Given the hostile climate, women writers had a difficult time establishing the credibility needed to gain a sympathetic audience for their ideas.

Consequently, many works by seventeenth-century women, particularly persuasive essays, exhibit a range of ingenious strategies to create an authoritative ethos in order to deflect attention away from the impropriety of the writing act and toward the content of their arguments. A fine example of these deflective tactics can be found in Bathsua Makin's *Essay to Revive the Antient Education of Gentlewomen* (1673), written under the anonymous persona of an English gentleman.

A History of Hostility

Before subjecting Makin's essay to a close examination, it would be useful to examine the religious roots of seventeenth-century hostility toward women who published their writings.[3] Rhetoric had long been recognized as a fundamental means of securing authority, and in an effort to keep them in a submissive position, women had long been excluded from exercising their power of speech. Patriarchal culture worked to keep women silent and subjected by ideologically undermining their moral and intellectual virtue and by consistently reinforcing divisions and inequalities between the sexes.

Separate gendered spaces, masculine public and feminine private spheres, and education, driven largely by pragmatic concerns, helped to cement the division between men and women. In the seventeenth century the worldly education of a gentleman included the study of ancient and modern languages, philosophy, logic, and rhetoric, a curriculum that would lead to engaging in public discourse. Since women were to remain within the household, the education of a gentlewoman was designed to help her perform the duties necessary to ensure the well-being of her family. She learned how to read the Bible, do a range of needlework, cook, preserve, brew, nurse, and manage the servants.[4] As long as the family structure mandated a sharp delineation of sex roles, women could have no opportunities to use an education modeled on that of men (Smith 1982, 48). The public world "naturally" belonged to men; a woman who left household duties undone while trying to compete with men in the public arena was perverting the social order and was perceived as committing a supreme act of disobedience.

By the seventeenth century women had a long history of ostensible disobedience to divine natural law and custom through an inordinate need to gain preeminence over men. Beginning with the early chapters of Genesis, woman's subordinated status is decreed in nearly the same breath as her creation and cemented by her participation in the Fall. By eating of the tree, Eve combines three punishable acts into one: she forthrightly disobeys God's command; she aspires to a higher state of knowledge; and she usurps her immediate superior's (Adam's) authority by giving him the forbidden fruit to eat as well. For all of this Eve is punished by losing the last vestiges of her autonomy: "thy desire shall be to thy husband, and he shall rule over thee" (3:16).

The Scriptural account of Eve's simple yet monumental act of disobedience and the interpretations of later exegetes have contributed greatly to woman's subjection. Succeeding generations of women were made to atone for Eve's sin, as her "seed" was passed from mothers to daughters. Early writers repeatedly castigate women as belonging to a morally inferior sex and bemoan their tendency to rebel against all decreed authority, that of God and man.[5] In a work from the thirteenth century, *Summa Theologica,* Thomas Aquinas offers another gloss on the problem when he adds that women's subordination is due to the necessity for wise government of her weak intellect: "Such is the subjection in which woman is by nature subordinate to man, because the power of rational discernment is by nature stronger in man" (1992, 93). Aquinas posits that Eve's inability to recognize the serpent's faulty reasoning leads to her act of sinful disobedience, an idea that Milton would later expand upon in *Paradise Lost.*

One of the key methods for keeping women subjected has been to deprive them of linguistic power, as a belief in the authoritative power of language would necessarily disallow a subject's access to speech. As woman has from almost the first moment of her creation shown herself unlikely to remain peacefully submissive, man's consequent task must lie in seeking ways to enforce her compliance to his governance. Saint Paul's injunctions against women's speaking held great authority for (and were frequently cited by) medieval and Renaissance writers who wished to keep women from speaking or writing publicly: "Let your women keep silence in the churches: for it is not permitted unto them to speak" (1 Cor. 14:34); and "Let the woman learn in silence with all subjection. But I suffer not a woman to teach, nor to usurp authority over a man, but to be in silence" (1 Tim. 2:13–14). Paul's words show the clear relationship between preeminence and discourse that underlies Scriptural mandates that women silently submit to male authority—speaking, teaching, and power usurpation all coexist within a single injunction.[6] By following Scripture and the early commentators, we can re-create a chain of reasoning which posits woman as a vessel containing weak discernment and weak obedience, whose own nature and behavior are responsible for creating the necessity for her control by the superior member of the species, man.

Renaissance England inherited the early Christian obsession with womanly obedience; it also continued to forbid women's access to speech that would grant them too much authority. One of the most popular conduct books for women throughout the sixteenth century was the 1528(?) *Instruction of a Christian Woman,* written in Latin by Juan Luis Vives, the humanist educator and friend of Erasmus, and translated into English by Richard Hyrde, a member of Thomas More's household. Vives warns women against teaching in much the same way as do the early churchmen: "Therfore bicause a woman is a fraile thynge and of weake discretion and that maye lightlye be disceyved: whiche thyng our fyrst mother Eve sheweth whom ye devyll caught with a lyght argument. Therfore a woman shulde nat teache leste whan she hath taken a false opinion and beleve of any thyng she spred this into the herars by the autoritie of maistershyp and lightly bringe other into the same errour" (qtd. in Wayne 1985, 19–20).[7] Vives extends the speech ban to a woman's everyday life by prohibiting her from taking part in group discussions; she should remain demure "and let fewe see her and none at al here her." In a gesture to Saint Paul, he says, "I gyve no licence to a woman to be a teacher nor to have authoritie of the man but to be in silence." Vives stands in vivid contrast to the relatively enlightened attitude toward women's education that Erasmus and More espoused (and from which More's daughters benefited).

By 1631, Richard Brathwait, in his *English Gentlewoman,* would almost entirely subsume silence into his concept of modest obedience. He never advocates directly for women to be silent, but, for contrast, he does describe a thoroughly improper woman as one who asserts herself vocally: "One of this ranke have I oft-times observed tracing the streets of this flourishing City; who, as one weary of her sexe, forbore not to unwoman her selfe. . . . *Quarrels* she would not sticke to bind upon. . . . Nothing desir'd she more than to *give affronts* in public places . . . where her *imperious tongue runne descant* upon every subject" (123–24, my emphasis). Whether by arguing (challenging male authority) or conversing upon every subject (teaching), a vocal woman is clearly viewed as an immodest one. Brathwait's negative example and Vives's overt reference to authority show the extent to which dominion and speech were still being conflated during the Renaissance.

The paradox at the heart of ethos for women writers of the seventeenth century thus stems from Paul's decree against women's speech and authority and from interpretations of Eve's initial lack of obedience as grounded in moral and intellectual weakness. Women were perceived as naturally deficient in both moral and intellectual virtue. Though Erasmus and More believed that education led to higher virtue for both men and women, Vives's ideal predominantly obtained: attention to retaining her chastity is study enough for all women.[8] The great triumvirate of desirable female attributes remained chastity, obedience, and silence; thus, a morally virtuous woman was a silent woman, and a woman who aspired to intellectual knowledge was suspected of the kind of moral weakness that led to Eve's disobedience. Finally, a woman who presumed to instruct others through her words usurped God-given male authority. Male ethos relied upon a fusion of both virtues, but the virtues themselves were in opposition for the woman writer.

Given this dilemma, the seventeenth-century woman writer's concern for ethos overwhelmed her project, sometimes leading her to the extreme measure of disguising her sex in order to receive a more sympathetic reading. The other artistic proofs employed by the contemporary rhetor, pathos and logos, were, for the woman writer, entirely dependent upon ethos. The fundamental question of whether a woman has the ability to reason and form logical arguments is at the root of her credibility as a persuasive writer, and she cannot possibly move the reader's passions if she is not considered a source of moral and intellectual virtue. Thus, women who wished to publish their writings were forced to circumvent this paradox in whatever ways they could.

Bathsua Makin

Bathsua Makin's own education was remarkable. The daughter of a schoolmaster and sister-in-law to a celebrated scholar, John Pell, Makin was adept in many languages and arts and held the position of governess to Charles I's daughter, Princess Elizabeth.[9] Late in life Makin opened the school for middling and upper-class girls that is advertised in her *Essay to Revive the Antient Education of Gentlewomen* (1673). In this essay Makin argues for the teaching of "Religion, Manners, Arts, and Tongues," a practice which, she assures us, has only recently been abandoned.[10] Faced with readers whose views were likely in opposition to her own, Makin carefully negotiates a rhetorical path while participating in the current debate over women's education. She inscribes a history for women in the learned arts and appropriates the humanist stance that education leads to virtue and piety. Under the veil of a male persona, Makin exhibits her own vast knowledge as she argues that an education for gentlewomen is possible, customary, and beneficial.

Although Makin makes a case for women's abilities, she does not want to be identified by the reader as female. The essay is ostensibly by an anonymous gentleman: the prefatory note to the reader asserts, "I am a Man my self, that would not suggest a thing prejudicial to our Sex" (5). This identification with the masculine is aimed at achieving what Kenneth Burke (1962) calls "consubstantiality"—a oneness with the dominant group, which, in this case, consists of gentlemen with potentially educable daughters. By linking herself to the reader's own group identification, she can achieve both credibility in the eyes of the reader, as a like-minded man, and a positive hearing for unorthodox views. By cutting off her identification with women, Makin removes any implication that she is complaining about her own situation and could therefore be perceived as an irate woman speaking for a radical few. Makin suppresses her authorial self in the interest of her cause of education, which, ideally, would make such suppression unnecessary in the future. Her subtextual message is that women will only be seen as respected and convincing orators after they are allowed the benefit of an education that teaches the necessary arts, an endeavor that does not preclude attention to virtue.

Beneath the simple title phrase, "Revive the Antient Education," lurks a contemporary philosophical debate between "custom" and "nature."[11] Some questions implicit in this debate include: Is a customary practice right simply because it is traditional, or must there be a foundation that is demonstrably rooted in nature in order to justify its continuance? Are traditions naturally received from God and our forbears, or is there evidence that some are perversely unnatural? "Custom," Makin pronounces, "when it is inveterate, hath a mighty influence: it hath the force of Nature it self" (3); thus, the difficulty of her endeavor to change or remove a custom through argumentation is immense and must be artfully done. Makin participates in this debate through the means of an anonymous letter from a "Friend" that introduces to the essay the conservative stance in respect to women's education. This "Friend" claims that "Women do not much desire Knowledge; they are of low parts, soft fickle natures." He continues to suggest that even if young girls could be allotted the time for studies, it would do them no good because, "the end of Learning is to fit one for publick Employment, which Women are not capable of. *Women must not speak in the Church*, it's against custom," and letting girls become bookish would "make them intolerably Proud" and unfit for their household duties.

Finally, he declares, "[I] would gladly have a fair answer to these things, or else shall breed up my Daughters as our forefathers did" (6). This letter, no doubt written by Makin for the purpose of providing specific grounds for the content and direction of her argument, resonates with all of the obstacles against women's learning and public discourse discussed earlier in this essay: Paul's injunctions against speech, gender-exclusive social roles, and women's lack of mental capacity. By grounding her argument against these obstacles in the nature versus custom debate, Makin can address many ills at once.

At the dawn of the scientific revolution, early feminists such as Makin joined in this debate in an effort to prove that the way women had been bred had no foundation in their natural abilities. Contemporary physiology maintained a conviction that men's minds were composed of a hard substance, suitable for learning difficult subjects, such as ancient tongues, rhetoric, and logic, while women's minds were inherently soft, unsuited for these studies. Early feminist writers accepted that men were, in Makin's terms, "the rougher Sex" and women were constructed of "softer and finer Materials," but she pursues the idea that the difference of materials would not significantly affect a woman's ability to learn. She refutes the usual objections that women's education is against custom by showing—through a catalog of exempla drawn from biblical, classical, and English history—that not only is it not unnatural for women to learn, but there are many precedents for this practice throughout history. While she overtly argues that there is indeed a purpose for education other than speaking in church or fitting one for public employment, she provides examples of women who did, in fact, participate in public life, albeit in times of crisis; indeed, she argues, it is only recently that this proper tradition of educating women has been broken and replaced with a "heathenish" or "barbaric" custom that keeps women in ignorance.

Makin's catalog of women is grounded in a long-standing tradition of defenses of women, beginning with the writing of female saints' lives and continuing through such early works as Geoffrey Chaucer's *Legends of Good Women* and Giovanni Boccaccio's *Concerning Famous Women*, and, in the Renaissance, Cornelius Agrippa's *Treatise of the Nobilitie and Excellencye of Woman Kynde* (1542), Sir Thomas Elyot's *The Defence of Good Women* (1540), Christopher Newstead's *Apology for Women* (1620), and Charles Gerbier's *Elogium Heroinium* (1651) (Hull, 1982).[12] Her knowledge of this tradition as well as her knowledge of the exempla themselves testify to her impressive education even as the exempla provide the proof for her arguments. Her use of more recent English history, particularly references to Elizabeth I and Jane Grey, allow her reader to see that in the last century highly esteemed women, immediate predecessors to seventeenth-century gentlewomen, excelled in learning. She insists that what has been commonplace in the past is not only possible but both customary and natural.

Makin diverges from the prior, more conventional catalogs of good women by categorizing these women by their contributions to or participation in the learned arts, in effect inscribing a history of learned women. Although Elyot generally praises women such as Zenobia for their wisdom and judgment, most catalogs list women remarkable for their piety, faithfulness, and chastity. The bulk of Makin's essay is organized around headings such as "Women Educated in Arts and Tongues, have been eminent in them" (9) and "Women have been profound Philosophers" (13), followed by discussions of the women who have achieved fame in these areas. Makin claims, "Women have not been meer Talkers: (as some frivolous Men would make them) but they have known how to use Languages, when they have had them. Many Women have been excellent Oratours," and she comments upon these:

> Valeria Maximus tells us of Amesia a modest Roman Lady, when she was accused of a great Crime, and ready to incur the Sentence of the Pretor, she in a great Confluence stept up amongst the People, and without any Advocate pleaded her own Cause so effectually, that by the publique Suffrage she was acquitted from all Aspersion whatsoever. . . . Hortensia was equal to her, the Daughter of Quintus Hortensius. When a grievous Fine was imposed upon the Roman Matrons by the Tribunes, when all Lawyers and Oratours were afraid to take upon them the Patronage of their Cause, this discreet Lady pleaded before the Triumvirate in the behalf of the Women, so happily and boldly, that the greatest Part of the Mulct [a fine, penalty, OED] imposed upon them, was remitted. (12)

Makin shows through these examples modest, virtuous women who were willing and able to defend themselves rhetorically (when no one else would rise to the task) in legal and political arenas. But the ability to do so, Makin implies in her essay, comes from solid study of the principles and practice of rhetoric and other arts, without which women are vulnerable to a host of wrongs and excluded from performing right actions: "She could not open her Mouth with Wisdom, and have in her Tongue the Law of kindness, unless she understood Grammar, Rhetorick, and Logick" (35).

Makin's task is one of universalizing—uniting—that which has been for too long separated into gendered space. Alongside her message that women can learn what men can learn is the often recurring argument that uneducated men are as liable to folly and error as uneducated women. It is not education, she insists, that ruins, but the lack thereof. She writes: "What is said of Philosophy is true of Knowledge; a little Philosophy carries a Man from God, but a great deal brings him back again; a little knowledge, like windy Bladders, puffs up, but a good measure of true knowledge, like Ballast in a Ship, settles down, and makes a person move more even in his station; 'tis not knowing too much, but too little that causes the irregularity" (32). Knowledge cannot and will not ruin women, as it does not hurt men, and though some women may "abuse" their education, there is a far greater likelihood that learning will have a positive effect on both men and women. Indeed, Makin argues that her project will not invert the social order: "My intention is not to equalize Women to Men, much less make them superior. They are the weaker Sex, yet capable of impressions of great things, something like to the best of Men" (29). In effect, women are lesser men, created as "help-meets" from Adam's rib, and, although they may not be capable of deeds that equal the best of men's, they are capable of lesser greatness that sometimes exceeds that of most men.

In a culture characterized by Scripturally mandated gender hierarchy, to argue for true egalitarianism would be fruitless, verging on blasphemy. Makin is well aware of these limits and makes use of the customary modesty topos. She argues up to (and not beyond) the margins of acceptability, assuring the reader that women's highest callings lie in support positions: women "may be very useful to their Husbands in Their Trades, and to their Children, by timely instructing them, before they be sent to School" (27). In fact, the greatest praise that can be bestowed upon women is to say, "How modest and chaste many have been; how remarkable in their love to their Husbands, how constant in Religion, how dutiful to their Parents, or how beneficial to their Country" (29). This last in a list of highly conventional female virtues alludes to a role in public life but is vague enough to pass unchallenged by a skeptical eye—still, it leaves room for pushing the boundaries of domestic life. According to Makin, all of these virtues are most successfully achieved not by women who spend their lives "dressing and trimming themselves" and "Painting and Dancing . . . and such like vanities" (30), but by women who receive a serious education which "perfects and adorns the Soul" (24). She claims: "God intended Woman as a help-meet to Man, in his constant conversation, and in the concerns of his Family and Estate, when he should most need, in sickness, weakness, absence, death, etc. Whilst we most neglect to fit them for these things, we renounce God's Blessing, he hath appointed Women for, are ungrateful to him, cruel to them, and injurious to our selves" (23). Education does not interfere with a woman's modest duties but actually turns young women away from dangerous vanity and toward the sober pursuits that befit a wife and mother. Thus, Makin responds to the pragmatic view that education must lead to adult duties.

Above all, Makin insists that education is not an end in itself, not intended to push women ahead in public life, but designed, in the great humanist tradition, to promote virtue and piety. She claims: "I acknowledge the great end of Arts and Tongues is the better to enable us to know God in Jesus Christ, and our own selves, that we may glorifie and enjoy him for ever. . . . Many Women have improved their humane Knowledge, so as by Gods Blessing hath been a means of their obtaining Spiritual Knowledge" (15). This most sacred and unopposable intention has long been used as the rationale for boundary-crossing, active pursuits undertaken by women. The choice of a religious subject is what allowed some women to publish their writings in the Middle Ages and Renaissance, creating, in effect, a loophole in the requirement for silence.[13] That Makin would make use of this topos testifies to her awareness of its power. She also links herself to the humanist tradition by discussing Erasmus's colloquy "The Abbot and the Learned Woman," a dialectical exploration of women's education. Makin summarizes the discourse:

[The Maid] gives many good Reasons why Women should be learned, that they might know God, their Saviour, understand his Sacred Word, and admire him in his wonderful Works; that they might also better administer their Household Affairs amongst a multitude of Servants, who would have more reverence towards them, because they were above them in understanding. Further, she found a great content in reading good Authors at spare times. [The Abbot] gives her one Answer to all this, *That Women would never be kept in subjection if they were learned.* (23)

Makin asks, "Seeing Nature produces Women of such excellent Parts, that they do often equalize, some-times excel men, in what ever they attempt; what reason can be given why they should not be improved?" (23). Of course, Makin has already answered her own question through Erasmus's Abbot: the only conceivable reason for keeping women uneducated is to keep them in subjection. Yet, since this subjection is a Scriptural mandate, Makin is in difficult territory. She must argue that the benefits of education will improve women's virtue but will not raise them above men socially.

To this end, Makin devises an approach in which women's education will ultimately serve men. As women bear sons and are responsible for boys' early education, an educated mother will be both more capable of giving her son a good early education and more likely to stand as an example of what he should plan to exceed. She explains: "If this way of Educating Ladies should . . . be generally practiced, the greatest hurt, that I fore-see, can ensue, is, to put your Sons upon greater diligence to advance themselves in Arts and Languages; that they may be Superior to Women in Parts as Well as Place. This is the great thing I designe" (5). The improvement of women will promote the improvement of men. By playing to men's own self-interest and concern for social preeminence, she issues a challenge to them to excel women in learning as well, as if to say that the only tolerable subjection is one in which the masters are truly superior to the servants. Makin also appeals to the masculine sense of sportsmanship and fair play: after all, "This favors not of a Manly Spirit, to trample upon those that are down" (5).

That Makin admits to men's right to dominion over women is not really in conflict with her numerous examples of women who are naturally capable of matching or excelling the feats of men. According to Makin's reasoning, men are certainly responsible for keeping women in a state of ignorance; if women have been wiser and more heroic in ages past, it is to men's disgrace that they have allowed women to become so "ill-bred." Yet women's natural abilities have been to a large degree disempowered by God's decree that women remain socially inferior to men. She admits, "I think the greater Care ought to be taken of [Females]: Because Evil seems to be begun here, as in *Eve*, and to be propagated by her Daughters" (7). Makin aims the thrust of her essay at the point at which women can benefit from a scholarly education, improve their piety and virtue, yet remain modest helpmates to their husbands. Although women have, long ago and in times of crisis, stepped beyond their prescribed space to perform public acts of bravery and self-defense—speaking aloud in order to right wrongs—in the interest of keeping her readers' goodwill, Makin stops far short of calling for wide-scale social change. This sort of call to action would take generations of increasingly secularized society to find an audience, in a time that would no longer uphold a literal reading of the Bible as supreme authority upon which to base all human actions.[14]

Finally, however, Makin leaves us with a small but significant defiance that undergirds her positive assertions about women's enduring natural abilities and subtly subverts her acquiescence to male authority. We must remember that Makin's entire project, a published persuasive essay advertising the offerings of a woman teacher and written by a woman (though not overtly so), stands as a prime example of that unsanctioned act of public oration and claimed authority. Bathsua Makin herself has become another member of her catalog of exemplary women; she joins the ranks of the newly acknowledged tradition of learned women as one who speaks out against the wrongs of her society when no one else would. She wrote, "I hope Women will make another use of what I have said; instead of claiming honour from what Women have formerly been, they will labour to imitate them in learning those Arts their Sex hath invented, in studying those Tongues they have understood, and in practising those Virtues shadowed under their Shapes; the knowledge of Arts and Tongues, the exercise of Virtue and Piety, will certainly (let men say what they will) make them honourable" (21–22).

In summary, seventeenth-century women were ideologically discouraged from publishing their writings, an act which was construed as an attempt to usurp male authority by presuming to "teach" others. Because women were considered morally and intellectually inferior to men, their potential readers were predisposed to find fault with their writings or to attribute them to male writers. Thus, women who wrote for a public audience were forced to devise strategies to gain a sympathetic reading. In an effort to present a credible ethos, Bathsua Makin chose to write her essay in the persona of an upstanding, well-educated English gentleman who encourages readers to educate their daughters in the arts and letters. Makin's essay serves two related ends: by describing the exemplary accomplishments of women of the past, it argues for the improvement of women's virtue and intellect through a humanist education; and, by subverting the injunctions against women's speech, Makin places herself within a tradition of women orators.

Notes

I would like to thank Lisa M. Klein and Nan Johnson for their comments on earlier versions of this essay.

1. According to Patricia Crawford (1985, 214), during the second half of the century, particularly during the Interregnum (1649–1660), no fewer than 653 first editions authored by women were published, nearly half of which are attributed to twenty-two prolific writers and the rest to women with only one or two publications apiece. During this historical period women wrote and published nearly every imaginable genre of works, including memoirs, spiritual and secular diaries, poetry, prose literature, essays, advice books, almanacs, plays, meditations, biographies, and petitions. For extensive bibliographies, see Crawford (1985, 211–82) and Hobby (1989).

2. Much of our evidence that women's published texts were received with hostility or otherwise attributed can be found in the prefatory material in those texts. Rachel Speght claims in a later work that her learned (anonymous) reply to Joseph Swetnam's misogynistic *The Araignment of lewde, idle, froward, and unconstant women* was attributed to her father: "I am now, as by strong motive induced (for my rights sake) to produce and divulge this offspring of my indevour, to prove them further futurely who have formerly deprived me of my due, imposing my abortive upon the father of me, but not of it. Their varietie of verdicts have verified the adage *quot homines, tot sententiae*, and made my experience confirme that apothegme which doth affirme Censure to be inevitable to a publique act" (1621, Sig. A2^v). See the epistle dedicatory to her *Mortalities Memorandum*. Her polemic reply to Swetnam is *A Mouzell for Melastomus*. For more on Speght, see Lewalski (1993).

3. I make a distinction between women who wrote for private or family perusal and those who made the effort to present their writings to the public; it was the movement from the domestic, feminine space to the public, masculine arena that produced the most anxiety.

4. Only at the highest social ranks would women have been able to remain ignorant of household work in this period. Although all upper-class households had servants (even most lower-class households took in a boy or girl to help with chores), wives were still expected to have a full range of housekeeping skills in order to oversee and work alongside their servants. Numerous household guides for gentlewomen were published in the seventeenth century. See Markham (1623) and Woolley (1673). For a catalogue of similar titles, see Hull (1982).

5. For a groundbreaking study of the belief that women inherently want to invert the social order and rule men, see Davis (1975, 124–51).

6. For a fascinating seventeenth-century defense of women's right to preach, see Fell Foxe (1990). For a discussion of Fell Foxe, Mary Astell, and biblical exegesis, see Thickstun (1991).

7. Wayne gives a thorough reading of Vives's highly proscriptive position on women's writing. The *Revised Short Title Catalogue* lists eight separate English editions of *Instruction* before 1600.

8. Baumlin (1994, 229–63) perceptively notes the contemporary conflation of silence and chastity. I maintain that these attributes were further conflated with obedience.

9. A controversy has arisen over the correct identification of Makin and the writings she produced. According to a recent study, Makin has been frequently identified incorrectly as Bathsua Pell Makin (rather than Bathsua Reginald Makin) and mistakenly named as the author of an anonymous treatise on debt. For the most current biographical information about Makin, see Brink (1991), Teague (1989, 285–304), and Fraser (1985, 130–31).

10. All quotations are taken from Makin (1673, Wing M309). For discussion of Makin's place in the history of linguistics, see Salmon (1987). For an investigation of Makin's essay from an eighteenth-century perspective, see Myers (1985).

11. Two other late-seventeenth-century women writers, Margaret Cavendish (Duchess of Newcastle) and Mary Astell, also investigate the custom versus nature debate in a number of their works.

12. Refer to Hull's bibliography for a list of other defenses before 1640.

13. See Hannay (1985, 1–14). The book of essays is dedicated to examining the ways religion allowed women to bypass injunctions of silence in order to write and speak publicly and become patrons to other writers.

14. More than a century after Makin's tract, Mary Wollstonecraft would argue in her *A Vindication of the Rights of Woman* (1792) much to the same purpose: against a still-widespread opposition to women (without even the religious need to justify their subjection).

References

Agrippa, Cornelius. 1542. *A Treatise of the Nobilitie and Excellencye of Woman Kynde.* London.

Aquinas, Saint Thomas. 1992. *Summa Theologia.* Trans. Edmund Hill, O.P. In *Woman Defamed and Woman Defended: An Anthology of Medieval Texts,* edited by Alcuin Blamires. Oxford: Clarendon Press.

Baumlin, Tita French. 1994. "'A good (wo)man skilled in speaking': Ethos, Self-Fashioning, and Gender in Renaissance England." In *Ethos: New Essays in Rhetorical and Critical Theory,* edited by James S. Baumlin and Tita French Baumlin, 229–63. Dallas: Southern Methodist University Press.

Boccaccio, Giovanni. 1963. *Concerning Famous Women.* Trans. Guido A. Guarino. New Brunswick, N.J.: Rutgers University Press.

Brathwait, Richard. 1631. *The English Gentlewoman.* London.

Brink, Jean R. 1991. "Bathsua Reginald Makin: 'Most Learned Matron.'" *Huntington Library Quarterly* 54.4: 313–26.

Burke, Kenneth. 1962. *A Rhetoric of Motives*. In *A Grammar of Motives and a Rhetoric of Motives*, 521–857. Cleveland: World Publishing Company.

Chaucer, Geoffrey. 1977. *The Legend of Good Women*. In *The Complete Poetry and Prose of Geoffrey Chaucer*, edited by John H. Fisher, 617–65. New York: Holt, Rinehart, and Winston.

Crawford, Patricia. 1985. "Women's Published Writings 1600–1700." In *Women in English Society 1500–1800*, edited by Mary Prior, 211–82. London & New York: Methuen.

Davis, Natalie Zemon. 1975. "Women on Top." In *Society and Culture in Early Modern France*, edited by Davis, 124–51. Stanford, Calif.: Stanford University Press.

Elyot, Sir Thomas. 1540. *The Defence of Good Women*. London.

Erasmus, Desiderius. 1923. "The Abbot and the Learned Woman." In *Twenty Select Colloquies of Erasmus*, translated by Sir Roger L'Estrange, 208–14. London: Chapman & Dodd.

Fell Foxe, Margaret. 1990. *Women's Speaking Justified*. In *The Rhetorical Tradition*, edited by Patricia Bizzell and Bruce Herzberg, 677–85. Boston: Bedford.

Fraser, Antonia. 1985. *The Weaker Vessel*. New York: Vintage.

Gerbier, Charles. 1651. *Elogium Heroinium*. London.

Hannay, Margaret P. 1985. "Introduction." In *Silent but for the Word: Tudor Women as Patrons, Translators, and Writers of Religious Works*, edited by Margaret P. Hannay, 1–14. Kent, Ohio: Kent State University Press.

Hobby, Elaine. 1989. *Virtue of Necessity: English Women's Writing 1649–88*. Ann Arbor: University of Michigan Press.

Hull, Suzanne C. 1982. *Chaste, Silent, and Obedient: English Books for Women 1475–1640*. San Marino, Calif.: Huntington Library Press.

Lewalski, Barbara Kiefer. 1993. *Writing Women in Jacobean England*. Cambridge: Harvard University Press.

Makin, Bathsua. 1673. *An Essay to Revive the Antient Education of Gentlewomen*. London.

Markham, Gervaise. 1623. *Country Contentments, and The English Huswife*. London.

Myers, Mitzi. 1985. "Domesticating Minerva: Bathsua Makin's 'Curious' Argument for Women's Education." *Studies in Eighteenth-Century Culture* 14: 173–92.

Newstead, Christopher. 1620. *Apology for Women*. London.

Salmon, Vivian. 1987. "Bathsua Makin; a Pioneer Linguist and Feminist in Seventeenth-Century England." In *Neuere Forschungen zur Wortbildung und Historiographie der Linguistik*, edited by Brigitte Asbach-Schnitker and Johannes Roggenhofer. Tubingen: Gunter Narr.

Smith, Hilda L. 1982. *Reason's Disciples: Seventeenth-Century English Feminists*. Urbana: University of Illinois Press.

Speght, Rachel. 1617. *A Mouzell for Melastomus*. London.

———. 1621. *Mortalities Memorandum, with a Dreame Prefixed*. London.

Swetnam, Joseph. 1615. *The Araignment of lewde, idle, froward, and unconstant women.* London.

Teague, Francis. 1986. "New Light on Bathsua Makin." *Seventeenth-Century News* 44.1–2: 16.

———. 1989. "Bathsua Makin: Woman of Learning." In *Women Writers of the Seventeenth Century,* edited by Katharina M. Wilson and Frank J. Warnke, 285–304. Athens & London: University of Georgia Press.

Thickstun, Margaret Olofson. 1991. "'This was a Woman that taught': Feminist Scriptural Exegesis in the Seventeenth-Century." *Studies in Eighteenth-Century Culture* 21: 149–58.

Wayne, Valerie. 1985. "'Some Sad Sentence': Vives's *Instruction of a Christian Woman.*" In *Silent but for the Word,* edited by Margaret P. Hannay, 19–20. Kent, Ohio: Kent State University Press.

Wollstonecraft, Mary. 1985. *A Vindication of the Rights of Woman.* London: J. M. Dent.

Woolley, Hannah. 1673. *A Gentlewoman's Companion.* London.

A Woman's Inventive Response to the Seventeenth-century *Querelle des Femmes*

Ekaterina V. Haskins

This Subject may be handled two ways, either in a flourishing, brisk, and complementive Stile, or otherwayes after the manner of Philosophers by Principles, to the end of being instructed therein to the bottom.

Such as have the true idea of eloquence, know well that these two stiles are almost inconsistent together, and that one cannot enlighten the mind, and tickle it by the same Methode.
François Poulain de la Barre

Thus, a seventeenth-century French scholar described the rhetorical difficulties of those who ventured to defend the equality of the sexes. According to Poulain (1988, 92), whom Simone de Beauvoir proclaimed "the leading feminist of the time" (1989, 107), poets and orators, when speaking of womankind, had been employing "Figures of Eloquence" and "Flowers of Rhetoric" only to "hinder the discerning of Truth" about women's real social position. To produce an unprejudiced defense of the female sex, therefore, an author was required not only to discard the notions of women's nature that were grounded in and legitimized by the literary tradition, but also to avoid any rhetorical flourishes that might impede the process of strict observation and reasoning.

Certain women authors of the late seventeenth century, nevertheless, prove the opposite of Poulain de la Barre's thesis. In their writings about women they offer noteworthy examples of rhetorical invention that draw on traditionally incompatible argumentative styles.[1] Yet, similar to Poulain and unlike most "benign" works written by men about women, early feminist[2] discourses sought to overcome the double standard fostered by literary discussions of womankind and aspired to reshape the idea of a woman in accordance with a new standard of rationality introduced in Europe by the philosophies of René Descartes and John Locke.

This essay explores the rhetorical and philosophical sources of *An Essay in Defence of the Female Sex*. This book was written anonymously by the Englishwoman Judith Drake in 1696, and several subsequent editions attest to its success with the public.[3] As part of the English cultural landscape of the Restoration period, Drake's essay exemplifies a kind of early feminist discourse that borrows its stylistic and argumentative features from two conflicting traditions of writing: an age-old genre of the controversy over women and the egalitarian argument of seventeenth-century rationalism.

Rhetorical Legacy of the Controversy over Women

At first sight, Drake's essay bears a strong resemblance to the writings of the so-called *querelle des femmes,* or controversy over women—a genre that was widespread in Europe in the late Middle Ages and Renaissance.[4] Such works feature defenses and attacks on women, supported by examples from classical history and the Bible and by the appeal to philosophical and religious authorities. Arguments for and against matters concerning the female sex were usually presented in the form of a dialogue between the author and his or her opponent or a sympathetic listener, as in the dialogues of Plato. The other rhetorical model was Quintilian's *Institutio Oratoria* (1921, 1: 235), which included panegyric and denunciation among the most prominent tools of the orator. Occasionally classical and biblical examples would be supplemented by a more versatile technique, a principle of characterization, dating back to Theophrastus's *Characters,* that was written in 319 B.C.E. This principle presupposed the use of a literary character to depict a particular human fault or virtue.

For instance, Joseph Swetnam's *Araignment of lewde, idle, froward, and unconstant women* (1615), an early-seventeenth-century specimen of literary misogyny, combined biblical and classical examples of female treachery and vanity with a Theophrastean character of the widow, a staple target for Renaissance satirists. Swetnam (1) also dwelled on a topos common to both literary attacks and defenses, the Creation story, which attributed the "froward nature" of women to the crookedness of the rib from which Eve was supposedly shaped. In contrast, a number of Renaissance vindications of women (Anger 1589, 8; Gosynhill 1985, 164; Sowernam 1617, 3–5, 15) used the Creation story as proof of womankind's superior value, for man was made of "vile earth," whereas woman got her flesh from the material already purified by God.

To support their claims of women's goodness and men's folly, the defenders frequently offered contesting interpretations of literary and historical personae who were attacked by literary detractors of the female sex. Jane Anger, for example, insisted that it was the folly of Vulcan and flattery of Paris that led Venus and Helen to flee their husbands; the author then marshaled historical examples of violent and lustful men to "persuade [the reader] that the hearts of men are most desirous to excel in vice" (1589, 12–13). Apology for women often took the form of invective, as in Ester Sowernam's caustic response to Swetnam, in which the misogynist himself is turned into a literary character who is arraigned before the feminine judges, Reason and Experience.

It must be granted, therefore, that *An Essay in Defence of the Female Sex* followed the conventions of the earlier "controversy" genre in several ways: it fostered a debate over women, addressed a sympathetic listener (Princess Anne of Denmark), and presented a Theophrastean gallery of male comic portraits. But while these features point to similarities between *An Essay* and the works of controversy that preceded it, Judith Drake in her defense of women undoubtedly went beyond the usual technique of balancing the examples of "bad" women with "good" female characters.[5] When the men of letters used this rhetorical device, they were not opposed to the inequality of women; they only hoped to promote the ideal of the obedient and mute wife. As Linda Woodbridge comments, "Most authors who delicately and wittily defended the fair sex against hypothetical slanders would have been merely baffled by talk of job discrimination or women's property rights" (1984, 129). Authors of the genre did not question the social status of women but concentrated instead on general "female" qualities such as shrewishness or modesty and inconstancy or faithfulness, portrayed by staple characters from Cleopatra to Griselda.

Drake makes clever rhetorical use of Theophrastean character to portray certain vices that were commonly attributed to women. She first presents the traits as universal human faults and then offers the reader a sequence of male portraits exemplifying these vices. Denouncing misogynist complaints of women's vanity, she brings in the examples of a "Bully," a "Fop Poet," and a "Beau" to prove that vanity is "an Ambition of being taken notice of, which shows it self variously according to the humor of the Persons" (75).

Following Theophrastean method, Drake gives a definition of a defect and then allows the character to expose the fault in his social environment. Impertinence, for instance, is described as "a humor of busying our selves about things trivial, and of no Moment in themselves" (84). Adversaries hypocritically accuse women of impertinence because of their preoccupation with such seemingly petty things as "Household Affairs" and "Government of Children and Servants" (85). In response to this charge, Drake offers the character of a "Coffee-House Politician," for whom the thrill of vicarious participation in political intrigues overshadows domestic necessities: "He is one whose Brains having been once overheated, retain something of the Fire in 'em ever after. . . . He lodges at home, but lives at the Coffee-House. He converses more with News Papers, Gazettes and Votes, than his Shop Books, and his constant Application to the Publick takes him off all Care for his Private Concern. He is always settling the Nation, yet cou'd never manage his own Family" (87–89).

The satirical force of her examples is produced by Drake's skillful use of metaphor and irony. Consider her portraits of the "Pedant" and the "Country Squire," which illustrate how English men "often Baffle and Frustrate the Effects of a liberal Education, as well by Industry as Negligence" (35). The Pedant, because of his "retired and inactive life" and "constant Conversation with Antiquity," appears as one of "the Ghosts of Old Romans rais'd by Magic"; he knows as much about the affairs of his native country as could "reasonably be expected from an animated Egyptian Mummy" (27–28). The Country Squire, on the other hand, "having made the usual Tour of Latin, and Greek Authors," returns home "to be made" a gentleman; thereafter "his Conversation . . . is wholly taken up by his Horses, Dogs and Hawks" (30–31).

The characters not only embody various follies but also seem to replicate real people living in seventeenth-century London. Although the author denies any "Malicious Design to characterize any Particular Persons," she has to acknowledge that "there is no Man, who is but moderately Acquainted with the World, especially this Town, but may find half a Dozen, or more Originals for every Picture" (Sig. B, B1). Comparing Drake's pen to those of her contemporaries, Myra Reynolds claims that the author of these caricatures "certainly deserves the credit of being the most brilliant woman writer of the period" (1964, 306). By creating portraits of her compatriots, Drake managed to comment on a larger society, distinguishing herself from many women's advocates who culled their exempla mostly from literary lore.

Drake, however, owes the method of character painting to a rich and ambivalent tradition of humor present in both strictly "literary" and popular folk genres.[6] The "Preface" to *An Essay* invokes the festive topsy-turvy atmosphere of fairs and puppet shows, where distorting mirrors and puppeteers can momentarily turn anyone into a ridiculous monster. The characters, then, given their function as an attraction, seem to be less of a pointed weapon against misogyny than a comic entr'acte entertainment inserted into the otherwise serious polemic. Only those who "play the Fool seriously in the World" are expected to take the joke as an insult, explains Drake, while "the Candid and Ingenious" men would not object to her observations (Sig. B).

The misogynist side of the debate over women used jest and humor as a primary method of attack, and the defenders often were forced to rebut jokes and anecdotes, which inevitably weakened their rhetorical thrust. Despite their passionate resistance to culturally entrenched negative archetypes, early feminist writers could not advance beyond praising virtuous women. Drake's forerunners either attacked verbal detractors of their sex personally or, in an equally generic fashion, paraded glorious female characters from days past. "Caught up in opposition to misogyny," writes Joan Kelly, "the feminists of the *querelle* remained bound by the terms of that dialectic" (1982, 27).

Apart from stylistic constraints of the controversy, these authors faced an ideological barrier of religion that preordained women's inequality in the name of God. Although female writers such as Anger and Sowernam did blame misogynists for their bad character and lack of courtesy, and even pointed out stylistic and logical flaws in the attackers' discourses, they nevertheless did not question the authority of the Bible and the validity of arguments by example.

Drake's distinctive style is shaped by her unusual treatment of charges against women. Before she launches her satirical attack on particular types of men, she lists a catalog of imperfections for which women were traditionally blamed: vanity, impertinence, enviousness, and inconstancy. Interestingly, Drake does not reject these charges immediately but presents them as characteristics that could be equally attributed to men and women. In her "Preface" to the essay Drake admits that "Vanity [is] almost the universal mover of all our Actions, and consequently of mine" (Sig. A [10]). After exposing vanity in its various forms, she concludes ironically: "I hope therefore the burden of this good Quality will not hereafter be laid upon us alone, but the Men will be contented to divide the Load with us . . ." (84). It is apparent that the author deliberately avoided staple examples of women's virtue to argue her point: for her, "tis very ill logick to argue from particulars to General, and where the Premises are singular, to conclude Universally" (134). Moreover, Drake openly dismisses an argument that is based solely on the ethos of a literary persona. Her reaction to a contemporary work, *Dialogue concerning Women* by William Walsh, is sarcastically cold:

> He has taken more care to give an Edge to his Satyr, than force to his Apology; he has play'd a sham Prize, and receives more thrusts than he makes; and like a false Renegade fights under our colors only for a fairer Opportunity of betraying us. . . .
>
> I have neither Learning, nor Inclination to make a Precedent, or indeed any use to Mr. W's labour'd Common Place Book; and shall leave Pedants and School-Boys to rake and tumble the Rubbish of Antiquity, and master all the Heroes and Heroins they can find to furnish matter for some wretched Harangue, or stuff a miserable Declamation with instead of Sense or Argument. (5)

Thus, criticizing one of the old controversy's main appeals, the author proceeds with quite a different line of argument—one that aligns her with followers of seventeenth-century rationalism.

Rationalist Complement to the Discourse on Women

In Drake's time Cartesian thought was rapidly gaining popularity among wide circles of the European literate population, especially women. Thomas M. Lennon notes, "because of its availability in the vernacular and its non-scholastic, relatively informal literary quality, Cartesianism was the philosophy of choice among women, especially in the salons" (1992, 53). Furthermore, Descartes's assumption of the genderless quality of the human intellect allowed, at least in theory, equality between the sexes. According to Ruth Perry, "Descartes had asserted that formal scholastic education was of no special use in apprehending reality or ascertaining how the mind functioned; any serious person might cultivate self conscious thought, which was marked by logic, clarity and inner certainty. This radical epistemology put women on a theoretical par with men" (1986, 70).

Since even upper-class women in the late seventeenth century were rarely trained in classical rhetoric and ancient languages, their ability to enter learned discussions was limited. But Descartes in *Discourse on Method* insisted that classical training was not an indispensable foundation for eloquence: "Those who reason most cogently, and work over their thoughts to make them clear and intelligible, are always the most persuasive, even if they speak only a provincial dialect and have never studied rhetoric" (1960, 7). It is not surprising, then, that female authors who could not enjoy a liberal education as often as men embraced the Cartesian idea of rhetoric with enthusiasm and popularized it in their writings.

Defending women's right to speak in a society of men, Drake also emphasized that "for Conversation, it is not requisite we should be Philologers, Rhetoricians, Philosophers, Historians, or poets; but only that we should think pertinently, and express our thoughts properly" (38). To reinforce this position, she challenged the traditional scholastic definition of the term *learning:* "Nor can I imagine for what good Reason a Man skill'd in Latin, and Greek, and vers'd in the Authors of Ancient Times shall be call'd Learned; yet another who perfectly understands Italian, French, Spanish, High Dutch, and the rest of the European Languages, is acquainted with the Modern History of all those Countries, knows their Policies, has div'd into all the Intrigues of the several Courts, . . . shall after all this be thought Unlearned for want of those two languages" (45).

Learning, in Drake's mind, meant one's capacity to form independent judgments about reality: "I take Nature to be the great Book of Universal Learning, which he that reads best in all, or any of its Parts, is the greatest scholar" (47). Because female rationality, in general, and the ability to argue sensibly, in particular, had been constantly questioned by learned men, Judith Drake attempted to persuade her readers of the merits that a conversation with ladies may bring to "an ingenious Gentleman" (6).

Exclusion from the educational system, for Drake, did not make women irrational and rhetorically inept. There is no special virtue in the knowledge of Antiquity, or of many foreign languages, the author argues, if a person cannot engage "in a Discourse that concerns the present Times, and their Native Country" (28). Books by English authors, if read with a goal of gaining proficiency in various conversational styles and topics, are as good as Plato and Aristotle. Drake invites aspiring women rhetors to study native masterpieces: in tragedy, no one can give "Nobler, or juster Pictures of Nature than Mr. Shakespear;" in comedy, Wycherley's "strong Wit, pointed Satyr, sound and useful Observations [are] beyond imitation" (48–49). Though farce and slapstick are thought of as "an inferior Class," they still "deserve commendation," for "even the worst of 'em afford us some diversion" (49). In addition, English readers have a good supply of serious literature: the essays of Lord Bacon, Sir Walter Raleigh, as well as translations of "Montagne, Rochefacaut, and St. Evremont" (52–53). Encouraging her female compatriots to read the best of their native writers, Drake promulgated Descartes's egalitarian approach to rhetorical invention. But she contributed to this approach a refreshing appreciation for stylistic diversity by adding comedy, satire, and farce to a legitimate array of rhetorical choices.[7]

In addition to Cartesian skepticism, yet another philosophical method provided a foundation for early feminists' egalitarian polemics. In 1690 John Locke's treatise on human understanding was published to the controversial but attentive reception of the public. The most famous work of empirical thought, *An Essay Concerning Human Understanding* won the sympathetic ear of women such as Judith Drake. Her assertion that "there are no innate ideas, but all the Notions we have, are derived from our external Senses, either immediately, or by Reflection" (11–12), is obviously borrowed from Locke.[8] Applying this thesis to her own discussion of women, Drake sets out to prove the natural equality of the sexes and the social causes of women's inferior position.

In order to discredit the misogynist assumption of the natural intellectual inferiority of the female sex, the author "appeal[s] yet further to Experience" (13) as an alternative to settling the dispute of "whether Men, or Women, be generally more ingenious, or learned" (6). It is quite obvious to Drake that men have had an unquestionable advantage over women due to "their Education, Freedom of Converse, and Variety of Business and Company" (6). These advantages are all attributable to experience. Given Lockean assumptions, the question remains: are men naturally the intellectual superiors of women?

Before Drake, Poulain de la Barre had attacked social custom from the position of Cartesian skepticism, "rejecting all which hath been hitherto believed upon the simple report of other Men, without Tryal, or Examination" (1988, 64). Drake accepts the Cartesian premise that "all Souls are equal" (1697, 11) but feels compelled to demonstrate this equality with the help of empirical evidence. Among animal species, she points out, "there is no difference betwixt Male and Female in point of sagacity" (14). If one looked at humans, the sexual difference increased with the degree of prosperity: among the "Country People" who "subsist upon their daily Labour . . . the Condition of the two Sexes is more level, than amongst Gentlemen, City Traders, or Rich Yeomen" (15–16). Since gender inequality was stronger among the propertied class, that proved the force of social custom in the shaping of male dominance. Considering that customs varied in different countries, Drake offers "our Neighbours the Dutch" as an example of an "improvement" in the relations between the sexes: there women were partners in business with their husbands, whereas in England women were bred "so ignorant of Business" (16–17).

Female intellectual inferiority and ineptness for business and politics, therefore, had distinctly social causes. The major cause, in Drake's view, was the lack of a serious education: in "tender years" boys and girls may receive the same training, but after the age of seven, they are separated, so that the boys can go to the grammar school, while the girls learn only such "accomplishments" as needlework, dancing, singing, or painting (36–37). Men who blame women for ignorance and other faults associated with inadequate training display the same "courage" as a person who beats a man whose hands are bound (20). It is men, Drake insists, who "compel us to a Subjection, Nature never meant" and "train us up altogether to Ease and Ignorance" (21).

The essay unambiguously asserts that accusations of vanity, impertinence, inconstancy, and other traditionally "female" faults are based on a double standard. To prove this, Drake offers a line of argument that amalgamates Cartesian and Lockean principles of investigation. However, her commitment to either methodology seems questionable; as Hilda L. Smith contends, Drake's essay was not a scholarly defense, "but a vigorous presentation of ideas that now needed less to be justified or proved than to be driven home" (1982, 144).

Entering the dispute concerning women in print, the author used those rhetorical tools that were most likely to attract public attention as well as influence popular opinion on the question of women's role in seventeenth-century English society. At the time there was no consistent theory that advocated women's intellectual as well as social parity with men. Even such philosophers as Descartes and Locke never ventured to apply their egalitarian premises to a serious questioning of the socially entrenched sexual inequality. Descartes's reconciliation of reason with the authority of the Church, evident in his late work "Meditations," and Locke's positive assessment of the government as the institution of male property owners[9] undermined the egalitarian potential of these philosophies. But their principles introduced what Lennon calls "a conception of reason to which women could lay full claim in theory and did lay claim to an unprecedented and increasing extent in practice" (1992, 54).

An Innovative Blending of Rhetorical Traditions
in *An Essay in Defence of the Female Sex*

"The defence of our Sex against so many and so great Wits as have so strongly attack'd it, may justly seem a Task too difficult for a Woman to attempt" (Drake 1697, 2–3), admitted the author of the defense, which prompted London society to ascribe it to the male publisher James Drake. Such a reaction was not unusual, if we consider popular notions of female rationality perpetuated in all sorts of literary productions of the era: "In the seventeenth century, . . . women were praised chiefly for their domestic capabilities and for their ability to function as static, passive exemplars of virtue. Because of historical developments, shifting economic structures, and the prescriptions of marriage manuals and courtesy books, seventeenth-century English women, though encouraged to work for the moral betterment of society, were consistently discouraged from becoming actively, directly involved in matters of public importance" (Latt 1977, 56–57).

The genre of the controversy over women, until it was creatively appropriated by Drake, had only helped to popularize the ideal of a chaste and obedient wife among Englishwomen of the Restoration period. The genre's lush, ornamental style ensured an easy literary success without ever creating a genuine controversy. For the most part, literary sympathizers of the female sex sought little more than public applause for their ingenuity in conjuring better examples of women's virtue. Theophrastean character proved to be a rich rhetorical source for the controversy: first, because it did not require any serious knowledge of classical history and mythology to create a literary persona; and second, because it allowed the author more freedom to manipulate the details in portrayal of a social type.

As we have seen, Judith Drake employed the advantages of Theophrastean character to break generic conventions of the controversy and to pursue a discussion of women's social role that combined sober realism and humor. Since she did not receive a standard liberal education, Drake was certainly at a disadvantage in her choice of classical rhetorical tools. She was keenly aware of the system of exclusion that prevented her female contemporaries from engaging in intellectual and political activity. Women can seldom defend their cause, she persisted, precisely "because through the Usurpation of Men, and the Tyranny of Custom (here in England especially) there are at most but few, who are by Education, and acquir'd Wit, or Letters, sufficiently qualified for such an undertaking" (Drake 1697, 3). Nevertheless, strong belief in reason and solid knowledge of English literature enabled Drake to enter public discussion even without the skills of a well-trained rhetorician.

The author's use of the Theophrastean technique in depiction of pedantism, ignorance, vanity, and other defects in men reveals a rare satirical talent. Yet, when presenting the reader with portraits of the "Pedant," the "Squire," the "Beau," the "Coffee-House Politician," or the "Fop Poet," she wisely did not generalize about the male sex, as the writers of the controversy style so clearly did when writing about women. Had she resorted to this device only, it would have been impossible for her to defend women as the intellectual equals of men. Instead, Drake introduced a rationalistic argument based on empirical evidence to establish a ground for her exposition of male comic portraits. Thus, she elegantly combined logic and metaphor, strict reasoning and satire, to produce a vigorous defense of her sex.

It may well be concluded, then, that in Judith Drake's work we have an example of a creative amalgamation of seemingly incompatible argumentative styles employed by seventeenth-century defenders of the female sex. Drake's innovative use of a hybrid genre transcended the stylistic constraints of the querelle des femmes by applying the same principle of characterization (i.e., the Theophrastean character) to support a fresh line of reasoning, pertinent to the enlightened discussion of women. Therefore, the sources of the author's feminist polemic could be discovered not only in the egalitarian philosophies of Descartes and Locke but also in the conservative discourse of the old literary controversy, which became an impetus for the rejection of the old norms that the genre itself had sustained.

Notes

1. Complex rhetorical constructions that are created by the blending of dissimilar generic features were termed by Jamieson and Campbell (1982, 147) "rhetorical hybrids."

2. It is difficult to apply the term *feminist* to the majority of defenses of women written in the late Middle Ages and Renaissance, since they mostly tended to exemplify the "better" side of female nature and hardly ever voiced the concerns of modern feminists: for example, the assumption of intellectual equality between the sexes and a demand for a just share in education, employment, and political activity. Toward the end of the seventeenth century, however, more women intellectuals started "to view women as a sociological group, not to stress, as had previous authors, the abilities of a few outstanding individuals or to view women as beings tied together primarily through biological or psychological natures" (Smith 1992, 28).

3. *An Essay* was first mistakenly attributed to Mary Astell, whose *Serious Proposal to the Ladies* appeared in print in 1694. James Drake, the publisher, was also suspected of the authorship. The third edition contains a gallant exchange between James Drake and the author, where James Drake claims to have been undeservedly "shin'd by the lustre of another's worth." "The Lady's Answer" gives a humorous description of this confusion: "Most Men pronounce it a Performance above the ability of a Woman," while other "nice Judges . . . think the Stile too Masculine: But . . . let them form themselves with equal Care, by the same Models, and they will no more be able to discern a Man's Stile from a Woman's, than they can tell whether this was written with a Goose Quill, or a Gander's" ([Drake] 1697). For further explanations of the authorship of the essay, see Perry (1986, 106, 490) and Ferguson (1985, 201).

4. For miscellaneous discussions of the genre, see Henderson and McManus (1985), Hull (1982), Kelly (1982), Rogers (1966), Utley (1944), and Woodbridge (1984).

5. I disagree with the opinion that Drake's essay is "hardly more than a frame for the 'characters'" (Reynolds 1964, 310). Drake structures her argumentative discussion in a manner that allows for the introduction of the comic portraits, and not vice versa. I argue that the essay's rhetorical poignancy is tied precisely to the strategic mixture of philosophical polemic and comic discourse.

6. On the ambivalence and liberating potential of laughter in the Middle Ages and Renaissance, see Bakhtin (1984).

7. Drake's contemporary Mary Astell, on the contrary, advocated a reserved and passionless style of argument and never would have risked the appearance of immorality for the purpose of entertainment. For Astell's contribution to women's rhetorical theory, see Sutherland (1991).

8. See especially Book I of *An Essay Concerning Human Understanding.*

9. As Smith (1982, 58) asserts, Locke's sexual egalitarianism collapsed in

his *Second Treatise of Government*, where the creation and control of property appeared as the foundation of a men's community of property owners, while women's roles were those of obedient wife and mother.

References

Anger, Jane. 1589. *Jane Anger her Protection for Women. To defend them against the Scandalous Reportes of a late Surfeiting Lover, and all other Venerians that complaine so to be overcloyed with womens kindnesse.* London: R. Jones and T. Orwin.

Bakhtin, Mikhail. 1984. *Rabelais and His World.* Trans. Helene Iswolsky. Bloomington: Indiana University Press.

Beauvoir, Simone de. 1989. *The Second Sex.* Trans. and ed. H. M. Parshley. New York: Vintage Books.

Descartes, René. 1960. *Discourse on Method and Meditations.* Trans. Laurence J. Lafleur. The Library of Liberal Arts. Indianapolis: Bobbs-Merrill.

[Drake, Judith]. 1697. *An Essay in Defence of the Female Sex.* 3d ed. London: A. Roper and R. Clavel.

Ferguson, Moira, ed. 1985. *First Feminists: British Women Writers, 1578–1799.* Bloomington: Indiana University Press.

Gosynhill, Edward. 1985. "The praise of all women, called *Mulierum Pean:* Very fruitful and delectable unto all the readers." In *Half Humankind: Contexts and Texts of the Controversy about Women in England, 1540–1640,* edited by Katherine U. Henderson and Barbara F. McManus, 156–70. Urbana: University of Illinois Press.

Henderson, Katherine Usher, and Barbara F. McManus, eds. 1985. *Half Humankind: Contexts and Texts of the Controversy about Women in England, 1540–1640.* Urbana: University of Illinois Press.

Hull, Suzanne W. 1982. *Chaste, Silent and Obedient: English Books for Women, 1475–1640.* San Marino, Calif.: Huntington Library.

Jamieson, Kathleen Hall, and Karlyn Kohrs Campbell. 1982. "Rhetorical Hybrids: Fusion of Generic Elements." *Quarterly Journal of Speech* 68 (May): 146–57.

Kelly, Joan. 1982. "Early Feminist Theory and the *Querelle des Femmes,* 1400–1789." *Signs* 8 (August): 4–28.

Latt, David J. 1977. "Praising Virtuous Ladies: The Literary Image and Historical Reality of Women in Seventeenth-Century England." In *What Manner of Woman: Essays in English and American Life and Literature,* edited by Marlene Springer, 39–64. New York: New York University Press.

Lennon, Thomas M. 1992. "Lady Oracle: Changing Conceptions of Authority and Reason in Seventeenth-Century Philosophy." In *Women and Reason,* edited by Elizabeth D. Harvey and Kathleen Okruhlik, 39–62. Ann Arbor: University of Michigan Press.

Locke, John. 1975. *An Essay Concerning Human Understanding.* Ed. Peter Nidditch. Oxford: Clarendon Press.

Perry, Ruth. 1986. *The Celebrated Mary Astell: An Early English Feminist.* Chicago: University of Chicago Press.

Poulain de la Barre, François. 1988. *The Woman as Good as the Man, or, the Equality of Both Sexes.* Trans. A. L. Ed. Gerald M. MacLean. Detroit: Wayne State University Press.

Quintilian. 1921. *The Institutio Oratoria of Quintilian.* 4 vols. Trans. H. E. Butler. New York: G. P. Putnam's Sons.

Reynolds, Myra. 1964. *The Learned Lady in England 1650–1760.* Gloucester: Peter Smith.

Rogers, Katharine M. 1966. *The Troublesome Helpmate: A History of Misogyny in Literature.* Seattle: University of Washington Press.

Smith, Hilda L. 1982. *Reason's Disciples: Seventeenth-Century English Feminists.* Urbana: University of Illinois Press.

———. 1992. "Intellectual Bases for Feminist Analyses: The Seventeenth and Eighteenth Centuries." In *Women and Reason,* edited by Elizabeth D. Harvey and Kathleen Okruhlik, 19–38. Ann Arbor: University of Michigan Press.

Sowernam, Ester. 1617. *Ester hath hang'd Haman: or An Answere to a lewd Pamphlet, entituled, The Arraignment of Women. With the arraignment of lewd, idle, froward, and unconstant men, and Husbands.* London: [T. Snodham] for N. Bourne.

Sutherland, Christine Mason. 1991. "Outside the Rhetorical Tradition: Mary Astell's Advice to Women in Seventeenth-Century England." *Rhetorica* 9.2: 147–63.

Swetnam, Joseph. 1615. *The Araignment of lewde, idle, froward, and unconstant women: Or the vanity of them, choose you whether.* London: G. Purslowe for T. Archer.

Theophrastus. 1960. *The Characters of Theophrastus.* Ed. R. G. Ussher. Loeb Classical Library. New York: St. Martin's Press.

Utley, Francis. 1944. *The Crooked Rib: An Analytical Index to the Argument About Women in English and Scots Literature to the End of the Year 1568.* Columbus: Ohio State University Press.

Walsh, William. 1691. *Dialogue concerning Women, being a Defense of the Sex.* Written to Eugenia by W. Walsh. London.

Woodbridge, Linda. 1984. *Women and the English Renaissance: Literature and the Nature of Womankind, 1540–1620.* Urbana: University of Illinois Press.

Part 5

Appropriating the Rhetorical Tradition

If the Western intellectual tradition is not only a product of men, but constituted by masculinity, then transformation comes not only from women finding women authors but also from a gendered re-reading of that masculine rhetoric.

Susan Jarratt

"As Becomes a Rational Woman to Speak"
Madeleine de Scudéry's Rhetoric of Conversation

Jane Donawerth

Madeleine de Scudéry, the most popular novelist of seventeenth-century Europe, was also, I shall argue, a rhetorical theorist. She was the first of a series of women in the seventeenth century to appropriate the Renaissance and adapt rhetoric to women's circumstances.[1] Scudéry devised a new rhetorical theory for women: she revisioned the tradition of masculine "public" discourse for mixed gender "private" discourse in salon society, emphasizing conversation and letter writing.

From 1642 to 1684 Madeleine de Scudéry developed a theory of rhetoric and composition in many of her writings: in prefaces; in a fictional speech titled "Sapho to Erinna"; and in dialogue essays on conversation, the art of speaking, raillery, invention, and letter writing. By appropriating rhetoric, Scudéry was appropriating the Renaissance, since rhetorical Latin education was the center of humanist culture. Furthermore, she viewed the Renaissance as a myth, a discursive or rhetorical strategy, one formerly used by male middle-class and lower-gentry humanists in the interest of social mobility, and one that could be used for women's ends as well.[2] Seizing the opportunity, she presented women's education and women's right to speech as existing in this past, needing only a new renaissance for her female contemporaries to reclaim them.[3]

Today Scudéry is of special interest to students of rhetorical history because she is a woman revising a much-studied male tradition, and also to students of composition theory, since she anticipates current feminist emphases on sophistic and private models of women's writing.

Entering the Conversation:
Defending Rhetorical Education for Women

Carolyn Lougee has argued, in *Le Paradis des Femmes*, that the salon of seventeenth-century France centered on women and provided men and women a means of social mobility: the salon assimilated the new nobility and some bourgeois into aristocratic French society through marriage across class lines and through redefining nobility as educated behavior, not lineage.[4] Addressed to women as an audience and published in 1642 under her brother's name, Madeleine de Scudéry's *Les Femmes Illustres or the Heroick Harangues of the Illustrious Women* promoted education for women rather than beauty and marriage as a means of social mobility. She offered to French women a justification for their participation in literary culture, especially speaking and writing.

Scudéry presents *Les Femmes Illustres* as a conservative text by appropriating a central tenet of the Renaissance: the return to classical literature. The volume contains twenty fictional speeches by women of classical antiquity, including Cleopatra, Mariamne, Sophonisba, Lucretia, and Volumnia. In the final speech the younger poet Erinna receives advice from Sapho (a character widely recognized as Scudéry's self-portrait, since "Sapho" was the name she used in précieuse society). Sapho urges Erinna to acquire an education and to write: "They who say that beauty is the portion of women; And that fine arts, good learning, and all the sublime and eminent sciences, are of the domination of men, without our having power to pretend to any part of them; Are equalie differing from justice and vertue" (Sig. V6ᵛ); for "Our Sex is capable of every thing that it would undertake" (Sig. X2ᵛ). In this fictional speech Scudéry presents two women from ancient Greece discussing standards of writing and, albeit privately, philosophical issues; thus she situates women in a valorized past and implies that French salon society can climb to intellectual eminence by imitating this past. Scudéry's recovery of the classics for women is safely nostalgic, since men's interests in philosophy had moved to empiricism and Cartesian rationalism by 1642, when *Les Femmes Illustres* was published.

Though Scudéry's text is presented as conservative, her goal is not. She aims to appropriate rhetoric for women as a means to political power: to appropriate the right to speak and so the opportunity to influence others. In the preface to *Les Femmes Illustres*, Madeleine and her brother Georges argue that eloquence is natural to women: "Certainlie among the thousands of rare qualities that the Ancients have noticed in your Sex: They have alwayes said that you [women] possesse Eloquence, without art, without Labour, and without Pains, and that nature gives liberallie to you, that which studie sells to us [men] at a dear rate: That you are born the same which we become at last, and that facilitie of speaking well is naturall to you, in place of being acquired by us" (Sig. A2ʳ). Reworking the stereotype that women talk too much, the Scudérys argue that women have always been naturally good at speaking and that the ancients recognized this quality as a virtue in women. In this sense their use of the Renaissance is mythic, since ancient Greece and Rome were notably misogynistic and women did not generally receive rhetorical education. The Scudérys' argument is not conservative, even though its form is nostalgic, because they advocate a profound change in French society: rhetorical education for women.

Because of the gender role assigned to women in Renaissance Europe, Scudéry's appropriation of rhetoric was a radical thing to do. At the time, the ideal woman was "chaste, silent, and obedient." As Lisa Jardine, Peter Stallybrass, and Margaret Ferguson have explored, conservatives feared education for women because they associated speech with sexual license: if a woman opened her mind and her mouth, she might very well choose to open herself in other ways.[5] Scudéry attempts to evade these cultural anxieties through her nostalgic appeal to the myth of the Renaissance.

In the context of seventeenth-century upper-class women's material and social circumstances, Madeleine de Scudéry develops a rhetorical theory for new female consumers by modeling discourse on conversation rather than on public speaking. This new rhetoric requires new standards for judging women's speech and writings, which she and her brother outline in the preface to *Les Femmes Illustres*. They raise the question, "If Ladies be so naturallie Eloquent why do not I make them punctually observe all parts of Orations, as Rhetorick teaches in the schools?" And they provide an answer: "I have not thought that the Eloquence of a Zadie should be the same [as] a Master of Arts" (Sigs. A2ʳ–A2ᵛ).[6] Women speakers, argue the Scudérys, should not talk like men who went through a humanist rhetorical education. The Scudérys disparage "Exordes, Narrationes, Epilogues . . . and all the beautiful figures which usuallie doe enrich works of this kind"; such rhetorical techniques reflect men's minds and the artificial excesses of masculine education (Sigs. A2ʳ–A2ᵛ). Instead, they offer: "The delicacie of art consists in making believe there is none at all" (Sig. A2ᵛ).[7]

The Scudérys playfully rehabilitate the disparaging comparison of sophistic rhetoric to cosmetics that Socrates constructs in Plato's *Gorgias*. They substitute a female art that changes nature but "with such a subtile negligence and agreeable cairlessness" that the audience sees only nature, not art (Sig. A2^v). They compare rhetoric specifically to women's hairdressing, where "it might be judged raither the wind, then your hands had been helping to nature" (Sig. A2^v). The "harangues" of women speakers in *Les Femmes Illustres* also cite another female craft as a model for this female speech and writing: "The skill of these who make nosegayes, who mixe by a regular confusion Roses and Jassamine, the flower of *Orange,* and the *Pomegranat,* the *Tulips* and the *Jonquille,* to the end that from this so pleasing mixture of coulors there appear ane agreable diversitie" (Sigs. A2^v–A3^r). The writer's goal is like this mixing of flowers: "Just so heir I have chosen in historie the finest mater and the most different that I could; And I have so orderlie mixed, and so fitlie concealed them, that it is almost impossible but the reader shall be diverted" (Sig. A3^r). Thus, the Scudérys celebrate female triviality and sophistic rhetoric, unashamedly arguing for pleasure as the end of their literary and rhetorical efforts.

In the speech by Sapho, Madeleine de Scudéry extends this daring comparison of rhetoric to female cosmetic arts, arguing that the very success of women's personal arts demonstrates women's potential capability in poetry: "We have a good fancie, a clear sighted spirit, a fortunate memorie, a solid judgement, and must we employ all these things to frisle our hair, and to seek after Ornaments which can add something to our beautie?" (Sig. X1^v). Through these metaphors in *Les Femmes Illustres,* Scudéry positions herself as a sophist, against the dominant Platonic-Aristotelian rhetorical tradition. Although women have the ability to be orators, philosophers, and poets, argues Scudéry, they will best achieve a balance between study and society as poets: "It is there, that you shall acquire beauty, which time, yeares, seasones, old Age, nor Death it self can robb you of" (Sig. X2^v). Instead of trusting to men's praises to immortalize her beauty, which fades, a woman may make "her own Pictur her self" in her speech and writings: "You need but speak Elegantylie, and you shall be sufficiently known" (Sig. X3^r). Scudéry offers women the same social mobility that the salon offers men, the ability to achieve social status through education, rather than through marriage. If beauty will gain a woman a good marriage, a means of achieving social standing through her husband, education will put her in control of herself, allowing her to achieve advancement through her own abilities: she will be known through her speech.

A Rhetoric of Conversation

After her brother's death, Scudéry continued her development of a new rhetoric in *Conversations*, a series of dialogues published in the 1680s. These *Conversations* treat popular subjects in salon society: conversation, the art of speaking, invention, raillery, and letter writing. She continues her appropriation of the Renaissance, imitating classical dialogues such as Plato's *Gorgias* or Cicero's *De Oratore*, although she often focuses on a woman—Valeria or Euridamia, rather than Socrates or Crassus. Constructing a nostalgia for a classical past through place names and names of speakers, Scudéry creates a mythical past where women have the right to speak, even to pronounce rules for speech. She re-creates history so that it will justify the ideal of one who "speaks as becomes a rational woman to speak" (Sig. F7). In this way she rewrites Renaissance dialogues, as well, such as Castiglione's famous *Courtier*, in which men speak and women serve as listeners. She incorporates into her view of the intellectual equality and autonomy of women many of the qualities that her society attributed to the *honnête homme* (the ideal representative of polite society) and salon culture. As Domna C. Stanton has suggested, the seventeenth-century French rhetorical ideal of the *honnête homme* was defined by the elitist space of the *cabinet* or salon; the conversational literary form as an indication of aristocratic leisure; and the classical names, the "crypto-classical morphology" suggesting "the emulation of an idealized past, a mythical place distant from the everyday, contingent world" (Stanton 1980, 81, 83, 91).

In these *Conversations* Scudéry revises classical rhetorical theory to accord with the lives of aristocratic women in seventeenth-century France, who were excluded from the bar, the pulpit, and public political speech. She centers her theory of rhetoric on conversation as the model for discourse. In the dialogue "Of Conversation" Cilenia throws out public speech, "when Men only speak strictly according to the exigency of their Affairs," in favor of the higher art of conversation, "the bond of all humane society, the greatest pleasure of well-bred People; and the most ordinary means of introducing into the World, not only Politeness, but also the purest Morals, and the love of Glory and Vertue" (Scudéry 1683, 1: Sig. B1ʳ). Here Scudéry returns the conception of speech as civilizing, which Cicero imported into Roman public oratory, back into salon conversation, where the sophists originally developed it.[8] She also follows the sophists in stipulating pleasure as a central goal of speech.[9]

Although she draws from the classical rhetorical tradition, Scudéry's revision is so thorough that it constitutes an original contribution. For example, she describes the ideal woman conversing by adapting Cicero's influential five divisions of oratory—invention, arrangement, style, memory, and delivery. Plotina, says Aemelius, is the ideal speaker, "for all her expressions are Noble and Natural at the same time; she studys not for what she is to say; there is no constraint in her words; her Discourse is clear and easie; there is a gentile turn in her ways of speaking; no affectation in the sound of her Voice; a great deal of freedom in her actions; and a wonderful coherence between her eyes and her words, which contribute highly to the rendring Speech the more agreeable" (Scudéry 1683, 1: Sig. F7^v). Plotina's speech shows her adept at invention ("she studys not"), arrangement ("clear and easie"), style ("expressions . . . Noble and Natural"), memory ("no constraint"), and delivery ("Voice," "actions" or gestures, and "eyes"). Elsewhere Scudéry adapts many other classical rhetorical conceptions to conversation: for example, Aristotle's division of sophistries (1: Sig. F2^v), Quintilian's advice on diction (1: Sig. F3^v), Cicero's on wit (2: Sigs. D5^v and D9^v), and, from Cicero and Quintilian, the debates on art vs. imitation and practice, and art vs. nature in the ideal speaker (1: Sig. F9^r and 2: Sig. D9^v).

Scudéry frequently borrows directly from the sophists, adapting to the needs of conversation the concept of *kairos*, timeliness, and the importance of circumstances.[10] Conversation "ought to be free and diversified, according to the times, places and persons with whom we are," suggests Valeria in one dialogue; and she adds:

> To speak with reason, we may for certain affirm, that there is nothing but may be said in Conversation, in case it be manag'd with Wit and Judgment, and the Party considers well where he is, to whom he speaks, and who he is himself. Notwithstanding though Judgment be absolutely necessary for the never saying any thing but what is to the purpose, yet the Conversation must appear so free, as to make it seem we don't reject any of our thoughts, and all is said, that comes into the fancy, without any affected design of speaking rather of one thing than of another.[11] (Scudéry 1683, 1: Sigs. B9^v–B10^R)

After a lengthy discussion with everyone participating, Valeria comes to the following conclusion about the subjects that should be excluded from conversation: none, after all, can be excluded, but all are appropriate only at some times and with some people, and when handled with judgment. Thus, although influenced by classical rhetorical theory, especially sophistry, Scudéry is original in her development of standards and strategies for communication in conversation: an art of rhetoric for "private" communication.

Scudéry transforms rhetorical precepts from "public" debate and lecture as she applies them to the "private" spaces reserved for women in seventeenth-century France. She reconceptualizes rhetoric to fit the circumstances of privileged women's lives. For example, in the passage just discussed, the topics of conversation to be appropriately included at some times cover what colors of cloth best suit one's complexion and how well one's children are doing, as well as gallantry and science.

Scudéry changes the dialogue form itself by introducing the ideal of "the agreeable" as a goal of the exchange. In the dialogues of classical rhetorical theory, authors typically present their explorations of rhetoric as a debate that is settled eventually by an authoritative answer. In contrast, Scudéry's dialogue imitates conversation: each speaker either agrees with some aspect of the previous person's speech or apologizes for differing, and the speaker who provides core definitions builds on the ideas of those who went before her, rather than overthrowing them. In Scudéry's form there is frequently room for more than one right answer. She expresses these rules of politeness through her central female speaker in the dialogue "Of Rallery," who denies the appropriateness of wit for most occasions, while also giving rules for it, the central rule being never to place it before politeness to friends. More often than requiring "spirit" or "esprit" (in context a borrowing of the Italian idea of *sprezzatura* for gentlefolk's conversation, [Scudéry 1683, 2: Sig. B10^v]), conversation requires of its practitioners the "agreeable," *l'agréeable* (2: Sig. B10^r and 1 & 2 passim). To agree could scarcely be farther from the purpose of classical masculine debate and argument.[12]

Extended Conversation: Writing Letters

In the end, however, Scudéry succeeds not in establishing separate spheres of influence for women and men, but in blurring the boundaries of public and private communication. Such blurring adapts rhetoric to Scudéry's political circumstances, since "private" salons offered much more opportunity to influence through speech than did the "public" court of an absolute monarch. In her dialogue on "The Manner of Writing Letters," for example, she disposes of all the volumes of classical and contemporary letters that her friend has sent her as cold, meant more for the general public than for the intimate friend (Scudéry 1685, Sigs. B2^r–B2^v). In their stead, she establishes the necessary genres of letter writing as mainly private ones. Besides business letters and serious letters of important affairs, the genres she establishes are private writing: letters of consolation, congratulation, recommendation, news, and gallantry; polite letters of compliment; and most important, *billets d'amour* (letters of love).

Scudéry centers her conception of proper letter writing on conversation. As a standard for letter writing, Scudéry's characters use spoken language, as opposed to more ornate written language. "I do not make a point of fashioning my notes," says Clariste; "I write as I speak, I speak what I think, and provided that I make myself understood, I am content" (Scudéry 1685, Sig. B3^v).[13] And Berise agrees: "In the case of letters one must simply say what one thinks and say it well" (Sig. B4^r). These aristocrats understand that speaking naturally is an art, not natural at all, and they establish standards for such speech: neither "grand words" nor the words "of the people" (Sig. B4^r) but wit "that tastes of books and the study," a style that is "easy, natural, and noble—all at once."[14] Indeed, letters of gallantry are called by Berise "a conversation between absent persons" (Sig. B8^v). By using these standards of spoken language for written language, Scudéry furthers the blurring of the line between private and public spheres, and so provides women letter writers with a rhetorical space in which to exercise their influence.

In her dialogue on letter writing, Scudéry again emphasizes the sophistic conception of kairos—timeliness or appropriateness, accommodation of the audience, and all the worldly circumstances that surround speaker and speech. Scudéry's Berise treats this quality as an inborn characteristic of the aristocrat, a marker of class:

> So that when one has wit and judgment, one thinks about each thing pretty much what it is appropriate to think, and consequently one writes what it is appropriate to write. In effect, if I am writing on important business, I will not write as if I had nothing more than a simple compliment to make; if I send some news, I will not play the wit; if I am composing a friendly letter, I will not express myself in high style, and if I wish to write love letters, I will consult only my heart. (Scudéry 1685, Sig. B4^r)

Avoiding self-expression, the successful speaker assesses the desires of each particular audience and fulfills those desires. Even in letters devoted primarily to news and gossip, the content must be appropriate to the audience: "It is very necessary to know the humour and the interests of the people to whom one writes, when one meddles in handing on some news to them" (Sigs. B7^v–B8^r).[15]

Scudéry also draws on the sophistic tradition by emphasizing the place of emotion in letter writing, especially by the preeminence she gives to love letters in this dialogue. Most private letters draw on emotions in ways that for public forms of writing would be called sentimental or sophistical, but which are appropriate to these forms. For example, her speakers give directions for expressing grief and sympathy in letters of condolence, for responding to another's good fortune in letters of congratulation, even for eliciting pride to do a favor in a letter of recommendation. Nowhere is emotion more significant, however, than in Scudéry's discussion of *billets d'amour*, where it overrules all other considerations. In love letters "the fire of wit" used elsewhere is replaced by "the heat of passion"; and "expression in these letters must be very tender and very touching, and one must always say those things that move the heart, mixed with that which entertains the spirit" (Scudéry 1685, Sigs. B9^v–B10^r).

Passionate love is not the only emotion, however, to be expressed in love letters, for the distracted aristocratic lover is not supposed to be able to control emotional response—that is how one tells sincerity in love. Once that is said, however, Scudéry's speakers agree to give practical advice on what emotions to include: "If I am not wrong, one should likewise include a little anxiety, because happy letters get you nowhere in love. It is not that one is not able to have joy; but, after all, it must never be a peaceful joy, and when one does not have a subject for complaint, one must make one up" (Sig. B10^r).

The emphasis on emotions in love letters makes love letters the most difficult to judge, since the excessive feeling and the disordered form will be comprehensible only to another lover, for the lover's "heart is so distressed that it does not very well know what it feels" (Sig. B11^v). The love letter thus presents Scudéry with some representative problems for dealing with private forms in rhetorical theory: to the degree that the form of the love letter is controlled by advice of theorists, in this case a group of characters in fictional private conversation, the letters become insincere; good letters are supposedly those that escape theory, that remain in an intimate private realm. Actually, of course, even love letters, it becomes clear during the course of the conversation, are documents to share with at least one other confidante, and some collections may even be printed.

Scudéry suggests that women are better writers of love letters than men. The material circumstances of her female contemporaries require them to be modestly private, and privacy is an important element of the successful love letter: "For when a lover has resolved to write openly about his passion, he does not require more art than to say 'I die for love.' But with a woman, since she cannot ever admit so precisely what she feels, and she must keep it a great secret, this love that one can only catch a glimpse of, she delights more than someone who puts [himself] on display" (Scudéry 1685, Sig. B10^v). In love letters the social requirement of modesty in women becomes an artistic benefit, since it helps to create the aesthetic quality of private mystery. In addition, women may be better writers of letters of news and gallantry, for while men excel in the kind of eloquence practiced in public assemblies, there is another eloquence "that sometimes conveys a more charming effect with less noise, principally among ladies; for, in a word, the art of speaking well about trifles is not known to all sorts of people" (Sig. B9^r). Here Scudéry slyly adopts what is usually attributed to women as a fault, their triviality, to the end of social gaiety, putting it in the service of communal pleasure.

The boundaries of private and public were also blurred in the seventeenth century by the custom of letter reading. Families and close friends expected to hear the letters received by any of their members, perhaps with the exception of love letters. Private letters were even likely to turn up in print, to be consumed by a wider public audience, if only, as in Scudéry's dialogue, as models for further "private" communications. In "On the Manner of Writing Letters" Aminte's friends send her a library of published collections of letters—by Cicero, Voiture, Balzac, Costar—to convince her to write letters to them. They argue that she has neglected a social responsibility in neglecting her correspondence with friends.

Under the government of an autocratic ruler in seventeenth-century France, there was little room for public speech that moved assemblies. Other rhetorical activities were more important for gaining political power: the public rhetoric of praise (Goldsmith 1988, 60), the private persuasion of people who might influence Louis XIV, and the private conversation and writing that circulated news. The line between private and public is thus especially blurred in the letter of gossip and news, and Scudéry is as attentive to the political potential of writing *les nouvelles du Cabinet* (the news of the salon) as to the news of *grand choses* (great events) (Scudéry 1685, Sig. B7ᵛ). Scudéry is careful to remind her readers that the notes sent while in town are often as important as the letters between far away places, for notes keep aristocrats in touch with the people they employ (perhaps an allusion to representatives placed at court to keep them informed of events and gossip). Notes are also important because they pass on to friends the small details of everyday life that at any moment might assume political significance—"a thousand little things they would not otherwise know, because one would have forgotten them by the time one saw them" (Sig. B12ʳ). Indeed, in seventeenth-century France, a despotic monarchy, power often operated through private rather than constitutional channels of communication: the letters of Paul Pellison, Madeleine de Scudéry's special friend and secretary to the disgraced Nicolas Fouquet, were seized as evidence, and while he was in prison, Scudéry says that she burned the nearly five hundred letters that he sent her, including poems. In her dialogue on letter writing, Scudéry suggests that in the letter of news there is always "something one should never hand on" (Sig. B8ʳ)—something one should never put into writing. Scudéry offers a rhetoric that takes into account such movements of "public" power through "private" communication.

Conclusion

Scudéry was skilled herself in the performance of conversational rhetoric. Through her dialogues she may very well have been initiating her audience into successful trade secrets, just as did Isocrates and Cicero. It was the conversational practices of Madeleine and her brother Georges at Mme de Rambouillet's salon that gained Georges his preferment and political post. Madeleine refused marriage: it was her conversation at the salons and her published works, not her beauty, that gained her eventual financial security—a pension from the king. And the letters from her and her friends did eventually help to gain Paul Pellison's release from the Bastille. Her texts helped to change the climate in France for education for women, as well: her *Conversations* were used to teach conversation to the girls at Mme de Maintenon's school from 1686 to 1691, and this school became a model for others (Goldsmith 1988, 66). Scudéry suggests that even private words are rhetorical: they are events with material and social consequences. Her life demonstrates what her writings claim: there is a great deal of power to be gained by one who "speaks as becomes a rational Woman to speak."

Notes

I would like to thank Stephanie Lenky for her comments on my English translations of Scudéry's dialogue, "*Conversation de la Manière d'Ecrire des Lettres.*"

1. On the life and achievements of Madeleine de Scudéry, see the biographies by Aronson (1978) and McDougall (1922). The standard histories of rhetorical theory include almost no women. Howell (1961, 166–67) mentions only Mary Queen of Scots, for a speech in defense of women's education in rhetoric. A recent anthology by Bizzell and Herzberg (1990) includes a few women before 1900—Christine de Pisan, Laura Cereta, and Margaret Fell from the Renaissance. I have developed the argument (1995) that a group of women in the seventeenth century—Margaret Cavendish, Margaret Fell, Bathsua Makin, and Mary Astell, as well as Madeleine de Scudéry—adapted the Renaissance as a rhetorical strategy to argue for women's rhetorical education. Other women of the Renaissance to consider as rhetorical theorists are Bettisia Bezzidini, a thirteenth-century Italian professor of rhetoric, and Beatrix Galindo, a professor of rhetoric at the University of Salamanca, who taught Catharine of Aragon (Bassnett 1989, 21).

2. Retha Warnicke (1983, esp. 100–101) argues that some sixteenth-century aristocratic English parents adopted this strategy for daughters who ranked high enough to become royal brides, educating those daughters in Latin, Greek, and humanist arts to make them attractive marriage partners.

3. On rhetoric as the center of Latin humanist culture, see Kristeller (1961), Howell (1961), Doran (1954, 26), and Waller (1986, 48–59). On women's exclusion from rhetorical training in favor of grammar alone, see Gibson (1989).

4. On the social mobility furthered by salon conversation, see also Goldsmith (1988, 2, 6, 8). Stanton (1980, esp. 90) alternately argues that it is the aristocrats who promote the ideal of *honnêteté* and the exclusivity of the salon as a means of regaining prestige from the bourgeoisie.

5. See Ferguson (1988, esp. 99–102); Jardine (1983, esp. 121–33); and Stallybrass (1986, esp. 126–27). See also Belsey (1985) and Grafton and Jardine (1986, 32). In fifteenth-century Italy, in a letter to a male humanist, Isotta Nogarola apologized for transgressing "those rules of silence especially imposed on women" (Grafton and Jardine 1986, 37–38).

6. It is unclear whether "Zadie" is a name for the heroine of the romance, since Scudéry frequently uses such classicized names in her dialogues, or a printer's mistake for "Ladie."

7. See Stanton (1980, 178) on the aesthetic of the invisibility of art for seventeenth-century French aristocrats: the aristocrat is aware how much art it takes to construct the natural, how art is the process of making itself invisible.

8. On the sophistic idea that language preceded and caused the civilization of humanity, see Isocrates' "Nicocles" (vol. 1 pp. 77–81) and "Antidosis" (vol. 2 pp. 327–29). On Cicero's adaptation of this goal exclusively to public speech, see *De Inventione* I.ii.2–3, *De Re Publica* III.ii.3, and especially *De Oratore* I.viii.23 (see Cicero 1960, 1928, 1948, respectively). Scudéry is also adapting the antiprofessionalism of the ideal of the *honnête homme* in salon society to the subject of rhetoric: the ideal speech is not the professional speech of the trained rhetorician, who speaks (for profit) as a lawyer, statesman, or priest, but the leisured woman who converses in the interest of knowledge for its own sake and graceful beauty. See Stanton (1980) on the antiprofessionalism of the ideal of the *honnête homme* (95–97) and on the art of conversation (139–46).

9. On pleasure as a central goal of speech for sophists, see Jarratt (1991, 110).

10. See Kennedy (1963) on Gorgias's discovery and Isocrates' development of *kairos*, "the concept of the opportune" (66); "'the adaptation of the speech to the manifold variety of life, to the psychology of the speaker and hearer: variegated, not absolute unity of tone'" (67, quoting Untersteiner on the sophists); "what is opportune and fitting and novel" in the good speech (68, quoting Isocrates, "Against the Sophists"). See Carter (1988) for an explanation of *kairos* that links it not only to relativism but also to communal decision and discourse.

11. Note that I am using a seventeenth-century English translation here that supplies the masculine pronouns—Scudéry's French does not gender this ideal.

12. See Stanton (1980, 124) on charm or agreeableness, not beauty, as signaling the status of the aristocrat in seventeenth-century France. See Goldsmith (1988, 10–13, 41–75) on reciprocity as an ideal of salon conversation throughout seventeenth-century handbooks, and especially in Scudéry's *Conversations*.

13. For the dialogue "*Conversation de la Manière d'Ecrire des Lettres*" I have found no seventeenth-century translation into English; the translations here are my own.

14. Scudéry (1685, Sig. B8ᵛ), recalling Quintilian's standard of "the language of educated men," *Institutio* I.vi.45; see Donawerth (1984, 35, 52–53 n. 66).

15. This section on adjusting the telling of news to the audience is worth quoting at length: "But in my opinion when one composes these letters where one recounts the latest news, one should think up some news that would please the people to whom one writes. For I am sure that there are people who do not love all the news with which fame is ordinarily burdened, and who do not desire to hear about battles won or lost, sieges of cities, fires, floods, shipwrecks, uprisings of the people, and other similar great events; there are those also who scarcely care about the great happenings that one finds in the newspapers, who prefer what one calls the news of the "*cabinet*" [salon, study, private sitting room,

dressing room, *boudoir*], which are not told except in a low voice, and which are not well known except to worldly, well informed people, who have exquisite judgment and delicate taste" (Sig. B7^v).

References

Aristotle. 1954. *Rhetoric and Poetics*. Trans. Rhys Roberts and Ingram Bywater. New York: Modern Library.

Aronson, Nicole. 1978. *Mademoiselle de Scudéry*. Trans. Stuart R. Aronson. Boston: Twayne.

Bassnett, Susan. 1989. *Elizabeth I: A Feminist Perspective*. Oxford: Berg.

Belsey, Catherine. 1985. "Silence and Speech." In *The Subject of Tragedy*, by Belsey, 149–91. London: Methuen.

Bizzell, Patricia, and Bruce Herzberg, eds. 1990. *The Rhetorical Tradition: Readings from Classical Times to the Present*. Boston: Bedford.

Carter, Michael. 1988. "*Stasis* and *Kairos*: Principles of Social Construction in Classical Rhetoric." *Rhetoric Review* 7.1: 97–112.

Castiglione, Baldassare. 1928. *The Book of the Courtier*. Trans. Sir Thomas Hoby. London: J. M. Dent & Sons.

Cicero. 1928. *De Re Publica*. Trans. Clinton Walker Keyes. London: William Heinemann.

———. 1948. *De Oratore*. 2 vols. Trans. E. W. Sutton and H. Rackham. London: William Heinemann.

———. 1960. *De Inventione*. Trans. H. M. Hubbell. Cambridge: Harvard University Press.

Donawerth, Jane L. 1984. *Shakespeare and the Sixteenth-Century Study of Language*. Urbana: University of Illinois Press.

———. 1995. "The Politics of Renaissance Rhetorical Theory by Women." In *Political Rhetoric, Power, and Renaissance Women*, edited by Carole Levin and Patricia Sullivan, 256–72. Albany: SUNY Press.

———. Forthcoming. "Conversation and Power: Rhetorical Theory by Renaissance Women." In *Women and the Arts in the Renaissance: Women and Power*, edited by Elizabeth Welles and Harriet McNamee. Rochester: University of Rochester Press.

Doran, Madeleine. 1954. *Endeavors of Art: A Study of Form in Elizabethan Drama*. Madison: University of Wisconsin Press.

Ferguson, Margaret. 1988. "A Room Not Their Own: Renaissance Women as Readers and Writers." In *The Comparative Perspective on Literature*, edited by Clayton Koelb and Susan Noakes, 93–116. Ithaca: Cornell University Press.

Gibson, Joan. 1989. "Educating for Silence." *Hypatia* 4.1: 9–27.

Goldsmith, Elizabeth C. 1988. *"Exclusive Conversations": The Art of Interaction in Seventeenth-Century France*. Philadelphia: University of Pennsylvania Press.

Grafton, Anthony, and Lisa Jardine. 1986. *From Humanism to the Humanities: Education and the Liberal Arts in Fifteenth- and Sixteenth-Century Europe.* London: Duckworth.

Howell, Wilbur Samuel. 1961. *Logic and Rhetoric in England 1500–1700.* New York: Russell & Russell.

Isocrates. 1928. *Isocrates.* 3 vols. Trans. George Norlin. Cambridge: Harvard University Press.

Jardine, Lisa. 1983. "Shrewd or Shrewish? When the Disorderly Woman Has Her Head." In *Still Harping on Daughters: Women and Drama in the Age of Shakespeare,* 103–40. Totowa, N.J.: Barnes & Noble.

Jarratt, Susan C. 1991. *Rereading the Sophists: Classical Rhetoric Refigured.* Carbondale: Southern Illinois University Press.

Kennedy, George A. 1963. *The Art of Persuasion in Greece.* Princeton: Princeton University Press.

Kristeller, Paul Oscar. 1961. *Renaissance Thought: The Classic, Scholastic, and Humanist Strains.* New York: Harper & Row.

Lougee, Carolyn. 1976. *Le Paradis des Femmes: Women, Salons, and Social Stratification in Seventeenth-Century France.* Princeton: Princeton University Press.

McDougall, Dorothy. 1922. *Madeleine de Scudéry: Her Romantic Life and Death.* London: Methuen.

Plato. 1952. *Gorgias.* Trans. W. C. Helmbold. New York: Liberal Arts Press.

Quintilian. 1966. *Institutio Oratoria.* 4 vols. Trans. H. E. Butler. Cambridge: Harvard University Press.

Scudéry, Madeleine de. 1681. *Les Femmes Illustres or the Heroick Harangues of the Illustrious Women.* Vol. 1. Trans. James Innes. Edinburgh.

———. 1683. *Conversations Upon Several Subjects.* 2 vols. Trans. Ferrand Spence. London.

———. 1685. *Conversations Nouvelles sur Divers Sujets, Dediées Au Roy.* 2 vols. La Haye.

Stallybrass, Peter. 1986. "Patriarchal Territories: The Body Enclosed." In *Rewriting the Renaissance,* edited by Margaret Ferguson, Maureen Quilligan, and Nancy J. Vickers, 123–42. Chicago: University of Chicago Press.

Stanton, Domna C. 1980. *The Aristocrat as Art: A Study of the Honnête Homme and the Dandy in Seventeenth- and Nineteenth-Century French Literature.* New York: Columbia University Press.

Waller, Gary. 1986. *English Poetry of the Sixteenth Century.* New York: Longman.

Warnicke, Retha. 1983. *Women of the English Renaissance.* Westport, Conn.: Greenwood Press.

The Uses and Problems of a "Manly" Rhetoric

Mary Wollstonecraft's Adaptation of Hugh Blair's *Lectures* in Her Two *Vindications*

Julia Allen

Generations of women have read Mary Wollstonecraft's arguments for women's rights in *A Vindication of the Rights of Men* (1790) and *A Vindication of the Rights of Woman* (1792) and have taken her statements—both on the lack of necessity of conventional feminine behavior and on the need for women to be educated—as blueprints for feminist revolutionary efforts.[1] However, Wollstonecraft's work has also been subject to disparaging comments. It is not well written, critics say; others counter with excuses, claiming that *A Vindication of the Rights of Woman* was produced in only six weeks. Moira Ferguson (1984), Carole Huber (1989), and Gary Kelly (1992) note that Wollstonecraft read the work of Hugh Blair (in fact, Blair's 1783 *Lectures on Rhetoric and Belles Lettres* was the only rhetoric text widely available to members of the developing middle class at this time), but they do not examine in detail the implications of this finding. The rhetoric historian Wilbur Samuel Howell, however, cautions that "the rhetorical theories of that era . . . are important to the modern critic in defining the standards which the participants in [a] debate themselves observed" (1971, 647 n.).

As a late-twentieth-century feminist rhetorician, I read Wollstonecraft's two *Vindications* texts as implicit commentaries on Hugh Blair's gendered rhetorical precepts in addition to the stated functions of these texts as arguments against the writings of Edmund Burke, J. J. Rousseau, and others. Looking at Wollstonecraft's references to language allows us to understand the limitations of Blair's rhetoric and the effects of these limitations on a feminist rhetorician. At the same time, given her clever response to these limitations, Wollstonecraft can be seen as a significantly more exciting and daring rhetorician than the redoubtable Hugh Blair.

Relying on the moral postulates of the Rational Dissenter Richard Price, Wollstonecraft negotiates the contradictory discourses of gender and rhetoric. She operates within Blair's dual rhetoric of both production and critique, using his system to create arguments—thus demonstrating her eloquence—and also taking advantage of his prescriptions to attack the discourses of those with whom she disagrees, showing her powers of discernment and taste. She accepts yet quibbles over Blair's definition of "manly" eloquence, responds to and elaborates upon his use of the standard "dress" metaphor in rhetoric, and both challenges and makes use of Blair's gender prescriptions.

Thus adapting Blair's rhetoric for her own purposes, Wollstonecraft argues in *A Vindication of the Rights of Men* and *A Vindication of the Rights of Woman* that the common idea that women should be weak is not based in nature but rather is linguistically constructed by men for their own purposes. Moreover, she holds that such an idea is detrimental to the development of Virtue through Reason on the parts of both men and women. In this essay I will explore the ways in which Mary Wollstonecraft appropriates the rhetoric of Hugh Blair to rewrite gender in eighteenth-century England.

Wollstonecraft's Use of Blair's *Lectures:* Background Influences

Wollstonecraft read Hugh Blair's *Lectures on Rhetoric and Belles Lettres* in 1787. In a letter to her sister, Everina Wollstonecraft, dated 12 February 1787 she says: "I am now reading some philosophical lectures, and philosophical sermons—for my own improvement. I lately met with Blair's lectures on genius taste &c &c—and found them an intellectual feast" (Wardle 1979, 138–39). Perhaps she found them a "feast" in part because she and Blair shared similar sociocultural and philosophic positions, though there were differences beyond those associated with gender (such as access to education and employment) and nationality. Both belonged to churches other than the state-sponsored Church of England: Blair was a minister in the Church of Scotland, and Wollstonecraft was a Rational Dissenter. Because religious and moral concepts are key to both Blair's and Wollstonecraft's texts, a simple explanation of their respective theological positions is in order.

Theological Issues

During the eighteenth century a number of religious groups existed outside of the Church of England. The Church of Scotland was presbyterian in structure and Calvinist in theology. Within the Church of Scotland the two main groups were the Evangelicals and the Moderates. Hugh Blair, the first Regius Professor of Rhetoric and Belles Lettres at the University of Edinburgh, was a member of the moderate wing of the church. In England proper there were the Evangelicals—both those who accepted Calvinism and those who, following John Wesley, rejected predestination—and the proto-Unitarian Dissenters. Wollstonecraft was a Rational Dissenter and was associated with the community at Newington Green, just outside London. She was active in the circles of Richard Price, Joseph Priestley, and Joseph Johnson, writing frequently for Johnson's publications. The Dissenters were by and large of the middle class, and Dissenters' schools (one of which was run by Wollstonecraft) were an attempt to provide "practical, progressive education designed to fit the sons of the middling sort to staff the professions and the world of business" (Langford 1984, 392). These schools also maintained ties with the Scottish universities (Goodwin 1979, 69). Philosophically, Wollstonecraft followed the Arian[2] belief system of the Reverend Richard Price.

The Rational Dissenters cannot be identified with any one doctrinal position. Most important for following Wollstonecraft's arguments about gender, morality, and discourse is an understanding of Price's philosophy. Richard Price contended that "without liberty, the power of self-determination, 'there can be no moral capacities'" (Watts 1978, 476). Moreover, he divided mind from body, claiming that the soul "is inseparably united with knowledge and virtue, which are themselves inseparable. Indeed, it is the perfect union of knowledge and of virtue in a man's spiritual being that forms the complete soul, which, once complete, is capable of infinite spiritual improvement" (Lincoln 1938, 107). In contrast, body—actually all matter—is of little consequence, a mere machine doing the bidding of the soul, according to Price. It is this principle that allows Wollstonecraft to detach the concepts of masculinity and femininity from male and female bodies.

Price's most important work is his *Principal Questions in Morals*, published in the 1750s. In it he posits that rectitude, or virtue, is a universal law (Lincoln 1938, 110). "'Virtue supposes determination and determination supposes a determiner: and a determiner that determines not himself is a palpable contradiction'" (113). Specifically regarding moral behavior and its political relevance, Price says later: "In this hour of danger [1776] it would become us to turn our thoughts to Heaven. This is what our brethren in the Colonies are doing. From one end of North America to the other they are fasting and praying. But what are we doing?—shocking thought—We are running wild after pleasure and forgetting everything serious and decent in Masquerades—We are gambling in gaming houses: trafficking in boroughs; perjuring ourselves at elections; and selling ourselves for places—which side is Providence likely to favour?" (Price 1784, 3). Price's philosophical and resultant political system emphasizing personal liberty, his privileging of mind over body, and his establishment of specific norms of behavior are all crucial to the arguments Wollstonecraft makes in both *Vindications* texts.

Hugh Blair's system of thought shares some features with those of Price and Wollstonecraft. Charles Camic points out that the Moderates of the Church of Scotland were generally tolerant and liberal, supporting religious freedom and "strongly opposed [to] both the institution of slavery and the lucrative African slave trade" (1983, 87–88), views shared by the Dissenters. Apparently Hugh Blair "identified himself with a party of lenient Presbyterian theologians . . . who took a somewhat relaxed and worldly view of the application of religious dogma to social conduct" (Howell 1971, 672). This suggests at least a modicum of philosophic agreement between the systems of Blair and Wollstonecraft. Furthermore, Paul G. Bator tells us that the connection between moral philosophy and belles lettres was established at the Scottish universities prior to Blair, in the lectures of William Cleghorn, who said that "decorum in poetry . . . can be measured in terms of its agreeableness of virtue with respect to the moral nature of man" (Bator 1989, 54); and most Dissenting ministers, including Price and Priestley, studied at Scottish universities (Lincoln 1938, 73). On the other hand, Scottish Moderates "continually affirmed the Calvinist orientation of dependency and the theological postulates that accompanied it" (88); and they criticized the intellectuals of the Enlightenment, claiming that answers to human questions lay not in philosophy but in a dependence upon God. For Wollstonecraft, such a dependency means that the individual does not assume sufficient personal responsibility for moral action, thus obviating the necessity of attaining virtue through the exercise of reason. This theological difference is significant and is reflected in Wollstonecraft's adaptation of Blair's rhetorical system.

Political and Class Considerations

Notions of improvement found in Blair may also be traced to specific cultural conditions—a certain nervousness about Scots speech and knowledge, particularly in view of the fact that Scotland since 1709 was no longer a separate country but was, instead, deeply economically and politically dependent upon England (Bator 1989, 40). This preoccupation with linguistic expression developed along with, and in relation to, industrialization and the growth of the middle class and of expectations of literacy. Thomas Miller has shown that the Scottish universities shifted in emphasis from a "classical-religious education to a 'practical' secular education" as a response to middle-class demands that "higher education should prepare students for their lives in society" (1984, 126). Rhetoric and belles lettres were particularly attractive to the Scottish middle classes because "they saw these as a means to promote polite learning in Scotland and thus improve themselves and their nation" (15).

Blair himself was a member of several philosophical societies that were typical of eighteenth-century Scottish middle-class efforts at self-improvement. So we should not be surprised to find Hugh Blair telling his readers: "That which men concur the most in admiring, must be held to be beautiful. His taste must be esteemed just and true, which coincides with the general sentiments of men" ([1783] 1965, 2: 30). However, while the issues of class—and improvement—were important in the work of both Blair and Wollstonecraft, Wollstonecraft, as the daughter of an impoverished master weaver and "gentleman farmer,"[3] wrote arguments about class demonstrating considerably less satisfaction with conditions as they existed at the time. And she had little patience with some methods of "improvement." In contrast to Blair's willingness to accept "general sentiments" as a guide to taste, Wollstonecraft says: "It would be an arduous task to trace all the vice and misery that arise in society from the middle class of people apeing the manners of the great" ([1790] 1960, 49). Despite her more radical position, however, Wollstonecraft apparently found Blair's rhetoric a useful guide in arguing against those who represented established English and Continental sensibilities and who had considerably more formal education than she did.

Blair's *Lectures:* Eloquence and Passion

The essence of Wollstonecraft's argument in both *Vindications* texts is an opposition to any form of social organization or behavior that impedes an individual's attempts to attain virtue. Virtue, she believes, is attainable only through the exercise of reason. And reason flourishes only in conditions of freedom. Thus both women and men must be free in order to attain virtue. And while virtue is displayed through behavior, reason is a discursive operation—hence the importance of rhetorical principles and advice.

Blair's *Lectures* tell the reader how to develop both eloquence and taste—in other words, how to *argue* and *critique* effectively. Yet Blair, following Quintilian, asserts that such eloquence is "manly." Wollstonecraft makes use of this assumption as she argues for her system while criticizing both the arguments and prose styles of her opponents. In fact, in addition to creating her own arguments, Wollstonecraft, both rhetorician and moralist, specifically critiques the *prose* of her opponents, thus impugning their characters *in the guise of critiquing their rhetoric.* For example, in *A Vindication of the Rights of Men* Wollstonecraft assails Edmund Burke's style when she says his "pretty jargon seems . . . unintelligible" ([1790] 1960, 123). The word "pretty" in this context resonates especially as Burke has associated women, beauty, and debility in *A Philosophical Enquiry into the Origin of Our Ideas of the Sublime and the Beautiful* (1759), claiming that beauty in women is due to their smallness and weakness. A few pages prior to her attack on his "pretty jargon," Wollstonecraft has castigated Burke for precisely this attitude about women.

Blair encourages the sort of gender-specific critique that Wollstonecraft is making here when he announces his assessment of Sir William Temple's writing: "No writer whatever has stamped upon his Style a more lively impression of his own character. In reading his works, we seem engaged in conversation with him; we become thoroughly acquainted with him, not merely as an author, but as a man; and contract a friendship for him. He may be classed as standing in the middle, between a negligent Simplicity, and the highest degree of Ornament, which this character of Style admits" ([1783] 1965, 1: 394).

Later readers of Wollstonecraft have turned the critique of prose style back on her, however. Virginia Sapiro, for example, wonders why Wollstonecraft's text "seems more raw and uncontrolled," guessing that perhaps "her youth and inexperience . . . meant that she had not yet learned to channel her anger constructively in print" (1992, 205). It is more likely, though, that Wollstonecraft is following Hugh Blair's dictum that passion is the driving force behind eloquence. Blair distinguishes conviction from eloquent persuasion by precisely the addition of emotional involvement on the part of the orator. "A man may convince, and even persuade others to act, by mere reason and argument," Blair says. "But that degree of Eloquence which gains the admiration of mankind and properly denominates one an Orator, is never found without warmth, or passion" ([1783] 1965, 2: 6). Likewise, he claims that "all laboured declamation, and affected ornaments of Style, which shew the mind to be cool and unmoved, are so inconsistent with persuasive Eloquence" (2: 7).

When we read Wollstonecraft's statement regarding her own rhetorical practice, we can hear echoes of Hugh Blair's advice:

> This is a rough sketch of my plan; and should I express my conviction with the energetic emotions that I feel whenever I think of the subject, the dictates of experience and reflection will be felt by some of my readers. Animated by this important object, I shall disdain to cull my phrases or polish my style;—I aim at being useful, and sincerity will render me unaffected; for, wishing rather to persuade by the force of my arguments, than dazzle by the elegance of my language, I shall not waste my time in rounding periods, or in fabricating the turgid bombast of artificial feelings, which, coming from the head, never reach the heart. I shall be employed about things, not words! and, anxious to render my sex more respectable members of society, I shall try to avoid that flowery diction which has slided from essays into novels, and from novels into familiar letters and conversation. ([1792] 1967, 34–35)

Yet *heart* and the related term *passions*, while used here in a positive sense, have a variety of meanings for both Blair and Wollstonecraft, meanings that seem to indicate a fundamental difference between the two. Wollstonecraft's use of terms is a result of her moral/political focus. Her primary aim is to demonstrate to her audiences the value of social equality, particularly for women. Blair, however, has no such agenda. To him the "passions," if gendered, are gendered male, and are, as such, an uncomplicated force. He merely says that the rhetorician seeking to persuade an audience must "address himself to (the) passions" (2: 189). In fact, he says, "the passions are the great springs of human action. The most virtuous man, in treating of the most virtuous subject, seeks to touch the heart of him to whom he speaks" ([1783] 1965, 2: 189).

Wollstonecraft is more careful, however, having to contend with the gendered qualities of the terms that Blair uses. While she does agree that the rhetorician must address the heart, she qualifies almost all of her references to the passions. At best, she says, "the passions are necessary auxiliaries to reason" ([1790] 1960, 29). Indeed, she sees the passions as considerably more problematic than does Blair. For example, she asks, "For what purpose were the passions implanted?" and answers, "That man by struggling with them might attain a degree of knowledge denied to the brutes" ([1792] 1967, 39). She views the passions as both beneficial and untrustworthy: "Passions are spurs to action, and open the mind; but they sink into mere appetites, become a personal and momentary gratification, when the object is gained, and the satisfied mind resets in enjoyment" (64). This latter passage shows both her debt to Blair (or their common debt to some other source)—"spurs to action" sounds very similar to "springs of human action"—and her own modification of the concept to include the question of the misuse of passion. She turns this modification of the concept into critique, announcing to Edmund Burke in *A Vindication of the Rights of Men* that he is "deceived ... by the passions that cloud [his] reason" ([1790] 1960, 109). Moreover, even Eloquence is suspect in Wollstonecraft's estimation. "Eloquence," she says, following Blair, "has often confounded triumphant villainy; but," she adds, "it is probable that it has more frequently rendered the boundary that separates virtue and vice doubtful" (126). Yet she still at some points maintains Blair's distinction between the head and the heart. "If the passion is real," she tells Burke, "the head will not be ransacked for stale tropes and cold rodomontade" (64).

Figures

Not even Blair, though, is entirely consistent on the subject of passion and its relation to style, especially to figurative language. Ian

Thomson points out a contradiction in the writings of Blair and other eighteenth-century rhetoricians: "To summarize, the contradiction is this: that rhetoric is, according to one major definition, the art of persuasion, and one of its resources is to move its audience, and figurative speech assists this end: on the other hand, genuine passion is supposed not to resort to figures, which are now seen as artifice" (1982, 144). Yet Blair appreciates figures, well used. His five styles—the Dry, the Plain, the Neat, the Elegant, and the Florid—are defined by a greater or lesser degree of figurative language. In fact, he seems to favor those styles, the Neat and the Elegant, that do admit of some "graceful" ornamentation. However, Blair also inveighs against ornamentation. He refers to over-ornamented prose as "pomp" ([1783] 1965, 1: 3) and "pomp and parade" (77), and he says that "the main secret of being sublime is to say great things in few and plain words" (77). Wollstonecraft agrees, warning her readers to maintain a "suspicious coolness" in order to "prevent our being carried away by a stream of natural eloquence, which the prejudiced mind terms declamation—a pomp of words!" ([1790] 1960, 138). Both the Church of Scotland and the Dissenters saw artifice as socially and politically suspect. Socially, artifice signaled class distinctions, as men and women of higher classes were more likely to adorn themselves. More disturbing, perhaps, to those concerned with souls, not bodies, were the masquerades, in which people disguised themselves by means of artifice and men often dressed in elaborate women's clothing. Hence we have Richard Price's invective against masquerades.

Both Wollstonecraft and Blair would have objected to ornamentation on political and philosophical grounds as well, the Dissenters and the Presbyterians demanding a plainer style as a matter of doctrine. For Wollstonecraft in particular the word *pomp* has considerable political resonance, referring to the hierarchical English political system that she specifically argues against in *A Vindication of the Rights of Men*. Yet both have inherited a rhetorical tradition that privileges tropes and figures as the defining matter of oratorical study.

Blair attempts to escape from this problem by suggesting that it is the passion "which lies under the figured expression" that makes such an expression worthwhile ([1783] 1965, 1: 277). Wollstonecraft seems to agree with his orientation, saying that "when the heart speaks we are seldom shocked by hyperbole, or dry raptures" ([1790] 1960, 66). The term "dry raptures" no doubt refers to Blair's first category of style—the Dry—which is devoid of imagination and is "a considerable defect" ([1783] 1965, 1: 380).

Likewise, Wollstonecraft, still engaging in critique, accuses her opponents on two occasions of producing "turgid bombast," a phrase that echoes Blair's dicta that "[the sublime] is equally an enemy to such as are turgid" ([1783] 1965, 1: 77) and "the faults opposite to the sublime are chiefly two: the frigid and the bombast" (78). Thus, in accusing Burke of writing "turgid bombast" ([1790] 1960, 65), Wollstonecraft is suggesting that he is writing from his head and not his heart. Such "unmoved" writing is not eloquent—and therefore not "manly" or virtuous.

Simplicity is the rhetorical quality stressed by both Blair and Wollstonecraft. Blair says, "Simplicity I place in opposition to studied and profuse ornament" ([1783] 1965, 1: 66) and "It will be found to hold without exception, that the most sublime authors are the simplest in their style" (77). Wollstonecraft often remarks that she is writing about "simple truths" ([1792] 1967, 39). But even simplicity is gendered in Blair's system. "I conceive nothing more incumbent on me in this course of Lectures," he says, "than to take every opportunity of cautioning my Readers against the affected and frivolous use of ornament and to introduce . . . a taste for more solid thought, and more manly Simplicity in Style ([1783] 1965, 1: 386).

However, in order to argue against Rousseau in *A Vindication of the Rights of Woman*, Wollstonecraft says that while *her* ideas are simple (hence "solid" and "manly"), his writing is so circuitous (hence unmanly) that she is required to write an elaborate response. "My comments," she says, "it is true, will all spring from a few simple principles, and might have been deduced from what I have already said; the artificial structure has been raised with so much ingenuity, that it seems necessary to attack it in a more circumstantial manner, and make the application myself" (128).

In general, she uses the twin concepts of truth and simplicity against Burke as well, such as when, at the beginning of *A Vindication of the Rights of Men*, she subtly attacks his response to Richard Price's sermon by referring to his (Burke's) essay on the sublime and the beautiful, saying: "for truth, in morals, has ever appeared to me the essence of the sublime; and, in taste, simplicity the only criterion of the beautiful" (2). On other occasions she accuses her opponent directly of figurative faults. For instance, she says to Burke: "I pause to recollect myself; and smother the contempt I feel rising for your rhetorical flourishes and infantine sensibility" (153). She seems to be attempting both to speak with passion herself yet charge Burke with excessive ornamentation.

Wollstonecraft often speaks of avoiding "flowery diction" ([1792] 1967, 34) or "the flowers of rhetoric" ([1790] 1960, 6) in her writing. While Blair calls the Florid style an affectation of youth, Wollstonecraft associates such diction with the feminine, and in doing so she excuses herself from the necessity of using feminine language simply because she is a woman. As we have seen, she says: "anxious to render my sex more respectable members of society, I shall try to avoid that flowery diction which has slided from essays into novels, and from novels into familiar letters and conversation" ([1792] 1967, 34–35). At the same time, she implies that the writer of whom she is speaking has committed the errors that she herself is avoiding and thereby implicitly questions the masculinity of that writer.

Thomson also points out that Blair uses a particular rhetorical dictum passed down from classical times: "Language is the dress of thought." Thomson adds that Blair and other rhetoricians then suggest "that figures serve to adorn the dress. The notion of figures as ornament, whether the object is pleasure or persuasion, is not compatible with a notion of figures as a natural and sympathetic correlative between transmitted and received trains of ideas" (1982, 147). Indeed Blair does say that "the figure is only the dress" ([1783] 1965, 1: 277), and Wollstonecraft follows him in her advertisement for A Vindication of the Rights of Men, saying that Burke has created "many ingenious arguments in a very specious garb" (iv). In A Vindication of the Rights of Woman, she says that these errors cause one to turn away from "simple unadorned truth" (35).

More than just a class or doctrinal issue, seeing figures as adornment becomes a feminist problem for Wollstonecraft, as women are encouraged to adorn themselves to the detriment of the development of their minds. "The conversation of French women . . . is frequently superficial," she admits, "but, I contend, that it is not half so insipid as that of those English women whose time is spent in making caps, bonnets, and the whole mischief of trimmings" ([1792] 1967, 125). Thus, adornment, like artifice, is doubly unacceptable, both a class and a gender marker, and insubstantial discourse becomes one with a preoccupation with physical excess.

In general, Blair's text demonstrates his acceptance—and strategic use—of conventional and uncomplicated notions of gender. Certainly

Blair identifies specific rhetorical moves—particularly having to do with ornamentation—as manly and others as the obverse. "'Let ornament be manly and chaste,'" he says, quoting Quintilian, "'without effeminate gayety, or artificial coloring: let it shine with the glow of health and strength'" ([1783] 1965, 1: 407). Earlier he has cautioned: "Now, when an author has brought us, or is attempting to bring us into this state; if he multiplies words unnecessarily; if he decks the sublime object which he presents to us, round and round, with glittering ornaments; nay, if he throws in any one decoration that sinks in the least below the capital image, that moment he alters the key; he relaxes the tension of the mind; the strength of the feeling is emasculated, the beautiful may remain, but the sublime is gone" (66).

This unproblematic merger of discourse and gender should not surprise us. As Bator points out, Edinburgh during Blair's time was a "close-knit, male-dominated, familial culture of convivial clubs and philosophical societies" (1989, 40). Throughout Blair's *Lectures* we find frequent use of the terms *man* and *manly* defining rhetor and rhetoric. And Blair, of course, was not alone in deploying these terms; they are often found in eighteenth-century prose, indicative of a general cultural conversation on the subject during that time. Indeed, G. S. Rousseau and Roy Porter introduce their anthology *Sexual Underworlds of the Enlightenment* by pointing out: "Categories and labels, emphasis and distinction, practice and discourse remain at the heart of the riddle and permeate the whole historiography of the Enlightenment" (1988, 13). However, Blair's use of the terms seems unquestioning; for him these terms are stable signifiers. Blair's rhetoric follows Quintilian's, which defines the eloquent rhetorician as the "good man speaking well" and which is constructed on the basis of a distinction between masculine and feminine discourses and behavior. He conflates the meanings of *man* and *manly* (though it could be argued that there is still some grammatical flexibility within the term *manly* as an adjective).

Wollstonecraft, however, clearly announces a separation of the terms *man* and *manly* or *masculine*. "What can be more disgusting," she asks, "than that impudent dross of gallantry, thought so manly, which makes many men stare insultingly at every female they meet?" ([1792] 1967, 190). By linking *manly* with *thought*, Wollstonecraft removes *manliness* from the realm of terms with concrete referents. Contrast this with Blair's discussion of "[t]hose who have never . . . been trained to attend to the genuine and manly beauties of good writing and are always ready to be caught by the mere glare of language" ([1783] 1965, 1: 8). Blair's phrase, linking "manly" with "genuine" and pointing to a contrast between those terms and "the mere glare of language," seems to promise a clear and knowable "thing"—good writing.

The Appropriation of a "Manly" Rhetoric

Indeed, Hugh Blair claims that "in order to be a truly eloquent or persuasive speaker, nothing is more necessary than to be a virtuous man" ([1783] 1965, 2: 228). Mary Wollstonecraft, however, says, in carving out a space for herself to speak:

> I am aware of an obvious inference:—from every quarter have I heard exclamations against masculine women; but where are they to be found? If by this appellation men mean to inveigh against their ardour in hunting, shooting, and gaming, I shall most cordially join in the cry; but if it be against the imitation of manly virtues, or, more properly speaking, the attainment of those talents and virtues, the exercise of which ennobles the human character, and which raise females in the scale of animal being, when they are comprehensively termed mankind;—all those who view them with a philosophic eye must, I should think, wish with me, that they may every day grow more and more masculine. ([1792] 1967, 33)

For Wollstonecraft, *manly* is a term signifying a particular enactment of moral rectitude. In contrast, she uses the term *effeminate* to signify a preoccupation with body, a sense of moral weakness. Having severed the concepts of masculinity and femininity from biological men and women, she then is able to disparage femininity and promote masculinity, viz. her wish that women "may every day grow more and more masculine" (33). Indeed, she appropriates the term for her own use and poses to Edmund Burke a question regarding the separation of Church and state: "And, Sir, let me ask you, with manly plainness—are these *holy* nominations?" ([1790] 1960, 84). In this sentence she has taken for herself "masculine" rationality, and she even emphasizes her possession of the masculine prerogative by addressing Burke as "Sir" and then describing her own rhetorical style as "manly plainness," surely a reference to Blair's Plain style and his call for "manly Simplicity."

Although Burke was most likely not amused, certainly Wollstonecraft participated in the general cultural debate taking place at the time. Discussing America during the Revolutionary period, Ruth Bloch points out the changing meaning of the word *virtue* and its attendant terms *manly* and *manliness* in the colonial and postcolonial context. She notes the origins of the concept of virtue in the "Homeric idea of *arete* or human excellence (later translated as 'virtue'), which stressed the physical strength and bravery displayed in athletic contests and in battles" (1987, 42–43). The linkage between the idea of virtue and maleness was reinforced, Bloch says, by such decisions as that by Gov. John Winthrop, who "defended the power of the Massachusetts magistrates against Henry Vane, a supporter of Anne Hutchinson by insisting on the superior judgment of the 'fathers of the commonwealth'" (41). While women were considered capable of private and personal virtues, only men were considered able to carry out virtuous public acts contributing to the common good (42). However, the association of manly virtues with the male body began to crumble in the mid 1770s. Having a need to castigate those not in support of the Revolution—and the English themselves—speakers and writers began to separate men as a category from virtue. "Whereas the Americans were 'a hardy virtuous set of men,' proclaimed a patriot orator in 1776, their corrupt British enemies had succumbed to 'that luxury which effeminates the mind and body'" (45). Bloch notes also that "[m]orally deficient American as well as British men were frequently depicted as feminine" (45 n. 21).

In her discussion of gender boundaries in the eighteenth century, Lynne Friedli suggests that we "shift emphasis from understanding the construction of effeminacy as a symbol of attacks on social decadence to evidence of a more general epistemological concern with clear-cut categorization" (1988, 250). Although Wollstonecraft was concerned with and used the language of morality and opposition to social decadence, she more importantly was attempting to change discursive categories in order to effect a revolution in social conditions affecting women. And Blair's *Lectures* provided some of the terms that allowed her to make this attempt. Thus, in writing what she believed was simple and plain prose, "wishing rather to persuade by the force of [her] arguments than dazzle by the elegance of [her] language," Wollstonecraft disrupted the necessary connection between femininity and women and claimed manliness with its attendant rationality and virtue—and need for education—for herself and for other women.

Notes

1. *A Vindication of the Rights of Woman* sold widely in several editions in the United States and as translations in France and Germany. "It was read by all the woman leaders of stature throughout the nineteenth century and into our own and was often the decisive force in crystallizing their determination to struggle for education and social and political freedom for their sex" (Flexner 1972, 165). Ralph Wardle reports that "Elizabeth Cady Stanton read The Rights of Woman with enthusiasm in 1840, although it was, as she said, 'tabooed by orthodox teachers.' And when she met Lucretia Mott in London a few months later, the two women eagerly discussed 'Mary Wollstonecraft, her social theories, and her demands of equality for women'" (1951, 340). In 1884 Elizabeth Robins Pennell wrote the first biography of Wollstonecraft and argued that *A Vindication of the Rights of Woman* was the first book of the women's rights movement. She refers to Wollstonecraft as the "first sower of seeds of female enfranchisement" (146). In 1909 the *Progressive Woman*, a socialist-feminist magazine, published an article claiming Wollstonecraft as a foremother to the movement. And in 1933 Inez Haynes Irwin, in her history of American women from 1833 to 1933, credits Wollstonecraft with first announcing women's suffrage (82). Since the early 1970s Wollstonecraft has been required reading in many women's studies classes.

2. Arians believed that Jesus was not part of God but also was not simply human; he preexisted the world and was created in order to create the world.

3. At the time that she read the *Lectures,* she was serving as a governess in Dublin for the daughters of Lord and Lady Kingsborough. She was already involved in the Dissenter movement, having met the Reverend Richard Price in 1783, the same year that she established, with her sister Everina and her friend Fanny Blood, a school at Newington Green, one of the centers of Dissenter activity. The school closed in 1786 due to financial problems, but she remained in contact with Price and others. When she moved to London in the fall of 1787 to make her living as a writer, she joined the Dissenting group that met at the publishing house of Joseph Johnson.

References

Bator, Paul G. 1989. "The Formation of the Regius Chair of Rhetoric and Belles Lettres at the University of Edinburgh." *Quarterly Journal of Speech* 75 (February): 40–64.

Blair, Hugh. [1783] 1965. *Lectures on Rhetoric and Belles Lettres.* 2 vols. Ed. Harold F. Harding. Carbondale: Southern Illinois University Press.

Bloch, Ruth H. 1987. "The Gendered Meanings of Virtue in Revolutionary America." *Signs* 13.1: 37–58.

Burke, Edmund. [1759] 1987. *A Philosophical Enquiry into the Origin of Our Ideas of the Sublime and the Beautiful.* Rev. ed. Edited by James T. Boulton. Oxford: Basil Blackwell.

Camic, Charles. 1983. *Experience and Enlightenment: Socialization for Cultural Change in Eighteenth-Century Scotland.* Chicago: University of Chicago Press.

Ferguson, Moira, and Janet Todd. 1984. *Mary Wollstonecraft.* Boston: Twayne.

Flexner, Eleanor. 1972. *Mary Wollstonecraft.* New York: Coward, McCann, and Geoghegan.

Friedli, Lynne. 1988. "'Passing Women': A Study of Gender Boundaries in the Eighteenth Century." In *Sexual Underworlds of the Enlightenment,* edited by G. S. Rousseau and Roy Porter. Chapel Hill: University of North Carolina Press.

Goodwin, Albert. 1979. *The Friends of Liberty: The English Democratic Movement in the Age of the French Revolution.* London: Hutchinson.

Howell, Wilbur Samuel. 1971. *Eighteenth-Century British Logic and Rhetoric.* Princeton: Princeton University Press.

Huber, Carole. 1989. "Hugh Blair and the Female Pen." Paper presented at the Conference on College Composition and Communication, 1988, St. Louis, Missouri. ERIC Document Reproduction Service No. 297331.

Irwin, Inez Haynes. 1933. *Angels and Amazons: A Hundred Years of American Women.* New York: Doubleday, Doran.

Kelly, Gary. 1992. *Revolutionary Feminism: The Mind and Career of Mary Wollstonecraft.* New York: St. Martin's Press.

Langford, Paul. 1984. "The Eighteenth Century." In *The Oxford Illustrated History of Britain,* edited by Kenneth O. Morgan. New York: Oxford University Press.

Lincoln, Anthony. 1938. *Some Political and Social Ideas of English Dissent.* London: Cambridge University Press.

"Mary Wollstonecraft—Pioneer Suffragist." 1909 (12 March). *Progressive Woman.*

Miller, Thomas. 1984. "Eighteenth-Century Scottish Rhetoric in its Socio-Cultural Context." Ph.D. diss., University of Texas.

Pennell, Elizabeth Robins. 1884. *Life of Mary Wollstonecraft.* Boston: Roberts Brothers.

Price, Richard. 1784. *Observations on the Importance of the American Revolution.* Vol. 3. Quoted in Anthony Lincoln. 1938. *Some Political and Social Ideas of English Dissent,* 133. London: Cambridge University Press.

Rousseau, G. S., and Roy Porter, eds. 1988. "Introduction." In *Sexual Underworlds of the Enlightenment.* Chapel Hill: University of North Carolina Press.

Sapiro, Virginia. 1992. *A Vindication of Political Virtue: The Political Theory of Mary Wollstonecraft.* Chicago: University of Chicago Press.

Thomson, Ian. 1982. "Rhetoric and the Passions, 1760–1800." In *Rhetoric Revalued: Papers from the International Society for the History of Rhetoric,* edited by Brian Vickers. Binghamton, N.Y.: Medieval and Renaissance Texts and Studies.

Wardle, Ralph. 1951. *Mary Wollstonecraft: A Critical Biography.* Lawrence: University of Kansas Press.

―――, ed. 1979. *Collected Letters of Mary Wollstonecraft*. Ithaca: Cornell University Press.

Watts, Michael R. 1978. *The Dissenters*. London: Oxford University Press.

Wollstonecraft, Mary. [1790] 1960. *A Vindication of the Rights of Men*. Gainesville, Fla.: Scholars' Facsimiles and Reprints.

―――. [1792] 1967. *A Vindication of the Rights of Woman*. Ed. Charles W. Hagelman Jr. New York: W. W. Norton.

Textbooks for
New Audiences
Women's Revisions of Rhetorical Theory
at the Turn of the Century

Jane Donawerth

In this essay I will examine the theories of women who wrote rhetoric textbooks for new audiences at the turn of the century in the United States. I will survey the research already published on Gertrude Buck, adding some of my own analysis, and compare and contrast the rhetorical writings of two other women who wrote in the late eighteenth and early nineteenth centuries—Hallie Quinn Brown and Mary Augusta Jordan.

Composition and rhetoric studies as a field is now in the process of revisioning its history.[1] Although the standard histories and references still emphasize almost exclusively the theories and education of privileged white men in public speech and writing, women and African Americans did teach and publish their ideas on communication and, after the Civil War, increasingly designed textbooks for the new audiences of college students who were female, African American, or both.[2] As we look forward to enormous demographic changes in our classrooms in the next decade, it is helpful to recall this other time of change, when women and African American rhetorical theorists began writing for these new kinds of students admitted to United States colleges after the Civil War.

The women who wrote rhetoric textbooks for coed and female audiences at the turn of the century do not express the same kind of theory as do the majority of the men, writing for audiences of male students: they offer alternatives accommodating women's experience, most frequently by using conversation rather than public discourse as a model.[3] These women also represent a good cross section of possibilities for women in colleges in the nineteenth century. Gertrude Buck was educated at a coed institution for whites and taught at a white women's college; Hallie Quinn Brown was educated and taught at a coed college for blacks; and Mary Augusta Jordan was educated at one white women's college and taught at another. After an initial look at Gertrude Buck, I will compare and contrast Hallie Quinn Brown and Mary Augusta Jordan, examining the influences of race as well as gender on theory.

The Exceptional Woman Theorist?

Gertrude Buck (1871–1922) has received some attention from historians of composition and rhetoric (Allen 1986, 1989; Berlin 1984; Bordelon 1995; Burke 1978; Campbell 1996; Mulderig 1984; Vivian 1994) and has acquired the status of the "exceptional woman" in the history of rhetoric, the one who seems to have succeeded in an otherwise all-male field. Because of this status, her achievements are sometimes dismissed as mainly those of her teacher at the University of Michigan, Fred Newton Scott (Berlin 1984, 80). Other scholars have argued for her originality and contribution (Allen 1986, 1989; Bordelon 1995; Burke 1978; Mulderig, 1984; and Vivian 1994). I see her, as my essay will make clear, not as a lone exception but as part of a group of women who responded to the challenges of teaching new students with new kinds of textbooks and, consequently, new theories of rhetoric.

Having taken her Ph.D. at the coed University of Michigan and having taught at the women's school Vassar College, Gertrude Buck published her works nationally, and they exist today in many libraries, including the Library of Congress. In five textbooks, several theoretical treatises, and many articles on pedagogy, Buck revised standard sources by adapting the "scientific" progressive education theory of men such as John Dewey and William James (Bordelon 1995). Buck felt free to adapt this psychological theory to her own subject of composition, arguing for an organic, developmental model for learning language and writing. Her emphasis, like those of male theorists, was on formal composition and public speech, but she started in the classroom with informal dialogue and written exercises and used conversation as a model for teaching and learning writing, a model adapted, I propose, because of her new audiences of students at Michigan and Vassar.[4]

In this section I will sketch the character of Buck's work by examining her early treatise on metaphor and her later college textbook on argument. I will then summarize the recovery work already accomplished by other historians of rhetoric.

Buck's theoretical approach to language and rhetoric is already evident in her earliest work, *The Metaphor—A Study in the Psychology of*

Rhetoric (1899). In this study Buck refutes the classical idea of metaphor as a word for one thing transferred to another similar thing because of the poverty of language or a desire to ornament. She shows that in many cases there is no transfer, the metaphor occurring spontaneously as the only word for a thing (1–35). Borrowing from the new developmental psychology of William James and John Dewey (11–21), she outlines a history of the development of metaphor that applies to both individual growth and the growth of language: metaphor originates as radical metaphor, where two objects or experiences identified with each other are contained in a single word; in poetic metaphor the two are beginning to be differentiated; and in the simile the process of abstraction and differentiation is complete and the resemblance can be specified. Thus the function of metaphor is neither clarity nor ornament (the functions cited in classical treatments of metaphor) but rather communication and stimulation: either it is the only way the speaker can communicate an idea in the process of formation or it is stimulating to the reader (and the writer as reader) because of a release of tension when she/he perceives the resemblance in what was before inchoate (40–59). In this philosophical exploration of metaphor, Buck outlines several of the tenets on which she establishes all of her work: language is social, communication between a speaker and a hearer or a writer and a reader; language is in the process of evolutionary development both for the entire society and for the individual speaker; understanding and, therefore, education are based on an evolutionary psychological model rather than a mechanistic one.

In her textbooks this philosophy of language translates into pedagogical strategies that seem very contemporary. In *A Course in Argumentative Writing* (1899), for example, Buck teaches argument not as artificial techniques of dominance or manipulation but as a means of communicating belief or understanding from one person to another, with full respect for the other person's ability to judge. She defines argument not as persuasion but as "transplant[ing] your conviction into [the hearer's] mind" (2) or "establishing in the mind of another person a conclusion which has become fixed in your own, by means of setting up in the other person's mind the train of thought or reasoning which has previously led you to this conclusion" (3).

Buck advocates a developmental organization of what she teaches; later in the essay we will see this as a similarity to Hallie Quinn Brown's theory. In *Argumentative Writing* Buck teaches strategies for argument in an order which she believes parallels human development: from less abstract sensory experience (induction) to abstracted, more differentiated experience (classification and deduction, and analogy). As in the development of metaphor, simile comes last for Buck, so in logic analogy developmentally comes last. In teaching, Buck attempts to help students see that reasoning is not imposed on experience but rather arises from one's own experiences and thought processes (4–5); logic is thus "a knowledge of those typical activities of mind common to all thinking people" (5), while rhetoric supplements logic by considering the audience, by allowing the speaker to "put himself imaginatively in the place of the person he addresses" (7) in order to establish an appropriate train of reasoning for this different individual.

In this textbook on argument, Buck encourages a progressive pedagogy: she recommends subject matter for writing close to students' interests (iv, vii) and oral debate in class to establish a purpose and sense of audience for writing outside of class (vii). Like Brown and Jordan, who (we shall see) alternate "he" and "she," Buck often alternates "he" as a universal pronoun with "you" when she addresses the student, thus suggesting that she shared the other women's impulse to include women in the audience through pronouns. Clearly Buck opposes the theories of persuasion and correctness of many of her male contemporaries, and she models her teaching of writing on conversation, not lecture. As studies are beginning to show, women students do better with discussion rather than lecture models of teaching (Belenky et al. 1986, 215, 223; Hartman 1991, 23; Kramarae and Treichler 1990, 46; Maher 1985, 29–48). Buck's unusual pedagogy seems a response to her new audiences of students: mixed male and female at Michigan, female at Vassar.

Historians of rhetoric have recovered Buck as a crucial figure in opposition to mainstream emphases on grammatical correctness and forms of discourse in late-nineteenth- and early-twentieth-century composition theory, and as a precursor of pedagogical and theoretical reforms of the 1960s and 1970s. Rebecca Burke praises Buck for her modern view of speech as "'a living, growing, changing thing'" (Buck 1909, 22; Burke 1978, 11), and Burke traces this organic model of speech through all of Buck's textbooks—on narrative, on exposition, and on argument—in which Buck describes a process of writing that can be taught inductively, from students' own experiences (Burke 1978, 14–15). Buck's originality as a rhetorical theorist, according to Burke, lies in her desire to present rhetoric not as dominance but as a means of equalizing speaker and hearer, writer and reader (19). Gerald P. Mulderig finds Buck's greatest contribution in her development of a process view of writing, thus anticipating the much later work of composition theorists such as Janet Emig, Nancy Sommers, Sondra Perl, Linda Flower and John Hayes, and Frank D'Angelo (Mulderig 1984, 98, 100). He argues that Buck precedes Ken Macrorie in insistence on respect for student writing (98), and that Buck was the first advocate of writing across the curriculum, when she initiated a joint course between English and economics at Vassar in 1898–1899 (101). Virginia Allen, while agreeing that Buck anticipates modern composition theory and pedagogical methods (Allen 1986, 141, 145), also analyzes Buck's revision or subversion of nineteenth-century theories. She suggests that Buck opposes mechanistic theories of language by the first psycholinguistic theory of metaphor. Allen further points out Buck's recognition of a class basis for the doctrine of correctness (1986, 147–48) and argues that Buck revises the developmental psychology of Wilhelm Wundt, James, and Dewey in the service of rhetoric by subverting the neo-Darwinian theory of evolution as resulting not in survival of the fittest through competition but, instead, in cooperative social behavior through "'the speaker's primitive social instinct for sympathy'" (Allen 1986, 150–57; Allen 1989, 10–11; Buck 1901, 174). By a different route, then, Allen sees Buck's rhetoric of equality as her most important contribution to rhetoric. Vivian suggests that Buck's contribution lies in her highly inventive application of psychology to explain the origin and working of metaphor (Vivian 1994, 96, 100). Suzanne Bordelon also argues that Buck contributes to the development of turn-of-the-century rhetorical theory through her founding of composition theory on democratic social ethics and an "organic concept of society" (1995, 13). Bordelon traces Buck's development in rhetoric of the tenets of progressive education as outlined by John Dewey, Johann Friedrich Herbart, and Friedrich Froebel (1–7): the importance of stimulating students' interest, student-oriented approaches in the classroom, a reliance on psychology, and "rejection of 'traditional' education methods" (13).

I would add that Buck's moves toward equality in her teaching of audience theory directly promote the interests of the group of students relatively new to college training: women. Buck shares with contemporary feminist pedagogues an emphasis on discussion and collaboration and an understanding of the hierarchies at work in persuasion (Belenky et al. 1986, 214–29; Bricker-Jenkins and Hooyman 1987, 41; Donawerth 1996, passim).

New Students, New Theories

Now I would like to introduce two theorists who have had little attention: Hallie Quinn Brown and Mary Augusta Jordan. Like Gertrude Buck, they wrote for new audiences after the Civil War, Brown attending and teaching at the all-black Wilberforce College and Jordan attending Vassar and teaching at Smith, two all-women colleges. They also represent a crucial late-nineteenth-century split in rhetoric between speech and composition. In the following analysis I will look not only at what these two women share with Buck, in attempting to incorporate or establish a female audience for rhetoric, but also how they differ from each other, according to their acknowledgments of the role of race in the politics of rhetoric. I will quote much more liberally from their works than I did from Buck's because so little has been published on them and because their textbooks are so rare in today's libraries.

Hallie Quinn Brown (1845–1949) was a professor at Wilberforce College in Ohio, a black coed college opened in 1856, sponsored by the AME (African Methodist Episcopal) Church. She had also been educated at Wilberforce. She developed her books for this college audience, printing them locally. She published three on elocution: *Bits and Odds*, most likely from the 1880s, probably her repertoire as an elocutionist with the Wilberforce Concert Company, including a preface on elocution; *Elocution and Physical Culture*, about 1910, a textbook for elocution classes; and *First Lessons in Public Speaking*, 1920, now apparently lost. She also left an unpublished essay on elocution—perhaps from the 1920s.[5]

Mary Augusta Jordan (1855–1921) was a professor at Smith College, a white all-women secular college opened in 1875. She was educated at Vassar College. Jordan published her book, *Correct Writing and Speaking*, in 1904 as part of a national series called "The Woman's Home Library."[6] Absent from standard references, both Brown's and Jordan's work required archival research: Jordan's text exists in no more than a dozen copies in United States libraries, Brown's only in copies at Central State University in Ohio.

Brown and Jordan did not write the same theory as their male contemporaries: they both revised for their new audiences. In particular, they shared conversation as a model for discourse, as did many other early women rhetorical theorists.[7] For Brown this meant conceiving of the relation between the reader and her text for performance as dialogic: "We adapt ourselves to the creations of the author, and the creations of the author to ourselves" (1880s?, 6). In addition, conversation as a model allowed her to transform the distance of public performance into an individualized relation between speaker and listener: speakers must be "as earnest and sincere upon the platform as we are in private conversation," and even in public recitation the reader must "speak to the individual, not to the multitude" (1910?, 21, 39).

For Jordan conversation as a model meant revising the "kinds" of discourse that she inherited: the familiar, description, narration, exposition, and argumentation, or the classical speeches of praise/blame (epideictic), legal (forensic), and deliberative (judicial). Rather than using these public forms, she classifies private forms of discourse, including conversation. She constructs, in fact, a rhetoric of conversation: "*Fair play* may be offered as the brief advice for the conduct of private conversations," she suggests; "[i]f your voice is tired, at least consider whether you have given anybody else time for the proper exercise of hers" (232). Jordan enlarges the feminine principle of self-effacement into a general principle of social harmony: "Be careful not to sacrifice to your own feeling of interest in what you are saying or thinking, or to the expression you are making of yourself, the convenience and pleasure of others in working out similar expressions of themselves" (234–35). How improbable such a sentence would be in a nineteenth-century rhetoric directed at men![8] In addition, Jordan acknowledges the socialization of women, re-presenting it as a nonacademic education: "Few women are ignorant of the education they have undergone in the effort to fit themselves for the discharge of their purely private obligations. It probably takes as many years to learn to keep one's temper with an exasperating companion as it does to acquire control of the pitch and carrying tones of one's voice" (67–68). I read "companion" as a code word for "male," perhaps as specific as "husband."

Jordan extends the boundaries of conversation as an artful form to areas of women's experience usually left silent, implicitly acknowledging the functions that middle-class women and lower-class servants have in common: "Don't fear to speak politely and interestingly to those who happen to serve you. The relation might be reversed" (235). Jordan addresses, I think, the shifting class position of middle-class women in her culture, at one moment "master" of servants, at another moment servant to the masters. Jordan also suggests that degrees of friendship are reflected in conversational etiquette: "The familiar intercourse of intimate friends permits, by common consent, waste of time, display of personal weakness, or the expression of strong feeling that should never be imposed on general society, even in private" (233). I think the puzzling phrase "general society, even in private" is another code, indicating a woman in company with male family members. Although very different in their use of it, Brown and Jordan use conversation as a model in ways no male theorist in the nineteenth century—or earlier—attempted.

Brown and Jordan are also similar in revising their own writing styles to include women in their language. In particular, both alternate masculine and feminine pronouns to include their women readers and to bring in women as potential speakers and writers. (I had no idea any writer before the 1960s had tried this strategy.)[9] We have already seen that Buck alternates "one/he" with "you" when addressing her textbook audience, similar in fashion to this alternation of pronouns in Brown and Jordan.

In her lecture on elocution Brown says, "*Man* manifests the three states of *his* being through voice, muscle and speech" ("Untitled," 159), but on the next page a baby develops: "*she* begins to think . . . *She* separates herself from the objects that surround *her*." Brown represents universal experience by both pronouns. She was a committed feminist, won over by hearing Susan B. Anthony speak at Wilberforce (McFarlin 1975, 22). She applies her politics to her theory: "Thanks to elocution," she writes, "the sickly, young lady with her puny form and wasp waist, is being supplanted by the strong, vigorous woman, who is to preside in the home and to move to and fro over the land as a queen among men" (1920s?, 163). Brown's alternation of pronouns, then, seems to be a means of including women in the same quest for cultivation of power that she offers her male students.

Jordan also alternates pronouns, but with a different effect. Jordan says, "The average citizen in the United States aims to have a mind of *his* own" (228), but in a passage we have already read, a speaker with a tired voice must allow someone else "the proper exercise of *hers*" (232). Jordan sometimes speaks of intellectual experience as universal, and at other times she directly addresses women's gendered experience, as in a passage on women's work of child care, with the conclusion that a good speaking voice requires maintaining health, health conceived of as women's work, not men's (126–27, 133–35, 146). I think her pronoun use, then, depends on a complicated application to language of a doctrine of separate spheres of influence for women and men.[10] Thus both women revise the formal constraints of the language they use in order to include women, but Brown puts her revision to more radical use.

Overcoming Barriers to Free Speech for New Students

Although Brown and Jordan share much, they experienced the barriers to speaking quite differently. In her diaries Brown records race, but not gender, as a barrier: on 14 November 1882, for example, the Wilberforce Concert Company is kept from finding a sponsor for a stop at Des Moines by one vote of the Women's National Temperance Union (WNTU), and on 8 May 1883 a white landlady refuses to honor a reservation when she sees her customers are black. In her book Jordan sees gender as the barrier to speaking: even though "[t]he old teaching that women should not be heard in the congregation has given way before necessity," a woman "is often without training for the task laid upon her, but she is expected to use her motherwit to take the place of technique and somehow make her voice heard" (67).[11] While Brown seeks to further both blacks' and women's speaking, Jordan would preserve speech for white men and women: "It does not follow that a negro exhorter is a model of natural eloquence in using cadence as he does" (173).

Hallie Quinn Brown centers her revision of rhetoric on the enabling power of elocution. In *Elocution and Physical Culture* she states her purpose: "Breath is life, breath is speech. It is the chief source of power" (14); "The aristocracy of eloquence is supreme and in the land of the free can never be suppressed" (28). Brown is surer of her right to claim this power than are the other women discussed in this chapter, and I think her claim is a strategy for social change. These are dangerous ideas to teach to a black student in a racist society—dangerous because effective, recalling the political influence of the many nineteenth-century male and female black orators against slavery and for black education and the vote.[12] Indeed, from her earlier *Bits and Odds* we can see that Brown's repertoire for her own elocutionary tours was arranged with political designs on the audience and included poetry by blacks and abolitionists as well as "classics" and comic dialect pieces. In her later manuscript she sets eloquence in the larger context of education for blacks: "If the Negro Race is to come to real freedom and true spiritual power and progress; men and women trained to large knowledge, broad vision and lofty spiritual purpose . . . shall lift the standard and lead people into a larger life" (176). This rhetorical phrasing drawn from sermons and moral tracts is subversively applied to a larger life here and now. Such an education "means equipping the individual with certain powers and forces to earn his own living"; it also means "education that can be translated into *action;* that through cultured powers, makes for higher living" (1920s?, 175). She acknowledges the necessity of education to address survival, and she defines survival broadly as the development of a well-fed, whole, free person who thinks for herself.[13] In elocution she finds this education: elocution "gives mental and moral strength, great power, and a wide social influence to all who will take the time and patience to master it" (171).

The word *master* recurs in Brown's works: her elaborate program of physical and mental exercises bestows mastery of a discipline on the student, and, even more important, it bestows mastery of self. As do the later modernist writers that Houston Baker describes in *Modernism and the Harlem Renaissance,* Brown proposes "mastery of forms and defor-mation of mastery" (Baker 1987, 15–16; cf. Washington 1963, 176)—the one a means to the other for Brown. "But let us remember," she cau-tions, "when we have mastered these difficulties and made ourselves proficient, we are bound by the strong law of . . . [o]bligation to the man who is down" (1920s?, 176). She reminds her black audience at Wilberforce in the post–Civil War United States that "the cry" of fellow African Americans and former slaves "come[s] from those who sit in darkness" in the South, in "delta, canebrake, cotton field and rice swamp" (176). Indeed, power is defined not as dominance for Brown, but as self-mastery in concert with the powers of others: in her earliest work the elocutionist gives "forth those thoughts and feelings he has created in his mind, suggested by the expressed words of another, and causing the listener on the other hand to start the kindred chords vibrating in uni-son with his own" (1880s?, 5).

In her earliest journal, begun at the start of a speaking tour, Brown promises the reader "the odds and ends of a travelling career, begun March 16th in the year of our Lord 1881, by a girl who has an idea that she is not a cipher nor a figurehead" (1881–1885, 1). Drawing on the implicit metaphor of quilting, this diary describes Brown's method of self-construction throughout her career: piecing together the odds and ends of a fragmented life into a powerful life of social influence through vocal training and traveling performance. It is also Brown's method of mastering her sources: she weaves together such disparate elements as classical rhetoric, Delsartean elocution, theories of evolutionary devel-opment, and a spirituality arising from her African Methodist Episcopalian religion. She draws from works on eloquence by Cicero, Quintilian, Augustine, and Emerson, and she frequently cites her debt to Delsarte, "the master-teacher" (1910?, 7, 30; 1920s?, 159). She builds her conception of education in eloquence on the idea of evolutionary child development taken from progressive white educators (1880s?, 5; 1910?, 6; 1920s?, 156, 159–61). And she sees education as standing on a Christian foundation, "The study of the Word" (1910?, 35). But she then transforms the elements through her synthesizing revision and thus masters them: her theory proposes the teaching of speech through physical and mental exercises designed to prepare speakers to be instruments of spiritual powers; scientifically teaching these exercises in stages designed to imitate the original evolutionary development of speech in humans, from gesture to voice to articulation; and teaching them to the end of ethical use. Her synthesis no longer looks like white male theory, for she revises out of feminist and black experience. For example, in *Elocution and Physical Culture* she derives the origin of all speech from "the mother-tone": the long rounded "a" of "mama," the mother-tone is "the first cry of babyhood, of mother-love, of home-love and home-longing. This mother-tone runs like a scarlet thread through the lullabies of many primitive peoples. It is heard in the folk-songs, in the simple ballads, and in the passion of the opera" (15–16). Her theory allows her to piece together and claim all her heritages—classical, African, and United States—and in the process to validate herself as a free, speaking person.

In contrast, Mary Augusta Jordan at first glance seems to be mastered by her sources. Her work is rhetoric on its way to twentieth-century language studies, a combination of belletristic rhetoric, nontraditional grammar, physiology of voice, and education theory. She achieves an uneasy synthesis of her old-fashioned humanist ideals with her readings of progressive authorities such as A. J. Ellis on phonetics and H. G. Wells on education. Most surprising, especially in comparison to Brown, are Jordan's slavish word-for-word quotations of male authorities: Ellis for three pages in a row (54–56), for example, or Wells—socialist but snobby—for a full six pages (113–18). What are we to make of this?

What Jordan made of it, I think, was a rhetorical strategy for presenting a revision of rhetoric for women—in disguise. The white women colleges of the end of the century had engaged in a debate about their mission: whether it was to educate women, adapt curricula to women's experience, or dispense knowledge—up to that time male knowledge—to women. Many decided in favor of the latter, seeking to give women an education equal to men's, which they took to mean the same as men's. I think Jordan's rhetorical theory reveals the problems in this solution.

Since men's knowledge was not always relevant for her women students, she attempts to provide men's knowledge to authorize her textbook but also to include something new that truly applies to women's situations. Thus, I read her elaborate quotations of men as an attempt to prove that she is dispensing a theory as sound as the men's. Then she can fit women's experience, her revision of rhetoric, into the gaps and spaces and cover it with a code language. Her strategy of revising and disguising appears even in her title; *Correct Speaking and Writing* is actually a text denying the title: there is no "correct" or standard English (36, 71) because language changes and individuals express themselves individually (83–87). Jordan is opposing the dominant trend in college composition theory written for men: after the "Harvard Report," published in 1892, which criticized students' grammatical errors, correctness became a major goal of most composition textbooks (Kitzhaber 1953, 73–77, 346–52). Jordan is quite aware of the class basis for the desire to speak "correctly" (101, 103),[14] and I think she revised the concept of "correctness" out of her understanding of her audience of women: either reading at home with no education or contained within the home after college, the readers of "The Woman's Home Library," the series in which Jordan's text was published, were expected to speak "correctly," as if they belonged to the class of their husbands, when they did not have the same experience as their husbands. Jordan's doctrine of correctness seems to me designed to reassure women that their efforts to act their class roles are not in vain. Since there is no "correct" English, one learns to speak and write by "study, discipline, and practice," not by rules (100), and the person who has knowledge, curiosity, and moral values will speak best (229).[15]

Having presented her male authorities, Jordan offers a rhetorical theory that is far from the prescriptive and psychologically manipulative eighteenth-century rhetorics most often taught in nineteenth-century male colleges (see Kitzhaber 1953; Berlin 1984). "The audience is not to be dominated, cajoled, or bullied," Jordan insists. "It is to be interpreted, and made to know its own self in terms of something else than prejudice, or passion, or lazy self-indulgence. . . . The successful speaker of the present will use all his art to enable him to discern the signs of the spiritual forces coming into action in his presence. His aim will be to conserve them, to let as little as possible real energy go to waste" (69). This model for speech is based on private, not public, discourse and revises the goal of classical rhetoric—persuasion—into the goals of social harmony and self-knowledge. I read this as a feminization of rhetoric—despite the masculine pronouns in this passage—in the context of Jordan's culture, one that comes dangerously close to enforcing the status quo of rigid gender roles for women: "unselfishness" is a quality of Jordan's ideal speaker (229), and, to paraphrase Rachel Blau DuPlessis on nineteenth-century women writers, "Being a [speaker] is . . . reinterpreted as self-sacrifice for the woman, and thus aligned with feminine ideology" (DuPlessis 1985, 87).

Jordan comes close to enforcing the status quo but finally does not. Instead, in the interstices between the male authorities, she constructs a theory of kinds of discourses for women: besides the feminization of public speaking and the rhetoric of conversation that we have already looked at, Jordan treats letters and even diaries. She argues that discourse lies on a continuum from private to public and that letters are "closest to the personal character of the writer" (60), diaries and journals being a subgenre of letters (238). She sees letters as, at once, a personal "gift" (61, 238) and potentially a published literary form (61)—she cites Esther Edwards (63) and Lady Mary Wortley Montagu (24) as examples, along with many men. Jordan notes a new style of "suggestiveness in contemporary letters" (61) and sets forth standards for this private-public genre: letter writing requires "skill in presentation, vividness of detail, choice of significant subject matter, evidence of delicate and precise knowledge of the reader's taste and character, and just so much revelation of the writer's self and interests as shall really serve the reader's" (62). She uses the model of conversation for such writing: "In a letter, as in conversation, the other person should be left something of the topic to deal with. Letters should not be simply 'unpublished works,' but part of a pleasurable give and take, of suggestion, comment, interested question, and generous self-expression. The form might be after this sort: Something about me, something about you, something about the wide world" (239). It is in such a context that she justifies the necessity of (women) learning to write well: "Nearly everybody professes hatred of writing. Yet nearly everybody admires and enjoys good writing in others and depends upon it as one of the consolations or resources of life" (237). Jordan seems to be including a subtext here: through writing, her women students will be able to continue over the years friendships made at college.[16]

Conclusions

If we consider Hallie Quinn Brown, Mary Augusta Jordan, and Gertrude Buck together, we can begin to make a few generalizations about the women writers of rhetorics at the turn of the century. They write because they have new audiences who are not well served by the existing textbooks for white men. They experiment with pronouns in their own writing to indicate the inclusion of women. More than male theorists, they rely on conversation as a model for discourse and teaching. Their conception of the purpose of rhetoric is less dominance in the forms of persuasion or manipulation than consensus in the form of the speaker's gathering of power from her audience. And they experiment with pedagogy, borrowing from other disciplines or from nontraditional literature to adapt their classrooms to new students and revising classroom structure to incorporate more active student participation. Operating from the margins of traditional theory, they make new theories for new students. Coming from different backgrounds and different generations, they nonetheless work toward similar goals: to make the curriculum in rhetoric more responsive to the experiences of their nontraditional students, and to include women in the turn-of-the-century United States ideal of democratic free speech.

Notes

I would like to thank all the students in my graduate courses on the history of rhetorical theory, spring 1985 and 1990, who helped me redefine rhetorical theory and recover women theorists by responding to my assignment: "Find the first woman rhetorical theorist." Later in my notes I will thank individual graduate students for their contributions to this essay. I would also like to thank Virginia Beauchamp, Bob Coogan, Sue Lanser, and Kevin Meehan for reading and commenting on early versions of this essay.

The librarians of the Hallie Quinn Brown Library of Central State University in Wilberforce, Ohio, were very helpful, especially George T. Johnson, the director. In addition, I would like to thank the archivists at Smith's library for their help in finding material on Mary Augusta Jordon.

1. In order to include women as theorists, we must redefine rhetorical theory to cover areas other than the kinds of speeches that men historically made to each other in the public business of law, government, and preaching, where women were excluded. Recent calls for a revision of the history of rhetorical theory include Schilb (1986), Donawerth (1992), and Blair (1992).

2. None of the standard histories of rhetorical theory includes more than brief mention of one woman, and there are only a handful of articles on women

theorists, mainly on Gertrude Buck: Allen (1986, 1989), Burke (1978), McFarlin (1975, 1980), and Mulderig (1984). Historians of rhetoric who fail to mention female teachers of rhetoric or women rhetorical theorists include: Guthrie (1948), Howell (1971), Nan Johnson (1991), Kennedy (1972, 1980, 1983), and Murphy (1972). Historians of rhetoric who mention only one woman teacher or theorist include Berlin (1984, 80—Gertrude Buck), Howell (1961, 166–67—Mary Queen of Scots), Kennedy (1963, 158–64—Aspasia; 1983, 301–2—Anna Comnena). The recent anthology edited by Bizzell and Herberg (1990) includes excerpts from a few women before 1900: Christine de Pisan, Laura Cereta, Margaret Fell, and Sarah Grimké. For a study of nineteenth- and early-twentieth-century feminist rhetoric that does not treat rhetorical theorists (only speakers), see Campbell (1989). For other women rhetorical theorists, see my "Bibliography" (1990).

   3. Examples of theorists who model their rhetoric on conversation, rather than public discourse, include Pan Chao and Mary Astell, as well as the theorists discussed in this paper. This is not to say that no men discussed conversation before 1900: see Arnauld (1675, 93, 337) and De Quincey ([1890] 1967, 264–88). But Arnauld and De Quincey discuss conversation as a separate art, not as a model in general for discourse.

   4. Mary Yost, who later also received her Ph.D. from Michigan and taught at Vassar, developed the earliest sociological analysis of the speech situation, arguing for harmony as the goal of communication in an essay in the *Quarterly Journal of Public Speaking*; see Cohen (1994, 67–72).

   5. I owe my finding of Hallie Quinn Brown to the article by Annjennette McFarlin. Biographical information comes from McFarlin's article and dissertation (1980, 1975), notes by George Johnson (1982), and Wesley (1971). The dates of *Bits* and of *Elocution* are my own estimates, from the biographical information in the opening of *Bits* and from the 1908 copyright date on the premanufactured cover of *Bits*, a cover very similar to the undated cover of *Elocution*.

   6. I owe finding Mary Augusta Jordan to Susan Joseph, a graduate student at the University of Maryland. In my graduate course, "Readings in the History of Rhetorical Theory," we had read Gertrude Buck, who taught at Vassar. When she responded to my assignment to "find the first woman rhetorical theorist," Susan Joseph, an alumna of Smith, longed to find a Smith equivalent—and did, with help from the archivists at Smith's library. For biographical information, I am indebted to Susan's unpublished paper, "Mary August Jordan, 1855–1921," submitted as a course requirement. I regret that Susan felt unable to write further on Mary Augusta Jordan and appreciate very much her supplying me with a copy of Jordan's text.

   7. Male theorists later used conversation as a model for public discourse: see Cohen (1994, 25–26) on the views of William Mathews's *The Great Conversers* and George Hervey's *The Rhetoric of Conversation*; (94) on conversation not distinctly separate from public speaking in J. A. Winans's *Public Speaking* (1915);

(103) on conversation as an art in Everett L. Hunt's "Academic Public Speaking" in *The Quarterly Journal of Public Speaking* (1917); (110–12) on conversation as a model for speaking style in E. D. Shurter's *The Rhetoric of Oratory* (1911); and (275) on group discussion and reaching consensus in A. D. Sheffield's *Joining in Public Discussion* (1922).

8. Contrast Thomas De Quincey in his 1847–1860 essay on conversation, for example, who sees the art of conversation as a basis for individual performance and display, even though he cautions against the vices of indulgence or vanity of individual speakers ([1890] 1967, 264–88).

9. Cohen (1994, xii) explains that "Almost all the authors of this period [1914–1945], including women authors, made almost exclusive use of the masculine third person pronoun. If one did not know the usage of the time, one could assume from these publications that all students and all readers were male." Brown, Jordan, and Buck, then were exceptional in developing strategies that resisted the universality of the masculine pronoun.

10. Indeed, Barbara Miller Solomon, in her study of American women's education, finds this difference between generations of college women: first-generation college women are serious social reformers; third-generation college women are somewhat adrift until marriage and homemaking (1985, 84–85). This may also characterize a difference in Brown's conception of her audience as serious social reformers and Jordan's conception of her audience as "ladies." Of Irish descent, and of feminist persuasions, Jordan would not necessarily have approved of this difference.

11. The passage from Jordan is worth quoting in full, since it is a woman's bitter response to changing social customs in the second half of the nineteenth century with regard to women's license to speak in public:

> Indeed women may be said to have come into entirely new duties and responsibilities. The question of their increased enjoyment is, perhaps, still open. The old teaching that women should not be heard in the congregation has given way before necessity. Probably few women who speak in public began by choosing to do so as the gratification of any taste or desire for publicity. But circumstances forced the effort upon them, repetition made its difficulties less formidable, and gradually the feeling has grown in the community that women ought to be able to do what public speaking naturally comes in their way. The attitude of conservatism in regard to the pleasure that they should display in the exercise of their powers is not retained when their success or skill is under discussion. A woman may be forgiven for saying nothing, or even for publishing her incapacity for public address, but nothing justifies or quite excuses her saying her say badly. She is often without training for the task laid upon her, but she is expected to use her motherwit to take the place of technique and somehow make her voice heard. The resulting strain and distortion are regretted, are often considered necessary incidents to the

transition state of women's social influence, but by degrees they are coming to be looked upon as indications of the exorbitant price following bad or no training. The fact is that public relations are as normal and as dignified and, therefore in their degree, as pleasurable as private or personal ones. (1904, 66–67)

On the development of women's speaking in public and feminist rhetoric, see Campbell (1989).

12. I am indebted to Shirley Logan for this understanding of Brown's theory, and also to her work on nineteenth-century black women orators for my understanding of the historical context of Brown's theory; see Logan (1991a, 1991b, 1995).

13. Thus, Brown seems to take a middle position in the debate on post–Civil War education for blacks: whether mainly liberal arts or mainly industrial. On the debate, see Booker T. Washington's *Up from Slavery* (1963, esp. 64–65, 85, 88, 91, 112). In 1893 Brown served as "Lady Principal" (dean of women) at Tuskegee Institute under the leadership of Washington (McFarlin 1975, 51).

14. For an analysis of the importance of class to the nineteenth-century concept of "correctness," see Berlin (1984, ch. 6).

15. Alternatively, speaking correctly may be, for Jordan, a disguise that some women adopt: "The low sweet voice of the society woman bears almost as little relation to her real character as it does to her real voice without the restraints and conventions of social form" (1904, 83).

16. I am thinking of these women in the context described in Carroll Smith-Rosenberg's "The Female World of Love and Ritual: Relations Between Women in Nineteenth-Century America" (1985, 53–76).

References

Allen, Virginia. 1986. "Gertrude Buck and the Emergence of Composition in the United States." *Vitae Scholasticae: The Bulletin of Educational Biography* 5 (Spring/Fall): 141–59.

———. 1989. "Gertrude Buck's Rhetoric for the New Psychology." Unpublished paper, Conference on College Composition and Communication, Chicago.

Arnauld, Antoine. 1676. *The Art of Speaking.* London.

Astell, Mary. [1701] 1970. *A Serious Proposal to the Ladies, Parts I and II.* New York: Source Book Press.

Baker, Houston A., Jr. 1987. *Modernism and the Harlem Renaissance.* Chicago: University of Chicago Press.

Belenky, Mary Field, Blythe McVicker Clinchy, Nancy Rule Goldberger, and Jill Mattuck Tarule, eds. 1986. *Women's Ways of Knowing: The Development of Self, Voice, and Mind.* New York: Basic Books.

Berlin, James. 1984. *Writing Instruction in Nineteenth-Century American Colleges.* Carbondale: Southern Illinois University Press.

Bizzell, Patricia, and Bruce Herzberg, eds. 1990. *The Rhetorical Tradition: Readings from Classical Times to Present.* Boston: Bedford.

Blair, Carole. 1992. "Contested Histories of Rhetoric: The Politics of Preservation, Progress, and Change." *Quarterly Journal of Speech* 78.4: 403–28.

Bordelon, Suzanne. 1995. "Gertrude Buck's Participation in a Pedagogy of Democratic Ideas and Social Ethics." Unpublished paper, Conference on College Composition and Communication, given in Washington, D.C..

Bricker-Jenkins, Mary, and Nancy Hooyman, eds. 1987. "Feminist Pedagogy in Education for Social Change." *Feminist Teacher* 2.2: 36–42.

Brown, Hallie Quinn. 1880s(?). *Bits and Odds — A Choice Selection of Recitations for School, Lyceum and Parlor Entertainments.* Xenia, Ohio: Chew Press.

———. 1881–1885. *Diaries of Elocutionary Tours in Manuscript.* Hallie Quinn Brown Library at Central State University of Ohio. Wilberforce, Ohio.

———. 1910(?). *Elocution and Physical Culture: Training for Students, Teachers, Readers, Public Speakers.* Wilberforce, Ohio: Homewood Cottage.

———. 1920s(?). "Untitled Manuscript on Elocution." Rpt. as Appendix D, "Sample Manuscript of Text." In Annjennette S. McFarlin. 1975. "Hallie Quinn Brown—Black Woman Elocutionist: 1845(?)–1949." Ph.D. diss., Washington State University.

Buck, Gertrude. 1899. *A Course in Argumentative Writing.* New York: Henry Holt and Co.

———. 1899. "The Metaphor—A Study in the Psychology of Rhetoric." In *Contributions to Rhetorical Theory,* no. 5, edited by Fred Newton Scott. Ann Arbor, Mich.: Inland Press.

———. 1901. "Recent Tendencies in the Teaching of English Composition." *Educational Review* 22 (November): 371–82.

———. 1909. "Make-Believe Grammar." *School Review* 17 (January): 21–33.

Burke, Rebecca. 1978. "Gertrude Buck's Rhetorical Theory." In *Occasional Papers in the History and Theory of Composition,* edited by Donald C. Stewart, 1: 1–26. Manhattan: Kansas State University.

Campbell, Joann, ed. 1996. *Toward a Feminist Rhetoric: The Writing of Gertrude Buck.* Pittsburgh: University of Pittsburgh Press.

Campbell, Karlyn Kohrs. 1989. *Man Cannot Speak For Her.* Vol. 1: *A Critical Study of Early Feminist Rhetoric.* New York: Greenwood Press.

Cohen, Herman. 1994. *The History of Speech Communication: The Emergence of a Discipline, 1914–1945.* Annandale, Va.: Speech Communication Association.

De Quincey, Thomas. [1890] 1967. *Selected Essays on Rhetoric.* Ed. Frederick Burwick from David Masson's edition. Carbondale: Southern Illinois University Press.

Donawerth, Jane. 1990. "Bibliography of Women and the History of Rhetorical Theory to 1900." *Rhetoric Society Quarterly* 20.4: 403–14.

———. 1992. "Transforming the History of Rhetorical Theory." *Feminist Teacher* 7.1: 35–39.

———. Forthcoming. "Changing Our Originary Stories: Renaissance Women on Education, and Conversation as a Model for Our Classrooms." In *Attending to Early Modern Women*, edited by Adele Seeff et al. Wilmington: Delaware University Press.

DuPlessis, Rachel Blau. 1985. *Writing Beyond the Ending: Narrative Strategies of Twentieth-Century Women Writers*. Bloomington: Indiana University Press.

Guthrie, Warren. 1948. "The Development of Rhetorical Theory in America, 1635–1850." *Speech Monographs* 15.1: 61–71.

Hartman, Joan E. 1991. "Telling the Stories: The Construction of Women's Agency." In *(En)Gendering Knowledge: Feminists in Academe*, edited by Joan E. Hartman and Ellen Messer-Davidow, 11–34. Knoxville: University of Tennessee Press.

Howell, Wilbur Samuel. [1956] 1961. *Logic and Rhetoric in England 1500–1700*. New York: Russell & Russell.

———. 1971. *Eighteenth-Century British Logic and Rhetoric*. Princeton: Princeton University Press.

Johnson, George T. 1982. "Hallie Quinn Brown." In *Dictionary of American Negro Biography*, edited by Rayford W. Logan and Michael R. Winston, 67–68. New York: W. W. Norton & Co.

Johnson, Nan. 1991. *Nineteenth-Century Rhetoric in America*. Carbondale: Southern Illinois University Press.

Jordan, Mary A. 1904. *Correct Writing and Speaking*. The Woman's Home Library. Vol. 6. New York: A. S. Barnes & Co.

Joseph, Susan. 1990. "Mary Augusta Jordan, 1855–1921, Considered as an Early Female Rhetorician." Unpublished paper, University of Maryland at College Park.

Kennedy, George A. 1963. *The Art of Persuasion in Greece*. Princeton: Princeton University Press.

———. 1972. *The Art of Rhetoric in the Roman World 300 B.C.–300 A.D.* Princeton: Princeton University Press.

———. 1980. *Classical Rhetoric and Its Christian and Secular Tradition from Ancient to Modern Times*. Chapel Hill: University of North Carolina Press.

———. 1983. *Greek Rhetoric Under Christian Emperors*. Princeton: Princeton University Press.

Kitzhaber, Albert Raymond. 1953. "Rhetoric in American Colleges 1850–1900." Ph.D. diss., University of Washington.

Kramarae, Cheris, and Paula A. Treichler. 1990. "Power Relations in the Classroom." In *Gender in the Classroom: Power and Pedagogy*, edited by Susan L.Gabriel and Isaiah Smithson, 41–59. Urbana: University of Illinois Press.

Logan, Shirley. 1991a. "Rhetorical Strategies in Ida B. Wells's 'Southern Horrors: Lynch Law in All Its Phases': Roots of Current Practice in the Rhetoric of Protest." Unpublished paper, Conference on College Composition and Communication, Boston.

————. 1991b. "Converging and Diverging 'Communities of Interest' in the Speeches of Frances E. W. Harper." Unpublished paper, Pennsylvania State University Conference on Rhetoric and Composition.

————, ed. 1995. *With Pen and Voice: A Critical Anthology of Nineteenth-Century African-American Women*. Carbondale: Southern Illinois University Press.

Maher, Frances. 1985. "Classroom Pedagogy and the New Scholarship on Women." In *Gendered Subjects: The Dynamics of Feminist Teaching*, edited by Margo Culley and Catherine Portuges, 29–48. Boston: Routledge & Kegan Paul.

McFarlin, Annjennette S. 1975. "Hallie Quinn Brown—Black Woman Elocutionist: 1845(?)–1949." Ph.D. diss., Washington State University.

————. 1980. "Hallie Quinn Brown: Black Woman Elocutionist." *Southern Speech Communication Journal* 46 (Fall): 72–82.

Mulderig, Gerald P. 1984. "Gertrude Buck's Rhetorical Theory and Modern Composition Teaching." *Rhetoric Society Quarterly* 14.3–4: 95–104.

Murphy, James J. 1974. *Rhetoric in the Middle Ages*. Berkeley: University of California Press.

————. 1989. *Medieval Rhetoric: A Select Bibliography*. 2nd ed. Toronto: University of Toronto Press.

————, ed. 1972. *A Synoptic History of Classical Rhetoric*. New York: Random House.

Pan Chao (aka Ban Chao). 1968. "Lessons for Women." In *Pan Chao: Foremost Woman Scholar of China, First Century* A.D., translated by Nancy Lee Swann, 82–99. New York: Russell & Russell.

Schilb, John. 1986. "The History of Rhetoric and the Rhetoric of History." *Pre/Text* 7.1–2: 11–34.

Smith-Rosenberg, Carroll. 1985. *Disorderly Conduct: Visions of Gender in Victorian America*. New York: Oxford University Press.

Solomon, Barbara Miller. 1985. *In the Company of Educated Women: A History of Women and Higher Education in America*. New Haven: Yale University Press.

Vivian, Barbara G. 1994. "Gertrude Buck on Metaphor: Twentieth Century Concepts in a Late Nineteenth-Century Dissertation." *Rhetoric Society Quarterly*. 24.3–4: 96–104.

Washington, Booker T. 1963. *Up from Slavery: An Autobiography*. Garden City, N.Y.: Doubleday and Co.

Wesley, Charles H. 1971. "Hallie Quinn Brown." In *Notable American Women 1607–1950, A Biographical Dictionary*, edited by Edward T. James, 1: 253–54. Cambridge: Harvard University Press.

Epilogue

We need to know the writing of the past, and know it differently than we have ever known it; not to pass on a tradition but to break its hold over us.

Adrienne Rich

The Future of Feminist Rhetorical Criticism

Diane Helene Miller

Histories are powerful; much is at stake in their writing, and in writing about their writing.

Susan Jarratt

Among the humanistic disciplines, feminist work in rhetoric, as Susan C. Jarratt has pointed out, "has come rather lately into the conversation" (1990b, 193). Feminist literary critics have been actively critiquing their canon and excavating women's lost writings for over two decades, while feminist historians have been building a considerable body of scholarship, tracing the lives of women whose activities have been ignored by traditional approaches to history. In contrast, while notable feminist work in rhetoric first appeared at approximately the same time,[1] feminist rhetorical critics began a similar "re-vision" less than a decade ago. Calling upon their faith in interdisciplinary practice, feminists in rhetoric have used the insights of those in other fields as both a means of catching up and a way of overcoming disciplinary limits. As H. Leslie Steeves explains, feminist scholarship in communication studies is particularly indebted to this sort of borrowing: "feminist studies in communication are relatively new, and most scholars who explicitly utilize feminist theory must draw upon at least some works by scholars in other fields of study" (1988, 13). For Steeves this necessity is a fortunate one, for "feminist communication scholars have much to learn from what is being done in many other disciplines."

However, some of the forays of feminist communication scholars into other disciplines have been blamed for the relative lag in gaining feminist ground within the field. Barbara A. Biesecker, for example, claims that "in following too closely the tracks opened up by feminist theorists working in disciplines other than Speech Communication . . .

feminist rhetorical critics have had a tendency to derail Rhetoric" (1992b, 88). The result has been an uneasy fit between scholarly goals and critical methods, characterized by omissions and gaps that leave a feminist rhetorical criticism wanting.

In the first part of this chapter I examine the ways in which such importations have characterized feminist critical practice in rhetoric thus far, and why borrowed methods have failed to produce a significant upheaval in traditional practice or even to yield an identifiable feminist critical practice. I look first at the evolution of feminist literary criticism, from which rhetoric has primarily borrowed feminist insights, examining its key approaches in order to identify the ways in which these have been adopted by feminist rhetorical critics. By internalizing the priorities of feminists in other fields, feminist scholarship has achieved some visibility in major speech communication journals. Nevertheless, this work has often been dismissed or ghettoized because it is, in essence, an answer to a question we have not adequately articulated. I conclude that in rhetoric a reinvention of a new kind is needed and that while it may borrow from without, it must be generated and find its principles from within. In the second part of the chapter I examine what I perceive as a growing pattern of approaches that undertake such a task, engaging with canonical texts as a means of articulating the nature of an oppression and a rebellion that is specifically rhetorical.[2] I conclude with a consideration of some future trends in feminist rhetorical criticism.

Feminist Literary Criticism:
The Roots of Feminist Rhetorical Criticism

The literary critic Elaine Showalter has identified two "distinct modes" of feminist criticism that, she suggests, are often misunderstood and conflated. The first, "feminist critique," represents an ideological engagement with traditional texts that uncovers how these texts have marginalized or excluded women. This critical mode affirms the "authority of experience" in rereading such texts, rejecting adherence to any one theory in favor of an unmitigated commitment to pluralism. For Showalter such an approach represents only an evolutionary phase in feminist literary criticism; it is limited both by its rejection of theory and by its dependence on the very texts it seeks to undermine. Its value for feminists, therefore, is finally negligible: "So long as we look to androcentric models for our most basic principles—even if we revise them by adding the feminist frame of reference—we are learning nothing new . . . I do not think that feminist criticism can find a usable past in the androcentric critical tradition" (1985, 247).

Instead, Showalter suggests, feminist critics must redirect our efforts to a second mode of criticism, one "that is genuinely women centered, independent, and intellectually coherent" (1985, 247). Showalter coins the term "gynocriticism" to describe this second and more highly evolved critical approach, claiming that the move from androcentric to gynocentric criticism is, in the 1980s, already under way. Gynocriticism is not simply *a* feminist critical approach but, for Showalter, *the* feminist critical approach. Locating its emergence as far back as Patricia Meyer Spacks's *The Female Imagination* (1975), she suggests that Spacks's study "inaugurated a new period of feminist literary history" in which women's writing became "the central project of feminist literary study." This "new" project revolves around a clearly articulated, and privileged, set of questions that center on one primary issue: "the essential question of difference" between women and men, masculinity and femininity (Showalter, 1985, 248).

Entering late into the conversation, feminist rhetorical critics naturally took advantage of the progress already made by feminist literary critics. For rhetorical scholars the emphasis on the rediscovery and re-reading of women's texts at once affirmed the priority of such a project and minimized or dismissed the value of earlier literary critical approaches. Nor were feminists in rhetoric alone in privileging this approach. A focus on differences between men and women had also gained status in the work of feminists in psychology, most notably in Carol Gilligan's much cited *In a Different Voice* (1982) and Mary Field Belenky et al.'s successor to Gilligan, *Women's Ways of Knowing* (1986). An emphasis on sexual difference likewise informed European feminism, despite its notable dissimilarities from American feminism (Showalter 1985).

Unacknowledged in these methodological importations, and perhaps unrecognized by feminist literary and rhetorical critics alike, was the way that the earlier feminist critique of literature grounded and justified the gynocritical project that subsequently evolved by linking the practice of feminist criticism with the particular configuration of patriarchal literary history. By looking back at the literary tradition, feminists articulated with some specificity the history and means of their disciplinary exclusion. They uncovered the operation of patriarchal systems and chronicled the precise ways in which women's voices were suppressed or omitted from the historical record, as well as how views of women were consistently distorted through literary stereotypes.[3] In other words, they enumerated the forms of their exclusion and crystallized the nature of their oppression, so as to achieve an understanding of what, precisely, they were struggling against. In so doing, they began to formulate the most effective means for their resistance. This insight has been overlooked in later discussions of feminist criticism and disregarded in the adoption of more recent approaches by rhetorical critics.

Feminist rhetorical critics have, to put it simply, borrowed a revolution. The move was not entirely unfounded; earlier feminist work in other fields had identified the patriarchal, hierarchical structure of objectivism that undergirded the history of Western intellectual inquiry and pervaded traditional epistemology. It took little imagination to extend this critique to rhetoric: judging by the absence of women from the pages of our scholarship and history, it was all too apparent that "the canon in history of rhetoric, as in the rest of the European intellectual tradition, excludes women" (Jarratt 1990a, 27). The justification for feminist intervention was thus abundantly provided by observing that women had been silenced and that, even when they found or created opportunities to speak, their words were largely erased from or hidden by history. It was enough to know that the history of rhetoric was oppressive, without entangling ourselves in the depressing work of examining precisely where or how. Instead, following Showalter, it seemed much more productive to seek out another tradition, a recovery of what had been lost. It is this goal, characterized by the exclusive focus on excavating and revaluing women's texts, that has largely guided feminist rhetorical criticism thus far.

In rhetoric, the failure of this gynocritical approach to enhance our understanding of women's communicative practices significantly, or to account for the force and nature of women's exclusion from history adequately, now compels us to question its limitations for feminist rhetorical scholarship. Despite what Carole Spitzack and Kathryn Carter (1987) identify as the increased visibility of feminist work within the discipline of speech communication, many feminists agree that to date the overall effects of feminist criticism on the field have been minimal. Karlyn Kohrs Campbell suggests that despite the appearance of feminist-oriented articles in major journals, "the influence of such critiques on theory, criticism, and pedagogy has remained small" (1989b, 212). Spitzack and Carter caution that "although female visibility and diversity *may* contribute to a knowledge of women's communication, the suggestion that mere presence of strength in numbers signals understanding may be overly optimistic" (1987, 401).

Such observations echo those of historian Joan Wallach Scott when she describes both the value and the limitations of a focus on recovering women in history, an approach she terms "her-story." Scott claims that this approach, "by piling up the evidence about women in the past . . . refutes the claims of those who insist that women had no history . . . [however,] it tends to isolate women as a special and separate topic of history" (1988, 20). This reinscription of women's marginal status remains a risk in any gynocritical feminist enterprise, as historian Linda Gordon observes: "One of the worst things about the emphasis on difference is that it allows the development of new 'fields' and the adoption of new styles of critique that do not fundamentally challenge the structure of the disciplines. It does not force the reinterpretation of all existing interpretation on the basis of new evidence but instead creates, potentially, pockets of women's literature, women's psychology, women's morality, and so forth" (1986, 27). By focusing narrowly on individuals to the exclusion of structures, gynocriticism prevents the recognition that women are not only *told* not to speak or prevented, as individuals, from speaking, but that their silencing is effected by configurations of gender that are built into the very definition of rhetoric as it has been conceived in Western society from its beginning.

By assuming and emphasizing the differences between women and men, feminists limit themselves to approaching history as a "battle of the sexes." Their struggle becomes one that is therefore only addressed by a search for role models, as the liberation of women and other oppressed groups is seen as dependent upon the ability of those groups to "win equality." The focus is directed to the "great men and women" whose individual achievements are interpreted as steps toward ending inequality. The problem with looking at such success stories is that it reinforces a view of institutions and structures as given or invariable, so that change consists only in the movement of individuals and groups to greater or lesser status within those institutions. This approach, therefore, encourages tokenism and reinforces the invisibility of other minority group members.

Such an approach has characterized much of feminist rhetorical criticism thus far.[4] Campbell, the most widely published and well-known feminist rhetorical critic, represents this approach to feminist criticism by recovering the work of great women speakers in history. Her two-volume work, *Man Cannot Speak for Her* (1989a), highlights "key texts" of women who spoke out in favor of causes such as suffrage, abolition, and temperance in the late eighteenth and early nineteenth centuries. Campbell's work is largely responsible for introducing feminist criticism to the field of rhetoric and has made a tremendous contribution in terms of recovering women's voices and recognizing the achievements of important historical figures whose texts were nearly lost.

Biesecker at once applauds Campbell's work for its contribution and cautions against a too-hasty alignment with her views. Biesecker characterizes the project of supplementing the canon with women's texts as an "affirmative action approach," noting that accumulating women's texts does not necessarily result in challenging existing epistemology. She warns that a continuing focus on individual subjects may reinforce, rather than undermine, accepted principles of canon formation, in particular the focus on individuals at the expense of collective contributions: "The mere accumulation of texts does not guarantee that our ways of knowing will change when the grounds for their inclusion and, likewise, our way of deciphering them, remain the same" (1992a, 144–45). Other feminist rhetorical critics have echoed her concerns about an approach that is characterized by a turning away from oppressive structures rather than an engagement with them.[5]

The consequence of this approach is an absence of feminist rhetorical self-knowledge. A focus on the difference between men and women, which Showalter advocates as a means of putting women at the center of study, has for rhetorical scholars instead pushed women again to the margins in an ultimately ineffective theoretical intervention. Recent discussions of this problem have, as a result, focused on the need to engage with dominant disciplinary concepts and to confront traditional texts. Spitzack and Carter express this new imperative: "Improved understanding becomes possible when taken for granted assumptions concerning the questions asked and the strategies employed by researchers are critically examined. Such analysis not only demands attention to *women's* communication, but in the process of critique, dominant assumptive bases in communication research come under scrutiny" (1987, 401). Campbell agrees that "in the end, a feminist critique of rhetorical studies is not simply a demand for the inclusion of materials by and about women; it is a challenge to rethink fundamental assumptions in our theory, criticism, and pedagogy" (1989b, 214).

This shift in focus clearly reverses the direction of change Showalter (1985) supports for literary criticism. Yet it is precisely because feminist literary critics have already critiqued the received categories of their discipline that they are ready to revise the inherited tradition or even to create new categories.[6] When seen in this light, their earlier efforts were not misdirected but, instead, crucial in providing a foundation and a direction for the work ahead. Showalter's advocacy of gynocriticism, from this perspective, represents not a break with the past but an emergent approach, fundamentally interconnected with and dependent upon previous approaches.

The process through which the gynocritical approach in literary criticism emerged has no parallel in feminist rhetorical criticism thus far. This, then, is the juncture at which feminist rhetorical criticism and feminist literary criticism must, at least temporarily, part company. At this point in our history, some feminist rhetorical critics recognize a need to challenge the foundations of our own work, questioning the stability of the very categories—"woman" and "authorship"—upon which investigations of women's history have been built (Jarratt 1992, 1). In taking seriously these new questions, scholars turn from the issue of the inclusion of neglected women speakers to the investigation of how gender itself is present in the organization of historical knowledge, a shift marked by a (re)turn to our own history and texts. This not only enables us to articulate for others in our field how a feminist perspective fundamentally challenges traditional rhetorical criticism. Perhaps, more importantly, this engagement with the past, *our* past, is a key to self-knowledge and to moving beyond received history. It permits us to disclose the nature and the structure of our oppression, and to see how it operates, how it has been perpetuated and reinscribed through history, and how we might conceive of it, and ourselves, otherwise.

Feminist rhetorical critics must return to the phase we have omitted, and some have already set out in this new direction, recognizing now that "in rhetoric as well as in other disciplines we needed not only women's history but gendered readings of male authored texts" (Jarratt 1990b, 192). While affirming that an emphasis on retrieving women's texts "was both politically necessary and unquestionably powerful at a certain political-historical moment" in feminist rhetorical criticism (Biesecker 1992a, 87), feminist critics have recently (re)turned to the project that some had thought unnecessary, tracing the origins of their oppression and so identifying the means of an effective resistance.

Feminist rhetorical critics have thus arrived at the stage of critique and revision. If, as Biesecker notes, the objective of feminist criticism "is not only to reveal the manner in which seemingly universal and disinterested standards . . . disguise sexist commitment," but "also to reinvent them otherwise" (1992b, 88), this phase involves undertaking both of these projects at once. On the one hand, feminists reread traditional texts for the purpose of pointing out the exclusion of women, the structures of gender that are hidden by claims of objectivity, the marginalization of women's voices, and the privileging of male interests. On the other hand, they "reinvent them otherwise," engaging in strategies of rereading that permit the infusion of their own experiences into their interpretations of the texts, revalidating their role in the history of rhetoric. Such work relies on a perspective that the historian Joan Kelly (1984) has called "doubled vision," a way of seeing that permits scholars to read themselves back into history even as they catalog the means by which they have been excluded from it.

This dual project of critique and revision is the source of promising possibilities. This sort of project creates a space in which feminists in rhetoric can undertake their own revolution, rejecting a stance of isolation and articulating a resistance to the rhetorical powers that be. Such a multivalent project that at once reads one's *ex*clusion from a text while simultaneously rereading the possibilities for one's *in*clusion in the text relies implicitly on particular conceptions of the nature and structure of language, the relation between text and reader, and the possibilities inherent in the reading process itself. It requires, first, a move to regarding the "masterpieces" or "great works" of the field in a nontraditional way. It is a move Roland Barthes (1979) would identify as a shift from "work" to "text," from "great works" unavailable for appropriation (and thus subject only to critique) to "texts" available for a variety of readings and thus subject to revision. By availing themselves of his notion of text, feminist critics introduce a space for themselves in the writings of the rhetorical canon, soliciting an invitation for their own engagement in the process of reinventing history.

For Barthes and those who follow him, meaning results from an active collaboration between reader and text. Language is viewed as "polysemic" and unstable, comprised of dominant meanings that can remain privileged only so long as they continually suppress alternate meanings. This insight has generated a cluster of concepts, loosely collected under the heading "deconstruction." In this view language can be interrogated and pulled apart to free those alternate, subordinated meanings. Feminist critics involved in critical/revisionary projects engage this deconstructive understanding that language is inherently plural and that it thus permits a variety of decodings. In recognizing this character of texts, the focus of criticism itself shifts so that "the quality of *reading* rather than the quality of the object then takes center stage and the critic is more producer than evaluator or consumer" (Schudson 1991, 58). Deconstruction thereby introduces the possibility of reading a text *both* in a manner that exposes the workings of the dominant culture *and* for the purpose of generating resistant readings that oppose or modify that dominant meaning.

In the remainder of this essay I will examine the status of the feminist critique of rhetoric as it appears in published scholarship in the field. More specifically, I will survey representative articles of feminist criticism that have turned to critique and revision as a means of redressing rhetorical history, and I will examine the ways in which such texts have begun the project of rethinking the rhetorical canon through the lens of gender. In elaborating some shared approaches among these articles, I will borrow terms and concepts from deconstructionists working in related fields to illuminate particular dynamics of various author-text-critic interactions.

Current Trends in Feminist Rhetorical Criticism

In their "Introduction" to Joan Kelly's *Women, History, and Theory,* Blanche W. Cook et al. write, "feminist theory represents a transcendence, a turning of 'alienation into a positive position, a chosen stance.' Woman's social experience as outsider provides a different reality that can illuminate the social nature of her existence" (1984, xxv). In terms of reading historical texts, this outsider's view offers the potential for new insights, the possibility of liberating versions of history that have remained suppressed thus far. To undertake the project of reading history from an outsider's perspective calls implicitly upon a deconstructionist view of historical narrative, a belief that the language in which history has been preserved has the potential to yield different interpretations and multiple readings. In what follows, I describe some of the approaches critics have employed in undertaking these rereadings.

Susan C. Jarratt advocates a practice she calls "gendered analysis," which seeks out the influence of gender where the subject of women does not appear in history. She identifies a shift among feminist critics characterized by a "movement from a discovery of women's history— i.e., women in history—to a diversification of projects focused not only on the presence of biological women but on gender as a discursive and social category" (1990b, 192–93). She calls for a rereading of traditional discourse with the intention of seeking out not (only) "woman" as a category, but the structures of gender that relegate some meanings to marginal status while elevating others to high visibility and positions of importance. In addition, Jarratt wants to ask different questions of history than are raised by a women's history approach: "I feel we should be asking not only 'Who are the neglected women rhetoricians?' but also 'How does gender give meaning to the organization and perception of historical knowledge?'" (1990b, 193). She explicitly distinguishes her project from that of such critics as Campbell (1989a), who clearly focuses on answering the former question. Jarratt, by choosing instead the latter, "rejects a universal, ahistorical definition of gender" while regarding "gender as a position from which to act politically" (1990b, 197).

Campbell's work, in fact, emerges in some recent essays as a foil against which feminist critics define their own challenges to traditional rhetorical history. Biesecker argues that Campbell's approach "resolidifies rather than undoes the ideology of individualism that is the condition of possibility for the emergence of the received history of Rhetoric" (1992a, 144). Invoking poststructuralism, she reiterates Jarratt's advocacy of a critical approach that "shifts the focus of historical inquiry from the question 'who is speaking' . . . to the question 'what play of forces made it possible for a particular speaking subject to emerge?'" Only when we come to understand "subjectivity as an historical articulation," she explains, will we recognize our need for "a new history of Rhetoric that begins by thinking the subject as 'historical through and through'" (148).[7]

Jarratt's work is driven by her belief that "If the Western intellectual tradition is not only a product of men, but constituted by masculinity, then transformation comes not only from women finding women authors but also from a gendered rereading of that masculine rhetoric" (1992, 2). Jarratt elsewhere advocates a method she calls "'overreading' an 'underread' text" (1990a, 38), a means of disrupting the smooth transmission of historical discourse by challenging received meanings. Her aim is to locate specific instances of exclusion in their historical contexts: "The goal of overreading is not only to retrieve a text from an anonymity it may have been forced into by a philosophical or 'masculine' discourse; it seeks to recover a fuller narrative, to identify the social conditions of its production." By taking a step beyond the search for women in history, this practice addresses itself to structures, offering "a way to reread hegemonic texts . . . tracing the itinerary of male desire with a new critical perspective" (1990a, 39).

In this way the terminology and procedures of deconstruction are useful feminist tools. As John Fiske explains in his article "Television: Polysemy and Popularity," from a deconstructive point of view, language is unstable as a result of its emergence from particular sociopolitical contexts. His explanation reveals how language may be a key to recovering struggles that have otherwise disappeared from the historical record: "terms (in language) bear the history of social conflict and negotiation and whenever and wherever used they enter that conflict once again" (1991, 349). Any given meaning of a term, therefore, is established only by successfully suppressing other meanings, which nevertheless remain part of its history and are available for reclamation in subsequent struggles. In this way the apparent endurance of meaning is illusory, for as Joan Wallach Scott explains, "Any unitary concept rests on—contains—repressed or negated material and so is unstable, not unified" (1988, 7).

Thus when language is used by a dominant group its meaning is never finally established or resolved. All texts have a quality Fiske terms "semiotic excess," so that although "dominant ideological values are structured into the text by the use of dominant codes and thus of dominant encodings of social experience," at the same time "the dominant reading does not exhaust the semiotic potential of the text" (1991, 359). What remains after a dominant reading is an "excess" that awaits an oppositional group to activate its potential. In Fiske's view, the encounter with dominant historical texts by a subordinate group need not lead only to a negative hermeneutics, because all texts are open to negotiation by their readers.

With a notion of semiotic excess, the author's control over meaning is mitigated by the instability of language, so that an author's ideology and intention can never finally circumscribe the potential "legitimate" readings of the text. For members of a subordinate group reading a dominant text, semiotic excess marks the failure of the hegemonic inscription of dominant ideology and opens up the possibility of constructing or "collaborating in" alternative, and subversive, readings. For feminist scholars, semiotic excess provides a means through which to defamiliarize accepted meanings of traditional texts and unearth forgotten struggles and long-hidden alternatives, providing a premise upon which feminist intervention into the canon may proceed. Specifying the ways in which our disciplinary history has been constructed upon unrecognized and unexamined assumptions about gender thus provides an entrée for the feminist foray into the traditionally male territory of rhetorical history.

In her article "The Taming of *Polos/Polis:* Rhetoric as an Achievement without Woman," Jane Sutton takes feminist criticism on a whirlwind tour of this territory as she highlights competing and contradictory meanings of history as a rich source of feminist insight. Sutton traces a route through rhetoric's history as it parallels and intersects with the history of the category of "woman," arguing that neither the subjugation of rhetoric nor the disappearance of woman from history was a natural or inevitable process. Sutton sets out to read the history of women's rebellion against her subjugation. She employs a notion she terms "undertow," describing a semiotic excess that works against and undermines hegemonic meaning. "Even though there is a text of rhetoric held together by chronological sequence, an undertow will not let the image of rhetoric stay on the proper track" (1992, 110). The undertow provides the mechanism through which, in true polysemic fashion, "Plato's writing resists his intentions" (112) with respect to the taming of desire, of rhetoric, and of woman.

Sutton engages the intertwined texts of rhetorical history and of "woman" in a project that re-visions as well as critiques rhetorical history. Describing her approach as one that works against the grain of traditional textual logic, she warns that in her essay, "there will be 'turns'—deviations from customary or literal usage—against the 'logic' sanctioned by the narrative, a 'logic' that entails the possibility of rhetoric's conceptualization" (98). Sutton's deconstructive practice encompasses not only resistant reading but resistant writing. In exposing the struggle that underlies the language of history, she finds the means through which to dramatize a rebellion of her own.

A conception of language as the source of potentially empowering contradictions is widely shared by this group of feminist critics.[8] Such critics see multiplicity as the key to empowerment, as the process of feminist reading reveals the imprint of gender in patriarchal discourse and the remnants of an alternative and largely suppressed view of history. To explore the possibilities inherent in this view, to shift from an outsider stance into the role of participant or collaborator, is to move from a project of feminist critique to that of feminist revision, encompassing Showalter's "revisionary imperative" and "feminist reading." Having elucidated some of the ways that dominant meanings are informed by gender, critics involved in this endeavor theorize alternate reading practices in order to discover other possible configurations of gender, and thus other possible meanings.

For ultimately it is not only the opportunity for critique but the potential for reinvention that provides the impetus for a feminist engagement with the texts of the rhetorical tradition. To read in this way is to usurp power from the dominant ideology, and Fiske offers an optimistic view of how such a practice can empower members of nondominant groups. He identifies "a power relationship between text and reader that parallels the relationship between the dominant and subordinate classes in society. In both instances authority attempts to impose itself but is met with a variety of variously successful strategies of resistance or modification that change, subvert or reject the authoritatively proposed meaning" (1991, 349). Fiske's insistence on the availability of oppositional readings within dominant texts lends support to Susan Jarratt's (1992) call for a gendered rereading of history. Fiske notes, "varying readings need not work by rejecting the dominant ideology, but rather by articulating their oppositionality in relation to it. The dominant and the oppositional are simultaneously present in both the text and its readings. The dominant is found in the preferred reading, the oppositional in the semiotic excess that the preferred reading attempts to marginalize, but that can never be finally or totally controlled by the dominant" (1991, 359–60).

The revisionary imperative is well served by deconstructive practice, for as Fiske explains, "The main enterprise of deconstruction is to deconstruct texts to reveal their instability, their gaps, their internal contradictions and their arbitrary textuality, and thus their potential for readings that are produced by the audiences" (356). Deconstruction enables critics to challenge received meanings of traditional texts by locating the instabilities within them. Deconstruction discloses the particular oppositions a text embraces and the ways in which such oppositions are ordered hierarchically and function oppressively. Such a practice has obvious utility for nondominant groups who wish to disclose the power dynamics of dominant texts. As a strategy for feminist rereading, deconstruction is authorized by the notion that women's invisibility in history results from their position in spaces "inbetween" [sic] language, hidden in such a way that their existence goes unnoticed even while it "shores up the center and makes *it* visible" (Biesecker 1992b, 91).

More than tools for identifying the suppression of women and the influence of gender, deconstructive readings provide means of attaining Joan Kelly's "doubled vision" (1984) in order to transform women's marginalized status in traditional texts into a position of empowerment. Biesecker, quoting Hélène Cixous, asserts that "by using, without indulging in or celebrating, her marginalization as that which marks both a contact with and a detachment from the system of linguistic forces positioning her, woman can 'become *at will* the stand-taker and initiator, for her *own* right, in every symbolic system, in every political process'" (1992b, 91). For Cixous, women's invisibility permits them to "steal" self-serving meanings from discourse while escaping detection until it is too late to stop them. Their elusiveness is guaranteed, Biesecker explains, because women's "presence can be detected only to the extent that it opens a horizon and a center that effects its disappearance," thus insuring that "they can pilfer the discourse that regulates the system and move it in a new direction" (1992b, 91).

Cixous's adoption/adaptation of the French word *voler*, which means both "to fly" and "to steal," offers a deconstructive approach designed to empower women to speak and write of their own experiences, to create *écriture féminine* (feminine writing). Biesecker, with Cixous, advocates "'stealing' or unfixing the syntax, the grammar, and the signs of the dominant discourse so as to make it possible for new meanings to circulate and 'fly'" (1992b, 93). Given that there is no "pure" point of departure for developing a feminine language, Biesecker quotes Jacques Derrida's instruction that we must "begin wherever we are." A deconstructive practice provides a place from which to start, a means of "win[ning] a rhetorical beginning by 'stealing' back and recoding particular signs within the phallocentric system" (Biesecker 1992b, 93). When the phallocentric system in question is rhetorical history, Cixous's method provides a means through which feminists can transgress established boundaries by "stealing" meanings that lie buried beneath dominant discourse, in order to generate possibilities for alternative views of history.

Sutton locates the possibility for resistance to rhetoric's / women's subordination in precisely the sort of illegitimate activity Cixous advocates. In her rereading of rhetoric's history, Sutton takes advantage of the inherent plurality of language as a means of "flying" with it elsewhere than its intended destination. Discussing Sutton's critical method, Janice Hocker Rushing writes that even as she demonstrates how woman and rhetoric resist their own subjugation, "Sutton enacts a sort of resistance herself," in an essay that "replaces the usual recitation of material facts with analogical collages and elevates tropology over *logos* as the most appropriate means of articulating an alternative history of Rhetoric" (Rushing 1992, 84).

The various conceptions of reading proposed by feminist scholars illustrate that there is no one prescription for feminist re-vision, no single set of practices that constitute *the* methodology for gendered rereading. Instead, re-visionary reading is an umbrella term encompassing a variety of approaches, some already delineated and many more yet to be articulated or attempted. Just as resistance and struggle in other contexts are continual processes rather than end products, so feminist practices of reading must be understood as ongoing and never completed. Such an understanding goes beyond the more traditional hermeneutic goal of producing a definitive reading or, more bluntly, "mastering" a text. Instead, the text may be seen as forever "in process," comprised of configurations of identity that change with varying sociohistorical locations. Even the concept of gender itself, and thus any approach of gendered rereading, must take into account the way that gender is variously structured with respect to other variables, including race, class, and sexual orientation.

The adoption of deconstructionist insights in feminist critical practice has yielded a conception of "women" that differs significantly from the construction of the subject in traditional rhetorical approaches, or even in the approaches of earlier feminist work. Differing conceptions of identity provide the fulcrum around which the debate over feminist historiographic methods takes place. A "women's history" or "her-story" approach relies upon a politics of gender as identity, whereas a deconstructionist approach regards gender as signification, a discursive category rather than an identifiable class. Those feminist historians of rhetoric who fall into the latter camp explicitly distance themselves from the politics of identity approach, instead articulating gender in terms of specific sociohistorical configurations.

The reconceptualization of identity in terms of discursive categories introduces a space within which feminists can transcend a focus on differences between men and women and redirect their attention to differences among and within women. In practice, a few feminist critics do discuss the importance of accounting for differences among women, though oddly without ever discussing the specific configurations (i.e., race, class, sexual orientation) whose articulation would contribute to a comprehensive feminist analysis. That is, despite acknowledgment of the *need* to address other forms of difference, only gender is ever addressed. Biesecker, for example, explains that by employing a conception of subjectivity that is not premised on individualism, "the critic taking up the project of rewriting the history of Rhetoric would be required to come to terms with rather than efface the formidable differences between and amongst women and, thus, address the real fact that different women, due to their various positions in the social structure, have available to them different rhetorical possibilities and, similarly, are constrained by different rhetorical limits" (1992a, 157). Yet neither she nor any of these other critics went beyond comment to pursue an area of analysis that, it would appear, offers such promise for expanding the insights of a feminist critical practice.

Conclusions

As recently as 1989 Campbell was able to assert, "There is, as yet, nothing that can be clearly identified as feminist rhetorical criticism" (1989b, 218). To date, few would contest her claim. Self-consciously feminist scholarship has appeared with varying frequency in mainstream journals and in special journal issues devoted to feminist criticism. Nevertheless, in relation to the dominant rhetorical tradition, feminist criticism remains marginalized, having failed thus far to achieve a radical revision of any fundamental rhetorical concepts. Thus, while a "women's history" approach to criticism has made some progress in increasing the availability and even the status of women's texts within the field, this very "success" has often prevented serious consideration of other feminist challenges.

While literary critics such as Showalter (1985) have dismissed the role of the feminist critique of traditional texts in identifying a "usable past" for feminist critics, rhetorical critics have begun to recognize that a period of direct confrontation and engagement with the texts of the dominant tradition is a crucial step in articulating the nature of our own disciplinary struggle and in formulating a strategy for change. If we fail first to challenge the critical assumptions grounded in the ancient origins of rhetoric and reinforced by centuries of exclusionary practices, we have only the inherited critical categories through which to examine and evaluate women's texts. In fact, then, the feminist critique and revisionary imperative are necessary for rhetorical criticism, as they were for literary criticism, precisely because they prevent us from unreflectively employing traditional categories.

Nevertheless, breaking the hold of the past does not mean rejecting that past entirely, for its stories have also been our stories, holding clues to the ways many different women have lived. Whatever is of value in that past thus belongs to us as well. With this in mind, recent feminist engagements with the works of the rhetorical tradition have aimed at moving beyond a women's history approach to a feminist criticism that employs the tools of deconstruction as a means of re-visioning the past. Calling upon an understanding of historical discourse as at once "works" and "texts," feminists critique the "great works" in terms of their marginalization and exclusion of women, while collaborating with these same texts to generate alternative readings. By taking a nontraditional view of language, this project reconfigures traditional author/text and critic/text relationships. Moreover, such an approach has the potential to overcome the limitations of earlier critical work further by reconceptualizing gender as a discursive category, a "fluctuating identity" (Riley 1988) continuously (re)constituted by and subject to changing social, political, and historical configurations.

The idea that categories long understood to designate characteristics of individual and group identity may in fact be built into the very conception of such fundamental notions as "speakers," "texts," "history," and even "rhetoric" itself, has profound implications. Even the basic assumption that rhetoric must be persuasive is challenged by the suggestion that there are types of influence that, while not intended to persuade, still fall within the domain of rhetoric.[9] Similarly, the need to see rhetoric as comprised of multiple, and at times discordant, realms is introduced by the suggestion that rhetoric is fundamentally divided into a foreground and a background, with public, "masculine" communication characteristic of the foreground and private, "feminine" communication relegated to a separate and distinctive background realm.[10] Such a view calls for distinct rhetorical theories to account for the specific kinds of communicative behavior found in each of these two realms and points to the possibility of identifying even more intricately layered realms of rhetoric. Once we begin to envision alternatives to traditional understandings of rhetoric, we begin to glimpse the vast array of possibilities that have been suppressed by too-rigid definitions of basic disciplinary concepts.

A commitment to exploring the ways in which identity categories *constitute* rhetoric requires a willingness to reconceptualize the field from the ground up—not dismissing nor, certainly, forgetting the past but "seeing it again" by looking for gendered structures and institutions, rather than gendered individuals, and seeking out changes as well as continuity in representations of gender. However, such a commitment must mean looking beyond gender as an isolated category to the intersection of gender with variables of race, class, sexual orientation, and other variables of stratification—looking, therefore, to the differences *among* and even *within* women rather than focusing exclusively, or even primarily, on the differences between the sexes. For example, multicultural perspectives argue against using white women's communication to draw universal conclusions about *all* women's communication, because elements such as race and class interact with gender to influence communicative practices. Thus feminist scholarship must define its boundaries and limit its generalizations within the local contexts and configurations of identity upon which it draws. Multicultural scholars urge that we need theories and methods that are developed for, and suitable for exploring the experiences of, women who are marginalized and oppressed by other factors in addition to gender.[11] Precisely because the dominant tradition has failed to acknowledge or identify differences among women, feminist criticism of women's texts requires first a consideration of these previously ignored differences and an effort to theorize the interdependence of these variables as they influence conceptions of subjectivity, discourse, and knowledge.

It is too soon to judge what effect this new direction will have on mainstream rhetoric, and, as always, the forces aligned against change are numerous, varied, and powerful. Yet through these feminist interventions, at least, "tradition" is no longer entirely on the opposing side. Through their rereadings and recuperations, feminist scholars have laid claim to a multifaceted view of history that leaves its status ambiguous, no longer so clearly marked by sameness and unrelieved suppression. Whether this newly re-formed history will eventually force a broader questioning of the dominant tradition, as many feminist critics hope, or will continue to be marginalized remains to be seen. What has been achieved, in any case, is no less than a revolution in the conceptual possibilities available for retracing a rhetorical history, animating a potential for creating anew our history in a way that permits us to create, anew, our future.

Notes

An earlier version of this chapter was presented at the annual meeting of the Speech Communication Association, November 1994, New Orleans. I am grateful to Cindy Jenefsky, Celeste Condit, and Linda Grant for their helpful comments and suggestions.

1. For example, Campbell (1973) and Kramer (1974).

2. I use the word *pattern* here in a deliberately ambiguous fashion. I do not wish to overemphasize continuities between approaches at the expense of discontinuities, nor to suggest a singularity of methods or intentions.

3. Similarly, in other fields, the feminist focus on recovering voices was preceded by analyses of the particular ways in which such voices were devalued or omitted. For example, Carol Gilligan (1982) studied the work of Lawrence Kohlberg, and her work responds specifically to the marginalization of women in his model of moral development.

4. See Biesecker (1992a), Campbell (1989b), Jarratt (1990b, 1992), and Spitzack and Carter (1987).

5. Susan Jarratt (1990b, 192), for example, warns of the danger "of developing a separate women's canon, or of simply adding a few titles to a list constructed within a masculinist system of knowledge and value."

6. However, this is not to suggest that such work is completed nor that feminist literary critics have overcome all of the problems involved in critiquing a tradition of which one is largely a part.

7. Peaden (1992) expresses a similar critique.

8. However, see Ballif (1992) for a dissenting view.

9. For example, the term *invitational rhetoric* has been applied to a particular sort of unintended influence, to convey the sense that opportunities for change may be made available ("invited") even where there is no intent to change the beliefs or behavior of others; see Foss and Griffin (1993), Foss and Foss (1994).

10. Griffin (1993). I have placed "masculine" and "feminine" in quotation marks to indicate that these terms refer to traditional stereotypes about masculinity and femininity, rather than to qualities that inhere in real men and women.

11. Stanback (1988). For example, Victoria Chen (1992, 226), examining the

identity construction of Asian-American women, notes the tension involved in maintaining what she terms a "bicultural" gender identity. She suggests that the differences between Chinese and American traditions are so vast that "Not only do these two realms of discourse have a limited basis for comparison, they also lack a shared vocabulary to even address the differences between [them]." Chen urges communication scholars to examine Asian-American women's identities to understand better how particular cultural differences affect women's communicative styles and strategies.

References

Ballif, Michelle. 1992. "Re/Dressing Histories: Or, On Re/covering Figures Who Have Been Laid Bare by Our Gaze." *Rhetoric Society Quarterly* 22.1: 91–98.

Barthes, Roland. 1979. "From Work to Text." In *Textual Strategies*, edited by Josué V. Harari, 73–81. Ithaca: Cornell University Press.

Belenky, Mary Field, Blythe McVicker Clinchy, Nancy Rule Goldberger, and Jill Mattuck Tarule. 1986. *Women's Ways of Knowing: The Development of Self, Voice, and Mind.* New York: Basic Books.

Biesecker, Barbara A. 1992a. "Coming to Terms with Recent Attempts to Write Women into the History of Rhetoric." *Philosophy and Rhetoric* 25.2: 140–61.

———. 1992b. "Towards a Transactional View of Rhetorical and Feminist Theory: Rereading Hélèn [*sic*] Cixous' *The Laugh of the Medusa*." *Southern Communication Journal* 57.2: 86–96.

Campbell, Karlyn Kohrs. 1973. "The Rhetoric of Women's Liberation: An Oxymoron." *Quarterly Journal of Speech* 59.1: 74–86.

———. 1989a. *Man Cannot Speak for Her: a Critical Study of Early Feminist Rhetoric.* 2 vols. New York: Praeger.

———. 1989b. "The Sound of Women's Voices." *Quarterly Journal of Speech* 75.2: 212–20.

Chen, Victoria. 1992. "The Construction of Chinese American Women's Identity." In *Women Making Meaning: New Feminist Directions in Communication*, edited by Lana F. Rakow, 225–43. New York: Routledge.

Cook, Blanche W., Alice Kessler-Harris, Clare Coss, Rosalind P. Petchesky, and Amy Swerdlow. 1984. "Introduction." In *Women, History, and Theory*, edited by Joan Kelly, xv–xxvi. Chicago: University of Chicago Press.

Fiske, John. 1991. "Television: Polysemy and Popularity." In *Critical Perspectives on Media and Society*, edited by Robert K. Avery and David Eason, 346–64. New York: Guilford Press.

Foss, Sonja K., and Cindy L. Griffin. 1993. "Beyond Persuasion: a Proposal for an Invitational Rhetoric." Unpublished paper, Speech Communication Association Convention Miami Beach, Florida.

Foss, Sonja K., and Karen A. Foss. 1994. *Inviting Transformation: Presentational Speaking for a Changing World.* Prospect Heights, Ill.: Waveland Press.

Gilligan, Carol. 1982. *In a Different Voice*. Cambridge: Harvard University Press.

Griffin, Cindy L. 1993. "Women as Communicators: Mary Daly's Hagography as Rhetoric." *Communication Monographs* 60.2: 158–77.

Gordon, Linda. 1986. "What's New in Women's History?" In *Feminist Studies/ Critical Studies*, edited by Teresa de Lauretis, 20–30. Bloomington: Indiana University Press.

Jarratt, Susan C. 1990a. "The First Sophists and Feminism: Discourses of the 'Other.'" *Hypatia* 5.1: 27–41.

———. 1990b. "Speaking to the Past: Feminist Historiography in Rhetoric." *Pre/ Text* 11.3–4: 190–209.

———. 1992. "Performing Feminisms, Histories, Rhetorics." *Rhetoric Society Quarterly* 22.1: 1–5.

Kelly, Joan. 1984. *Women, History, and Theory*. Chicago: University of Chicago Press.

Kolodny, Annette. 1985. "Dancing Through the Minefield: Some Observations on the Theory, Practice, and Politics of a Feminist Literary Criticism." In *The New Feminist Criticism: Essays on Women, Literature and Theory*, edited by Elaine Showalter, 144–67. New York: Pantheon Books.

Kramer, Cheris. 1974. "Women's Speech: Separate but Unequal?" *Quarterly Journal of Speech* 60.1: 14–24.

Peaden, Catherine. 1992. "Understanding Differently: Re-reading Locke's *Essay Concerning Human Understanding*." *Rhetoric Society Quarterly* 22.1: 75–90.

Rich, Adrienne. 1979. *On Lies, Secrets, and Silence: Selected Prose 1966–1978*. New York: W. W. Norton.

Riley, Denise. 1988. *Am I That Name? Feminism and the Category of Women in History*. Minneapolis: University of Minnesota Press.

Rushing, Janice Hocker. 1992. "Introduction to 'Feminist Criticism.'" *Southern Communication Journal* 57.2: 83–85.

Schudson, Michael. 1991. "The New Validation of Popular Culture: Sense and Sentimentality in Academia." In *Critical Perspectives on Media and Society*, edited by Robert K. Avery and David Eason, 49–68. New York: Guilford Press.

Scott, Joan Wallach. 1988. *Gender and the Politics of History*. New York: Columbia University Press.

Showalter, Elaine, ed. 1985. "Feminist Criticism in the Wilderness." In *The New Feminist Criticism: Essays on Women, Literature and Theory*, 243–70. New York: Pantheon Books.

Spacks, Patricia Meyer. 1975. *The Female Imagination*. New York: Alfred A. Knopf.

Spitzack, Carole, and Kathryn Carter. 1987. "Women in Communication Studies: a Typology for Revision." *Quarterly Journal of Speech* 73.4: 401–23.

Stanback, Marsha Houston. 1988. "What Makes Scholarship about Black Women and Communication Feminist Communication Scholarship?" *Women's Studies in Communication* 11.1: 28–31.

Steeves, H. Leslie. 1988. "What Distinguishes Feminist Scholarship in Communication Studies?" *Women's Studies in Communication* 11.1: 12–17.

Sutton, Jane. 1992. "The Taming of *Polos/Polis:* Rhetoric as an Achievement without Woman." *Southern Communication Journal* 57.2: 97–119.

Contributors

Julia Allen is an assistant professor of English at Sonoma State University, where she teaches courses in writing, rhetorical history and theory, and women's studies. Her research focuses on alternative or nontraditional rhetorics and has appeared in *Women's Studies Quarterly* and *Rhetoric Review*.

Virginia Allen is an associate professor of English and secondary education at Iowa State University, where she serves as graduate English examiner and teaches courses in history of rhetoric, pedagogical linguistics, and science fiction. She is co-author with Merriellen Kett of *College Writing Skills* and *How to Avoid Sexism: A Guide for Writers, Editors, and Publishers*. Her other publications include works on rhetorical memory and on the ethos of English departments, some short fiction, and biographical essays on turn-of-the-century writers. She is an active book reviewer and has done editorial work for *Vitae Scholasticae: The Bulletin of Educational Biography*.

Robert W. Cape Jr. is an assistant professor of classics and the director of gender Studies at Austin College, where he teaches a variety of courses in classical languages and rhetoric. He has published essays on Roman oratory and women in Antiquity. Currently, he is finishing a text, translation, and rhetorical commentary on Cicero's Catilinarian speeches and a book on oratory and social values at Rome.

Laurel Carrington is an associate professor of history at St. Olaf College, where she teaches courses in medieval and renaissance history. Her primary research area is Erasmus studies and she has published articles in the *Erasmus of Rotterdam Society Yearbook* and the *Archiv für Reformationsgeschichte*. Presently, she is preparing a manuscript, "Erasmus on the Way to Language: The Postmodern Critique of Western Humanism," and exploring the debate between Erasmus and Strassbourg reformer Martin Bucer.

Vicki Tolar Collins is an assistant professor of English at Oregon State University, where she directs the Writing Intensive Curriculum and teaches courses in rhetoric and composition, writing across the curriculum, and British literature. She is the author of articles on women in the history of rhetoric and writing across the curriculum.

Julia Dietrich is a professor of English at the University of Louisville, where she teaches courses in rhetorical theory, medieval literature, and medieval culture. Her research is on the social uses of literature in different historical eras, and her most recent book is *The Old Left in History and Literature*.

Jane Donawerth is an associate Professor of English and affiliate faculty in women's studies at the University of Maryland at College Park, where she teaches courses in early modern literature, history of rhetorical theory, and science fiction by women. Her books include *Shakespeare and the Sixteenth-Century Study of Language, Daughters of Frankenstein: Women Writing Science Fiction*, and *Utopian and Science Fiction by Women*. She is presently co-editing a volume, *Women, Writing, and the Reproduction of Culture in Tudor and Stuart Britain*, and is working on an anthology of rhetorical theory by women before 1900.

Cheryl Glenn is an associate professor of English at Oregon State University, where she teaches courses in rhetorical history and theory, composition theory, British literature, and grammar. Winner of her institution's 1992 Teaching Excellence Award and the 1996 Distinguished Professor Award, she will direct the College of Liberal Arts Center for Teaching Excellence from 1996 to 1998. She also received the 1995 Richard Braddock Award for the best article in *College Composition and Communication* and a 1995–1996 National Endowment for the Humanities research grant. Her books include *Rhetoric Retold: Regendering the Tradition from Antiquity through the Renaissance* (forthcoming) and *St. Martin's Guide to Teaching Writing* (co-authored with Robert Connors). She is currently at work on a first-year writing textbook.

Ekaterina V. Haskins is a doctoral student in the rhetorical studies department at the University of Iowa. Her research areas include the rhetoric of political movements of the early to mid–twentieth century, and ancient Greek language and rhetoric.

Clella I. Jaffe is an assistant professor of communication at George Fox University, where she teaches a variety of speech communication courses. Her research in rhetoric and culture has resulted in articles on the ethical precepts found in mothers' manuals, on the Russian Old Believers' chronemic system, and on the communication strategies of Jehovah's Witness students.

Barbara S. Lesko is the administrative research assistant in the Department of Egyptology at Brown University. Author of *The Remarkable Women of Ancient Egypt*, Lesko also edited, with both NEH and Mellon support, *Women's Earliest Records*, the proceedings of an international conference at Brown in 1987. She has contributed articles to numerous journals, magazines, and anthologies and has collaborated with her husband, Leonard H. Lesko, on a five-volume *Dictionary of Late Egyptian*.

Shirley Wilson Logan is an assistant professor of English at the University of Maryland, College Park, where she directs the Professional Writing Program and teaches courses in language, writing, and rhetoric. She is the editor of *With Pen and Voice: A Critical Anthology of Nineteenth-Century African-American Women* and has published articles on computers and writing, feminism and composition, Ida B. Wells, Frances E. W. Harper, and nineteenth-century black women's uses of literacy. She is currently writing a book on black women's persuasive discourse at the turn of the century.

Diane Helene Miller is the director of the Writing and Composition Center at East Tennessee State University. She recently completed a study examining the rhetoric of lesbian and gay civil rights discourse in the 1990s. She is a recipient of the Berkeley Fellowship, the University of Georgia University-wide Assistantship, and the AAUW Athenian Award for Outstanding Scholarship. Her publications include book chapters in the rhetoric of abortion and a co-authored essay on Southern women's rhetorical initiatives during the Civil War.

Nancy Weitz Miller is a visiting assistant professor of English at the University of Maine, where she teaches courses in early modern British literature and composition. She is the author of essays on Milton and Vives and is currently working on a book-length study of female chastity in early modern English literature.

Malcolm Richardson is a professor of English at Louisiana State University, where he directs the Writing Center and Technical Writing Program and teaches courses on Chaucer, Shakespeare, and professional writing. He is co-author of *An Anthology of Chancery English*, and the author of *The Chancery under Henry V* (forthcoming). His articles on the history of the English language and on rhetoric have appeared in *Speculum*, *Chaucer Review*, *American Journal of Legal History*, *Disputatio*, and elsewhere.

Christine Mason Sutherland is an associate professor in the Faculty of General Studies at the University of Calgary, where she teaches courses in rhetoric. Her publications include essays on the rhetoric of St. Augustine as well as on women's rhetoric, including a chapter on Mary Astell. She is also co-editor with Beverly Rasporich of *Woman as Artist: Papers in Honour of Marsha Hanen*.

Barbara Warnick is a professor and the chair of the Department of Speech Communication at the University of Washington. Her areas of interest include early modern rhetoric, contemporary rhetoric, and argumentation. She has written two books on the early modern period: a translation of Fénelon's *Letter to the French Academy* and *The Sixth Canon: Belletristic Rhetorical Theory and Its French Antecedents*. She is presently editor of *Quarterly Journal of Speech*.

Molly Meijer Wertheimer is an associate professor of speech communication and women's studies at the Pennsylvania State University, Hazleton Campus, where she teaches courses in public speaking, gender communication, and women in the humanities and the arts. Her research interests include the history and philosophy of rhetoric, listening, and women's rhetoric. She is co-author with John F. Wilson and Carroll C. Arnold of *Public Speaking as a Liberal Art* and has published articles and reviews on Augustine, Campbell, Woolbert and Winans. She is currently the book review editor of *Philosophy and Rhetoric*.

Index